THE CAMBRIDGE COMPANION TO

PHILOSOPHICAL METHODOLOGY

The Cambridge Companion to Philosophical Methodology offers clear and comprehensive coverage of the main methodological debates and approaches within philosophy. The chapters in this volume approach the question of how to do philosophy from a wide range of perspectives, including conceptual analysis, critical theory, deconstruction, experimental philosophy, hermeneutics, Kantianism, methodological naturalism, phenomenology, and pragmatism. They explore general conceptions of philosophy, centred on the question of what the point of philosophizing might be; the method of conceptual analysis and its recent naturalistic critics and competitors; perspectives from continental philosophy; and also a variety of methodological views that belong neither to the mainstream of analytic philosophy, nor to continental philosophy as commonly conceived. Together they will enable readers to grasp an unusually wide range of approaches to methodological debates in philosophy.

GIUSEPPINA D'ORO is Reader in Philosophy at Keele University. Her publications include *Collingwood and the Metaphysics of Experience* (2002), *Collingwood's An Essay on Philosophical Method* (2005) and *Reasons and Causes: Causalism and Anti-Causalism in the Philosophy of Action* (2013).

SØREN OVERGAARD is Associate Professor of Philosophy at the University of Copenhagen. His recent publications include *Wittgenstein and Other Minds* (2007) and *An Introduction to Metaphilosophy* (2013).

Continued at the back of the book

The Cambridge Companion to

PHILOSOPHICAL METHODOLOGY

Edited by Giuseppina D'Oro and Søren Overgaard

CAMBRIDGE
UNIVERSITY PRESS

CAMBRIDGE
UNIVERSITY PRESS

University Printing House, Cambridge CB2 8BS, United Kingdom

One Liberty Plaza, 20th Floor, New York, NY 10006, USA

477 Williamstown Road, Port Melbourne, VIC 3207, Australia

314-321, 3rd Floor, Plot 3, Splendor Forum, Jasola District Centre, New Delhi - 110025, India

79 Anson Road, #06-04/06, Singapore 079906

Cambridge University Press is part of the University of Cambridge.

It furthers the University's mission by disseminating knowledge in the pursuit of education, learning and research at the highest international levels of excellence.

www.cambridge.org
Information on this title: www.cambridge.org/9781107547360

© Cambridge University Press 2017

First published 2017

A catalogue record for this publication is available from the British Library

Library of Congress Cataloging in Publication data
Names: Overgaard, Søren, editor.
Title: The Cambridge companion to philosophical methodology /
[edited by] by Giuseppina D'Oro and Søren Overgaard.
Description: New York : Cambridge University Press, 2016. |
Series: Cambridge companions | Includes bibliographical
references and index. Identifiers: LCCN 2016045341|
ISBN 9781107121522 (hardback: paper) |
ISBN 9781107547360 (pbk.: paper) Subjects: LCSH: Methodology.
Classification: LCC BD241. C3255 2016 | DDC 101–dc23
LC record available at https://lccn.loc.gov/2016045341

ISBN 978-1-107-12152-2 Hardback
ISBN 978-1-107-54736-0 Paperback

CONTENTS

vii

CONTRIBUTORS

HERMAN CAPPELEN is Professor of Philosophy at the University of Oslo and at the University of St Andrews. He is the co-author of many papers and seven monographs, including *Insensitive Semantics, Relativism and Monadic Truth, Philosophy without Intuitions*, and *The Inessential Indexical*. He is the Co-Director of ConceptLab and the Editor-in-Chief of the journal *Inquiry*.

DAVID R. CERBONE is Professor of Philosophy at West Virginia University. He is the author of *Understanding Phenomenology, Heidegger: A Guide for the Perplexed*, and *Existentialism: All That Matters*, as well as numerous articles on Heidegger, Wittgenstein, and the phenomenological tradition. He also co-edits the *Routledge Research in Phenomenology* series.

GIUSEPPINA D'ORO is Reader in Philosophy at Keele University. Her research interests lie at the intersection between idealism, philosophy of mind, and metaphilosophy. She is the author of *Collingwood and the Metaphysics of Experience*, the editor (with Constantine Sandis) of *Reasons and Causes: Causalism and Anti-Causalism in the Philosophy of Action*, and has published many papers on Collingwood's contribution to philosophical methodology and action theory.

FABIAN FREYENHAGEN is Professor of Philosophy at the University of Essex. His research interests include the Frankfurt School, ethics, and political philosophy. He is the author of *Adorno's Practical Philosophy* and has published articles in journals such as *Hegel Bulletin, Kantian Review*, and *Politics, Philosophy & Economics*.

KRISTIN GJESDAL is Associate Professor of Philosophy at Temple University. Her publications include *Gadamer and the Legacy of German Idealism* and a number of articles on Herder, post-Kantian philosophy, hermeneutics, and aesthetics. She is the co-editor of the *Oxford Handbook of German Philosophy in the Nineteenth Century*, the editor of *Key Debates in Nineteenth-Century Philosophy*, and the co-editor of the forthcoming *Cambridge Companion to Hermeneutics*.

HANS-JOHANN GLOCK is Professor of Philosophy at the University of Zurich (Switzerland) and Visiting Professor at the University of Reading (UK). He is the author of *A Wittgenstein Dictionary*, *Quine and Davidson*, *La mente de los animals*, and *What is Analytic Philosophy?* He has edited *The Rise of Analytic Philosophy*, *Wittgenstein: a Critical Reader*, *Strawson and Kant*, and co-edited *Wittgenstein's Philosophical Investigations*, *Wittgenstein and Quine*, *Wittgenstein and Analytic Philosophy*, and *The Blackwell Companion to Wittgenstein*.

ROBERT HANNA is an independent philosopher, co-director of the *Critique & Contemporary Kantian Philosophy* project, and a visiting research professor at PUC-PR, Brazil. He is a philosophical generalist with a broadly Kantian orientation, and has authored or co-authored six books, including *Kant and the Foundations of Analytic Philosophy*, *Kant, Science, and Human Nature*, *Rationality and Logic*, *Embodied Minds in Action* (co-authored with M. Maiese), and *Cognition, Content, and the A Priori: A Study in the Philosophy of Mind and Knowledge*.

FRANK JACKSON is an Emeritus Professor at The Australian National University. He works in the philosophy of mind and language, and ethics. His publications include *Language, Names, and Information*, *Conditionals*, *Perception*, and *From Metaphysics to Ethics*.

HILARY KORNBLITH is Professor of Philosophy at the University of Massachusetts, Amherst. His work has focused on ways in which a scientific understanding of the mind can shed light on traditional philosophical problems in epistemology and related areas. He is the author of *Inductive Inference and its Natural Ground*, *Knowledge and its Place in Nature*, *On Reflection*, and *A Naturalistic Epistemology: Selected Papers*.

LEONARD LAWLOR is Edwin Erle Sparks Professor of Philosophy at Penn State University. His research interests are in contemporary continental philosophy, especially French philosophy of the 1960s. He is the author of seven books, among which are *This is not Sufficient* and *Derrida and Husserl*. His new book is called *From Violence to Speaking out*.

DAVID MACARTHUR is an Associate Professor in the Philosophy Department at the University of Sydney. He works on liberal naturalism, contemporary pragmatism, scepticism, metaphilosophy, and philosophy of art and architecture. He is editor of the forthcoming *Pragmatism as a Way of Life* by Hilary and Ruth Anna Putnam.

A. W. MOORE is Professor of Philosophy at the University of Oxford. He is the author of four books: *The Infinite, Points of View, Noble in Reason, Infinite in Faculty: Themes and Variations in Kant's Moral and Religious Philosophy*, and *The Evolution of Modern Metaphysics: Making Sense of Things*. He is also co-editor of the journal *MIND*.

SØREN OVERGAARD is Associate Professor of Philosophy at the University of Copenhagen. He is the author of *Husserl and Heidegger on Being in the World* and *Wittgenstein and Other Minds* and co-author (with Paul Gilbert and Stephen Burwood) of *An Introduction to Metaphilosophy*.

ROBERT PIERCEY is Associate Professor of Philosophy at Campion College of the University of Regina. His interests include hermeneutics, pragmatism, metaphilosophy, and the philosophy of history. He is the author of *The Uses of the Past From Heidegger to Rorty* and *The Crisis in Continental Philosophy*.

JEAN-LUC PETIT is Professor of Philosophy at the Université de Strasbourg. He has organized a series of workshops and conferences intended to promote dialogue between phenomenology and cognitive (neuro)science. In collaboration with Alain Berthoz at the Collège de France (Paris), he has co-authored *The Physiology and Phenomenology of Action* and edited several collected volumes at the interface between these same topics.

NICHOLAS RESCHER is Distinguished University Professor of Philosophy at the University of Pittsburgh. Author of over one hundred books covering virtually every branch of philosophy, he has served as President of the American Philosophical Association, the American Catholic Philosophical Association, and the Metaphysical Society of America. His many years of contribution to philosophy have been recognized by honorary degrees from seven universities on three continents.

JACK REYNOLDS is Professor of Philosophy and Associate Dean (Research) of the Faculty of Arts and Education at Deakin University, Australia. His recent books include: *Phenomenology, Naturalism and Science* (forthcoming), *Chronopathologies: The Politics of Time in Deleuze, Derrida, Analytic Philosophy and Phenomenology*, and *Analytic Versus Continental: Arguments on the Methods and Value of Philosophy* (with James Chase).

PATRICK STOKES is Senior Lecturer in Philosophy at Deakin University. He works on issues of personal identity, moral psychology, time, memory, and death, with a focus on bringing continental work (particularly Kierkegaard) into analytic debates. He is the author of *The Naked Self* and *Kierkegaard's Mirrors*.

ROBERT B. TALISSE is W. Alton Jones Professor of Philosophy at Vanderbilt University. His research interests include pragmatism, contemporary political philosophy, and social epistemology. He is the author of many articles and several books, including *A Pragmatist Philosophy of Democracy* and *Democracy and Moral Conflict*.

ALESSANDRA TANESINI is Professor of Philosophy at Cardiff University. She is the author of *An Introduction to Feminist Epistemologies*, of *Wittgenstein: A Feminist Interpretation*, and of several articles in feminist philosophy, the philosophy of mind and language, epistemology, and on Nietzsche.

AMIE THOMASSON is Professor of Philosophy and Cooper Fellow at the University of Miami. She is the author of *Ontology Made Easy*, *Ordinary Objects*, and *Fiction and Metaphysics*, as well as of more than sixty articles on topics in metaphysics, philosophical methodology, philosophy of mind, social ontology, and aesthetics.

JONATHAN M. WEINBERG is Associate Professor of Philosophy and the Program in Cognitive Science at the University of Arizona. He works in epistemology, philosophy of psychology, and aesthetics, as well as in experimental philosophy and philosophical methodology.

ACKNOWLEDGEMENTS

We would like to thank Hilary Gaskin at Cambridge University Press for her invaluable help on this project. We would also like to express our gratitude to Christofere Fila and Stephen Leach for their assistance in the last stages of the production of this volume. We owe a special debt of gratitude to our anonymous readers.

Introduction

I

Despite countless substantive differences in terms of style, general outlook, and much more, most philosophers – whether 'analytic' or 'continental' – arguably used to agree on one thing: that the activity of philosophizing differed in significant ways from the typical activities of empirical scientists. Even Quine, for whom philosophy was straightforwardly 'a part of science', held that the former belonged at 'the abstract and theoretical end' of the latter (Quine, in Magee 1982: 143). Thus, unabashed methodological naturalists, their explicit doctrines notwithstanding, did not necessarily *do* philosophy any differently from the way it had traditionally been done: in the main without relying substantively on – let alone actively collecting – empirical data. In practice, if not always in theory, it was assumed that philosophy could, indeed perhaps should, be done from an 'armchair'.

In recent years, however, this erstwhile consensus – or near-consensus – has shattered. The rise of experimental philosophy (see Knobe and Nichols 2008) has challenged deeply entrenched ideas about how analytic philosophy is to be done. Instead of offering *a priori* arguments for and against philosophical theses, experimental philosophers use the standard methods of social psychology and other empirical sciences to test such theses. Across the analytic/ continental divide, a comparable trend can be seen, for example, in calls for the 'naturalization' of phenomenology, as well as in recent, naturalistically motivated bids to discard post-Kantian continental philosophy altogether.[1]

These challenges to the traditional 'armchair' practices of the philosopher have moved methodological questions – questions concerning the methods of philosophizing – towards the top of the philosophical agenda. Such questions have not always been considered important. Gilbert Ryle, for example, notoriously argued that 'preoccupation with questions about methods tends to distract us from prosecuting the methods themselves. We run, as a rule, worse, not better, if we think a lot about our feet' (Ryle 2009 [1953]: 331). Ryle seems to be suggesting two distinct reasons for thinking it a bad idea to pay much attention to methodology. First, it may simply distract us from presumably more important work in other areas of philosophy: we get too caught up in thinking *about* the methods of philosophizing and neglect to *use* them. Second, Ryle also suggests a sort of centipede effect: that the more we worry about how to philosophize the less well we are able to do it. Neither argument seems conclusive, however. First, there simply is no reason to think a philosopher could not make important contributions to other areas of philosophy, while also (occasionally, say) addressing methodological issues. Second, since critical reflection is central to what philosophers do, it is far from obvious that the centipede effect applies. Perhaps too much reflection will impede one's performance when skiing or cycling, but surely not when the task at hand is to think. In this way, philosophizing, as Timothy Williamson writes, 'is not like riding a bicycle, best done without thinking about it' (Williamson 2007: 8).[2]

Ryle's dismissive attitude towards philosophical methodology is perhaps somewhat understandable, given that he was writing at a time when philosophers – at least at Oxford – believed they had already attained the methodological tools to solve all the traditional problems of philosophy.[3] In such a situation, perhaps, it is best just to get on with it. For after all, as Karl Popper – a contemporary of Ryle – put it, 'a philosopher should philosophise: he should try to solve philosophical problems, rather than talk about philosophy' (Popper 1968: 68).[4] But obviously, the current situation is a very different one that makes Ryle's and Popper's attitudes difficult to justify. For when it is entirely up for grabs what the proper methods of philosophizing, if there are any such, might be, then there is little chance of making much headway with the philosophical problems that Popper is referring to. At any rate, any suggested solution is likely to be controversial. For when philosophers disagree over whether there is a place for experimental methods within philosophy, say, their disagreement is in part precisely about which sorts of evidence bear on philosophical problems. Someone who thinks of philosophizing as consisting entirely in *a priori* conceptual analysis will hardly accept that experimental data has any bearing on her research. Conversely, someone who believes such 'armchair' methods are in serious need of supplementation and potential replacement by experimental research is not, without further ado, going to accept the deliverances of the armchair analyst's musings as evidence for anything other than what that particular individual is inclined to say.

There are other, more general reasons to be sceptical of Popper's and Ryle's dismissive attitude towards philosophical methodology. Ryle and Popper seem to assume a neat distinction between philosophical problems or questions proper and questions about philosophy and its methods. But – quite part from the fact that in practice, as just seen, the former cannot be entirely isolated from the latter – it is unclear what philosophical justification might be given for assuming this distinction. To be sure, questions about *how* philosophy is (to be) done belong to a part of philosophy often referred to as 'metaphilosophy'. This name suggests, perhaps, that methodological enquiry 'look[s] down on philosophy from above, or beyond' (Williamson 2007: *ix*), and thus that methodological questions belong to 'a distinct higher-order discipline' (Glock 2008: 6).

But the term 'metaphilosophy' is not mandatory – it is just a term – and some reject it precisely because it suggests that when we are discussing philosophical method we are no longer doing philosophy proper.[5] Presumably, few people would deny that questions concerning the nature of science and its methodology belong to philosophy proper. Certainly Popper would accept that much: 'the critical inquiry into the sciences, their findings, and their methods', he writes, 'remains a characteristic of philosophical inquiry' (Popper 1975: 53). Yet if this is part of philosophical enquiry proper, then surely the corresponding questions about philosophy must be as well. (After all, it is hard to see where else such questions might belong.) This ought to be particularly obvious to someone like Popper who thinks philosophy 'ought never to be, indeed ... never can be, divorced from science' (ibid.).

While this is of course strictly *ad hominem*, the general point here is one that everyone ought to accept: if questions about the nature of science and art, say, are genuine philosophical questions, then corresponding questions about philosophy must be as well. As Cavell puts it, then, 'philosophy is one of its own normal topics' (2002: xxxii). Surely one does not beg any major (meta-)philosophical questions if one takes philosophy to include the critical examination of the varieties of human knowledge and understanding, and of the methods by which such knowledge and understanding may be acquired. But if so, the philosophical project must remain incomplete unless it includes a critical examination of philosophy itself. It is for this reason that Wilfrid Sellars asserts that it is 'this reflection on the place of philosophy itself, in the scheme of things which is the distinctive trait of the philosopher', so that 'in the absence of this critical reflection on the philosophical enterprise, one is at best but a potential philosopher' (Sellars 1991: 3).

II

This volume aims to provide an overview of the most important positions and debates on philosophical methodology. While naturalistic challenges have been instrumental in terms of putting methodological issues firmly on the agenda, the issues that are thereby raised go beyond the specific debates about whether or not to 'naturalize' one or another traditional method. For if the orthodox philosophical methodology is in question, this could be a sign that philosophy has taken a wrong turn somewhere. 'Naturalizing' some version of that methodology, then, is not the only alternative to business as usual. Another option is to explore other perspectives on how to do philosophy. Consequently, the chapters in this volume approach the question of how to do philosophy from a wide range of perspectives, including conceptual analysis, critical theory, deconstruction, experimental philosophy, hermeneutics, Kantianism, methodological naturalism, phenomenology, and pragmatism.

Within philosophical methodology, one can distinguish between descriptive and normative questions. Descriptive questions concern the methods that philosophers actually use (or advocate), or have

[handwritten margin note at top: WHAT PHILOSOPHY IS WILL SHAPE WHAT METHOD IS "RIGHT"?]

used (or advocated) historically. We might inquire, for example, how large a proportion of the current philosophical community design and conduct experiments as part of their philosophical research. By contrast, normative philosophical methodology concerns not what philosophers actually do, but what they *ought* to be doing: what the *correct* or *proper* methods of philosophizing are. Since most will agree that the majority of philosophers actually conduct their research from the armchair, arguably the most interesting challenge that methodological 'naturalists' raise is a normative one. Consequently, this volume addresses normative methodology: the chapters present, discuss, and often defend particular views on how philosophy ought to be done.

As mentioned, philosophical methodology belongs to a part of philosophy – mostly called 'metaphilosophy', but perhaps more felicitously labelled 'the philosophy of philosophy' – in which the topic is philosophy itself. Other important questions in this area include the questions of what philosophy *is* and why it might be thought valuable.[6] These questions are obviously connected. If one thinks of philosophy as an empirical science along the lines of experimental psychology, certain conclusions about the proper method would – *ceteris paribus* – follow. Furthermore, a certain view about the value of philosophy would also suggest itself: like other empirical sciences, philosophy advances our knowledge in a particular domain or set of domains. Conversely, suppose you believe that the task of philosophy 'is not to add to the sum of human knowledge, but to enable us to attain a clear understanding of what is already known' (Hacker 1996: 272–3). Such a view on the value of philosophizing seems to have clear negative implications with respect to methodology – as empirical methods are precisely designed to 'add to the sum of human knowledge', they would (*ceteris paribus*) seem unsuited for philosophy, on the current understanding. For the same reason, it seems philosophy would have to be construed as an enterprise fundamentally distinct from the sciences within which such methods are essential.

[handwritten margin note: STYLE MATTERS ALONG w/ WHAT PHILOSOPHY IS ∧ WHAT ITS METHOD(S) SHOULD BE (EVEN NEW GENRES MAY MATTER)]

Ultimately, then, one cannot separate the question of how we should do philosophy from the question of what we can expect philosophy to do for us. Consequently, although our focus is on philosophical methodology, the essays in this volume place this topic in the wider metaphilosophical context. That context notably

[handwritten note at bottom: WHAT IS PHILOSOPHICAL METHODOLOGY (DESCRIPTIVE ∧ NORMATIVE), ∧ WHAT IS PHILOSOPHY? WHY IS PHILOSOPHY VALUABLE?]

also includes questions concerning style. Depending on what one thinks philosophy is, and how one thinks it is best carried out, different literary styles – and perhaps even genres – might be called for. If one thinks that a central task of philosophizing is to effect some change in the way we lead our lives, say, then the style and format of a scientific research article may not be as appropriate as the current majority of philosophers seems to think it is.

III

The volume is divided into four parts. The chapters in Part I offer general conceptions of philosophy, centred on the question of what the point of philosophizing might be. Philosophy is sometimes claimed to be concerned with abstract theoretical discussions that are only tenuously connected with any concerns of real life, and are all the more pointless for being seemingly irresolvable. The contributions of Alessandra Tanesini, Nicholas Rescher, and A. W. Moore discuss the first part of that rather disparaging view of philosophy, while Herman Cappelen's contribution questions the common assumption that philosophy is marred by persistent disagreement. The topic of Part II is the method of conceptual analysis – arguably still the most widely used tool in the analytic philosopher's toolkit – and its recent naturalistic critics and competitors. Hans-Johann Glock, Amie L. Thomasson, and Frank Jackson present and defend contemporary varieties of conceptual analysis, while Hilary Kornblith and Jonathan M. Weinberg articulate naturalistic programmes according to which the traditional methods of 'armchair' analysis must be guided and constrained in various ways by empirical research.

The chapters in Part III address a variety of methodological views that belong neither to the mainstream of analytic philosophy, nor to continental philosophy in the usual sense of that word. Robert Hanna conceives of philosophy as 'rational anthropology' and argues that its proper methodology can be extracted from Kant's critical philosophy. Giuseppina D'Oro's contribution presents and defends a philosophical methodology derived from the English idealist philosopher R. G. Collingwood. According to Robert B. Talisse's contribution, there is a tendency within pragmatist philosophy to relocate standard (first-order) philosophical disputes to the metaphilosophical level, which Talisse argues can be resisted by embracing a 'metaphilosophically minimalist' conception of pragmatism. David Macarthur defends a variety of 'metaphysical quietism' – roughly, the view that philosophers should critically reflect on the problems of metaphysics, not attempt to solve them – inspired by Wittgenstein. Robert Piercey's contribution contends that the notorious divide between analytic and continental philosophy is best seen as a metaphilosophical divide, and suggests that it is bridged in the metaphilosophies of Rorty and Ricoeur, both of which maintain that philosophy and the history of philosophy are inseparable.

Part IV turns to perspectives from continental philosophy. David R. Cerbone discusses whether the method of phenomenology involves a break with everyday life and experience, which undermines the phenomenologists' aim of articulating everyday experience in a way their readers will recognize. The contribution by Jack Reynolds and Patrick Stokes articulates and defends key aspects of existentialist methodology, including existential philosophers' use of unconventional forms of dissemination. Centred on a reading of the eighteenth-century German hermeneutic philosopher J. G. Herder, Kristin Gjesdal outlines a hermeneutical methodology and defends it against Gadamer's influential criticisms of methodological approaches to hermeneutics. Fabian Freyenhagen's contribution addresses the uneasy relationship between critical theory – typically associated with the so-called Frankfurt School – and traditional philosophy, focusing in particular on the case of Adorno. Developing and extending ideas from Bergson, Deleuze, Derrida, and others, Leonard R. Lawlor outlines a deconstructionist methodology aimed at liberation from conventional modes of thought. Finally, Jean-Luc Petit's contribution adopts the perspective of 'naturalized phenomenology' and discusses whether the experience of patients with Parkinson's disease poses a problem for traditional Husserlian phenomenology.

This collection provides a useful snapshot of the contemporary methodological debates. In analytic philosophy, such debates have traditionally tended to revolve around a dispute between philosophers who seek to construct theories about reality and those who on the other hand are intent on dissolving philosophical problems by showing that they are grounded in misuses of language. An implication of this way of cutting the cake is that if the task of philosophical analysis is not to construct theories which contribute to the advancement of human knowledge then conceptual analysis is relegated to a purely therapeutic function. A number of contributions in this collection, however, question the view that philosophy can have a positive role to play only in so far as it makes substantive claims about the structure of reality. What emerges here is a variety of nuanced attempts to articulate some middle ground between armchair metaphysics and linguistic therapy.

The methodological angle on the analytic/continental divide also reflects a growing view that while the distinction is useful in some ways, it is problematic in others because it cuts across more kosher philosophical distinctions such as those between realists and anti-realists, naturalists and anti-naturalists. As A. W. Moore points out, the continental tradition, working in the shadows of Kant's Copernican turn, has been, at least historically, less inclined to align philosophy with the natural sciences, and more predisposed towards distinguishing between the first-order level of the special sciences and the second-order level of philosophical reflection. But apparent differences and similarities between the two traditions should be handled with care, for the devil, as the saying goes, is always in the detail. Much as one should not infer from the phenomenological slogan 'to the things themselves' that continental phenomenologists are consorting with analytic metaphysicians in advocating constructive theories about the nature of reality, one should also be wary of inferring from the influence the Copernican turn has exercised on the continental tradition that all continental philosophers endorse a robust distinction between empirical and transcendental levels of analysis. The naturalizing movement, as Petit's paper shows, is in no way the preserve of the analytic tradition. As membership to a common tradition (be it analytic or continental) is not necessarily indicative of genuine philosophical affinities, the absence of a common tradition does not rule out the existence of genuine methodological affinities. Phenomenology may make explicit the structures of experience rather than the rules of language, say, but phenomenologists and conceptual analysts are endeavouring to expose underlying structures (be they existential or linguistic) which are in some sense 'always already' implicitly known. Examining philosophical methodology on both sides of the analytic/continental divide – as well as paying attention to

methodological questions in those parts of philosophy that do not
fit neatly into either camp – may enable us to gain a new perspective
on an old and arguably problematic distinction.

NOTES

1 For examples of the former, see (Petitot *et al.* 1999) and the papers
collected in (Noë 2007), a special issue of the then-recently founded
journal *Phenomenology and the Cognitive Sciences*. Parts of the so-
called speculative realist movement in recent European philosophy
exemplify the latter, although it is probably too soon to attempt to form
any clear picture – let alone gauge the philosophical merits – of this very
heterogeneous movement. See (Zahavi 2016) for critical discussion.
2 In fact, Williamson questions whether the centipede effect even applies
in the latter case: 'the best cyclists surely *do* think about what they are
doing' (Williamson 2007: 8).
3 P. F. Strawson relates that Oxford philosophers in the 1940s and 50s,
armed with the method of linguistic analysis, would 'speculate about
how long it would take to "finish off" traditional philosophy' (Strawson
2011: 72).
4 Consequently, Popper declares that he, for one, 'should not bother much
about' such questions as what philosophers 'are doing or might do' (Popper
1968: 68).
5 Glock and Williamson reject the term 'metaphilosophy' for this reason,
as does Stanley Cavell: 'If I deny a distinction, it is the still fashionable
distinction between philosophy and meta-philosophy, the philosophy of
philosophy. The remarks I make *about* philosophy … are … nothing more
or less than philosophical remarks' (Cavell 2002: xxxii). Apparently, the
term 'meta-philosophy' was coined by Morris Lazerowitz – a student of
Wittgenstein – in 1940 (Lazerowitz 1970: 91).
6 (Overgaard, Gilbert and Burwood 2013: Ch. 1) suggest that the three
central 'metaphilosophical' questions are the 'What', 'How', and 'Why'
questions.

Part I

Visions of Philosophy

1 Doing Philosophy

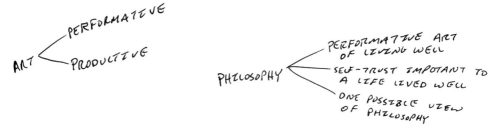

ART < *PERFORMATIVE* / *PRODUCTIVE*

PHILOSOPHY < *PERFORMATIVE ART OF LIVING WELL* / *SELF-TRUST IMPOTANT TO A LIFE LIVED WELL* / *ONE POSSIBLE VIEW OF PHILOSOPHY*

The main aims of this paper are: 1) to present and defend a view of philosophy as the performative art or craft of living (well);[1] and 2) to argue that in contemporary Western societies self-trust is an essential component of a well-lived life. I take this to be one possible account of what philosophy may amount to, rather than the only one that can justifiably lay claim to the title.

This paper consists of three main sections. In the first I contrast a 'doctrinal' conception of philosophy as a body of knowledge with an 'artistic' conception of philosophy as a craft. I trace the Socratic origins of the latter, and argue that the art of living is a performative art, like dance, rather than a productive art, like shoemaking. In the second section I show that an attitude of self-assured conviction is an essential part of living well. I also argue that self-confidence is a manifestation of intellectual self-trust. In the third section I defend the identification of the art of living with philosophy. Finally, I draw some of the methodological implications of this identification.

I

The view that philosophy is a craft or an art can be traced to Greco-Roman roots as far back as Socrates. It finds its main expression in various Hellenistic schools but especially within Stoicism. More recently it has influenced the works of Nietzsche, Wittgenstein, and Foucault.[2] It has often been identified with a conception of philosophy as the art of living.[3] This view stands in contrast to another understanding of philosophy as a body of theories or doctrines. In this section I explain these two contrasting views of philosophy and argue that the art of living is a performative art, like dance, rather than a productive art like making shoes.

Doctrinal and artistic conceptions of philosophy. I reserve the term 'doctrinal' for the conception of philosophy as a collection of philosophical claims which purport to be true. This is the most popular approach in the contemporary English-speaking scene; it can take one of many forms. It finds its purest expression in Timothy Williamson's view that philosophy is a science like other sciences and that philosophical knowledge is knowledge of reality, typically of its modal and abstract features (Williamson 2007). But it is also exemplified in Wilfrid Sellars' conception of philosophy as offering a synoptic view of everything there is, which would enable one to relate the findings of some natural and social sciences to those of others (Sellars 1991). Even Bernard Williams' conception of philosophy as a humanistic discipline is doctrinal since its task, in his view, is to provide a reflective understanding of our ideas about ourselves, our customs and values so that we can form a true picture of what they are (Williams 2006).

I adopt the term 'artistic' for any conception of philosophy as a craft or an art. This was arguably the dominant view in classical antiquity. The approach has its origins in the Socratic analogy of philosophy with various arts and crafts.[4] In a number of Platonic dialogues Socrates is portrayed as enjoining his interlocutors to engage in the craft of taking care of one's own soul.[5] In *Alcibiades I* (hereafter, *Alc. I*) Socrates compares a number of crafts such as shoemaking, horsemanship and navigation.[6] These are skills which assist in taking care of one's shoes, horses and passengers. In addition to these skills which take care of one's belongings, there is – Socrates urges – a distinct art for taking care of oneself (*Alc. I*: 127e ff.). Since one is identical with one's soul rather than one's body, this art must concern taking care of one's soul. In the same dialogue but also in the *Gorgias* (hereafter, *Gorg.*), Socrates claims that skills presuppose knowledge of principles. Thus, the shoemaker must know facts about shoes and their manufacture in order to make good shoes. By analogy, the art of taking care of oneself presupposes self-knowledge (*Alc. I*: 129c). The ability to provide a rational account, which presupposes the possession of relevant propositional knowledge, is in Socrates' words the main distinguishing characteristic between those who have a skill and those who possess a knack or a routine (*Gorg.*: 465a). Since knowledge of this sort can be imparted to one's apprentices, Socrates appears to conclude that crafts can be rationally taught (cf. Irwin 1977: 74).

The art of taking care of one's soul is the art of taking care of oneself. It is, in other words, the art or craft of living. This approach is further developed by the Stoics who latch onto the Socratic analogy of the art of taking care of one's soul with the art of taking care of one's body (medicine).[7] In their view philosophy is the therapy for the diseases of the soul which if successful permits one to live well. It is a therapy which one must practice on oneself.

Performative and productive arts. There are at least two different kinds of craft: productive and performative. Productive arts, like shoemaking or medicine, are the crafts of making something; they are practised in order to make excellent products. Expertise in the craft is measured by the quality of the product and the reliability of its production. Shoemakers, for example, produce footwear, whilst doctors produce health (*Charmides*: 166a). The product thus provides an objective measure of success by which one can tell apart those who have the skills, from learners and impostors. One can judge whether a pair of shoes is good by seeing how they fare when worn. One does not need to be a shoemaker oneself to be able to decide whether the craftsperson is any good at what she does.

Other arts are performative because they are exhibited in performance. Music making is Socrates' favourite example of a performative art; dance is another example. The characteristic activities of the productive arts have a distinctive structure since they culminate in a terminus or goal whose achievement determines whether the whole process has been successful. For example, the completion of the manufacture of a pair of shoes is the goal of the activity of shoemaking. The performative arts involve activities which are often, although perhaps not always, not structured by a terminus. For example, both dancing and music playing can continue indefinitely since they do not need to be performances of existing pieces of music or choreographed ballets. But even when the musician is following a score and thus stops playing when she has come to the end of the piece, the success of the performance is not determined by its ending or by any other single moment during, before or after the performance.

The characteristic activities of productive and performative arts thus have different shapes. The activities which one does well when one is a productive craftsperson have the shape of projects; those which are done well by the skilled performer have the shape of performances. In what follows I explain several of the features that distinguish projects from performances before arguing that life has the shape of a performance rather than a project. I conclude that the art of living, which is the craft of doing well the activity of living, is a performative art.

Projects and performances. The main difference between activities which are projects and those which are performances is that the former but not the latter are wholly constituted by their relations to goals.[8] A project is a complex set of activities carried out over time which has a constitutive goal. For example, writing a paper is a project since it is an activity with various components each of which purports to contribute to achieving the aim. The goal is, thus, a criterion for separating the acts that belong to the project from those which do not. In addition, the correct description of each act that is a component of the project must make a reference to its contribution to the achievement of the aim of the project as a whole. Performances do not have this goal-directed structure. An act of performing a given step, for instance, is not always carried out in order to achieve a separate goal. The dancer may improvise but even when she is not, because she is executing choreography, the point of the movement is in its contribution to the whole of which it is a constituent rather than its contribution to a goal. This is not to say that the dancer may not also treat the dance as a project. If she does, she may, for example, have the goal of completing a particularly difficult set of moves. When this happens the same movement may belong to two different activities. As a component of a performance a step is intelligible for its contribution to a more comprehensive whole, as a component of a project the same step has the significance of a means to achieving a goal. In short, when carrying out a performance individual acts are *for the sake of* the whole performance, but when one engages in a project individual acts are executed *in order to* achieve a goal.[9]

Two main differences between projects and performances flow from the fact that the former are structured by means–ends (in order to) relations while the latter by subordinate–superordinate (for the sake of) relations. First, the motivation for engaging in a project is a desire whose satisfaction is brought about by the achievement of the goal which completes the activity. Thus, when the shoemaker has made the shoes she wanted to make she can stop working until she wants to make another pair of shoes. The motivation to perform takes a different shape. There is no end state which counts as the desired outcome of the activity so that once it is achieved the activity stops. Instead, the motivation must be something more akin to love than to desire. Thus, whilst desire stops once it has been satisfied, love does not end when one has obtained what one loves. If I love reading, my love for the activity does not stop when I am doing it. However, if I want an ice-cream, my desire stops when it has been satisfied.[10]

Second, the value of the activities which are constituents of projects is, *qua* parts of projects, merely that of tools for achieving the goal. For instance, the value of making shoes is that of a means to an end (a good pair of shoes) from which it derives its value. The value of a component of a performance such as a dance, instead, is *qua* constituent of the larger activity, a matter of its contribution to the value of the whole activity. Thus, the part has value because it is part (rather than cause or tool) of a whole to whose value it contributes.[11] In other words, because projects are structured by means–end relations the value of component activities will be instrumental, whilst given that performances are structured by subordinate–superordinate relations the value of constituent activities will be contributive.

The art of living. In the remainder of this section I argue that the craft of living must be a performative art because (i) living is the activity done well when one manifests this art, and (ii) life is a performance rather than a project. I shall address the question whether it is plausible to claim that philosophy can be identified with this craft in the final section.

Both Socrates and the Stoics, however, seem to have thought of this art as productive. They are likely to have been motivated by two considerations. First, they talked about the art of living as the project of learning how to live well. Second, they thought that expertise in this art must be objectively assessable. Productive arts fulfil this requirement since even those who lack the craft can often judge whether a person can carry out projects to a successful completion. Performative arts instead are opaque to the non-initiated. It is practically impossible for someone who is not herself an expert to appreciate the difference between an excellent and a merely competent performance. This feature of the performative arts may lead one to doubt that there is any such thing as genuine expertise. The Stoics and Socrates feared this conclusion and for this reason they may have been inclined to press the view that the art of living is productive.

There are two plausible candidates as the goal of the art of living conceived as a productive art. These are: some specific state of one's soul whose achievement guarantees that one's life goes well, or the well-lived life itself. The Stoics adopted the first of these two positions and proposed that the state of the soul that one must aim at to live well is an attitude of acceptance towards everything that happens to one.

In order to assess the plausibility of the view under discussion, it is helpful to consider an analogy with medicine as the productive art concerned with bringing about, and maintaining a healthy state. Health is the goal of therapeutic activities since its achievement individuates the activity, determines its success, satisfies the desire that motivated it, brings it to an end, and confers instrumental value to the activity as a whole and to its components. The goal of the art of living cannot be an attitude, since if it were its achievement would terminate the activity. So if acceptance were the goal of living, once one has acquired this attitude and therefore satisfied the desire to have it, there would be no reason to continue living. One may object that obtaining the attitude is not sufficient as one may also desire to preserve it, so that the project of accepting life cannot ever be completed. But if so, the project would never be successful, since successful projects require that their goal is achieved. Hence, since the well-lived life cannot be a failed project, then its goal cannot be the preservation of an accepting attitude.[12]

Perhaps, however, the goal may be to adopt an accepting attitude as long as one lives. Whilst this goal is achievable, if one thinks of life as a project aimed at this goal, the value of one's current activities wholly depends on one's future ability to maintain an accepting attitude. Hence, it is only at the moment of death that it might turn out that a life was well-lived (or not). Whilst it is not implausible to claim that the future may be part of what determines whether the present is well-lived, it is implausible to claim that a necessary feature of a well-lived life is the presence of a desire (to adopt an accepting attitude as long as one lives) which must remain unsatisfied until death. These considerations, however, are not telling against the possibility that acceptance may be the goal of the project of *learning* to live well because it may be a necessary part of a life well-lived without being its goal.

We are thus left with the possibility that the goal of the art of living is simply a life well-lived. In this context I wish to remain neutral about what must be the case for a life to be well-lived.[13] My concern is with a more abstract issue: namely whether an art of living could have a goal that brings it to completion, given that a well-lived life is the most plausible candidate for that role. In order to answer the question we need to bear in mind that the aim of an activity is the end to which the activity is a means so that the activity is carried out in order to achieve the aim. That is, projects are carried out in order to bring into existence a good, which one previously lacked, whose production successfully completes the activity. For instance, the shoemaker who is able to make shoes initiates her shoemaking activity with the goal of producing a new pair of shoes which she did not have before.

Suppose that the art of living were the craft of executing well a project whose aim is obtaining a good (the well-lived life) which one currently lacks. If so, once the goal is achieved and the desire to live well is satisfied, the person would no longer want to live well. Hence, if life were the project whose goal is the well-lived life, one could not live well. Either one would desire to live well because one is currently not living well or, if one's desire were satisfied one would no longer desire it and therefore not engage in the project of living. The paradox disappears if living well is the object of love rather than desire. If one loves living well, having a well-lived life will offer a motivation for continuing to live. This is because living well is not something one is aiming to achieve (because one does not have it), it is that for the sake of which one lives. That is to say, the value of each activity that is part of living is at least partly a matter of its contribution to a whole which is the well-lived life (cf. Blattner 2000).

A comparison with another performative art may be of assistance here. Consider the example of someone who is learning to play the piano. The learner may have a number of projects whose goals are to achieve clear outcomes such as being able to play a given piece without error. Once the learner has acquired some level of expertise, she may play the same piece for the sake of playing. In this instance, playing the piece well is no longer the goal of her playing activity whose achievement completes it. Rather, even though she may also have other motives for playing at any given time, playing well is the end for the sake of which she engages in the activity. She plays because she loves playing. It is her love of playing that motivates her to play and to improve. The success of her playing is not determined by the achievement of a goal. Instead, success depends on the quality of the performance as a whole to which its parts contribute.

These considerations show that if living is an activity which can be done well by those who have mastered the art of living, it must have the structure of a performance since living (well) is that for the sake of which one lives rather than the goal of living. In the next section I turn to the more substantive question about what it may take to live well; for now I wish to address four outstanding questions for the account developed so far. First, one may object that it presupposes that for any activity there is a corresponding craft of doing it well. Second, one may argue that living is not an activity. Third, one may claim that possession of the craft is not a guarantee that one will perform well in every instance. Fourth, one may object that well-lived lives are often shaped by projects.

In response to the first objection, I want to distinguish activities from mere succession of events. We have a succession of events, when one thing merely follows another in time. Activities instead also have some organizational structure since they are either projects or performances. Either way activities can be a success or a failure; whilst successions of events cannot. A project is a success if and only if its goal is achieved. A performance is a success if and only if it embodies that for the sake of which it is undertaken. So both projects and performances can be carried out well or badly. Consequently, for every activity there is a craft which consists in the ability to do it well.[14]

One may accept this response but argue further that life is not an activity but is a mere succession of events. I do not wish to deny that a life that goes extremely badly may degenerate into a mere sequence of events. My contention is rather that living well minimally requires some purposive structure to one's life.[15] If this is right, life must possess the characteristic structure of activities. Therefore, there must exist an art of living.

I agree with the claim that possession of the relevant art does not guarantee success in the activity. Nothing in the account offered so far suggests otherwise. It may be the case that misfortune conspires and that, as a result, a life goes badly or at least less well than it otherwise would even though the person in question has the relevant skills. I also agree with the view that well-lived lives often involve projects. For all I have said so far, it could even be true that a life goes well if and only if it is made to coincide with a project. In that case, the performance of living for the sake of living would be also organized as a project with a goal such as that of writing philosophy, or of being the person who discovers the cure for cancer, or any other goal that one may think is extremely worthwhile and whose value would imbue one's activity with meaning.

II

I have argued so far that, according to one plausible conception, philosophy is the art of living. I have also defended the view that since life is a performance rather than a project, the art of living is a performative art. Living well, Socrates claimed, requires taking care of oneself. In this section I show that to look after oneself one must adopt a self-trusting attitude. I also argue that taking care of oneself is not a goal to be pursued in order to live well. Rather one looks after oneself when one treats oneself as an end for the sake of which one lives. Thus, a well-lived life is a performance motivated by love for oneself, rather than a project motivated by the desire to change oneself.

In contemporary Western societies the unreflective yet well-lived life is no longer an option. With the advent of secularism – as the view that human flourishing may be the yardstick by which to measure value (cf. Taylor 2007) – it is inevitable that individuals ask themselves how they should live. Once this question is posed, it needs to be answered if a person is to live well. In this paper I shall not discuss the considerations one may adduce which would count as reasons to live in some way or other. Instead, my focus is on two other requirements that any answer must fulfil to be satisfactory: it must motivate one to act; and it must prevent the question from obsessively recurring. I argue that only a self-assured answer could satisfy these requirements. I reach this conclusion by considering and rejecting two alternatives: certainty and resoluteness of will.

Once I have established that to answer the question of how one should live one must have the confidence of one's own convictions, I argue that this confidence is the manifestation of intellectual self-trust understood as a cognitive and affective ability. I rely on these considerations to argue further that taking care of oneself requires that one trusts oneself. Hence, a well-lived life is a self-trusting life. Self-trust, however, may be appropriate or a manifestation of arrogance. When it is warranted, a trusting attitude directed towards the self is an expression of self-love understood as a form of self-respect.[16]

The Socratic question and the original doubt. In *Ethics and the Limits of Philosophy* (1993), Williams famously raised sceptical doubts about whether ethical theory (and by implication philosophy) could answer the Socratic question about how to live.[17] I concur with Williams' pessimism that one may be able to answer the question in a manner that generates the required conviction to act solely by reference to theory, insight, or understanding. Knowledge or understanding on their own lack the motivational force that an answer must possess to help one to live well.[18] This pessimism need not infect philosophy itself, however, if one abandons its doctrinal conception.

To live well one must live in a manner which is supported by all those considerations one may adduce in answer to the Socratic question. In addition, one must be able to quell the doubts that have led one to ask the question in the first place. The latter is required because the posing of the question is itself symptomatic of disorientation about what is of value. Hence, one cannot live well if one keeps asking the question about how one should live. For this reason what is required to live well is not merely an answer to the question (once the question has been asked) but an answer that will give peace to the questioning so that it does not endlessly recur.

Similar considerations in my view motivate Williams' scepticism about the ability of theories to animate ethical thought (Williams 1993: 112). The answer to the Socratic question, once it has arisen, must take the form of conviction. But, as Williams also notes: 'ethical conviction is not to be identified with knowledge or certainty' (ibid.: 169).

Certainty, resoluteness, assuredness. There are, generally speaking, three compatible ways of solving doubts: certainty, resoluteness, and assuredness. On occasions, one is in a state of doubt because one lacks the information required to form a firm belief on the issue. In such instances doubt is born out of ignorance; it is addressed by certainty. For instance, I may be in doubt as to whether I am on time for my class. Upon learning that it is 9.30, the doubt disappears. In cases such as this one, knowledge dissipates doubt. Certainty would solve it once and for all.

On other occasions doubt is born of indecision; it is addressed by resoluteness. Suppose I face two slices of cake that are identical in all relevant respects. I want one slice (and one slice only) but I am in doubt about which one to have. No amount of knowledge will make this doubt dissipate. Instead, I must make a decision and follow it through. Finally, doubt may be indicative of a lack of confidence. I may remember clearly locking the front door, and yet a doubt can take hold of me, forcing me to double or triple check. In this instance, knowledge does not quell doubt because it is born out of the incapacity to rely on oneself rather than out of ignorance.

These three ways of solving doubt are not mutually incompatible and some doubts require a combination of knowledge, resoluteness, and assuredness. For example, we usually gather evidence before making a decision. Similarly, assuredness which is not backed by the facts is a symptom of arrogance. Nevertheless, not even certainty can guarantee confidence.

Given that in order to live well one must dissipate the doubt that prompts the Socratic question, it is only if we become clearer whether this doubt is born out of ignorance, indecision, or lack of confidence, that we can make progress towards understanding the kind of answer that would resolve it. In what follows I consider all three options and conclude that the Socratic doubt is primarily generated by a lack of confidence and that therefore it can only be addressed by the cultivation of assuredness.

Replacing ignorance with certainty. A prominent philosophical attitude to the Socratic question takes it to be a doubt that can be answered by way of a theory, insight, or understanding alone.

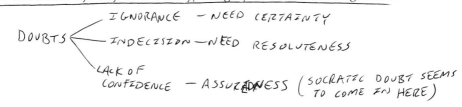

According to this view when one wonders about how one should live, one's questions are generated by a lack of knowledge about various ways of living, and all the possible reasons in favour of or against adopting them. For instance, one may wonder whether one should pursue a rewarding and well-paid career or follow a different path which one finds less interesting but which would make a more significant contribution to the well-being of others. The approach considered here proposes that these doubts are addressed by weighing up all the relevant considerations.

Reasoning, understanding, or insight alone, however, cannot prevent the doubts that motivate the Socratic question from recurring. Suppose that one formulates an answer to the Socratic question by these methods. One will as a result believe one's answer. In addition suppose, *per absurdum*, that one's answer possesses some kind of epistemic immunity such as infallibility. The answer, therefore, is certain in the sense that it cannot be mistaken. Nevertheless, even certainty cannot guarantee that a person will not lose faith in her convictions.[19] If she does, the doubt that motivates the Socratic question reappears to torment her.

Replacing indecision with resoluteness. If it is granted that reason, understanding, and theory cannot on their own offer a satisfactory answer to the Socratic question, one may presume that the will can achieve this feat. This option may be particularly tempting if one believes that values are made or created, rather than discovered (Mackie 1977: 106; Nietzsche 1974: §301). Nietzsche's views, that nihilism is defeated by adopting an affirming attitude towards life as a whole, illustrate how this is meant to work.

According to this position, one makes one's life worthwhile by conferring value upon it. If values are created by the will, one can transform every event that happens to one into something valuable merely by willing it to be such. Suffering is one of Nietzsche's favourite examples in this regard. One may think that suffering is bad, and that is why no one wants to suffer. However, if what we want is good because wanting it (in the right way) makes it good rather than because being good makes it desirable, then provided we want it, even suffering can be good.[20] What makes these exercises of the will effective is their resoluteness. That is, suffering can be good only if we continue to want it, when it happens. If the strength of our will gives way at any point, the values it creates will dissolve with it.

Upon reflection there is something deeply unsatisfactory about any answer to the Socratic question which is based exclusively on a decision. Once it becomes clear that one could have decided to value something else altogether, the arbitrariness of the chosen answer undermines its ability to prevent doubt from recurring. What is required is an answer that carries the force of conviction rather than the stubbornness of a resolute decision.[21] Hence, at least in those societies where reflective scrutiny is inevitable, resoluteness alone cannot supply the motivational force required of any satisfactory answer to the Socratic question.

Replacing self-diffidence with assuredness. The discussion so far has shown that neither certainty nor resolution can dissipate the doubt which prompts the Socratic question. Each of them fails individually; further, there is no reason to think that they will succeed together since resolution is needed precisely when the available evidence falls short of certainty. Hence, I conclude that the doubt that motivates the question about how one should live is generated by a loss of faith or confidence in those convictions that have animated one's life up to the moment of doubt. One asks the Socratic question again and again because one keeps losing faith in what one previously took to be one's response. It follows that any satisfactory answer to the question of how one should live must take the shape of a self-assured conviction.[22]

Self-trust and self-respect. If the claims made above are correct, what is required to answer the Socratic question is confidence or assuredness in one's judgements and choices.[23] I take this optimistic stance towards one's own cognitive capacities to be a manifestation of self-trust (Jones 2012). The person who trusts herself thinks that she is reliable.[24] However, belief in the reliability of one's doxastic capacities is not enough to guarantee that one trusts one's judgements, even when that belief is warranted. Witness the person who is certain that she has locked the front door, but double checks anyway. In addition, the person who trusts herself adopts an affective stance of feeling secure towards the products of one's intellectual capacities. As a result, the person who has self-trust is disposed to assert in public what she believes (because she is not intimidated); also, she will not endlessly doubt her own views. Self-trust, therefore, is an intellectual ability with cognitive and affective components which manifests itself as a positive stance towards one's own cognitive capacities combined with a favourable assessment of their reliability.

Assuredness is not always warranted. There is such a thing as excessive confidence, often born out of arrogance. But when confidence is appropriate it is an expression of the kind of self-trust which is a component of recognition self-respect (Dillon 2007; Tanesini 2016). Unlike evaluative self-respect, which is respect based on the evaluation of one's admirable features, recognition self-respect is based on the recognition that one is an agent deserving to be treated as such. There are many aspects to what it means to treat an agent as an agent. These include thinking of oneself and others as capable of forming opinions that must be given a fair hearing (whatever that may entail in the given circumstances).

Taking care of oneself as self-respect. I began this paper by noting Socrates' claim that philosophy is the craft of living. He compares philosophers with cobblers. Shoemakers possess the art of taking care of shoes; philosophers have the craft of taking care of oneself.[25] Socrates, however, presses the analogy too far by treating philosophy as a productive art. Once it is appreciated that it is a performative art, it becomes clear that one does not take care of one's soul in the way in which the cobbler takes care of shoes. The shoemaker's care for shoes is a desire to produce good shoes. It is thus a motivational state directed towards the goal which constitutes her activity as a project. The care for one's soul exhibited by the person who has the art of living is also a motivational state, but it is not a desire directed towards a goal (such as one's own well-being or achievements).[26] It is a state that is directed towards one's soul as an end, as that for the sake of which one lives. Thus, when one takes care of oneself, one relates to one's soul as a self-existing end, which is to say something which is the object of a motivating attitude that values it as it already is (Velleman 2006: 91). In sum, to take care of oneself is to love one's soul.

The soul of which one takes care is not a substance; it is a set of abilities. In the case of human beings, intellectual abilities are among those which are fundamental to the soul. These comprise cognitive capacities but also affective and emotional states. To love one's soul is to cultivate and appreciate for what they are the abilities that constitute it. Hence, taking care of one's human soul is predicated on intellectual self-trust which is a manifestation of self-respect.

We are now in a position to offer an account of the art of living (well). A good life is a complex activity which is performed for the sake of the person who lives it. It is shaped by a love of one's soul. The excellent performer, the person who lives well, is the person who has the skills and motivations required to execute the performance well. The overarching motivation is love of oneself.[27] The skills are those required to take care of, or love, one's distinctive abilities. These skills include self-trust since one cannot look after oneself unless one trusts one's own judgements and emotions. Self-trust, I have argued, is required to answer questions about how to live in the assured manner that stops doubts from endlessly occurring.

NB Z

III

Why should someone believe that philosophy is the art of living (well)? The short answer is that there is a tradition extending as far back as Socrates that interprets the tasks of philosophy to be (i) providing answers to the question of how to live, and (ii) supplying training for the skills required to live in accordance with these responses. The long answer concerns the means by which self-trust is first acquired and then secured.

Learning and securing self-trust. The ability to trust oneself is a basis of autonomy and self-reliance. It is, however, an ability which is socially developed. Thus, one acquires it initially by trusting others precisely because one is not yet in a position to trust oneself. One develops a belief in one's own reliability by having the products of one's perception, memory, or reasoning confirmed by individuals in positions of authority over one, such as teachers or parents. One acquires confidence in one's views by noticing that others have confidence in them. Thus, one learns to trust oneself as a response to the trust that authoritative others place in one.

This trust may be commensurate to our reliability or it may not. If we are not trusted as much as we should, we are unlikely to become self-confident due to underdeveloped self-trust. If too much confidence is placed in us, we will become excessively self-trusting and thus unwarrantedly self-assured. In the first case, we shall be deprived of an ability which is a necessary component of a life well-lived. The second case is harder to assess. Individuals who are arrogantly self-confident may not lead moral lives, but it is not clear

HOW TO LIVE WELL?

PHILOSOPHY PROVIDES ANSWERS

SUPPLIES TRAINING FOR SKILLS NEEDED TO LIVE OUT THE ANSWERS

that they cannot all things considered live well. Much depends on whether an excess of self-trust and the arrogant confidence which is one of its expressions are compatible with the kind of self-respect and self-love that are necessary to live well.[28]

Once some amount of self-trust is acquired it needs to be sustained over time. We preserve self-trust by a certain amount of self-reflection.[29] Primarily we secure it socially by obtaining an uptake for the demand that others trust us. The claim that we are entitled to be trusted can take several forms. It at least involves expecting others to adopt a positive affective stance towards us, and to treat us as being authoritative assertors (Tanesini 2016).

I have claimed above that self-trust is manifested in a disposition to assert in public what one believes. Public assertion carries commitments to having the suitable epistemic standing with regard to the content of the assertion.[30] But it also involves claiming entitlements for oneself including that of being treated as a possible source of warrant. That is to say, by making an assertion, I expect that others will treat my having asserted that thing as a reason to repeat the assertion on the grounds of my authority. The recognition of one's claim to authority does not require that authority is attributed to the claimant in every instance; rather, what must always be acknowledged is the possibility that the claim is authoritative. In a word, speaking *as* a member of a community requires that one has the authority to speak, at least at times, *for* the community (Cavell 1979: 18, 28).

Sustaining self-trust is not easy. It requires the cultivation of numerous intellectual and emotional skills. Prominent among these are the dialogical and reasoning skills required to argue for one's own position and the imaginative skills required to forge new concepts which make novel ways of seeing possible. These have been since its inception the skills associated with philosophical activity because they are the kind of intellectual abilities that serve well a gadfly who, like Socrates, is unafraid to assert authoritatively views that are contrary to current opinion. It should be unsurprising that the same skills are an essential part of the art of living since they are the basis for intellectual self-trust and without it one cannot sustain conviction in one's answer to the question of how one should live.

In conclusion, granted that it is the art of living, philosophy is constituted by a characteristic motivation which is self-love and by a set of abilities that prominently include self-trust and the emotional, dialectical, and imaginative skills required to sustain it. Hence, there are no specifically philosophical methods but there are philosophical skills some of which philosophers have always used. What philosophers have not always managed to do is to deploy them in conjunction with the right motivation. As a result, they have often treated philosophical activity as a project whose product would be philosophy as doctrine. In this paper I have shown that there exists an alternative conception of the discipline, one which is worthy of being performed.[31]

NOTES

1 In this paper I use the terms 'art' and 'craft' interchangeably. I do not understand crafts to be mere skills or know-hows. Instead, they can involve characteristic patterns of desire, emotion, and motivation.

2 I lack the space to address their views here. I have discussed Wittgenstein's conception of philosophy as a kind of therapy in (Tanesini 2004).

3 Or more accurately, in order to be faithful to the Greek origin of this conception, philosophy is the activity of trying to acquire the art of living. Excellence would be the preserve of the sage who has achieved wisdom rather than of the philosopher who seeks to *learn* how to live well. In this paper I shall write as if philosophy were the art itself rather than the training for the acquisition of this art.

4 My overview of the Socratic position is greatly indebted to (Sellars 2011).

5 It should be noted that ancient philosophers usually thought of the soul as the set of abilities such as self-locomotion, perception, or thinking possessed by an organism. As such the soul was not thought of as a substance that would survive the death of the body.

6 Here, and throughout this paper, I shall not address the question whether these were the views of the historical Socrates as opposed to the character in Plato's dialogues.

7 The Platonic source is (*Gorg.*: 464c).

8 Performances can include goals but the activity as a whole is not constituted by its relation to the goal.

9 The expressions 'in order to' and 'for the sake of' are often used in the literature to refer to the same distinction between means and ends (or goals), instrumental and final values (Korsgaard 1983: 170). Instead I wish to use them to mark two distinct notions. I reserve 'in order to' for the relation of means (which have instrumental value) to goals or ends (which have final value). I use the expression 'for the sake of' to mark the connection between parts (whose value is contributory) and wholes (which have final value). The distinction between an end as a

goal of an action and an end as that for the sake of which one acts has been discussed by (Velleman 2006: Ch. 4). (Blattner 2000) finds similar concerns in the work of Martin Heidegger.

10 Some desires may be persistent because they are impossible to satisfy since they are directed towards unachievable goals.

11 Of course, the activity as a whole and its parts may also be valuable as means to further ends such as health or pleasure.

12 One may take these considerations to show that a well-lived life is impossible. I think that this conclusion is unwarranted unless all other options have been shown to fail.

13 So I shall not discuss whether a well-lived life must be a happy one, or one in which one's desires are satisfied, or one that manifests a variety of objective goods.

14 I ignore the possibility that for some activities one may simply acquire the knack of how to do them.

15 I take this claim to be initially plausible. I shall not provide arguments directly to support it here.

16 As I indicate below, there may be cases in which inflated self-trust is compatible with recognition self-respect. My claim here is that warranted self-trust is a manifestation of this kind of self-respect.

17 The question does not presuppose that to live well one must live morally, in accordance with duty, or live happily. The question only presupposes that some ways of living are better *for* one than other ways.

18 This comment should not be read as claiming that desires as well as beliefs are required to motivate action. Rather, the argument offered here illustrates how love rather than desire can supply the required motivational force. The comment, however, commits me to some kind of reason internalism which says that any reason to act must bear some relation to some motivational factor. I shall not defend this commitment in this paper.

19 There is another kind of certainty which is psychological rather than epistemological in character. Understood in this sense certainty is a matter of *feeling* sure. I take this feeling to be identical to the notion of assuredness or self-confidence which I discuss below.

20 I have discussed these issues in greater detail in (Tanesini 2015) where I have defended the plausibility of attributing these views to Nietzsche. In that paper I provide textual evidence in favour of this interpretation.

21 I hasten to add that Nietzsche's actual position is more nuanced and defensible than that presented here. See (Tanesini 2015) for an elaboration and an answer to this objection.

22 This may explain why some have thought that resolute decisions can survive critical scrutiny. One may realize that one's answer to the Socratic question is arbitrary but nevertheless embrace it in its arbitrariness. When doing so, however, one exhibits assuredness or self-confidence in one's decisions.

23 I have however said nothing about how one acquires and then preserves self-trust. I discuss this issue in the final section.

24 Trust and self-trust are relative to domains of discourse or cognitive capacities. Thus, I may trust my perceptions but not my memory. I have generic self-trust when I trust myself on most important things.

25 I shall assume here that the self is identical with the set of abilities which make up one's soul. Thus, I use 'self' or 'oneself' as approximations for the notion of character.

26 Hence, love of oneself is not to be confused with exclusive concern for one's own interests.

27 There will be others. These may include desires such as the desire that one is healthy. What these other motivations may be depends on one's specific answer to the question of how to live.

28 Reasons of space prevent me from addressing the topic here. For a discussion of related issues, see (Tanesini 2016).

29 However, as Jones notes (2012: 244), self-trust is a corrective for excessive self-analysis.

30 This may be knowledge or warranted belief. I shall not take a stance on this question here.

31 I would like to thank the editors and an anonymous referee for their insightful comments.

2   Philosophy as Rational Systematization

I. PHILOSOPHY AS A VENTURE IN RATIONAL ENQUIRY

The definitive mission of philosophy is to provide a basis for understanding the world and our place within it as intelligent agents – with 'the world' understood comprehensively to encompass the realms of nature, culture, and artifice. The aim of the enterprise is to provide us with cognitive orientation for conducting our intellectual and practical affairs. And the data of philosophy by whose means this project must be managed include alike the observation-based science of reality, the imaginable realm of speculative possibility, and the normative manifold of evaluation. Given this massive mandate, the prime flaw of philosophizing is a narrowness of vision. Granted the issues are complex and specialization becomes necessary. But its cultivation is never sufficient because the details must always be fitted into a comprehensive whole.

Philosophy is a potentially many-sided enterprise. Some philosophers want to energize action, some to edify aspiration, some to clarify thinking, some to enhance knowledge, some to improve living. Some are concerned primarily for the body, some for the intellect, some for the spirit. But common to the affective pursuit of all these objectives is understanding – understanding ourselves, the world we live in, and the linkage between the two.

Philosophy is a venture in question-resolution – a cognitive enterprise addressing the traditional 'big questions' about ourselves and our place in the world's scheme of things. At the centre of its concern lie the traditional issues of correct believing, appropriate valuing, right acting, good living, and the like, that have formed the core of the subject since its inception in classical antiquity.

The development of understanding is a matter of rational enquiry, a cognitive enterprise subject to the usual ground rules of cognitive and practical rationality.[1] The discipline seeks to bring rational order, system, and intelligibility to the often confusing diversity of our cognitive affairs enabling us to find our way about in the world in a practically effective and cognitively satisfying way. Philosophy is indeed a venture in theorizing, but one whose rationale is eminently practical. A rational animal that has to make its evolutionary way in the world by its wits has a deep-rooted demand for speculative reason. It is rooted in human curiosity – in the 'fact of life' that we have questions and feel a need to obtain cognitively satisfying answers to them.

Philosophizing in the classical manner – exploiting the available indications of experience to answer those big questions on the agenda of traditional philosophy – is predicated on the use of reason to do the best we can to align our cognitive commitments with the substance of our experience. In this sense, philosophizing involves an act of faith: when we draw on our experience to answer our questions we have to proceed in the tentative hope that the best we can do is good enough, at any rate for our immediate purposes.

In the final analysis there is no alternative to philosophizing as long as we remain in the province of reason. The salient point was already well put by Aristotle: '[Even if we join those who believe that philosophizing is not possible] in this case too we are obliged to inquire how it is possible for there to be no Philosophy; and then, in inquiring, we philosophize, for rational inquiry is the essence of Philosophy' (Aristotle 1955: vii).[2] To those who are prepared simply to abandon philosophy, to withdraw from the whole project of trying to make sense of things, we can have little to say. (How can one reason with those who deny the pointfulness and propriety of reasoning?) But with those who *argue* for its abandonment we can do something – once we have enrolled them in the community as fellow theorists with a position of their own. F. H. Bradley hit the nail on the head: 'The man who is ready to prove that metaphysical knowledge is impossible ... is a brother metaphysician with a rival theory of first principles' (Bradley 1897: 1). One can abandon philosophy, but one cannot *advocate* its abandonment through rational argumentation without philosophizing.

2. THE DATA OF PHILOSOPHY

In perusing a philosophical discussion, the first question that should figure in the reader's mind is: 'What problem is this discussion endeavouring to solve – what questions is it trying to answer?' And then two others fall naturally into place, namely 'What sort of answer is being offered to us?' and 'Does this way of dealing with the issue make good sense, or does it pose more difficulties than it resolves?'

In philosophizing we strive for rational coherence in achieving answers to our questions. But how is one to proceed in this venture? It is clear that here, as in other branches of enquiry, we must begin with data.

Neither individually nor collectively do we humans begin our cognitive quest empty handed, equipped with only a blank tablet. Be it as single individuals or as entire generations, we always begin with a diversified cognitive heritage, falling heir to that great mass of information and misinformation afforded by the 'knowledge' of our predecessors – or those among them to whom we choose to listen. What William James called our 'funded experience' of the world's ways – of its nature and our place within it – constitute the *data* at philosophy's disposal in its endeavour to accomplish its question-resolving work. These specifically include:

- common-sense beliefs, common knowledge, and what have been 'the ordinary convictions of the plain man' since time immemorial;
- the facts (or purported facts) afforded by the science of the day; the views of well-informed 'experts' and 'authorities';
- the lessons we derive from our dealings with the world in everyday life;
- the received opinions that constitute the worldview of the day; views that accord with the 'spirit of the times' and the ambient convictions of one's cultural context;
- tradition, inherited lore, and ancestral wisdom (including religious tradition);
- the 'teachings of history' as best we can discern them.

There is no clear limit to the scope of philosophy's potentially useful data. The lessons of human experience in all of its cognitive dimensions afford the materials of philosophy. No plausible source of information about how matters stand in the world fails to bring grist to the mill. The whole range of the (purportedly) established 'facts of experience' furnishes the extra-philosophical inputs for our philosophizing – the potentially usable materials, as it were, for our philosophical reflections.

And all of these data have much to be said for them: common sense, tradition, general belief, and plausible prior theorizing – the sum total of the different sectors of 'our experience' in the widest sense of the term. They all merit consideration: all exert some degree of cognitive pressure in having a claim upon us. Yet while those data deserve respect they do not deserve acceptance. And they certainly do not constitute established knowledge. There is nothing sacred and sacrosanct about them. For, taken as a whole, the data are too much for tenability – collectively they generally run into conflicts and contradictions. The long and short of it is that the data of philosophy constitute a plethora of fact (or purported fact) so ample as to threaten to sink any ship that carries so heavy a cargo. The constraint they put upon us is thus not peremptory and absolute – they do not represent certainties to which we must cling at all costs. Even the plainest of 'plain facts' can be questioned, as indeed some of them must be, since in the aggregate they are collectively inconsistent. And so for the philosopher, nothing is absolutely sacred. The difficulty is – and always has been – that the data of philosophy afford an embarrassment of riches. They engender a situation of cognitive overcommitment within which inconsistencies arise. For they are not only manifold and diversified but invariably yield discordant results. And here philosophy finds its work cut out for it.

In philosophy, we cannot accept all those 'givens' as certified facts that must be endorsed wholly and unqualifiedly. Every datum is defeasible – anything might in the final analysis have to be abandoned, whatever its source: science, common sense, common knowledge, the whole lot. In view of such tensions those data cannot be viewed as truths but only as plausibilities. They are merely suggestive and indicative in their bearing and significance rather than decisive. Nothing about them is immune to criticism and possible rejection; everything is potentially at risk. One insightful commentator has affirmed that: 'No philosophical, or any other, theory can provide a view which violates common sense and remain logically consistent.

For the truth of common sense is assumed by all theories ... This necessity to conform to common sense establishes a constraint upon the interpretations philosophical theories can offer' (Kekes 1980: 196). But this is very problematic. The philosophical landscape is littered with theories that tread common sense underfoot. There are no sacred cows in philosophy – common sense least of all. As philosophy goes about its work of rendering our beliefs systemically coherent, something to which we are deeply attached will have to give, and we can never say at the outset where the blow will or will not fall. Systemic considerations at the global level may in the end lead to difficulties at any particular point.

For these data do indeed all have some degree of merit and, given our cognitive situation, it would be very convenient if they turned out to be true. But this is unhappily not the case, for they all too often give conflicting indications. And yet philosophy cannot simply turn its back on these data without further ado. Its methodology must be one of damage control and salvage. For as regards those data, it should always be our goal to save as much as we coherently can.

3. PHILOSOPHY CANNOT AVOID SPECULATION

The use of data in philosophy is necessary and unavoidable. But it is not sufficient because for philosophical purposes these data are merely suggestive and inconclusive. They invariably fall short of providing answers to our questions. For those 'big questions' are large and far-reaching while those data are particularized, limited, and circumscribed in their bearing. They lie within the horizons of our experience, while the questions we propose to settle by their means are large and experience transcending in scope. Even as in natural science observation cannot *demonstrate* a theory but only *evidentiate* it, so in philosophy our data can do no more. They need to be extended and transcended – supplemented by speculative conjecture.

But of course those philosophical conjectures should not be unfounded and arbitrary. Our claims must coordinate with those data in a rationally harmonious way. And this is where systematization comes into it. For the reality of it is that if our philosophizing is to proceed in a cogent and convincing way, these issue-resolving speculations must achieve a condition of an optimally best-fit with the data at our disposal.

4. PHILOSOPHY PIVOTS ON RATIONAL SYSTEMATIZATION

That the prospect and promise of coherentism as a cognitive methodology is nowhere more clearly manifest than in philosophy itself has been – or should have been – reasonably clear ever since Kant's critical rejection of Spinoza's sequential axiomatic *more geometrico* reasoning in philosophy.[3] For in philosophy there is and can be nothing that is basic, axiomatic, self-evident, and exempt from question. We have no choice but to begin here with data whose status is largely tentative and presumptive. Charles Sanders Peirce rightly noted this aspect of network systematization when he wrote:

Philosophy ought to imitate the successful sciences in its methods, so far as to proceed only from tangible premises which can be subjected to careful scrutiny, and to trust rather to the multitude and variety of its arguments than to the conclusiveness of any one. Its reasoning should not form a chain which is no stronger than its weakest link, but a cable whose fibers may be ever so slender, provided they are sufficiently numerous and intimately connected.

(CP5: 265)[4]

In philosophy, our acceptance policy is based on considerations of overall best-fit, where the fit at issue is one of consonance and coordination with our prevailing commitments.

On such an approach we begin with a philosophical question, say: 'Are there ever cogent excuses for doing something morally wrong?' We then make a systematic canvas of the range of plausibly available answers (say 'never', 'rarely', 'often'). And thereupon we examine what argumentative pros and cons can be produced for each of the alternatives. Next, we weigh out, case by case, how smoothly the ramifications and implications of the reasons (pro and con) that are involved in each case fit into the overall indications of the data – of that which we otherwise know and believe – assessing what sort of discord and dissonance each of them would engender. Our philosophy thus does not in general ignore or suspend the cognitive materials obtained on other fronts (e.g., a science or everyday life experience). Rather it tries to accomplish its cognitive work with maximal overall utilization of and minimal overall disruption to the relevant information that our other more familiar cognitive resources provide.

Philosophers generally pursue their mission of grappling with those traditional 'big questions' regarding ourselves, the world, and our place within its scheme of things by means of what is perhaps best characterized as *rational conjecture*. Conjecture comes into it because – ironically – those questions arise most pressingly where the available information does not suffice – where they are no straightforwardly available answers in terms of what has already been established.

Rational conjecture based on systematic considerations is the key method of philosophical enquiry, affording our best hope for obtaining promising answers to the questions that confront us. Our philosophical view of reality's nature is thus taken to emerge as an intellectual product achieved under the control of the idea that systematicity is a regulative principle for our theorizing. Here, evidentiation and systematicity are inextricably correlative. Philosophizing is a matter of the systematizing of question-resolving conjecture and the products of 'experience' – in the broadest sense of this term. The object of the exercise is to determine the best candidates among competing alternatives – searching for that resolution for which, on balance, the strongest overall case can be made out. And seeing that a fundamentally reductive approach typifies the procedure of philosophy, it is not 'the uniquely correct answer' but 'the least problematic, most defensible position' that we can hope to secure. The appropriate goal is the problem resolution that fits most smoothly and harmoniously within our overall commitment to the manifold 'data' at stake in these philosophical matters.

What is needed here is a methodology of enquiry that is *ampliative* in C. S. Peirce's sense of underwriting contentions whose assertoric content goes beyond the evidence in hand.[5] We need to do the very best we can to achieve resolutions that transcend accreted experience and outrun the reach of the information already at our disposal. It thus becomes necessary to have a plausible means for obtaining the best available, the 'rationally optimal', answers to our information-in-hand-transcending questions about how matters stand in the world. And experience-based conjecture – theorizing if you will – is the most promising available instrument for question-resolution in the face of imperfect information. It is a tool for use by finite intelligences, providing them not with the best *possible* answer in some rarified sense of this term, but with the best *available* answer, the putative best that one can manage to secure in the actually existing conditions in which we do and must conduct our epistemic labours.

Here as elsewhere there is no categorical assurance that the 'best available' answers that we obtain through best-fit systematization are in fact correct. Nevertheless, the 'best available' answer at issue here is intended in a rather strong sense. We want not just an 'answer' of some sort but a viable and acceptable answer – one to whose tenability we are willing to commit ourselves. The rational conjecture at issue is not to be a matter of *mere guesswork*, but one of *responsible estimation* in a strict sense of the term. It is not *just* an estimate of the true answer that we want but an estimate that is sensible and defensible: *tenable*, in short. We may need to resort to more information than is actually given, but we do not want to make it up 'out of thin air'. The provision of reasonable warrant for rational assurance is the object of the enterprise.

In the information-deficient, enthymematic circumstances that prevail when philosophical questions must be resolved in the face of evidential underdetermination, we have and can have no logically airtight *guarantees*. We must recognize that there is no prospect of assessing the truth – or presumptive truth – of philosophical claims apart from using our imperfect mechanisms of enquiry and systematization. And here it is *estimation* that affords the best means for doing the job. We are not – and presumably will never be – in a position to stake a totally secure claim to the definitive truth regarding those great issues of philosophical interest. But we certainly can – and indeed must – do the best we can to achieve a reasonable *estimate* of the truth.

Philosophizing thus consists in a rational rebuilding of the structure of our beliefs in the effort to do what we can to erect a solid and secure edifice out of the ill-assorted contents placed at our disposal by our initial restrictions to belief. On this approach, the validation of an item of knowledge – the rationalization of its inclusion alongside others within 'the body of our knowledge' – proceeds by way of exhibiting its interrelationships with the rest: they must all be linked together in a connected, mutually supportive way (rather than having the form of an inferential structure built up upon a footing of rock-bottom axioms).

5. A NEED FOR THE 'LARGER VIEW'

In philosophy, as in various other cognitive domains, two very different approaches to problem-solving can be implemented. The first is a narrower, localist course of opting for the least risky – and thus the least informative – answer to our immediate questions that can accommodate the putative facts of the case (minimalism). The second is the more ambitious course of opting for the globally most adequate – and thus most risky – among the 'available' answers that is compatible with the facts (maximalism).

Against this background, various schools of epistemic minimalism go about posting signposts that put all risk of engaging larger issues OFF LIMITS. Such theorists turn Occam's razor into Robespierre's guillotine. Their tumbrels carry off a wide variety of victims:

- *sets* in the philosophy of mathematics;
- *abstracta* in semantics;
- *unobservable entities* in the philosophy of physics;
- *dispositional theses* in the philosophy of language;
- *obligations* that reach beyond the requisites of prudence in moral theory, etc. etc.

Reluctant to venture beyond the immediate, local, case-specific requisites of the first-order agenda epistemological demands, the philosophical minimalist is content to accept incomprehension on the larger issues. All too often, observability alone is the standard of reality and causal and explanatory questions are ruled out. Why do phenomena have the character we observe? Don't ask. What accounts for the lawfulness of their interrelationships? Don't ask! Why are they uniform for different observers? Don't ask! What of factual claims that go beyond observability? Throw them out! What about claims that transcend the prospect of decisive verification? Eject them.

But such an approach is not without its problems. The fact is that, in philosophy, as elsewhere, minimalism proves to be a very questionable bargain. Here – as elsewhere – some investment in added capacity is generally required for extra capability. In philosophy, as in life, the economies of a minimalism are unwise practices that frequently produce long-term waste.

To be sure, one can readily imagine a narrowly focused specialist who is prepared to say something like this:

As far as I am concerned, the limits of my core interests are the limits of my world. Having worked out what I see as the optimal solution for the local issues of my chosen field of primary specialization, I simply don't care about its ramifications anywhere else. Local optimization is all that concerns me – global implications and ramifications are a matter of indifference to me.

One can readily *imagine* someone having this attitude. But certainly one cannot *approve* of it. For it imports into philosophy a fanaticism and narrow-minded unconcern for wider ramifications that sensible people reject in virtually every other context.

The systematic nature of philosophy-as-a-whole has far-reaching implications for the proper cultivation of the discipline. In particular, it means that we should not – nay cannot – rest satisfied with isolated piecework, with single pieces of doctrine whose merits do not extend beyond immediate adequacy in a local problem area. For in philosophizing, as in economic matters, externalities may come into play. A seemingly elegant solution to the difficulties posed by one problem may carry in its wake hopeless difficulties for the satisfactory resolution of some other problem. Its ramifications in another, seemingly remote, area may require one to pay an unacceptable price for the neat resolution of a problem in a given domain. One may, for example, feel compelled to be forced into accepting an epistemology that one does not much like for itself (say, value intuitionism) in the interests of possibilizing an ethical position (here moral objectivity) that one deems essential.

Philosophizing is, in this regard, akin to cognitive engineering. For the sensible philosopher, like the sensible engineer, must proceed holistically with a view to the *overall* implications of his or her particular ventures in problem solving. An engineer who allows one particular desideratum (cost, safety, fuel economy, repair infrequency, or the like) to dominate his or her thinking, to the exclusion of all else, would not produce a viable product, but an absurdity. We would certainly laugh at someone who offered to build us a supersafe car – but one that would go only two miles per hour. Surely a similar derision is deserved by the sceptic who offers to build us a supersafe, error-excluding epistemology that would not, however, allow us to maintain a line of distinction between science and pseudoscience. In philosophy as in economics, engineering, and medicine we cannot avoid concern for externalities and have to come to grips with incidental interactions and side-effects. In chess, we cannot play rooks independently of what we do with bishops; in medicine, we cannot treat one organ independently of the implications for others; in political economy, we cannot design policies for one sector without concerning ourselves with their impact upon the rest. In almost any problem-solving context we do well to keep all our commitments in reasonable coordination overall. Why should philosophy be any different?

A philosopher who achieves her proximate, localized ends at the cost of off-loading difficulties onto other sectors of the wider domain is simply not doing an adequate job. With rationally cogent philosophizing, it is not local minimalism but global optimalism that is required. To be acceptable, a philosophical problem-solution must form an integral part of a wider doctrine that makes acceptably good sense overall. Here only systemic, holistically attuned positions can yield truly satisfactory solutions – solutions that do not involve undue externalities for the larger scheme of things.[6]

6. PHILOSOPHICAL DISAGREEMENT IS UNAVOIDABLE

The preceding discussion has argued that philosophizing is a matter of endeavouring to answer the subject's 'big questions' on the basis of considerations of best-fit harmonization with the data of experience. But if this – or anything like it – is indeed so, then it must be acknowledged and accepted that there is bound to be doctrinal disagreement in this field. For the corpus of experience of different individuals is not just likely but virtually certain to differ on the basis of their exposure to historical, cultural, and circumstantial developments. Here there can be no 'one size fits all' resolution. And where evidentiating considerations differ it is inevitable that the conclusions that can rationally be based upon them must do so as well.

The crucial fact here is that different people living in different conditions are bound to differ in regard to what their experience affords them. And even where they have many experiences in common, they can still differ in their view of significance and priority: what things are central or peripheral, what are significant or insignificant, and the like. And this circumstance will of course orientate them very differently in their approach to the data.

But this view of the matter is not an indifferent relativism. It is not a matter of taste or personal inclination which sorts of consideration are significant or insignificant, central or peripheral, inductive or incidental, and so on. Rather the crux is – or should be – a matter of rational assessment on the basis of the burden of available experience. So what we have is a rationally grounded experimental contextualism where, in philosophy as in science, a kind of empiricism obtains. For here too it is experience in the widest sense of the term that can and should determine the considerations by whose means we resolve the questions that concern us.[7]

A tenable philosophy must be a systematically dovetailed whole. For in the end the range of our philosophical concern is a network where everything is systematically interconnected with everything else.

NOTES

1 There are, of course, very different ways of *doing* philosophy even as there are different ways of cooking food. But the enterprise itself is characterized by its defining objective: if one isn't doing that sort of thing, then one isn't pursuing it. (Sewing is not cooking food, nor is journalism philosophy.)

2 For the text, see (Aristotle 1955: 28). But see also (Chroust 1969: 48–50).

3 Kant 1933: see the section on 'The Architectonic of Pure Reason'.

4 Following the standard reference system to Peirce, *Collected Papers*.

5 For Charles Sanders Peirce, 'ampliative' reasoning is synthetic in that its conclusion goes beyond ('transcends') the information stipulated in the given premises (i.e., cannot be derived from them by logical processes of deduction alone), so that it 'follows' from them only inconclusively (cf. CP2: 680, *et passim*).

6 Some of these themes are also discussed in (Rescher 1994: Ch. 2).

7 The author's position on metaphilosophy is developed in a series of books published over many years: (Rescher 1985, 2000, 2006a, 2006b).

3   Sense-making From a Human Point of View

I.THE ARTISTIC CONCEPTION OF PHILOSOPHY

A view famously held by Bernard Williams is that philosophy is a humanistic discipline (Williams 2006b).[1] I entirely endorse this view – and the reasons he gives for it. I have tried to defend something similar elsewhere (Moore 2012: esp. 602–4).[2] I shall not try to offer any further defence here. For the purposes of this essay I shall take the view in question as a kind of datum. I am concerned with what follows from it, or rather with what follows from one particular embellishment of it, and with certain problems that this embellishment poses.

But I must begin by saying something about what the view is; or rather, what it is not. It is not the view that philosophy is one of the human sciences. One might think that this barely needs saying. For one thing, is there not a familiar and well entrenched distinction, within academia, between the humanities and the human sciences? Maybe there is (although it is worth remembering that there are at least two disciplines, history and linguistics, which are standardly included in the humanities and which might also reasonably be classified as human sciences).[3] However, that is beside the point. For the point is not simply to classify philosophy as one of the humanities either. (Williams makes this clear right at the beginning of his essay.) The point is rather, as Williams himself puts it, to signal 'what models or ideals or analogies [we] should … look to in thinking about the ways in which philosophy should be done' (Williams 2006b: 180). A slogan that helps to convey the point is this: philosophy, though it is not anthropological, is anthropocentric. That is to say, philosophy, though it is not the scientific study of human beings or of any of the peculiarities that mark their way of

44

life, has a fundamental concern with human beings and with what it takes to be one and is properly pursued, at the deepest level, from a human point of view. Philosophy is an attempt, by humans, from their unique position in the world, to make sense both of themselves and of that position.

But 'make sense of' is a polymorphous term. One respect in which I would want to go beyond what Williams says is by urging that we take seriously the term's overtones of invention rather than discovery in this context. I believe that the sense-making involved in philosophy, at least in philosophy of the best sort, is, quite literally, sense-*making*: not an exploration of something antecedently given, but a creation of something, most notably a creation of concepts by which to live (such as Kant's concept of a kingdom of ends, or Nietzsche's concept of eternal return, to pick two signal examples).[4]

Let us call the conception of philosophy on which it is both humanistic in Williams' sense and creative in the sense just indicated the 'artistic' conception. (This is what I had in mind when I referred to an embellishment of Williams' view.) Now if, as I hold, the artistic conception is correct, then we can straight away identify two things of which philosophers need to beware: one of these relates primarily to the element of humanism in the conception, the other to the element of creativity in it. The first thing of which they need to beware, the one that relates primarily to the element of humanism in the conception, is scientism. That is, they need to beware of the unwarranted appropriation of procedures that are suited to the natural sciences. *Sometimes* the appropriation of such procedures in the pursuit of philosophy is perfectly acceptable and not precluded by anything that I have said on behalf of the conception. For instance, among the many things in which philosophers can quite properly show an interest are the natural sciences themselves, these being (after all) a very significant part of human life; and such an interest may well include self-conscious engagement with them (cf. Williams 2006b: 182 and Williams 2006c: 203). But there can be no presumption that procedures suited to the natural sciences will in general serve philosophy well.

The second thing of which philosophers need to beware, the one that relates primarily to the element of creativity in the artistic conception, is conservatism. If one of the purposes of philosophy is sense-making, understood quite literally as the production of something, then philosophers had better not be too beholden to extant forms of sense-making. They had better feel no compunction about modifying these, extending them in various ways, establishing new connections between them, supplementing them – or even challenging, disrupting, discarding, and replacing them.[5] This I take to be an anti-Wittgensteinian idea. Wittgenstein is not in general a conservative with respect to sense-making (see e.g., Wittgenstein 1967: §132). But he *is* a conservative with respect to sense-making in philosophy, which he famously says 'leaves everything as it is' (ibid.: §124). For Wittgenstein, the purpose of philosophy is to cure us of the confusions that arise when we mishandle our own conceptual apparatus (ibid.: §§89–133). Innovation in our sense-making can only ever bring with it the risk of new confusions whereas, on Wittgenstein's view, philosophers should be looking to minimize that risk. That is contrary to the spirit of the artistic conception.

2. THE DISTINCTION BETWEEN ANALYTIC PHILOSOPHY AND CONTINENTAL PHILOSOPHY: A PROBLEM FOR THE ARTISTIC CONCEPTION

It is instructive, in the light of these twin dangers of scientism and conservatism, to consider how the artistic conception relates to the distinction that is standardly drawn between 'analytic' philosophy and 'continental' philosophy.

Now I am, in common with many others, impatient both with the connotations that the drawing of this distinction typically has and with the absurd terminology that is used to draw it (cf. Williams 2006c: 201). But I do not deny that such a distinction exists; nor do I see any great advantage in trying, at this stage, to promote a new label for it. More to the point, I think that the distinction has something to teach us about the artistic conception. It does this by creating a paradox vis-à-vis that conception. For, as far as actual practice is concerned, it is continental philosophers whom we might expect to be more sympathetic to the conception. They are the ones who seem more ready to engage with other humanistic disciplines, such as history and literary theory, and to do so, moreover, in such a way as to suggest some continuity with their own endeavours. They are the ones whose practice is on the whole more playful.

Analytic philosophers are the ones who more often proceed as though they were mapping the features of something independent of the mapping, indeed independent of humanity altogether. They are the ones who are more likely to need reminding of the danger of scientism. On the other hand, as far as self-image is concerned, that is as far as the practitioners' own conception of the scope and limits of philosophy is concerned, it is, if not exactly the other way round, then at least more nearly the other way round. Analytic philosophers are the ones who are liable to think that what they do is regulated by appeal to, or with reference to, some such fundamentally human phenomenon as language or discursive knowledge.[6,7] It is among continental philosophers that we are more likely to find the view that what philosophy is, first and foremost, is pursuit of the great questions of ontology.[8]

Part of my response to this paradox is simply to acknowledge a failing in the practice of some analytic philosophers, a failing which does indeed suggest that they have paid insufficient heed to the danger of scientism. It is not just that their practice is not true to philosophy as I conceive it, that is to the artistic conception. Their practice is not true to philosophy as *they* conceive it. Nor is it true to their own heritage. A significant part of that heritage is the aim, not only to make sense, but to make clear sense, where clarity is a matter of presentation, and where presentation presupposes an audience. Analytic philosophers should be more self-conscious than they very often are, first about who their audience might be, and second about the need to make sense of things from some suitable point of view that they share with that audience. This shared point of view will typically be much more restricted than a human point of view. But it will not typically be less restricted.

For one prominent example of the failing that I have in mind, consider Derek Parfit's book *Reasons and Persons* (1984). In his conclusion to that book, Parfit discusses the various kinds of argument that he has invoked. He says that these lie between two extremes (where 'between' is understood in such a way that this includes the two extremes themselves): what he calls 'the Low Road', which 'merely appeals to our intuitions', and what he calls 'the High Road', which 'asks what is the meaning of moral language, or the nature of moral reasoning' (Parfit 1984: 447). Both extremes, and the territory between them, involve a human element of the kind to which I have alluded. Yet Parfit's conclusions in the book are notoriously detached from any relevant point of view that he might share with his audience. For instance, he argues that there are good reasons to induce in ourselves dispositions that will subserve a certain ethical theory while keeping the content of that theory hidden (Parfit 1984: Pt. I, *passim*); but he does little or nothing to say what this means from the point of view of those for whom, if he were right, the practicalities of inducing such dispositions (not least by suppressing reflective self-consciousness of the very kind that his own argument has instilled) would constitute a real social and political problem.[9]

Is there a mirror-image failing in the practice of some continental philosophers? Is there a similar mismatch between their practice and their self-image? That would afford an interesting symmetry, if it were so. In fact, however, there is no obvious reason to think that it is so – not if we focus on the anthropocentrism that is evidenced in their practice. The great questions of ontology can certainly be addressed in an anthropocentric way. Phenomenology provides the model. Heidegger at one point equates phenomenology with ontology (and each, in turn, with philosophy);[10] but he also insists that it should be executed with peculiar reference to the sort of being that each human being is, namely *Dasein* (Heidegger 1962: 61–2).

I said that we see no mirror-image failing in the practice of continental philosophers if we focus on the anthropocentrism that is evidenced in their practice. But what if we focus on the creativity that is evidenced in their practice – creativity being the other element in the artistic conception – and then reflect on the associated danger of conservatism? Is there perhaps, if not a tension between addressing the great questions of ontology and proceeding anthropocentrically, then a tension between doing both of those things and being radically innovative?

What tension do I have in mind? Well, consider this. Why should the radical innovation that I have suggested is a feature of the best philosophy not be *so* radical that it brings us to a new conception of who 'we' are and of what it takes to be one of 'us'; *so* radical, in other words, that it provides us with ways of making sense of things that leave our humanity behind? There are various things that might be at stake here. We might come to reassess the relations between human beings and other animals in such a way that the former no longer have the special significance for us that is required for there to be a distinctively human point of view. Or advances in technology might challenge the very application of the concept of a human being in such a way that we are eventually led to abandon the concept altogether. And there is indeed, in certain continental philosophers, a preparedness, if not an aspiration, to think beyond the human in this way. Foucault, Deleuze, and Guattari are among the clearest and most interesting cases in point.[11] How can philosophy be pursued in a spirit such as this, while remaining resolutely anthropocentric?

It is a good question. There is certainly a tension here. It is not, however, a tension that peculiarly afflicts any continental philosophers. I represented it above as a tension between three elements: the anthropocentrism evidenced in the practice of continental philosophers; the creativity evidenced there, where this is creativity of a kind that allows for radical innovation; and the pursuit of the great questions of ontology that many continental philosophers take to be their *métier*. But the third is not really relevant. The tension is already there between the first two. And this means that, if it afflicts anyone, it afflicts me. For those are precisely the two elements in the artistic conception. It is an urgent question for me, then, how this tension can be resolved.

3. THINKING BEYOND THE HUMAN IN PHILOSOPHY

Is the following a reasonable way of resolving the tension?

We should indeed be open to the possibility of thinking beyond the human in philosophy. But what this means is that we *humans* should be open to the possibility of thinking beyond the human in philosophy. We should be open to the possibility that our philosophy will one day no longer need to be, or may even one day no longer have the proper resources to be, anthropocentric. Nevertheless, we cannot oversee its becoming non-anthropocentric except by overseeing its evolution from something anthropocentric. And 'evolution' is the right word here. Nothing can happen in a metamorphic flash. Quite apart from whatever gradual transformation may have to be involved in our coming to embrace non-human possibilities outside philosophy, there is a gradual transformation that will certainly have to be involved in our coming to embrace non-human possibilities within philosophy. We cannot come to make radically new philosophical sense of things save through a progressive piecemeal process. (This is a conceptual point, not an anthropological point. There is a limit to how drastic and how rapid an upheaval in our philosophical sense-making can be while still counting as an upheaval in our philosophical sense-making – as opposed to our being as it were magically transported to some new position on the philosophical landscape.) So *for now* our philosophy needs to be anthropocentric. That is the only way, for now, in which we its practitioners can appropriate the sense that it helps us to make of things as distinctively ours, and the only way, therefore, in which we can recognize it as having the value and importance for us that it should. The tension between philosophy's anthropocentrism and its creativity is resolved by our recognizing the former as provisional.

Yes, I think that *is* a reasonable way of resolving the tension, at least in outline. Even so, I am uncomfortable with letting the matter rest there. For I also think we should be extremely *wary* of thinking beyond the human in this way. I have already remarked on Wittgenstein's conservatism and Deleuze's anti-conservatism; and I have made it clear that my sympathies are with the latter. However, there is a further, related disparity between the two thinkers with respect to which my sympathies are more with the former. And this inclines me towards a conservatism of practice, if not of principle.

The disparity that I have in mind turns on Wittgenstein's and Deleuze's different conceptions of *the given*. Wittgenstein says that what are given are forms of life (Wittgenstein 1967: 226). Deleuze says that what are given are differences (Deleuze 1994: 222). It is not obvious that there is any conflict between these – not least because it is not obvious that they mean the same by 'the given'. Even so, there is. For Wittgenstein, a form of life, which he relates very closely to a language (Wittgenstein 1967: §§19, 23, and 241), provides a kind of framework within which sense is made of things. The limits of our form of life, we might say, are the limits of our world.[12] That would be an anathema for Deleuze, for whom all unity – including the unity of any framework of this kind – has to be constituted *within* multiplicity, that is to say within what he counts as the given,[13] and must itself, accordingly, be made sense of in the same way as everything else.

I lean towards Wittgenstein in this conflict. There seems to me something fundamentally right in the idea that, for sense to be made of things, there must first of all be some such framework for it to be made within, a framework determining whose sense it is. And if there *is* something fundamentally right in this idea, then any disruption of the sort that would be required for us to think beyond the human in philosophy would have to be a disruption to more than just our sense-making. There would have to be, beyond whatever new sense we made of things, a new 'we' making it. For Deleuze, too, there would have to be a new 'we'. But, for Deleuze, this new 'we' would itself be a product of our sense-making, a sort of self-creation. The changes that would be involved in our thinking beyond the human, however extreme, would be of a piece with the changes that would be involved in our extending our sense-making in any other way. On a more Wittgensteinian conception, however, something more radical would be at stake. And the radicalness would be an ethical radicalness. For, in so far as the primary ethical question is the question of what it is for 'us' to live well, ethics itself would be called into question. None of this is a conclusive reason to eschew all such disruption. But it is a reason, an ethical reason, to tread extremely carefully.

4. SPINOZA: A CASE STUDY

Let us take the case of Spinoza.[14] Spinoza might be reckoned an opponent of anthropocentrism in philosophy. One of his best known doctrines is that our supreme virtue involves our making sense of things *sub specie æternitatis* (Spinoza 2002a: Pt. V, Props 29ff.). In fact, however – be the interpretation of that doctrine as it may – there is something profoundly anthropocentric in Spinoza's philosophy. Nowhere is this more blatant than in his account of the difference between good and bad. Spinoza denies that these are anything 'positive considered in themselves' (ibid.: Pt. IV, Pref.). Rather, they are ways we have of thinking of things, according to our desires. Thus, in Spinoza's view, we judge a thing to be good because we desire it; we do not desire it because we judge it to be good (ibid.: Pt. III, Prop. 9, Schol.). This, of course, entails a kind of relativism, as Spinoza freely acknowledges (e.g., ibid.: Pt. III, Prop. 39, Schol., and Pt. IV, Pref.). Nevertheless, because he believes that there is a 'model of human nature that we all set before ourselves', *and because he is writing from a shared human point of view,*

Spinoza is able to bypass the relativism and define the good as 'that which we certainly know to be the means for our approaching nearer to the model' and the bad as 'that which we certainly know prevents us from reproducing the said model' (ibid.: Pt. IV, Pref.). Such anthropocentrism is striking in its own right. But it is striking also for a more indirect reason, highly pertinent to the caution that I am now urging. It counteracts what would otherwise be a disturbing and sinister aspect of Spinoza's philosophy, itself a natural attendant of the relativism to which he is committed, namely the doctrine that the right of each thing extends as far as its power does (Spinoza 2002b: Ch. 16, §4).[15] Thus the right of a tiger on the loose extends as far as its power does; the right of a cancerous growth extends as far as its power does; the right of a repressive regime extends as far as its power does. Spinoza's anthropocentrism provides a bulwark here. As soon as we can see that an exercise of one of these powers is preventing us from reproducing the model of human nature in some way, we can see that it is bad; and we can accordingly resist it. To quote Max Stirner: 'The tiger that assails me is in the right, and I who strike him down am also in the right. I defend against him not my *right*, but *myself*' (Stirner 1982: 128, emphasis in original).

By the same token, were we to start trying to extend Spinozism beyond the human, we would undermine the assurances that such anthropocentrism provides and exacerbate that which is troubling in Spinoza's power-centred vision. We might, for instance, begin to take seriously a point of view from which the flourishing of individuals was subordinate to the flourishing of the state.[16] Admittedly, 'assurances' and 'troubling', like 'good' and 'bad', are to be understood from a human point of view. But that, in a way, is the point. The point is not that there is some neutral position from which to evaluate different forms of philosophizing; precisely not. The point is that our philosophizing and our evaluating are, at least for now, from a common point of view, a human point of view, and, as long as that is the case, we are bound to acknowledge the dangers, that is to say the *human* dangers, in its being otherwise.

To be sure, the sheer fact that there is no Archimedean point means that it is equally important for us to acknowledge the dangers, perhaps the *non*-human dangers, in our remaining beholden to one particular philosophical paradigm.[17] But that does not gainsay the conclusion that philosophy is, at least for now, an exercise in making sense of things from a human point of view. It merely reinforces the conclusion that we must proceed with care when doing philosophy. Only, let us not underestimate the force of this conclusion. For if philosophy *is* an exercise in making sense of things from a human point of view – if, as I put it earlier, philosophy is an attempt, by humans, from their unique position in the world, to make sense both of themselves and of that position – then the care with which we must proceed when we are doing philosophy is the care with which we must proceed when our very humanity is in question.[18]

NOTES

1 See also (Williams 2014) for associated reflections on the nature of the humanities.

2 Something similar but not the same, because my concern in that book is specifically with metaphysics and not with philosophy more generally. Still, my concern is with metaphysics on a somewhat idiosyncratic and very generous characterization of metaphysics, as the most general attempt to make sense of things (a characterization that many people would in fact take to be more appropriate for philosophy as a whole). And much of what this excludes within philosophy – such as aesthetics, ethics, political philosophy, and philosophy of religion – gives the discipline, if anything, an even greater claim to the title of being humanistic.

3 It is also worth remembering that Collingwood took metaphysics to be a branch of history: see (Collingwood 1998). (That said, he did not take *philosophy* to be a branch of history: see (Collingwood 2005: Ch. 10, §3).)

4 This too is a view that I have tried to defend elsewhere, in relation specifically to metaphysics but with implications for philosophy more generally (see Moore 2012: esp. Intro., §7, and Concl., §4). I say that I am going beyond what Williams says. But am I in fact doing something more radical than that? Am I contradicting what he says? In particular, does the view that philosophy is creative in the sense indicated conflict with Williams' insistence that 'there has to be such a thing in philosophy as *getting it right*' (Williams 2006c: 202, emphasis in original)? I do not think so. This is because I do not think that answering to something antecedently given is the only way of 'getting it right' (see Moore 2012: 381, 393–4). Certainly, my view does not conflict with the idea that there is such a thing in philosophy as *doing it well*.

5 Williams spends a great deal of time issuing warnings against scientism in philosophy, for example (Williams 2006b) and (2006c: *passim*). Warnings against *conservatism* in philosophy, unsurprisingly, are less visible in his work; unsurprisingly, because the corresponding idea that philosophy is creative is not there. But such warnings are not absent from his work altogether. They hardly could be, given that there is a closely associated

idea that is quite certainly in his work, namely that reflection must sometimes be allowed to disturb the concepts by which we live: see, for example (Williams 2006e, esp. Chs 8 and 9).

6 Cf. Dummett's contention that 'the philosophy of language is the foundation of all other philosophy' (Dummett 1978: 442), or Quine's suggestion that 'philosophy of science is philosophy enough' (Quine 1966: 151), where by 'science' he means not much more than organized knowledge (see e.g., Quine and Ullian 1978: 3).

7 Admittedly, these phenomena can be objects of (non-anthropocentric) scientific study. But their relevance to analytic philosophy is of a different ilk. If an analytic philosopher, reflecting on how (say) the word 'causation' is used, denies that there is any such thing as backward causation, then he or she is not announcing the result of an empirical investigation into the use of the word 'causation'; he or she is enunciating a rule for its use. (Here I am betraying my Wittgensteinianism, my earlier complaint about Wittgenstein notwithstanding: cf. (Wittgenstein 1967: §383); cf. also (Hacker 1996, esp. Ch. 8), and (Hacker 2007: 7–11).) For a sustained discussion of the relations between analytic philosophy and language from a deeply opposed perspective see (Williamson 2007: *passim*). What *may* be true is that the kind of attention that analytic philosophers pay language shows that they have not indulged in that suspension of our natural-scientific modes of thought which phenomenologists take as their starting point: what they call the *epochē* (cf. Moore 2012: 431; and for an explanation of the *epochē* see Husserl 1970: §35). But that is not, in itself, any offence to the artistic conception. There are all manner of ways in which philosophy might distance itself from the natural sciences without going as far as suspending their very modes of thought. (Some phenomenologists are perhaps insufficiently sensitive to this point: see e.g., Husserl 1962: §62.) Note that a yet different approach to philosophy has recently emerged, under the title 'experimental philosophy', which retains a broadly analytic interest in language but which also involves significant use of empirical investigation, notably the empirical investigation of people's linguistic intuitions (see e.g., Knobe and Nichols 2008).

8 Cf. Heidegger's claim that 'ontology and phenomenology are not two distinct philosophical disciplines among others' but rather that they 'characterize philosophy itself' and that 'philosophy is universal phenomenological ontology' (Heidegger 1962: 62). I shall have a little more to say about this shortly.

9 Parfit's book may also contain another prominent example of what I have in mind. He argues that personal identity is nothing over and above certain impersonally understood facts of bodily and psychological continuity (Parfitt 1984 III, *passim*). And he tries to draw conclusions about persons, in particular ethical conclusions, that can themselves be understood impersonally. But there is good reason to think that only from a certain point of view involving a set of values that run contrary to these conclusions can there be any meaningful talk of persons in the first place (see further Moore 1997: 229–32).

10 See above, n.8.

11 See, for example (Foucault 2001: Ch. 10, §6), and the discussion of 'becoming-animal' in (Deleuze and Guattari 1987: Ch. 10). The notion of 'a body without organs' which permeates the latter work is also relevant.

12 This is of course an allusion to Wittgenstein's early work, in particular to (Wittgenstein 1961: 5.6), where he says, 'The limits of my language mean the limits of my world' (emphasis removed). The suggestion that some fundamental aspect of this idea survives into the later work is associated above all with (Williams 2006d). (Williams 2006a) is also relevant: it provides a compelling elucidation and defence of the idea that a human form of life is, for us humans, 'given' (though Williams does not himself put it in those terms).

13 There is an echo of this in his attitude to empiricism. At one point he says that what marks a position out as empiricist is that it has an account of how the subject is constituted within the given (Deleuze 1991: 109); elsewhere he makes clear that he sees his own position as empiricist, for example (Deleuze and Guattari 1994: 47–8).

14 One of the many reasons why Spinoza is worth considering in this connection is the high regard in which he is held by Deleuze, for whom he is 'the 'prince' of philosophers' (quoted in Joughin 1990: 11; cf. Deleuze and Guattari 1994: 48).

15 For discussion, see (Curley 1996).

16 It is instructive at this point to recall Mao Zedong's remarkable claim, quoted in (Chang 1993: 293): 'Even if the United States ... blew [the earth] to pieces ... [this] would still be an insignificant matter as far as the universe as a whole is concerned.' There are times when trying to make more objective sense of things verges on the catastrophic.

17 We might hear talk in this connection of 'the human prejudice', the phrase appropriated by Williams as the title for his essay on related themes (Williams 2006a).

18 I am very grateful to Yuuki Ohta for comments on an early draft of this essay.

4 Disagreement in Philosophy
An Optimistic Perspective

Many philosophers (and non-philosophers) think persistent disagreement is a characteristic feature of philosophy. This thought is central in much scepticism about philosophy as a discipline: *Surely,* the thought goes, *if the goal is to find answers to important questions, philosophers have failed: they've been at it for more than 2000 years and they haven't managed to agree on anything!*

This paper is an extended response to that line of thought and also an exploration of the sources of persistent disagreement in philosophy.[1] I argue for three central theses:

1. We have no evidence that there is more persistent disagreement in philosophy than in relevantly similar disciplines.
2. There is *some* persistent disagreement in philosophy, but it is: (a) inevitable (because of the failure of *Evidence Neutrality*) and (b) intellectually valuable.
3. Convergence is irrelevant to the intellectual value of any view – the value of the views in for example, contemporary physics has nothing to do with the convergence on those views within academia.

THE VIEW THAT PHILOSOPHY IS PLAGUED BY PERSISTENT DISAGREEMENT

In 1933 Ferdinand Schiller wrote:

We are all aware that philosophers are even more prone to disagree than doctors, and probably all of us are ready upon occasion to contribute our quota to the disagreements that mark, and scar, the face of philosophy.

(Schiller 1933: 118)

Here is a similar sentiment expressed in 2004 by Peter van Inwagen:

Disagreement in philosophy is pervasive and irresoluble. There is almost no thesis in philosophy about which philosophers agree. If there is any philosophical thesis that all or most philosophers affirm, it is a negative thesis: that formalism is not the right philosophy of mathematics, for example, or that knowledge is not (simply) justified, true belief. That is not how things are in the physical sciences.

(Van Inwagen 2004: 332)

Chalmers (2015) defends a related view. Chalmers' focus is on what he calls 'the Big Questions of philosophy'. These are questions like:

- *What is the relationship between mind and body?*
- *How do we know about the external world?*
- *What are the fundamental principles of morality?*
- *Is there a God?*
- *Do we have free will?*

According to Chalmers there hasn't been what he calls 'large collective convergence' on answers to the Big Questions. Here is his account of *collective convergence*:

We can define collective convergence on an answer over a period as the increase in degree of agreement on that answer from the start of the period to the end of the period. Degree of agreement can be defined using one of various mathematical measures of agreement across a group of people on a set of issues. Collective convergence (*simpliciter*) over a period is defined as the collective convergence on the dominant answer at the end of that period over the period.

(Chalmers 2015: 5–6)

Here is the account of *large collective convergence*:

We can say that *large* collective convergence over a period requires as much convergence as there has been over big questions in the hard sciences in the same period. Here I will take the hard sciences to include at least mathematics and the natural sciences: paradigmatically physics, chemistry, and biology.

(Ibid.: 6)

What is the evidence that there hasn't been large collective convergence on the big questions in philosophy? This is an empirical claim and there isn't much empirical work on this issue. Almost the only effort in this direction is the 2009 PhilPapers Survey (published as Bourget and Chalmers 2014). This was an online survey sent to 2000 professional philosophers in North America, Europe, and Australasia. Respondents were asked about their views on thirty important questions in philosophy. I won't go through the details of the responses here, instead I report Chalmers' summary:

The degree of disagreement here is striking, if unsurprising. Only one view (non-skeptical realism about the external world) attracts over 80% support. Three views (*a priori* knowledge, atheism, scientific realism) attract over 70% support, with significant dissent, and three more views attract over 60% support. On the other 23 questions, the leading view has less than 60% support.

(Ibid.: 9)

CHALLENGES TO THE EMPIRICAL EVIDENCE FOR PERSISTENT DISAGREEMENT

Claims about how practitioners of a discipline like philosophy compare to practitioners of other disciplines raise very complicated empirical questions. This is even more so when such claims invoke difficult notions like 'agreement' and 'disagreement' – and the idea that this can be measured in the relevant comparative way. This section raises some concerns about the data in Bourget and Chalmers (2014). Most of what I have to say here is quite tentative and at best adds up to the rather non-controversial conclusion that we need much more empirical work in order to be confident in making the comparative claims.

First note a couple of very obvious limitations of Bourget and Chalmers (2014) (these points are also mentioned in Chalmers 2015):

a) The study covers only a single point in time so it doesn't tell us anything about convergence over time.

b) Convergence, as Chalmers and others think of it, is comparative. The claim is that philosophers converge less than some other people (e.g., those who work in 'the hard sciences'). But Bourget and Chalmers (2014) has no comparative component.

So their study is completely silent on the crucial comparative question: is the situation in philosophy significantly different from that in similar disciplines? What we would need would be a series of diachronic studies of several disciplines and then a comparison. That's missing.

So even if we take the study at face value, it is at best extremely weak evidence for Chalmers' empirical claim. Of course, many philosophers have a hunch that there's a lack of convergence in their discipline, but hunches about empirical matters even (or maybe in particular) about ourselves and our own disciplines are horrifically unreliable (this is one of the points Bourget and Chalmers (2014) correctly emphasize). One point all parties to this debate should agree on is that more empirical work is needed. At this point there's simply no genuine evidence for the claim that philosophy is significantly different from other disciplines with respect to the amount of disagreement.

That's not all: there are at least four additional reasons for concern about how Chalmers (2015) uses the data from Bourget and Chalmers (2014).

(i) **Verbal disputes are not real disagreements (and Bourget and Chalmers (2014) doesn't screen for verbal disputes):** The study assumes that if two respondents gave divergent answers to one of the questions asked, they disagree. But that's a naive assumption. It follows only if they interpret the words in the same way. Take, for example, the question, 'Physicalism or non-physicalism?' Suppose one respondent says 'yes' and another 'no'. Do they disagree? Only if they interpret the word 'physicalism' the same way. If they mean different things by that word, then we have no evidence they disagree.[2] Do we have reason to believe that participants in the study interpret the words in the question in a uniform way?

No, we don't. What follows is in danger of looking like an *ad hominem* argument, but it's not: I happen to wholeheartedly agree with Chalmers (2011). In that paper, Chalmers argues that a) verbal disputes are pointless, and b) almost all the questions that are mentioned in Bourget and Chalmers (2014) have been involved in verbal disputes. Chalmers says:

In the Socratic tradition the paradigmatic philosophical questions take the form 'What is *X*?'. These questions are the focus of many philosophical debates today: What is free will? What is knowledge? What is justification?

What is justice? What is law? What is confirmation? What is causation? What is color? What is a concept? What is meaning? What is action? What is life? What is logic? What is self-deception? What is group selection? What is science? What is art? What is consciousness? And indeed: What is a verbal dispute?

(Chalmers 2011: 531–2)

He continues in a footnote: 'I think that the philosophical literature over almost all of the questions in the last paragraph is beset by verbal disputes, in a fashion that is occasionally but too rarely recognized' (ibid.: 532).

Suppose Chalmers is right in this. If so, an alternative interpretation of the Bourget and Chalmers (2014) results is that they provide additional evidence of widespread verbal disputes in philosophy. The differences in replies do not reflect differences in substantive views, but instead differences in how crucial terms are used.

I should mention that Chalmers briefly mentions verbal disputes in his 2015 paper. He asks: *Why is there so much disagreement in philosophy?* and one of the replies he considers is this:

there is little convergence because participants are talking past each other. Each side is using key terms in different ways and each is correct where their own use of the term is concerned. In 'Verbal Disputes' I argued that verbal disputes are common in philosophy. For example, I think many debates in the philosophy of free will and the philosophy of language have a significant verbal element. And I think that resolving verbal disputes can lead to philosophical progress. Still, often when we clarify the key terms in a partly verbal dispute, we find that a substantive dispute remains. And there is a core of fundamental questions (including many normative questions, as well the mind–body problem and other issues involving 'bedrock' philosophical concepts, in the terms of 'Verbal Disputes') for which the diagnosis of a verbal dispute seems quite implausible.

(Chalmers 2015: 26)

Two thoughts about this:

a)   Verbal disputes don't explain disagreement. They undermine the idea that there is disagreement in the first place. Verbal disputes are not genuine disagreements, they are pointless verbal confusions.

b) The appeal to bedrock is unhelpful for two reasons: first, we now have a new empirical assumption: *that there are substantive bedrock disagreements.* We have no evidence of that. The questionnaire in Bourget and Chalmers (2014) certainly doesn't support that, since it is not conducted at the bedrock level. Second, one can question whether there is a bedrock level and, if there is, whether it is purged of verbal disputes. It would go beyond the scope of this paper to explore those issues further, but they are important issues to get clear on for those who want to understand the connection between disagreement in philosophy and verbal disputes in the way Chalmers hints at.

(ii) **Why compare to 'hard sciences' and not instead to the social and cognitive sciences?** Van Inwagen, Chalmers, and others take the relevant comparison class to be 'the hard sciences' and go on to claim that philosophy compares unfavourably to those disciplines. But why is that the relevant comparison? Why not instead compare to the cognitive and social sciences? The remit of philosophy is, taken as a whole, much more closely related to those fields than to theoretical physics and mathematics. Here is a **bold empirical conjecture**: if we were to pick a set of 'core' (or 'Big') questions within economics, political science, sociology, or psychology, we would find as much (if not more) disagreement as in philosophy.

With that comparison in mind, two connected points are worth noting: a) practitioners of these disciplines – for example, economics and psychology – have the highest *social* standing of any disciplines. So-called experts in these fields are given enormous decision-making powers. Economists run the infrastructures of our societies and psychologists are given immense power over individual lives. In this respect they have much higher standing than theoretical physicists and mathematicians. If persistent disagreement is a negative aspect of a discipline, then, if my conjecture is correct, we are no worse than practitioners of those highly respected disciplines. b) It is striking that self-doubt isn't nearly as prevalent in for example, economics and psychology.[3] That's one respect (maybe the only) in which we should learn from those disciplines.

In the light of a) and b), here is a psychological/sociological conjecture about why there's so much more self-doubt in philosophy than in economics and psychology: it's not because there's more progress or more convergence in those disciplines. It's because they have high social standing (and are given lots of responsibility) and philosophers don't. It's this lack of social standing (and role) that triggers rather than any objective features of philosophy.

(iii) **Convergence leads to special sciences:** In the history of philosophy, the following has happened many times: philosophers work on a set of problems and then at some point they converge on precise questions and develop some shared methodological standards. Then, *under certain hard to understand conditions,* that set of issues becomes a new discipline. At some point in history, central issues in what we today describe as economics, psychology, sociology, theology, linguistics, and biology were considered philosophical questions. They then developed into what we today consider separate disciplines. This 'spawning function' of philosophy is undeniable, but very difficult to understand in detail. However, for current purposes the details don't matter much. What matters is that, speaking roughly, *there is some correlation between increased convergence and the spawning of a new discipline.* So when philosophers start to converge on a cluster of issues, then, under hard to predict and explain conditions, that cluster tends to become identified as a separate discipline. It seems a bit arbitrary, then, to not treat that as an instance of philosophical convergence. Insofar as these other disciplines count as converging disciplines, philosophy should share in some of that 'glory' (if you think that is what it is.)

(iv) **There's more consensus on 'small questions', negative claims, and conditional claims (and these are just as important as answers to 'Big Questions'):** Chalmers and van Inwagen focus on the 'Big Questions' and treat the adjective 'Big' in a somewhat normative way. It's as if being 'Big' (with a capital 'B') makes a question more valuable or interesting or central to philosophy. So if we measure disagreement in philosophy, we should measure it with respect to the Big Questions. Here are some reasons to resist that attitude towards the Big ones: first, there's more convergence on the 'smaller' questions in philosophy. There is also more convergence on negative claims (e.g., 'the meaning of a word isn't an associated mental image' or 'disagreement data fails to establish that truth is relative') and conditional claims (e.g., 'if evidence for distinctive de se attitudes is just evidence of opacity, then there are no good arguments for an essential indexicality thesis'). Chalmers recognizes this. He says:

> This is not to deny that we have attained a great deal of collective knowledge in philosophy. As Timothy Williamson (2006) has said, we knew much more in 2004 than in 1964, much more in 1964 than in 1924, and so on. But this collective knowledge typically does not involve answers to the big questions. It is mainly knowledge of the answers to smaller questions, of negative and conditional theses, of frameworks available to answer questions, of connections between ideas, of the way that arguments bear for and against conclusions, and so on. In the absence of convergence on the big questions, collective knowledge of the answers to those questions eludes us.
>
> (Chalmers 2015: 15–16)

For the sake of argument, let's assume that the last sentence is right – without convergence on the Big Questions we don't get *collective* knowledge[4] of the answers to the Big Questions. That, however, doesn't address the question: why focus on the Big Questions? Why does only the convergence on those questions matter? Again, comparison with economics might be useful. There's no more consensus on 'Big Questions' in economics, but to the extent that there's a sense of progress it's connected to the little questions – they get lots of little questions worked out. It's important for us philosophers to emphasize that we too get lots of little questions worked out. We know much more now about how semantics for relativist treatment of modals would have to go, or how scoping arguments can try to respond to the modal argument, or what Lewis' triviality argument tells us about the interaction between probabilities and conditionals. We just are less likely to count that as 'progress', because we're taking progress to mean solving the Big Questions. That bias is a mistake – the 'smaller' questions are just as important (and maybe what we need is to give up the entire category of 'Big Questions').

In sum: so far no one has made the case that there's persistent disagreement in philosophy that distinguishes the field from other relevant disciplines. That said, I don't take these doubts to undermine the plausible idea that there is a set of philosophical questions that there's persistent and genuine disagreement about. The next section provides an account of why there will always be a set of questions like this.

FIRST SOURCE OF PERSISTENT DISAGREEMENT IN
PHILOSOPHY: FAILURE OF EVIDENCE NEUTRALITY

There are some philosophical questions there's persistent
disagreement about. One important reason for this is the failure of
what Williamson calls *Evidence Neutrality*. Here is Williamson's
helpful introduction to the idea:

As far as possible, we want evidence to play the role of a neutral arbiter
between rival theories. Although the complete elimination of accidental
mistakes and confusions is virtually impossible, we might hope that
whether a proposition constitutes evidence is in principle uncontentiously
decidable, in the sense that a community of inquirers can always in
principle achieve common knowledge as to whether any given proposition
constitutes evidence for the inquiry. *Call that idea Evidence Neutrality*.
Thus in a debate over a hypothesis h, proponents and opponents of h should
be able to agree whether some claim p constitutes evidence without first
having to settle their differences over h itself.

(Williamson 2007: 210, my emphasis)

If Evidence Neutrality were true, then we should expect those
debating philosophical issues to be able to converge on answers,
given time and good will. If, however, Evidence Neutrality is false,
then we should not expect to reach agreement – we should expect
those who disagree about central philosophical questions to be
deadlocked.

Next step: *Evidence Neutrality is false*. Here, again, is
Williamson:

Having good evidence for a belief does not require being able to persuade
all comers, however strange their views, that you have such good evidence.
No human beliefs pass that test. Even in principle, we cannot always
decide which propositions constitute evidence prior to deciding the main
philosophical issue; sometimes the latter is properly implicated in the
former. Of course, we can often decide whether a proposition constitutes
evidence prior to deciding the main issue, otherwise the notion of evidence
would be useless. But the two sorts of question cannot be kept in strict
isolation from each other.

(Ibid.: 203)

This paper will assume, with Williamson, that Evidence Neutrality
is false. It would take us too far afield to engage in a full-blown

argument for denying Evidence Neutrality, but briefly: first-order and second-order philosophy are intertwined. So in many cases, to take a stand on a core philosophical issue is also to take a stand on what the correct way to do philosophy is and also on what counts as evidence in philosophy.

The assumption that Evidence Neutrality is false provides a partial explanation of persistent disagreements in philosophy. Often the following will be the case, call this a Paradigmatic Irresolvable Philosophical Dispute:

Paradigmatic Irresolvable Philosophical Dispute: A believes that p and B believes that not-p. If p is true, then q counts as strong evidence for p. If p is not true, then q doesn't count as evidence for p (i.e., the question of what counts as evidence for p is in part settled by the truth or falsity of p). A and B might agree that q, but that won't help resolve their disagreement. B will discount q as evidence (since she doesn't endorse p) and A will cite q as evidence (since she endorses p).

The beliefs of A and B could both be the best supported by the evidence given what their theories treat as evidence. 'The role of evidence as a neutral arbiter is undermined' (ibid.: 213).

The details of how an irresolvable philosophical dispute is grounded in different views of what counts as evidence will always be complex. A full presentation of a single case would require a level of detail that takes us beyond the scope of this contribution. However, it's not too hard to get a rough sense of what I have in mind. Here are five simple illustrations of junctures where first- and second-order philosophy intersect in the relevant ways:

- Different views of the nature of knowledge will affect what you think counts as evidence (and even more obviously: different views of what evidence is will affect what you think counts as evidence).
- Whether you think there is an external world or not will affect how you think about evidence (and how to collect it).
- Whether you are a dualist, panpsychist, or a reductive materialist will affect how you think about evidence.
- What you think concepts are will have consequences for how you think about philosophical methodology – in particular it

will have consequences for whether you think philosophers can and should be engaged in *a priori* conceptual analysis.

- Different views about the semantics of 'intuition' and the metaphysics of intuitions can have direct consequence for how you think of philosophical evidence and methodology – in particular it can have consequences for whether you think intuitions can and should serve as evidence in philosophy.

Often the connections between first-order and second-order issues won't be quite as obvious as in these cases, but I suspect that in many of the cases Chalmers lists as 'Big Questions', such connections can be unearthed with a bit of work.

A final point to note before leaving the topic of Evidence Neutrality and Irresolvable Disagreements. Not only does the falsity of Evidence Neutrality explain persistent disagreements, but it also tends to exacerbate those disagreements: 'both the good fortune of being right and the misfortune of being wrong are magnified' (ibid.: 213). Those who are right are also right about what counts as evidence and so are in a good position to improve their theory: they know where to look for additional evidence. However, those who are wrong are also wrong about what constitutes evidence and so are not in a good position: their further theorizing will be contaminated by their false beliefs about what counts as evidence.

SECOND SOURCE OF PERSISTENT
DISAGREEMENTS: INSTITUTIONAL IMPARTIALITY

The second explanatory component for disagreement is institutional/sociological. It's simply this: as a matter of fact, philosophy departments don't tend to hire just people who agree with each other. We hire people who fundamentally disagree. We also educate and supervise students who fundamentally disagree with us. There's no doctrinal or methodological entry-ticket to becoming a professional philosopher. Throughout our 2000-year history, we see a spectacular array of different views represented across the world among those who would self-describe as professional philosophers.

It could have been different. We can imagine an alternative development in which one set of answers and one methodology became institutionally dominant. That would mean we had a form of institutional partiality, where hirings required allegiance to a specific conception of philosophical methodology and also agreement on substantial issues.

In the light of the failure of Evidence Neutrality, institutional impartiality is a very good thing for at least two reasons: (i) non-experts are not in a position to choose between competing philosophical views. The people building up academic institutions are, in large part, non-experts. They are also not in a position to adjudicate between competing experts. So it's good that they stay impartial and don't try to force philosophy into one direction. (ii) Pluralism is good even for those who are right. When they have around them people who disagree with them, they are constantly challenged to sharpen their arguments. If, by some miracle, those who are right got to be in a position to make all philosophy hires and just hired other people who were right, that wouldn't be good for them: they need people who challenge them fundamentally.

CONVERGING DISCIPLINES, INSTITUTIONALLY CONSTRUCTED CONSENSUS, AND THE VALUE OF PERSISTENT DISAGREEMENTS

In the light of the points made in the previous section, the concern should be with the converging disciplines rather than the non-converging disciplines. Structurally, what happens in converging disciplines is often something like the following: they start with fundamental assumptions, both methodological and substantive. Those assumptions then provide a framework for a research programme and the basis for assessing both contributions and participants. What is not questioned or investigated are those fundamental assumptions. Typically, practitioners are not in a good position to justify their fundamental assumptions: when challenged about these, they can't provide reasons that aren't just internal to the framework. When challenged about the framework as a whole, they would have no clue what to say.

It helps here to distinguish two rough models of how to generate convergence: *institutionally constructed convergence* and *genuine intellectual convergence*. Let's take contemporary physics as an illustration. In what sense is there consensus about their views? First notice that there isn't broad consensus across the population of humans. Focusing just on the USA, a recent Gallup poll shows that 'More than four in 10 Americans continue to believe that God created humans in their present form 10,000 years ago'.[5] This contradicts what contemporary physics tells us about the origin of the universe. So if 'communal agreement' requires agreement across society as a whole, then there's no consensus on core views in contemporary physics. Those who take physics as a paradigm of a converging discipline will reply: *what we mean is that people who are hired as physicists in universities agree that the universe is more than 10,000 years old.* That's true, but the restriction is problematic. Here is why: institutional consensus is very easily generated in intellectually irrelevant ways. You just make sure that people who are hired in the institution agree with each other. So, for example, the people who are hired by the Church of Scientology all agree that humans have an immortal spirit who used to live on other planets. That there's consensus among those working in the Church of Scientology about this is of course entirely unsurprising and gives no kind of epistemic boost to those views. It's an institutionally constructed consensus. That, in itself, has no intellectual value.

What we are looking for is some form of intellectual consensus – consensus generated just by the force of the arguments. However, when we focus on institutions such as universities and their physics departments, it is very hard to make the empirical case that it is the force of arguments that has generated consensus. Disentangling the institutional pressures from the intellectual force is practically impossible.

What's the upshot of this? I take the upshot to be that what we should focus on are the arguments and the evidence for a theory. There are great arguments and impressive evidence for general relativity. That's what's important. Whether a majority of people hired by a particular kind of institution happens to endorse the view doesn't matter. Here is a thought experiment to make that clear: suppose horrific political developments result in religious fanatics taking over physics departments. As a result, the consensus among those employed as physicists ends up being that the world was constructed 10,000 years ago. That's unfortunate, of course, for many reasons, but it doesn't undermine any of the evidence for physics as we know it. Its intellectual value remains, no matter how many of those hired in physics departments believe the world was constructed 10,000 years ago. What matters isn't consensus or convergence. That's irrelevant to the intellectual value of the view.

Moreover, given the failure of Evidence Neutrality in philosophy, some persistent disagreement is unavoidable. To aim for convergence is to aim for something impossible. To have an impossible goal is irrational. Moreover, there are good institutional reasons for having this reflected in the people hired as professional philosophers. In other words, we have good reason to not let academic institutions try to force convergence – that would be a dreadful system and an enormous intellectual risk. In sum, it seems rational to aim for an institutional structure that preserves divergence (even when we know that means employing some people who are wrong – i.e., paying people to work out views that eventually turn out to be blind alleys).

I now go on to consider two objections to the views just expressed. According to the first objection, peer-disagreement undermines knowledge. According to the second, disagreement undermines 'collective knowledge' and collective knowledge is valuable.

DOES LACK OF CONVERGENCE UNDERMINE KNOWLEDGE?

I have just argued that convergence is something we shouldn't care about. Chalmers disagrees – he thinks it's very important. But why? Chalmers considers two replies and endorses the second. The first reply, that he rejects, is this:

> One obvious answer is that we value knowledge, agreement is required for knowledge, and convergence goes along with increases in knowledge. A strong version of this view, suggested by van Inwagen's discussion, is that where there is sufficient disagreement among experts, no individuals can be said to know the truth. Even if some individuals have hit on good arguments for true conclusions, how can they have justified confidence that these are good arguments, when so many of their peers disagree?
>
> (Chalmers 2015: 14)

Chalmers doesn't endorse this view. He says, even though lots of his colleagues deny the existence of consciousness, he still knows that he is conscious. So widespread disagreement about a view doesn't undermine knowledge. I agree. Given the very extensive literature on peer disagreement, the ideal way to address this would be to go through each and every account of peer disagreement currently on the market to see what it has to say on this issue. That would make this paper far too long and would also go beyond my area of expertise. Instead, I here simply want to flag the issue and to refer readers to other literature on this topic. The best and most thorough paper on this topic that I know of is 'Disagreement in Philosophy: Its Epistemic Significance' by Thomas Kelly. Kelly, in my view convincingly, argues that 'there is *no* plausible view about the epistemology of disagreement, on which philosophical agnosticism is compelling' (Kelly 2016: 375).[6] Those who want to explore this question further should refer to Kelly's paper and the literature he discusses.

COLLECTIVE VS. INDIVIDUAL KNOWLEDGE

In response to the question, 'Why is *convergence* to the truth important, and why should we be concerned about its absence?' Chalmers says:

> even if agreement is not required for individual knowledge, some degree of agreement is plausibly required for *collective* knowledge. If the community of experts on a question has serious disagreement over the answer to that question, then that community cannot be said to collectively know the answer to that question, and nor can the broader community of which they are a part.
>
> (Chalmers 2015: 15)

He adds:

> Furthermore, we value collective knowledge. One reason that progress of the hard sciences has been so impressive is that it has plausibly enabled us – the community of inquirers – to collectively know the answers to those questions. But in the absence of sufficient agreement on the answers to philosophical questions, we cannot be said to have collective knowledge of those answers.
>
> (Ibid.)

I think there are two questions worth disentangling here: (i) Can we describe a situation in which there is collective knowledge without large-scale collective convergence? (ii) If the answer to (i) is 'no', why should we care?

With respect to the first question, I think the issue is murky. Here is an illustration of the issue as I see it. Consider theories of truth. There are a number of alternative theories on the table (correspondence theories, coherence theories, pragmatic theories, deflationary theories, etc.), all of them very well worked out, but no consensus on the truth about truth. Suppose, for simplicity, that we have eight candidate theories, and suppose one of them is correct, say the deflationary theory. Is there any sense then in which we philosophers know the answer to the question: *What is truth?* I'll assume that if the answer is 'yes', then in some sense we have collective knowledge. If the answer is no, then we don't have collective knowledge. Here are some analogies to help you think about that kind of situation:

> **Analogy 1**: Suppose I'm looking for a golden coin together with 10,000 other people. I can say that *we* have found the coin even if just one of us found it and many are still looking for the coin in the wrong places.
>
> **Analogy 2**: As in 1, I've found the golden coin, but seven other people found fake-gold coins, and they think theirs is the golden coin and I can't argue them out of their false belief. I can still say that *we* have found the golden coin (though unfortunately, some people don't recognize it).
>
> **Analogy 3**: As in 2, I have found the golden coin and seven others have found fake coins. Now emphasize that there's no consensus among the 10,000 collaborators about who has found the genuine coin (they are evenly split between the eight of us). We can still, I think, say that *we* have found the golden coin – there's just the complication that we have no consensus about how to pick it out from some fake coins.

The relevance of these analogies is that we have a form of collective achievement by virtue of an individual achievement even when other members of the group fail to recognize that achievement (or even dispute it). In cases involving attitude verbs, we have something similar:

> **Analogy 4**: We can say that Apple knows how to improve Siri when some of the employees have figured it out, even if there's

extensive disagreement within the company about how to do it. It might even be that the disagreement is irresolvable (in that one group can't convince another).

My own judgement about the Apple case is clear: Apple knows how to improve Siri (and it is also true *that Apple knows that Siri can be improved by doing D* (where D is the correct improvement procedure)). However, some people's judgement about this case vacillates somewhat depending on how the details are worked out (e.g., who makes the final decision, what are the practical implications, etc.).[7] Much will depend on what the point of the collective attribution is. In the Apple case, maybe what matters is the production end: can they as a matter of fact change the software in the relevant ways or do they at least have the capacity to do that? There's no clear analogy to that in the case of philosophy. That said, my view is that widespread disagreement is in principle no obstacle to collective knowledge. However, the details of the conditions under which we can make such attributions are no doubt complex and a full discussion would go beyond the scope of this paper (for some recent discussion of related issues see Bird 2010, Lackey 2014).

I turn now to the second question: why should we care about collective knowledge attributions? Some people think individual knowledge attributions are important because they endorse some version of the knowledge norms of assertion, belief, or action.[8] Many of us reject all such views. For example, Cappelen (2011) and Pagin (2015) argue that there are no such norms at all (so in particular, the knowledge norm is wrong). Even if you're not on board with the anti-norm view, an account is needed of the value and significance of making collective knowledge attributions. Whatever you think about the significance of the individual knowledge attributions doesn't transfer to the collective case without argument (i.e., work is needed to show that what we say about the individual cases applies to the collective case).

My view is this: what matters in this context (i.e., understanding the development and nature of disciplines) is not to get clear on whether it's okay for members of a group to say 'We know that ...'. What matters is to understand the details of the interaction between the participants in a non-converging discipline. To focus on a general question such as 'Can we say that they have collective knowledge?', isn't helpful for understanding anything important. What we should focus on instead are questions such as these:

- What's the detailed source of the disagreement?
- How much agreement is there on conditional claims, negative claims, methodology, space of possible answers, and quality of arguments?
- How do the groups who disagree cluster and interact?

The answers will be sensitive to details and be messy. In a discipline like philosophy, the answer will vary between sub-disciplines, between academic communities, and over time. So trying to answer the very general question 'What is the value of collective knowledge in philosophy' isn't particularly helpful. What's helpful is to try to answer detailed questions such as those just listed for specific sub-disciplines, and specific academic communities at particular times.

Again, it's important to keep in mind that there's not much that's distinctive about philosophy here. Compare again to a discipline like economics. There's no more consensus about Big Questions in economics than in philosophy, but we don't find nearly the same level of handwringing and agonizing about that fact. Why not? Well, they have sub-groups, often centred around specific institutions (e.g., around so-called Freshwater and Saltwater schools). Within each grouping there is a higher degree of convergence (than in the discipline as a whole) and complex theories are developed based on the consensus within each group. So to understand contemporary economics, we need to look at the work within those clusters, the relationship between the clusters, and the sources of the disagreement between them. Just to try to answer the question 'Can economists say that they know that ...' (where '...' is some thesis that there's disagreement over) isn't very illuminating.

In sum: Chalmers asks 'Why is *convergence* to the truth important, and why should we be concerned about its absence?' The answer is twofold: a) that's the wrong question, and b) if you insist on focusing on the very general question, then the important observation is that in some important sense (or in some contexts) it's true to say: 'We have collective knowledge of the answers to all the Big Questions'.[9]

NOTES

1 Much of this paper can also be seen as a reply to (Chalmers 2015).
2 We might have some evidence that they disagree about what the words mean or should mean, but that's not what Bourget and Chalmers were testing for.
3 This is not to deny that there's often internal criticism and debate within economics and psychology. What they have significantly less of is a group of people (internal and external to the discipline) who practically make careers out of criticizing the discipline as a whole.
4 At this point I'm bracketing problems with the notion of collective knowledge – more on that topic below.
5 www.gallup.com/poll/170822/believe-creationist-view-human-origins. aspx
6 Chalmers agrees: 'I think that at least in some cases, a good argument can ground an individual's knowledge of a conclusion even when peers reject it. For example, I think that the presence of any number of peers who deny the existence of consciousness would not undermine my knowledge that I am conscious' (Chalmers 2015: 14–15).
7 For empirical evidence that people judge that a group can know how to do something without actual agreement about how to do it, see (Jenkins *et al.* 2014).
8 For example, those who endorse the knowledge norm of assertion think it is constitutive of assertion that one should assert p only if one knows that p. For those who endorse this view, the question of whether A knows that p is important when assessing A's assertion that p. For more discussion of and criticisms of this view see (Cappelen 2011) and (Pagin 2015).
9 In January 2016, Nancy Bauer, Paul Horwich, L. A. Paul, Patrick Greenough, Mark Richard, and Bjørn Ramberg participated in a workshop on Progress in Philosophy at the University of Oslo. I learned a lot about these issues from discussions during that workshop. I also got useful feedback from Olav Gjelsvik, Joshua Habgood-Coote, Torfinn Huvenes, Øystein Linnebo, Knut Olav Skarsaune, and Rachel Sterken.

Part II

Conceptual Analysis and the Naturalistic Challenge

5   Impure Conceptual Analysis

My contribution defends conceptual analysis both in general and with respect to a specific topic – animal minds. At the same time, it argues for a type of conceptual analysis that differs from classical variants in being not just non-reductive but also impure. This approach distinguishes the conceptual issues of philosophy from the factual issues of science, while being sensitive to the way in which these interact in specific questions, arguments, theories, and research programmes. Philosophy is distinct from science, yet the two cannot proceed in isolation with respect to topics which pose scientific and other non-philosophical challenges. The vocation of theoretical philosophy is critical thinking writ large: it is a means of improving debates extending beyond philosophy, by making them clearer and more cogent. To this end, philosophers must engage with the details of these debates, rather than legislating from above on the basis of preconceived generalities.

I.   CONCEPTUAL ANALYSIS AND ANIMAL MINDS

Ever since Socrates, Western philosophers have attempted to analyse, define, or explain concepts. They have adressed 'What is X?'- or 'What are Xs?'-questions, for example, 'What is justice?', 'What is truth?'. To those of a practical frame of mind, this activity may appear pointless right from the start. But for the most part, philosophers do not pose 'What is ...?'-questions for their own sake, they arise out of problems of a different kind. Thus Socrates' struggle with the question 'What is virtue?' was not *l'art pour l'art*. Instead he was driven by a prior question to which he attached overriding moral and political importance, namely: 'Can virtue be taught?'

This holds equally of 'What is ...?'-questions within analytic philosophy. A prime example is the analysis of mental notions. It is propelled by antecedent philosophical puzzles, such as the mind–body problem and the issue of free will. I shall take as my prime example another topic, animal minds. It has the advantage of illustrating the interaction between conceptual and non-conceptual problems and claims. Computers and robots raise analogous issues. But animals are cuter and face a greater threat of extinction.

The *question of animal minds*:
Do some (non-human) animals have minds/mental properties/ mental powers?
The *distribution question* renders the query more specifc:
What mental properties, if any, are possessed by what species of animal?

Just as *the* question of animal minds and *the* distribution problem concern the mind or mental properties in general, there are analogous questions, concerning specific mental properties. The answers depend on two factors: on the one hand, they depend on contingent facts about animals to be established by empirical science, whether through observations in the field or experiments in the laboratory. On the other hand, they depend on what one makes of heavily contested concepts like that of a mind, of thought, rationality, belief, consciousness, desire, perception, sensation, intention, behaviour, action, emotion, and so on.

Assume that all the relevant empirical facts about animals – their behaviour, neurophysiology, and evolutionary origins – have been established or can be taken for granted for the sake of argument. What these facts imply for the possession of mental properties (the satisfaction of mental concepts) will still depend on *what these properties* (concepts) *amount to*. Conversely, if all the pertinent properties have been determined, *which animals actually possess the properties* will depend on contingent facts.

The rationale for the involvement of both factual and conceptual factors is truistic and applies generally. Whether what is stated by an assertoric sentence *s* is true, normally depends both on how things are and on what *s* means. By the same token, whether an answer *s* to an interrogative sentence *q* is correct normally depends both on how things are and on what s and q mean. What is asked by the use of q depends (partly, in cases involving indexicals) on what q means; what is stated by the use of an assertoric sentence s depends (partly, in indexical cases) on what s means.

Both for an assertoric sentence s and an interrogative sentence q, their meaning depends at least partly on the meaning of their constituents. Furthermore, although concepts cannot simply be equated with 'meanings', to specify what general terms like 'mind', 'thinks', or 'is conscious' mean is to specify *what concepts they express*, and *vice versa*. Likewise, *what properties those terms signify* depends exclusively on what they mean and thereby on what concepts they express. Accordingly, how one should answer a question q depends partly on what its constituent terms mean, and hence on what concepts these constituent terms express, or what properties they signify.

This involvement of both linguistic and factual factors provides an unassuming rationale for the method of conceptual analysis as propagated by G. E. Moore: the 'difficulties and disagreements' that have dogged philosophy are due mainly 'to the attempt to answer questions without first discovering precisely *what* question it is which you desire to answer. ... [Philosophers] are constantly endeavouring to prove that "Yes" or "No" will answer questions, to which *neither* answer is correct.' The remedy of this malaise lies in the 'hard work' of conceptual 'analysis and distinction' (Moore 1903: *vi*). It has to be clear precisely *what question is being asked*, if attempts to answer that question are to make sense. By the same token, in order to establish what a given proposition, argument, or theory is about, it must be clear what concepts its constituent terms express.

2. CONCEPTUAL ANALYSIS AND PHILOSOPHY

Two ideas require more by way of support than semantic truisms. First, the factual and conceptual factors that impinge on the proper answer to questions can be held apart. Second, whereas empirical science tackles factual issues, conceptual issues constitute the proper domain of philosophy.

Allotting to philosophy the role of clarifying concepts is the trademark of a particular current within analytic philosophy, namely conceptual analysis (Glock 2008: Ch. 2). Furthermore, conceptual analysis appears to be a task for which contemporary analytic philosophers are particularly well equipped. Nonetheless, the procedure of conceptual analysis requires defence against two currently popular alternatives – essentialist metaphysics and naturalism. Essentialism contends that philosophy is distinct from science because it is capable of ascertaining the essential features of the world. Metaphilosophical naturalism maintains that philosophy is part of or directly continuous with empirical science; there are neither essences nor distinctively conceptual issues for it to investigate. Both concur, however, that philosophy should be concerned *with reality* rather than concepts or the meaning of expressions.

I reject both alternatives. The idea of *de re* essences independent of our concepts is spurious. And the specifically philosophical task regarding animal minds does *not* consist in collecting new data about animal behaviour or in devising new empirical hypotheses about its neurological causes and evolutionary origins. It does not even consist predominantly in synthesizing empirical findings at a general level. Instead, it consists in establishing *what it is* to possess mental properties. Theoretical philosophy is a *second-order discipline*. It does not directly describe or explain reality; instead it reflects on the concepts that we use outside philosophy, in everyday life, science, or other specialized domains.

Philosophy clarifies mental concepts, among others, notably by investigating their *conditions of application*, the conditions which something must fulfil to satisfy these concepts. Empirical science, by contrast, determines whether or not these concepts *do in fact apply* to organisms or systems of a certain type; it also provides causal explanations of *how the instances of these concepts come* to satisfy these conditions of application.

In addition to the application and the elucidation of concepts, there is conceptual *construction* or *concept-formation*, the devising of novel conceptual structures. It is one of the hallmarks of mathematics, which invents novel formal tools for describing and explaining empirical phenomena. Concept formation plays an important role in the empirical sciences as well, especially when these develop new paradigms during scientific revolutions. Indeed, it occurs whenever new ways of classifying or explaining phenomena are introduced. Philosophy is no exception. The concepts of analyticity and a priority, for instance, are philosophical innovations.

The moot question is whether concept-formation has the same purpose and importance in philosophy as in science, namely of furnishing novel tools for classifying and explaining phenomena in the world. Analyticity and a priority, at any rate, serve to characterize, respectively, the logical and epistemic status of statements or beliefs. They reinforce my ideal of a division of labour. The primary task to which philosophy can make a distinctive contribution over and above other disciplines, is elucidating existing concepts rather than applying them to reality on the basis of empirical data or devising novel concepts. These activities are related and often proceed in tandem. Moreover, individual thinkers and texts often combine them. Especially in confronting novel, seemingly intractable, issues, scientists profit from conceptual sensitivity and ingenuity. Furthermore, concept application and concept formation have been pursued extensively under the label 'philosophy'. After all, both intellectually and institutionally most special sciences used to be part of philosophy. These disciplines emancipated themselves one by one from the eighteenth century onwards, with the result that most of their problems no longer count as philosophical.

This concession invites an objection (see Russell 1967: 90). Rather than being a second-order discipline distinct from science, philosophy is a *proto-science*, dealing with questions not yet amenable to empirical methods. Now, 'kicking upstairs' (Austin 1970: 231–2) topics like infinity, matter in motion, types of learning, forms of reasoning, or linguistic universals by passing them on to specialized disciplines is a role that philosophy as an academic discipline has fulfilled admirably. Whether or not it is their queen, philosophy is the mother of all (non-applied) sciences, even though its children rarely go overboard with tokens of gratitude. Nevertheless, the fact that the special sciences developed out of philosophy does not entail that the questions exercising philosophy are invariably scientific after all. For while the *topics* may be shared, they can give rise to distinct *kinds of problem*.

Some problems have remained within the purview of philosophy ever since its inception. Among them are problems that concern topics investigated by independent academic disciplines. Accordingly, disciplinary secession from philosophy is no panacea for philosophical perplexities. Moreover, at present, philosophy as a distinctive intellectual pursuit is constituted in large part by such problems. These include questions like 'What is truth?', 'Is knowledge possible?', 'How is the mind related to the body?' and 'Are there universally binding moral principles?'. Such puzzles are of a peculiar kind. They continue to defy the otherwise highly successful methods of empirical science. What is more, in many cases there are straightforward reasons for this failure. For instance, there is a difference between the questions 'What is true?' (about a particular topic) and 'What is truth?'; one cannot without circularity allay sceptical doubts about the possibility of empirical knowledge by appeal to empirical scientific findings; one cannot by pain of a naturalistic fallacy deduce the (non-)existence of normative principles from the (non-)existence of a moral consensus among human beings; and so on. Such considerations provide a *prima facie* case for regarding philosophy as *a priori* in a minimal sense: the distinctively philosophical questions and disputes concern not the empirical findings themselves, but at most the *relevance* the latter have for such problems. Thus, the discoveries of the neurosciences, impressive though they are, have not solved either the mind–body problem or the problem of free will. Instead, they have provoked fresh disputes about the relation between mental and neurophysiological phenomena, and about notions like decision, liberty, responsibility, and rationality.

3. CONCEPTUAL ANALYSIS AND DEFINITION

In response to 'What is ...?'-questions, philosophers have traditionally sought *analytic definitions* of X(s). Such definitions specify conditions or features which are *individually necessary* and *jointly sufficient* for being X. Furthermore, these features should not just *in fact* be possessed by all and only things that are X; rather, it should be *necessary* that all and only things that are X possess them. Only things possessing all of the defining features can be X, and anything possessing them all is *ipso facto X*.

Analytic definitions can be understood either as *nominal* definitions, which specify the linguistic meaning of words, or as *real* definitions, which identify the nature or *de re* essence of the things denoted by them, something independent of the way we think and speak. Both traditional and contemporary metaphysicians have pursued real definitions capturing the mind-independent nature or essence of things. They try to discover substantive truths about reality that are more general and fundamental than those of science, truths about the nature or essence of things, yet without relying on experience. As Kant pointed out, this ambition is puzzling. How can we achieve 'synthetic' insights about reality independently of experience? After all, the latter provides our paradigmatic and least contestable epistemic access to the world we inhabit. To this day, the Kantian challenge awaits a compelling response. Within the analytic tradition the idea of *de re* essences has been rejected by figures as diverse as Wittgenstein, the logical positivists, 'ordinary language philosophers', Popper, and Quine. In their wake, many twentieth-century philosophers settled for nominal or *de dicto* definitions, definitions or explanations which specify the meaning(s) of *X*.

Alas, at present such a procedure will be greeted by the indignant complaint that serious philosophy is, or ought to be, interested not in 'mere words', but rather in the nature of the things they denote. Any sane conceptual analyst will recognize the difference between words and concepts on the one hand, and the things they denote or apply to on the other. Nonetheless, the question 'What is *X*?' often concerns the meaning of words. Admittedly, questions of this form can be requests for empirical information about *X*(s). One might be interested in the *nature* of *X*(s), the cluster of properties that causally explain the behaviour of *X*(s), yet as a matter of fact. But 'What is *X*?'-questions posed in philosophical reflection are not directed at contingent features of *X*(s), however fundamental, that is, at features which instances of the concept may or may not possess and which need to be established empirically by looking at these instances. They are directed instead at the *essence* of *X*, at *what makes something an X*. That kind of question is properly answered by an explanation of *what 'X' means*. For such an explanation will specify what counts as *X*, or what it is to be an *X*, independently of features that *X*(s) may or may not possess and which need to be established empirically. Similarly for questions of the form 'What makes something (an) *X*?'. These can be requests for a *causal* explanation that specifies how come that certain objects are *X*. But they can also be requests for a *semantic* explanation that specifies what *constitutes* being an

X, that is, conditions *by virtue of which something qualifies as X* in the first place. For this reason, there is no significant difference between what Carnap called, respectively, the 'material' and the 'formal mode'. It matters little, for instance, whether we answer the question 'What is a drake?' by saying that a drake is a male duck or by saying that 'drake' means *male duck*.

This defence invites an antipodal objection, namely that conceptual analysis no less than science describes and explains reality after all. Are concepts and meanings not equally part of reality, albeit of a sub-section, whether it be mental, linguistic, abstract, or neural? In so far as concepts feature in intellectual operations and expressions in linguistic activities, the answer is: yes! The empirical investigation of conceptual thinking – the abilities and processes it involves and its neurophysiological vehicles – is a task for psychology, cognitive science, and neuroscience. *Mutatis mutandis*, empirical investigations into what expressions in a given language mean or have meant are a matter for empirical linguistics – synchronic and diachronic. However, philosophy deals with the meaning of expressions not by describing how members of a particular linguistic community employ them or by explaining how they came to employ them. Instead, it reflects on them by spelling out or explicating the concepts that *feature in philosophical discourse*, notably by elucidating what the explananda in pertinent 'What is ...?'-questions mean. A conceptual analyst establishes neither whether a general term applies to an object, nor by what mental and linguistic processes subjects decide whether it does; instead, she explains what property a general term signifies and what concept it expresses. In doing so, she does not adopt the external empirical perspective of the diachronic linguist. Instead, she may spell out her own understanding of a philosophically pertinent expression. In addition, she may try to articulate the understanding operative in the questions, statements, and arguments of an interlocutor. These are the kinds of dialectical explication familiar from the Socratic *elenchus*. Normally, however, such philosophical explications will start out from the understanding of those expressions operative in the linguistic community to which the philosophical interlocutors belong. For the primordial and most fundamental philosophical questions are couched in terms of *shared natural languages*. This holds in particular for questions concerning the mind.

The knowledge conceptual analysis aspires to presupposes learning for its genesis. Nevertheless, it is not straightforwardly empirical, since its epistemic warrant is different. It articulates an understanding obtained as part of language acquisition and of enculturation, that is, of the immersion into a shared linguistic practice. Because conceptual analysis explicates intersubjective rules, it can profitably be regarded as articulating 'participatory knowledge'. Linguistic competence is akin to the knowledge we gain by mastering other social practices, such as a game or dance (Hanfling 2000: 52–5). As competent speakers of a natural language, we observe others using words; yet we have also been initiated into this practice ourselves, and we participate in it willy-nilly. In explaining what expressions from that language mean, we formulate the logico-semantic rules – however flexible and context-dependent – that govern it, rules we have mastered in learning the language.

4. CONCEPTUAL ANALYSIS AND ESSENCES

The connection between the nature of a phenomenon X and the meaning of an expression 'X' in a 'What is X?'-question is obvious. Still, a gap between nature and meaning looms if one adumbrates essentialism, revived through Kripke (1980) and Putnam (1975: Ch. 12). According to their 'realist semantics', the reference of natural kind terms like 'water' or 'tiger' is not determined by the criteria for their application specified in nominal definitions – notably perceptible features by which laypeople distinguish things as belonging to those kinds. Rather, it is fixed in acts of 'baptism', by a paradigmatic exemplar and an appropriate 'sameness relation' that all members of the kind must bear to this exemplar. 'Water', for instance, refers to all stuff which is relevantly similar to a paradigmatic sample, that is, any substance which has the same microstructure as that paradigm. Accordingly, natural kinds do not just possess a 'nominal' but also a 'real essence', in Locke's terminology (*Essay* III.3), in this case to consist of H_2O.

Emboldened by realist semantics, many contemporaries proclaim that they can get *de re* essences into the crosshairs of their intellectual periscopes. Whether or not such aspirations can be fulfilled, however, realist semanticists perforce rely on their understanding of philosophically contested *expressions*, both in rejecting other accounts of the pertinent phenomena and in proposing their own alternatives. To be sure, they often conceal this reliance on linguistic points by dressing it up as an appeal to 'intuitions'. Unfortunately, intensive efforts over the last thirty years have failed to bring to light what exactly a philosophical intuition of X is supposed to be. Unless it is *either* the 'intuitor's' subjective hunch about what X is like, something that is properly called an intuition yet lacks any epistemic authority; *or* an explication of his concept of X, something that is *not a bona fide* intuition but rather – by any other name – an explanation of what he *means* by 'X'. When a philosopher says 'It is my intuition that such-and-such is (not) a case of X', this can properly amount to one of two claims. One is that the individual speaker would (not) count such-and-such as X, would (not) call it 'X', and hence amounts to (partially) explicating *his* understanding of that term, its *speaker's meaning*. The other is that 'we', that is, competent users of the term, would not count this case as X, would not apply 'X' to it, and hence amounts to a claim about its established use in a language and thereby about its *literal* or *conventional*. It is ultimately an attempt to articulate participatory knowledge of a shared language. The two types of claim are not mutually exclusive; in fact, speaker's meaning and conventional meaning will normally coincide. Yet they part company in certain respects. First, speaker's meaning *can* diverge from conventional meaning, not least among philosophers. Second, with respect to speaker's meaning but not to conventional meaning we possess a certain kind of *first-person authority*.

By comparison to contemporary intuition merchants, the founders of realist semantics were laudably candid. Although Kripke and Putnam sought necessities which concern reality rather than our conceptual scheme, they identified these through the *workings of language*, notably the alleged fact that natural kind terms are 'rigid designators' that refer to the same phenomena in all possible scenarios. This is why they frequently appealed to 'what we would say' about certain counterfactual scenarios, for example, a 'Twin Earth' on which a substance which shares all the surface properties of water turns out to have a chemical composition other than H_2O. How else could they have proceeded? In order to establish whether certain types of expression are rigid designators, and whether they (purport to) refer to real essences, one must start out by characterizing how these expressions function in established practice.

Whether the realist account *actually fits* our use even of natural kind terms like 'water' for which there are concrete paradigms that can be investigated by science is contestable (Glock 2003: Ch. 3). Doubts are exacerbated when it comes to *mental* terms. To begin with, there is no thing or stuff called, for example, (a) pain, consciousness, or reasoning that one could point to as a paradigm and subject to scientific scrutiny. Even if our mental expressions were, or could be, defined through individual speakers baptizing their own private experiences (contrary to Wittgenstein's private language argument), these would defy intersubjective scientific inspection. What one can point to are only paradigmatic cases of individuals *being in a* mental state or *undergoing* a mental process. But these are precisely the cases in which the criteria specified by a *nominal definition* are fulfilled.

Realist semantics may allow that in the baptismal situation the reference of terms is fixed by description rather than ostension, for example, 'Pain is the sensation caused by injury and eliciting averse reactions.' This would be compatible, however, with the procedure advocated here, namely establishing what must hold of an organism for it to be in pain, whether it be because of an original baptism to which our current use is causally linked (as realist semantics has it) or because of the applications and explanations of competent speakers at present (as I maintain). A bone of contention remains, namely whether the macroscopic states or processes picked out by mental terms have underlying real essences, for example, the micro-structural neurophysiological phenomena caused by injury and causing pain behaviour. Elsewhere I have argued that the relation between mental and behavioural notions is tighter and between mental and neurophysiological notions looser than this proposal allows (Glock 1996: 93–7, 174–9). Yet this is a question concerning the *proper analysis* of mental notions, rather than the very *propriety of their analysis*. Finally, even if scientific labels and distinctions are capable of 'carving nature at its joints', in Plato's striking phrase (*Phaedrus*: 265d–266a), it is a moot question whether our mental concepts serve that purpose, at least exclusively. In order to decide that issue, there is once again no way around establishing what mental terms *mean*.

Even if one settles for nominal definitions, methodological choices remain. Nominal definitions divide into stipulative definitions on the one hand, and reportive or lexical ones on the other. *Stipulative* definitions simply lay down *ab novo* what an expression *is to mean* in a particular context, in complete disregard of any established use it may have. Barring incoherence, such definitions cannot be correct or incorrect. But they can be more or less fruitful, in that it may be more or less helpful to single out a particular phenomenon through a separate label. *Lexical* definitions are supposed to capture what an expression *does mean* in its ordinary use. However, 'ordinary use' is ambiguous. It may refer to either the *everyday* use of an expression as opposed to its specialist or technical employment or the *standard* use of an expression as opposed to its irregular use, in any area, science included (Ryle 1971: 301–4). Finally, one should recognize a halfway house between the extremes of unfettered stipulation and faithful articulation of established use: *revisionary* definitions regiment or modify the extant use of a term, yet without diverging from it completely.

5. MENTAL IDIOM AND REVISIONISM

What sort of definition is most appropriate for mental terms, in particular with regard to the question of animal minds? Making sense of one another in terms of our sensations, feelings, moods, beliefs, desires, intentions, and so on, is deeply ingrained in the warp and weft of our daily existence. The same goes for speakers annunciating their own state of mind to others. With respect to an idiom that is not just entrenched but pervades our whole lives, unfettered stipulation is ill-advised. For one thing, it invites confusion for no apparent gain. For another, existing terms, as actually employed, stand in relations to *other terms* that would have to be redefined as well. This holds not just for the conceptual relations between different mental concepts, but also for the connection between the latter on the one hand, and concepts from other domains such as epistemic, moral, medical, and legal discourse on the other.

Of course mental terms are employed not just in everyday parlance, but also in philosophy, the empirical sciences of the mind, and numerous other academic subjects. These disciplines must develop their own terminology and conceptual apparatus. While there is no case for sheer stipulation, there may nonetheless be reasons for *modifying* generally accepted explanations. One might feel, therefore, that for philosophical and scientific purposes we need to graduate from quotidian use towards a more specialized one based on more exacting scrutiny of the phenomena. Thus one might earmark mental notions for 'logical explication' à la Carnap (1956: 7–9). The aim of such an explication is not to provide a synonym for the *analysandum*, but to *replace* it by an alternative expression or construction. That alternative ought to serve the cognitive purposes of the original equally well, while avoiding drawbacks such as obscurity, ambiguity, vagueness, paradox, or undesirable ontological commitments.

Conceptual analysts tried to resolve such problems not through substituting artificial terms and constructions for the idioms of natural languages, but by clarifying the latter. To logical constructionists like Carnap and Quine, this appeared as a philistine cult of common sense and ordinary use, at the expense of scientific insights and terminology. Similarly, present-day cognitive and neuroscientists complain that conceptual analysts who criticize their philosophical conclusions prefer thought-experiments to real experiments, and that they pose obstacles to scientific progress by setting themselves up as 'guardians of semantic inertia' (Gregory 1987: 242–3).

But conceptual analysis does not extol the virtues of the mundane or everyday over the sophisticated specialized employment of a term. Nor does it prohibit the introduction of technical terminology in either science or philosophy. Persistent misinterpretations notwithstanding, prudent conceptual analysts have refrained explicitly from criticizing philosophical positions merely for coining novel terms or employing familiar words in ways that differ from their established employment in everyday or scientific parlance. Instead, they insist that such novel terms or uses need to be *adequately explained* by laying down clear rules for their use. They further allege that many philosophical questions and theories – no matter whether propounded by philosophers or scientists – get off the ground only because they employ terms in a way which is at odds with their official explanations, and that they trade on *deviant* rules *along with* established ones. Thus Wittgenstein confronted metaphysical problems and theories trading on divergent uses of familiar terms with a *trilemma*: their novel uses of terms remain unexplained – which leads to *unintelligibility* or *misunderstanding*; or it is revealed that they use expressions according to incompatible rules – old and new – the threat of *inconsistency*; or their consistent employment of new concepts simply passes by the ordinary use – including the standard use of technical terms – and hence the concepts in terms of which the original problems were phrased – a case of missing the question or *ignoratio elenchi*. In a similar vein, Ryle intimated that conceptual analysis is interested less in language as a system, than in the often obscure, slippery, and equivocal *uses* to which it is put in the course of a *specific line of reasoning* (1971: Chs 14, 24, 31). Conceptual analysis is neither conservative, nor is it atavistic linguistics masquerading as philosophy. It is a way of dealing with Socratic 'What is…?'-questions in a dialectic fashion, and is an indispensible tool of critical thinking, one that helps to prevent or rectify errors that vitiate the efforts of philosophers, scientists, and laypeople alike.

This is not to deny that it can be both desirable and feasible to modify concepts slightly in order to avoid paradoxes or conceptual traps. Thus the allure of Hegelian confusions about 'identity in difference' and Heideggerian confusions about 'being' might be curbed by adopting a notation which replaces 'is' by either '=', '∈' or '∃'. Yet for several reasons this does not remove the need for at least *starting out* from established use.

First, unless the relation between the novel and the established ways of using the pertinent expressions (between the new and the old concepts) is properly understood, the philosophical problems associated with these expressions will merely be swept under the carpet (Strawson 1963). Second, all neologisms and conceptual modifications, those of science included, need to be explained. By pain of regress, this can ultimately be done only in terms of everyday expressions which are already understood – the expressions of a mother tongue. The expressions of our first natural language we acquire not through explanation in terms of another language, but through training in basic linguistic skills, and through enculturation more generally. With respect to many specialized purposes, ordinary – in the sense of everyday – language is inferior to technical idioms. But it is *semantic bedrock* and our *ultimate medium of explanation*. It is only by mastering a natural language that we acquire the ability to learn and explain new and technical terms. As Austin put it, while 'ordinary language is *not* the last word ... it *is* the *first* word' (1970: 185).

Like many philosophical questions, those concerning the mind in general and animal minds in particular are phrased in *extant*, non-modified vocabulary; indeed, in this case the idiom is first and foremost part of everyday discourse. We would like to know, for example, whether animals can think or are conscious in *our* sense of these terms, not in a sense introduced by new-fangled philosophical or scientific theories. Answers that employ modified – let alone entirely novel – concepts will simply pass these questions by. They will *change the topic* or *miss* it entirely. In fact, unless these modified or novel concepts can be explained coherently through extant concepts, such answers will remain vacuous or obscure.

Our established concepts *determine* the subject area of most philosophical problems and even of many *scientific* ones. They are presupposed explicitly or implicitly not just in philosophical theories and arguments, but also in research projects, methods, and conclusions from the special sciences. For instance, the explanation of perception cannot be couched exclusively in everyday concepts; it must employ technical concepts ranging from behavioural psychology to biochemistry. Yet everyday statements like 'Maria *saw* that Frank had put on weight', 'Sarah *listens* to the *Eroica*', 'One can *smell* the wild strawberries', 'The sense of *taste* is not affected by age', and 'In the Müller-Lyer illusion two lines of equal length *appear* to be of unequal length' pick out the *phenomena that the science of perception seeks to explain*. Small wonder, then, that in presenting and interpreting the results of empirical research into perception, philosophers and scientists do not uniformly stick to technical terminology. Instead, they often employ everyday terms like 'representation', 'symbol', 'map', 'image', 'information', or 'language' in ways which either remain unexplained or illicitly combine ordinary with technical uses (Bennett and Hacker 2003).

Mental notions are notorious for giving rise to a whole raft of vexatious puzzles. It is therefore a precondition of any sober approach even to scientific problems involving them that it should pay attention to the established use of the relevant expressions within their normal surroundings. Without the propaedeutic of conceptual clarification, we shall be 'incapable of discussing the matter in any useful way because we have no stable handle on our subject matter' (Joyce 2006: 52). And in the absence of a definitive clarification, conscientious cognitive scientists should at least provide a 'working definition' of mental notions, as they employ them in a particular line of research (Griffin 1981: 6).

6. CONNECTIVE ANALYSIS

In pursuing questions of the form 'What is X?' we shall inevitably rely on a *preliminary notion* of X, an idea of what constitutes the topic of our investigation. In our case we presuppose a preliminary understanding of mental vocabulary. This is not a fully articulated conception, the latter would have to emerge from subsequent debates; instead it is an initial idea of what those debates are about. Such a pre-theoretical understanding is embodied in the established uses of the relevant mental terms. In tackling the animal mind and distribution questions, we therefore need to pay heed to our extant mental concepts, as manifested in the standard use of those terms. Both the explanations of mental concepts and claims about their applicability to animals should in the first instance be measured against the customary employment of those concepts in successful and reasonably controlled forms of discourse. In our case, the latter will include everyday parlance; yet they will also include specialized disciplines from the behavioural and life sciences, the social sciences, and jurisprudence.

Whether such investigations will yield analytic definitions in terms of necessary and sufficient conditions, is another matter. Certain contemporary opponents of conceptual analysis have delighted in pointing out that ever since Plato, philosophers have failed spectacularly to come up with convincing definitions of any but the most trivial concepts. Thus Fodor opines hyperbolically – though not without some licence – that 'the number of concepts whose analyses have thus far been determined continues to hover stubbornly around none' (2003: 6).

Fortunately, we need not lapse into such pessimism. For one thing, some central philosophical concepts allow of analytic definitions, once one bids farewell to unjustified assumptions. In other cases – for example, consciousness, intention, intelligence – analytic definitions are in the offing if one takes note of complex ambiguities. Still, many notions defy analytic definition entirely. This does not mean, however, that it is either impossible or superfluous to elucidate them. There are other respectable ways of *explaining* concepts, notably contextual, recursive, and ostensive definitions, surveys of family resemblances, and explanations by exemplification.

To promote the idea that definition and conceptual explanation are not confined to analytic definitions, Strawson has distinguished between 'atomistic' or more generally speaking 'reductive' and 'connective analysis' (1992: Ch. 2). The former seeks to break down concepts into simpler (in the case of atomistic analysis, ultimate) components and to unearth the concealed logical structure of propositions. Developments in the wake of Wittgenstein and Quine cast doubt not just on the quest for simpler let alone ultimate components but also on the idea of definite logical structures. In consequence, connective analysis abandons the analogy to chemical analysis. It is the description of the *rule-governed use of expressions*, and of their connections with other expressions by way of implication, presupposition, and exclusion. Connective analysis need not result in definitions, it can rest content with elucidating features which are constitutive of the concepts under consideration, and with establishing how they bear on philosophical problems, doctrines, and arguments.

Even connective analysis separates conceptual from factual issues, and the explanation of expressions from the investigation of reality. It also remains wedded to the idea that in clarifying conceptual issues we rely not on empirical data, but instead *explicate our understanding* of certain terms, drawing in effect on our linguistic competence. Both ideas have been vigorously challenged by Quinean naturalists. They deny that there is any significant difference between analytic or conceptual statements independent of experience and the synthetic or factual statements based on experience. As a result, they maintain that proper 'scientific philosophy' does not just emulate the methods of the deductive-nomological sciences, it is itself 'continuous with' or even *part* of science (Quine 1951, 1970: 2).

Elsewhere I have argued that the Quinean attacks on the analytic/synthetic, *a priori/a posteriori* and necessary/contingent distinctions fail. As a result, the naturalistic assimilation of the conceptual issues of philosophy to the factual issues of science is unwarranted (Glock 2003: Chs 2–3). What is correct is that the borders between the conceptual and the factual can and do shift, along with our ways of thinking and speaking. What is more, such changes of the conceptual framework can themselves be motivated by scientific considerations ranging from new experiences and the availabality of novel mathematical apparatus through simplicity and fruitfulness to sheer beauty. This does not mean, however, that empirical and conceptual propositions are on a par. For such *conceptual changes* can in turn be distinguished from changes of factual beliefs, notably the falsification of scientific theories by empirical evidence. Conceptual claims can be abandoned as result of empirical discoveries, yet without being falsified. For they are constitutive of the concepts involved, which means that they explicate concepts that differ (however slightly) from the ones which feature in the newly adopted empirical theories.

7. IMPURE ANALYSIS

The interaction between conceptual and factual issues is patent in the case of our distribution question. In tackling it we must pay heed to the *conditions for the applicability* of mental terms. At the same time, it is obvious that the question as to which creatures these terms *actually apply* also depends on contingent facts about these creatures to be established empirically.

This interaction necessitates modifications of the idea that the philosophy of animal minds revolves exclusively around the analysis of mental concepts. Indeed, these caveats apply to *any* topic on which science and philosophy *converge*. Such topics pose both philosophical and scientific problems, thereby occasioning science to gather fresh data, develop novel methods, and construct new theories. My caveats are not incompatible with classical conceptual analysis. Yet they have been insufficiently recognized in these quarters. Furthermore, they stand in tension with a received image of conceptual analysis, namely that it is a purely *a priori* exercise, unaffected in all respects by scientific findings. Accordingly, they lend succour to a type of conceptual analysis that I call 'impure'.

The *first* caveat is this. While conceptual and factual problems are distinct in principle even when it comes to topics researched by science, they *cannot be tackled in isolation*. Philosophers cannot engage in a second-order conceptual reflection on a mode of discourse without being acquainted with its first-order problems, claims, and methods. For instance, one cannot take neuroscientists to task for describing the brain or its parts as perceiving, inferring, deliberating, and so on, without at least an inkling of the information processing by neurons, which they (mis-)describe in this way and the methods through which these processes are diagnosed.

A *second* caveat. On the one hand, matters of meaning *antecede* matters of fact: it makes sense to investigate a phenomenon X only if it is clear what is to count as X, if only provisionally. In that sense conceptual claims are not subject to empirical refutation. On the other hand, whether a question posed in empirical science is indeed muddled needs to be established case by case, not by invoking a preconceived account of the constituent concepts in a high-handed manner. Conceptual analysis is *a priori*, yet without being infallible. And conceptual confusion is rife only when the novel or modified concepts scientists employ are either obscure or at odds with the concepts of the questions these findings are supposed to address.

Third, the antecedence of meaning to fact notwithstanding, we must avoid the Socratic mistake of thinking that one cannot establish empirical facts about X unless one already has an analytic definition of 'X'. Plato's *Meno* (80a–e) devises the following paradox. It is impossible to inquire into what X is, since one cannot look for or recognize the correct answer, without already knowing it from the start. The underlying argument runs as follows:

P$_1$ To recognize the correct definition of X we already have to know what X is.
P$_2$ To know what X is, is to know the definition of X.
C$_1$ We would already need to know the correct definition of X in order to recognize it.
C$_2$ The search for a correct definition of X is pointless.

P$_1$ is mistaken, at any rate in conjunction with P$_2$, which identifies knowing what X is with knowing a *definition* of X. As Kant pointed out, 'definition' marks at best the terminus of philosophical enquiry, not its beginning. And as Wittgenstein pointed out, to look for and recognize the correct explanation of X, all one needs is a pre-theoretical understanding of 'X', something we normally learn in acquiring a language, by coming to master the use of 'X'.

Any scientific theory of mental phenomena presupposes at least a certain *preconception* of the pertinent properties. But this does not mean that one needs a cast-iron, precise definition of these properties in advance of empirical theory-building. Our concepts are tools which we fashion for our purposes, in science the purpose of describing, explaining, and predicting phenomena. In scientific theory-building, definitions are to be read from *right to left*: we introduce labels for newly discovered or postulated phenomena. An example from ethology. Tomasello and Call differentiate types of 'social learning', such as 'emulative learning' and 'imitation' (1997: Ch. 9). These categories were not devised in the armchair to be subsequently tested through observation or experiment; rather, they were inspired by observing the interactions between primates confronted with novel situations and comparing them with those between children.

Fourth, considering their applicability to animals in the light of empirical data may lead us not merely to replace or modify our mental notions for the purposes of scientific theory building. It can also have a bearing on how we should construe our *extant* notions. Even when the *concepts* are held in place, empirical findings may alter our *conceptions* of the mind, sensation, perception, thought, behaviour, and so on. In line with Hume's treatment of animals as 'touchstones' for a conception of the mind, philosophers have written of such feedback as the 'animal test' or 'calibration method' (Andrews 2015). This is but a particular instance of the Socratic *elenchus* employed by conceptual analysis. If we conceive of the criteria for the applicability, for example, of 'perception' or 'attention' in a way precluding animals, while at the same time regarding some animals as paradigmatic subjects of perception or attention, we have reason to alter our conception of the criteria. But whether the criteria we initially proposed *in fact preclude* animals is an empirical matter.

Fifth, the conceptual bond between mental and linguistic capacities is less tight and far-reaching than many differentialists suppose. Creatures that resemble us very closely in *all respects apart from language* – as regards not just intelligent behaviour like tool-manufacture but also facial expressions and bodily demeanour – can in principle be credited even with rudimentary reasoning. It is probable that our closest evolutionary ancestors without language resembled us in many of these respects. Yet at present there are no creatures that are sufficiently close to us in all respects bar language for this consideration to get a grip. Philosophical anthropology needs to consider the *conceptual* connections between mind and language that hold given the *contingent capacities of extant species*. Ascribing beliefs of a certain complexity may presuppose their linguistic manifestability, but only *given* the absence of other behavioural manifestations close to ours or accessible to us. And one cannot investigate the impact of such presuppositions without recourse to empirical facts.

Such mutual dependencies of conceptual and factual considerations do not pose a threat to conceptual analysis as such. The late Wittgenstein, for one, distinguished not just factual and conceptual propositions, but also allowed that empirical discoveries can motivate conceptual change. He further pointed out that there is a 'framework' of contingent facts concerning our own nature and the world around us without which certain concepts or an entire conceptual scheme may be pointless or even unfeasible (Glock 1996: 135–9). What is more, empirical facts come into play once we consider the question of whether certain abilities – such as the ability to entertain beliefs and desires – presuppose certain other abilities – such as the ability to express such beliefs and desires in sentences. For whether one ability requires another will almost always depend on what *other abilities* are assumed. And what abilities can be assumed with respect to a biological species – whether extant or extinct – is an empirical question.

Even Strawson's 'descriptive metaphysics' pays heed to framework conditions. Strawson argues for the ontological priority of material bodies, with a crucial rider. 'As things are' (1959: 38), given our perceptual and intellectual capacities, the only way to ensure the possibility of distinguishing between subjective experiences and objective particular phenomena that they are experiences of is to locate the latter within a spatio-temporal framework constituted by material bodies. For only this framework is 'humanly constructible'. For radically different fictitional scenarios, like Strawson's hearer world or a super-human that can trace all the relevant causal relations with the immediacy with which we can perceive location and motion, other options exist.

Finally, conceptual and ethical issues are similarly intertwined. Some mental notions are 'essentially contested' in that a particular moral value or status attaches to them. Obvious candidates include 'reason' and 'person'. In such cases the very business of conceptual analysis cannot be kept apart from reflections on moral attitudes and values. Once again, there is no need to abandon conceptual analysis, but only to widen its scope. To resolve philosophical puzzles arising out of a concept, we need to take a look at the *overall role and function of that concept within our lives*.

9. METHODOLOGICAL PRINCIPLES BETWEEN PHILOSOPHY AND SCIENCE

There is a final respect in which the purity of conceptual analysis must be sacrificed for topics shared between philosophy and science. While the distinction between conceptual (*a priori*) and factual (empirical) questions and statements is crucial, it is not *exhaustive*, even leaving aside normative principles. There is a sphere of *methodological* considerations that straddles – or sits uneasily between – the two.

Turning to animal minds, one methodological issue concerns the respective merits of experiment and observation. Should we set more store by observations in the field or by controlled experiments? The latter allow of more reliable corroboration and of systematically alternating the parameters of the situation. The former are more significant for biological purposes. They possess greater 'ecological validity', to use a term from research design.

These are not straightforwardly empirical matters, since they concern *what kind of empirical evidence* should carry what kind of weight. Nor are they straightforwardly issues of a conceptual kind. It is not part of the meaning of 'mind' or 'behaviour' that behaviour observed under natural conditions should reveal more about a subject's mental capacities than behaviour elicited through experiment. Furthermore, within practical constraints ethologists can aspire to the best of both worlds by employing modern technology in order to control for relevant parameters even in the wild (Cheney and Seyfarth 2007).

Nonetheless the contrast carries a potential for philosophical quandaries. For one thing, while atypical behaviour by a specimen – for example, symbol use by enculturated bonobos under laboratory conditions – evinces mental capacities, it is less clear what the presence of such capacities under those conditions shows about the biological nature of the species, or about the proximity between bonobos and us. For the symbolic systems acquired by enculturated bonobos are remote from their systems of communication in the wild.

For another, a methodological dilemma looms. On the one hand, the more unrestricted and spontaneous the animal behaviour, the less rigorous the procedure and the more it relies on 'mere anecdotes'. There is also the danger of the notorious 'Clever Hans effect'. We need to exercise caution in interpreting experiments in which animals interact with humans, since the latter may unwittingly condition them to respond to unconscious signals. On the other hand, the more controlled and predictable the animal behaviour, the less ecologically sound the findings. Rigorous procedures such as duplication or 'double-blind strategies' to protect against the Clever Hans effect may vitiate the subject's willingness to cooperate (Dupré 2002: Ch. 11).

Another hot potato is 'Morgan's canon': 'in no case may we interpret an action as the outcome of the exercise of a higher psychical faculty, if it can be interpreted as the outcome of the exercise of one which stands lower in the psychological scale' (Morgan 1894: 53). Although it is a well-known methodological principle of comparative psychology, it is far from obvious what Morgan's canon actually entreats us to do, and on what grounds (see Starzak 2016). It is often regarded as an instance of 'Occam's razor', a principle of parsimony held to govern all academic subjects, from philosophy through cosmology to sociology. Alas, it is unclear what kind of economy is at issue. It is even less clear how parsimony relates to *other desiderata of theories*, such as explanatory power, simplicity, conservatism, modesty, precision, facility of computation, and avoidance of perplexities. As a result, Morgan's canon lends itself to competing interpretations and to exploitation by diametrically opposed positions.

These controversies defy neat classification into conceptual or factual. One rarely noted feature of Morgan's canon in particular and of canons of parsimony more generally is their *prescriptive* character. We are dealing with *regulative* principles for how to investigate a given domain rather than principles that are *constitutive* of that domain. Such regulative principles raise philosophical problems. Yet not all of these are conceptual in a straightforward sense. Should parsimony be the only or overriding methodological consideration? Or should *other desiderata* – explanatory power, simplicity, conservatism, modesty, precision, facility of computation, avoidance of perplexities – be given equal weight? The parameters for theory-building depend on what works in what specific area of enquiry. At the same time, the question of what *does* work in disciplines like ethology is in turn fraught with intricate conceptual and methodological issues.

We encounter an *interplay* between empirical, methodological, and conceptual aspects. But this challenge *reinforces* rather than diminishes the need for conceptual analysis. While philosophy is neither part of nor continuous with science, it has a contribution to make. Logic and mathematics are neither part of nor simply continuous with empirical science. Nonetheless they contribute to the latter by providing formal methods of proof and calculation. Philosophy can aid science by obviating confusions that lie in its path. With respect to the sciences, therefore, philosophy is no longer the queen (as in Aristotelianism). Nor is its role exhausted by that of a judge who holds the sciences accountable to standards of knowledge (Kantianism) or linguistic sense (Wittgensteinianism). It is more akin to that of the Lockean underlabourer (*Essay*: Epistle). Philosophical reflections on topics successfully investigated by empirical disciplines should not just be conceptually enlightening and methodologically scrupulous; they also ought to be relevant to factual questions and beneficial to empirical research. Such conceptual service is both indispensible and tricky. Philosophers ought not to shirk it by dabbling in science – let alone pseudo-science – instead, and scientists should be duly grateful rather than hostile.

6   What Can We Do, When We Do Metaphysics?

What are we doing, when we do metaphysics? A tempting answer – popular among contemporary metaphysicians – is to think of metaphysics as engaged in discovering especially deep or fundamental facts about the world. But there are familiar and formidable problems for this 'heavyweight' conception of metaphysics. First, it leaves the epistemology of metaphysics unclear: by what methods are we supposed to be able to discover these deep or fundamental features of reality? Second, it leaves metaphysics in danger of falling prey to a rivalry with science – for isn't it the purview of physics to discover the deep and fundamental facts about reality, and doesn't it do so better than metaphysics? Third, the radical and persistent disagreements that have characterized metaphysics for millennia lead to scepticism about whether metaphysicians are really succeeding in discovering such facts – which might encourage some to abandon metaphysics altogether.

In the face of these difficulties, deflationary positions about metaphysics have become increasingly prominent. The deflationist is suspicious of the thought that metaphysicians are like scientists in discovering 'deep facts' about the world and its nature. The deflationist also takes a more cautious view of the methods available to metaphysics, typically limiting what we can sensibly do in metaphysics to some combination of conceptual and empirical work – with the metaphysician's share of the work being largely a matter of conceptual analysis. But the idea that the core work of metaphysics is conceptual analysis makes it difficult to account for the felt depth, importance, and world-orientation of debates in metaphysics. Indeed many have thought that this leaves metaphysics nothing of interest to do.

I think this is too hasty, however. Here I aim to sketch a broader conceptualist model, on which metaphysics may undertake not merely descriptive but also normative conceptual work. This broader model, I will argue, enables us to preserve – and in some cases improve on – the advantages of the descriptive conceptualist approach in avoiding epistemic mysteries and rivalry with science. But it also enables us to give a more satisfying view than descriptive conceptual analysis can of what we can do when we do metaphysics: a view that does far better at explaining the radical disagreement that persists in metaphysics, and gives a much more satisfying account of the apparent world-orientation, depth, and potential importance of work in metaphysics. Yet it does so without sacrificing the demystifying advantages of deflationism.

I will begin by reviewing the problems faced by heavyweight conceptions of metaphysics, and the ways in which descriptive conceptual analysis has tried to avoid them. Then I will go on to develop and argue for the view that metaphysics has been, and can legitimately be, engaged in normative as well as descriptive conceptual work. Finally, I will make a pragmatic argument for adopting this broader conceptualist view of what metaphysics does, and what it can do.

DIFFICULTIES FOR HEAVYWEIGHT METAPHYSICS

Metaphysicians often think of themselves as making discoveries about what really exists, and about the persistence conditions or modal properties of things of various sorts. Those I will call 'heavyweight metaphysicians' think of these facts as 'epistemically metaphysical' (to use a phrase of Ted Sider's (2011: 187)), in the sense that they can be answered neither by direct empirical methods nor by conceptual analysis. But, as mentioned above, there are familiar and formidable epistemic problems in figuring out how we *are* supposed to come to know the relevant ontological and modal facts. The methods most often employed in metaphysical debates involve arguing that one's theory better handles certain thought experiments or imagined cases. Yet if we think of metaphysical facts as deep facts of the world, it is hard to see how we can be justified in using thought experiments to discover them (see Sosa 2008 and Thomasson 2012). Imaginative experiments certainly aren't thought to play a major role in deciding among scientific theories. If we think of metaphysics as similarly discovering worldly facts, it seems there is just as little reason for thinking imaginative experiments have a legitimate role there. Another prominent method of arguing for a metaphysical position is to argue that it better preserves certain 'theoretic virtues' than its rivals. In this regard, metaphysics better parallels the methods of the sciences, where theory choice is guided by appeal to theoretic virtues such as empirical adequacy, explanatory power, or simplicity. However, where metaphysical views (unlike most scientific views) are concerned, rival 'theories' are typically equivalent in empirical adequacy. Moreover, as Karen Bennett (2009) and Uriah Kriegel (2013) have argued, rival metaphysical theories often involve simply trading some of the remaining theoretical virtues off against others. Furthermore, as Phillip Bricker has argued (forthcoming), the remaining theoretic virtues (other than empirical adequacy) generally are a matter of the *usefulness* of the relevant theory *for creatures like us* – with our relevant cognitive capacities and limitations. But then it is hard to see how one could take those to be reasons for thinking the relevant theory correctly reports the metaphysical facts, rather than just thinking it is of greater pragmatic value.

Another threat to the heavyweight conception of metaphysics comes from the apparent rivalry with science that arises if we think of metaphysics as aimed at discovering deep facts about what exists and what the world is like. As Stephen Hawking and Leonard Mlodinow rather bluntly put the point:

people have always asked a multitude of questions: How can we understand the world in which we find ourselves? How does the universe behave? What is the nature of reality? Where did all this come from? ... Traditionally these are questions for philosophy, but philosophy is dead. Philosophy has not kept up with modern developments in science, particularly physics. Scientists have become the bearers of the torch of discovery in our quest for knowledge.

(Hawking and Mlodinow 2012: 5)

A third threat to the heavyweight conception of metaphysics comes from noting the radical and persistent disagreements in metaphysics. For in metaphysics, unlike science, there is nothing like convergence on the truth (or even progress on convergence) to show for our labours. Instead, there seems to be an increasing proliferation of metaphysical theories, with no agreement even on what might resolve the debates among them. This in turn might lead to a sceptical outlook – to denying that we ever could know the truth. Along these lines, Karen Bennett argues that for at least some metaphysical disputes, there is little justification for believing either side – it's not clear that we can ever find grounds for settling these disputes (Bennett 2009: 42). Bryan Frances (forthcoming) argues for a form of scepticism based on an analysis of the Philosophical Survey – a poll of over 3000 professional philosophers and graduate students, asking their opinions on thirty core philosophical questions. Based on the diversity of answers given, Frances argues that (assuming we think there are correct answers to these philosophical questions), where definite answers are given, the average philosopher can be thought to get 47–67 per cent right. Hardly an impressive score! As a result, he argues, we should suspend judgement indefinitely, refraining from believing anything on these issues (Frances forthcoming: 11). This sort of radical disagreement in metaphysics might then lead us to a sceptical torpor – thinking that, undiscoverable as such facts are, we may as well give up trying, and turn our attention elsewhere.

THE DESCRIPTIVE CONCEPTUAL APPROACH

Given the difficulties that arise for and from a heavyweight conception of metaphysics, one might turn to a more deflationary conception of what metaphysics does and can do. A time-honoured alternative to thinking of metaphysics as engaged in discovering deep 'epistemically metaphysical' facts is to think of it instead as involved in conceptual work. Call this approach (broadly construed) the 'conceptualist' approach, contrasted with the 'heavyweight' approach. A conceptualist approach of various forms was dominant in the early twentieth century in the work of philosophers such as Husserl, Ryle, Wittgenstein, and Carnap, and forms of the approach have been defended more recently by Frank Jackson (1998) and myself (Thomasson 2015).

The most common development of a conceptualist approach is to see the (proper) work of metaphysics as engaged in conceptual analysis: determining the contours of our conceptual scheme, the rules that govern our concepts, and/or the relations among our concepts. Details here of course vary among philosophers. As Peter Strawson described it (without endorsing it), a traditional vision takes the task as 'a kind of intellectual taking to pieces of ideas or concepts; the discovering of what elements a concept or idea is composed of and how they are related' (Strawson 1992: 2). Strawson himself describes the task as follows: 'the philosopher labours to produce a systematic account of the general *conceptual structure* of which our daily practice shows us to have a tacit and unconscious mastery' (ibid.: 7). Gilbert Ryle spoke of mapping the 'logical geography' of our concepts (e.g., of belief, intention, action, mind) (Ryle 1949: 8). Frank Jackson takes the role of conceptual analysis to be 'that of addressing the question of what to say about matters described in one set of terms *given* a story about matters in another set of terms' (Jackson 1998: 44) – for example, what to say about the world as described in moral terms given a description of the world in physical terms. And he takes the method for this to involve 'appeal to what seems to us most obvious and central' about the topic 'as revealed by our intuitions about possible cases' (ibid.: 31). While they may differ in the details, what these approaches have in common is the thought that a primary task of metaphysics – or perhaps even all of philosophy – is what we might call *descriptive* conceptual analysis, aiming to determine the actual rules governing our concepts and/or the relations among them.

A conceptualist approach is attractive for many reasons.[1] First, it has the potential to ease the epistemic problems of heavyweight metaphysics. It enables us to vindicate the use of traditional methods in metaphysics, such as consideration of imagined cases – since these plausibly enable us to determine the rules governing our concepts. More broadly, it enables us to demystify the epistemology of metaphysics. For on this model we can see how knowledge in metaphysics may be acquired by making use of our conceptual competence (often alongside ordinary empirical methods) – not requiring any distinctively metaphysical insights into a realm of covert metaphysical facts. I have argued at length elsewhere (Thomasson 2007b, 2013) that those modal questions of metaphysics that are answerable can be answered via a form of conceptual analysis, in some cases combined with empirical work. For (I have argued) the most basic metaphysical modal claims may be seen as object-language correlates of the constitutive semantic rules governing our terms or concepts, and so as learnable via a form of conceptual analysis. Thus by elucidating the rules governing our actual concept of *person* or *work of art*, we might hope to grasp when an individual would, and would not, count as the same person; what sorts of change a work of art would (and would not) survive, and so on. We can combine this with empirical information to get more detailed modal knowledge – for example, if we can tell (by conceptual analysis) that a painting couldn't survive the destruction of its canvas, and we acquire the empirical information that a canvas can't survive temperatures of 500 degrees Fahrenheit, then we can also tell that a painting couldn't survive such temperatures.[2]

It is perhaps a little harder to see how the existential questions of metaphysics can be answered through a combination of empirical and/or conceptual work. But I have argued at length elsewhere (Thomasson 2015) that they can – at least when such questions are taken in what Carnap would have called the 'internal' sense: that is, as questions asked *using* the relevant linguistic framework.[3] Given conceptual competence, many existence questions (Do tables exist? Do organisms exist?) can be answered by means of simple empirical observation. If you have mastered the concepts and so know what it takes for there to be tables or organisms, go have a look in that restaurant and you'll have your answer to the question 'Are there tables?' or 'Are there organisms?' In other cases, those competent with the concepts in question can engage in trivial reasoning from obvious premises to answer the existence question. So, for example, if conceptual analysis tells us that there is a link between concepts entitling us to reason from 'the dog is brown' to 'the dog has the property of brownness' to 'there is a property', then we can make use of that inference to easily answer the question of whether properties exist. To be clear, in the first instance, all that is needed is *competence* with the relevant concepts that we *use* in the relevant observations or inferences. If that is challenged, however, or if the cases are more difficult or borderline cases, explicit conceptual analysis might be employed to determine what it takes for things of the relevant kind to exist, or what rules govern the relevant concept(s), on the basis of which we can justify our claim that the concept is instantiated, or the inference valid.

Apart from its obvious advantage in demystifying the epistemology of metaphysics, another advantage of the conceptualist approach is that it avoids the sense that metaphysics and the natural sciences are rivals – in a rivalry metaphysics seems bound to lose. For it leaves a clear and legitimate role for metaphysics: the primary role of the metaphysician is to engage in conceptual work, while that of the natural scientist is primarily to engage in empirical work (though of course each can profitably learn from the other and take on the opposing role at certain stages). Indeed it was largely in order to respond to the question of what the role of philosophy could be given the success of the empirical sciences that so many early twentieth-century philosophers adopted a division of labour view, taking the sciences to be fundamentally engaged in empirical work, while philosophers primarily undertook conceptual work.[4]

So, if we aim to adhere to the deflationist's demystifying standards, and appeal to nothing more mysterious than conceptual or empirical work in our work in metaphysics, what can we do when we do metaphysics? The descriptive conceptualist gives us an initial answer: one thing we can do is to engage in conceptual work, combined with obvious empirical work or the empirical results of the sciences. Under that rubric, we might attempt analyses of how our concept of freedom works, of its relation to concepts of responsibility, punishment, rationality, consciousness, and the like. Or we might engage (with Jackson 1998) in the question of what to say about the world in moral terms, given what we say about it in physical terms. Or we might ask what to say about colours, given what we now know about the science of light, reflectance, and vision. We might ask whether apes or elephants count as conscious beings, moral beings, or rational agents, given some analysis of each of these key concepts, combined with recent findings about the brains, behaviour, or culture of these animals. All of that is important and useful work we can do, very much in line with the traditional metaphysical work.

Yet an underlying dissatisfaction remains – especially among many metaphysicians – with the idea that that is *all* metaphysics can be up to. For while this approach does well at avoiding the epistemic mysteries of heavyweight metaphysics and carving out a legitimate role for metaphysics vis-à-vis the natural sciences, it is not clear that it can do so well at handling the phenomena of radical and persistent disagreements in metaphysics. Or rather, to be clear: a virtue of the approach is that it seems capable of *resolving* longstanding disagreements, in some cases by simple and obvious conceptual and/or empirical work. But if metaphysical disputes really are resolvable so straightforwardly, what explanation can the deflationist give of why they have *seemed* so intractable, or of why disputes about central metaphysical questions have persisted across the ages?

In some cases, of course, descriptive conceptualists can appeal to the difficulty of analysing some of our most important concepts (such as *freedom, person*, or *art*), or even to the indeterminacies, vagueness, or open-endedness of these concepts, leaving room for competing precisifications or explications. But even then, the objection goes, this makes metaphysical work a matter of shallow and parochial conceptual explication. And so, it is commonly thought, the conceptualist view is unable to capture the felt world-orientation, depth, and importance of traditional debates in metaphysics.

PRESCRIPTIVE CONCEPTUAL WORK

There is, however, far more that the deflationist can say than is commonly acknowledged. Even if she aims to limit the proper work of metaphysics to conceptual work (perhaps combined with empirical work), we can do more than simply analyse how our concepts actually work. We also can, and do, work on determining what conceptual scheme we *should* adopt for some purpose or other – doing work in what Alexis Burgess and David Plunkett (2013a; 2013b) have called 'conceptual ethics'.[5] This needn't interfere with the epistemic clarity the deflationist aims for, since it still does not take us beyond conceptual and empirical work.

But while there is no doubt that normative conceptual work is something we (according to the deflationist) can legitimately do, there might be more doubt that this can count as doing work in *metaphysics*. Thus, in the work that follows I aim to show two things: first, that it is reasonable to see a great deal of historical work in metaphysics as doing normative or pragmatic conceptual work. Second, I aim to make clear the pragmatic advantages that we can get by treating metaphysical work as including normative conceptual work. This involves a sort of dialectical bootstrapping for this paper – for together these form the basis for a pragmatic conceptual argument that the work of metaphysics should be seen as including pragmatic conceptual work.

The idea that at least some metaphysical work is implicitly pragmatic conceptual work is not entirely new of course. Defenders of conceptual analysis have sometimes suggested a pragmatic side to it. David Chalmers notes that verbal issues often have 'serious practical import':

If the community counts an act as falling into the extension of 'torture' or 'terrorism', this may make a grave difference to our attitudes toward that act. As such, there may be a serious practical question about what we *ought* to count as falling into the extension of these terms.

(Chalmers 2011: 517)

But this is generally left as a side note, not further pursued.

Carnap distinguished 'descriptive' work in syntax, semantics, and pragmatics from the 'pure' work in these areas undertaken as what he called 'conceptual engineering' (Carus 2007: 39).[6] Moreover, Carnap famously suggested that what disputing metaphysicians are *doing* is most charitably understood as answering *external* questions, construed as *practical* questions about whether we should make use of the linguistic forms in question (Carnap 1956: 213). For example:

Those who raise the question of the reality of the thing world itself have perhaps in mind not a theoretical question as their formulation seems to suggest, but rather a practical question, a matter of a practical decision concerning the structure of our language. We have to make the choice whether or not to accept and use the forms of expression in the framework in question.

(Ibid.: 207)

More recently, David Plunkett has argued that 'some (perhaps many) philosophical disputes are metalinguistic negotiations' (Plunkett 2015: 853) in which the dispute turns out to be at bottom a pragmatic dispute about how certain central terms *ought to be* employed.

There are good reasons for thinking that many classic debates in metaphysics can be understood as implicitly involved in pragmatic conceptual work. Consider some odd features of metaphysical debates. First, they are typically not resolvable by empirical means – one cannot just wait for the decisive observation or experiment to determine whether a person can survive loss of memories or to determine whether numbers exist. Some have suggested that these debates are merely verbal disputes – cases in which the dispute is to be resolved not by discovering further empirical facts about the world, but by 'settling the facts about the meanings of key terms in our community' or 'distinguishing key senses of a term' (Chalmers 2011: 526). But another odd feature of many metaphysical debates is that, in the eyes of the disputants, they cannot be settled by such methods as these. Thus disputants in serious metaphysical debates typically deny that they are each using the disputed term ('number', 'person') in a different sense, and deny that their dispute could be resolved even if work in linguistics or experimental philosophy showed definitively how the term is used in our community.[7] The disputants, of course, think that this is because their debate is about the *real metaphysical* facts, not about our words or concepts. But as we have seen, this position leads to grave epistemic difficulties, a rivalry with science, and a despairing scepticism. In my view there is a better way to account for these features of classic metaphysical debates – a way that preserves their felt depth, worldliness, and importance.

These odd features of metaphysical disputes are also the hallmarks of what David Plunkett and Tim Sundell have called 'metalinguistic negotiations'(Plunkett and Sundell 2013: 1). 1. They don't go away even if the disputants agree on all other 'facts' – they can't be empirically resolved just by correcting misinformation or adding empirical information. 2. They don't go away even if the disputants agree about how the word is *actually* used, or are given full empirical information about how the word is used. 3. They don't go away even if disputants recognize that they are using the term differently. A metalinguistic negotiation is involved when speakers *use* a term with the pragmatic function of negotiating how (or perhaps whether) that very term *ought to be* used (ibid.: 15). So, for example, consider a debate among friends watching the Olympics about whether figure skating is a sport. The dispute is not about any of the 'facts' about what figures skaters do, what sorts of training and skills are required, or how the competitions are judged. Disputants might agree about all that. One might interpret the disputants as using the term 'sport' in different ways (for example, one will apply it where 'artistic impression' scores play a role and the other won't) and each speaking a truth in their own idiolect. But even if that is pointed out to them, they will not give up the dispute as merely verbal and go home. Similarly, even if we take them both (owing to semantic deference) to use the term with the same, public meaning, and could appeal to data from linguistics or experimental philosophy to show that (given actual usage) figure skating *does* (or doesn't) meet the relevant criteria, that would not end the dispute. For regardless of whether or not we see the speakers as literally asserting conflicting propositions, their real dispute arises at the level of what is pragmatically communicated. In uttering 'figure skating is/is not a sport' each is *pragmatically communicating* views about whether the term 'sport' *should* be applied to figure skating. And such disputes may be very much worth having. For how we use words *matters*, both given their relations to other aspects of our conceptual scheme, and to our non-verbal behaviour. Treating figure skating as a sport, for example, is connected to a range of types of societal honours and rewards – to appearing in the Olympics, to receiving sponsorships and television coverage, to honouring its practitioners in all the ways athletes are honoured. What is at stake in arguments about whether figure skating is a sport, then, is a range of *normative* issues about how the skaters, fans, competitions, and so on *are to be treated*.

Once metalinguistic disputes are identified as a category, it is easy to see that they abound in our ordinary debates. Disputes about whether waterboarding is torture, whether the Oklahoma City bombing was terrorism, whether alcoholism is a disease, whether autism is a disability, and more can all be understood on this model.[8]

But on what grounds can we advocate changes in the way our terms or concepts ought to be used? The grounds for pressing one view or another are at bottom pragmatic. Often the grounds – made explicit – would involve an appeal to the *function* those terms have for us – and to what rules for using the term would best serve that function. Consider a daughter who says 'my parents are Bob and Jim'. Even if she lives in a state that does not permit gay marriage, she needn't just be seen as saying something trivially false given the legal definition in play. Instead, she may be seen as *negotiating* a revision in the use of a term by *using* it in an extended way – and perhaps even by refusing to use it in its more limited legal definition. Made explicit, the grounds for extending the term 'parent' to include both members of same-sex couples who raise a child together might naturally appeal to the function of the term 'parent'. Presumably that function is to mark certain close relationships and grant them the legal rights, responsibilities, and protections that we think should govern such close care-giving relationships, in which case the term can better fulfil its function if its meaning is extended from the old legal definition to a new one. The case of the daughter who *uses* the term 'parent' to negotiate such a change in the rules is not unlike cases of civil disobedience where protestors negotiated the change of rules about who could sit at the front of the bus by *using* the bus in ways conflicting with the old rules. By sitting in the front of the bus, Rosa Parks didn't *say* that the rules should be changed; she *pragmatically* advocated their change by refusing to follow the old rules. Similarly, by using the term 'parent' in saying that Bob and Jim are her parents, the daughter doesn't *say* that the rules for the use of 'parent' should be changed, she *pragmatically* advocates their change by refusing to follow the old rules, where this change might be explicitly justified by appeal to the term's function.

Many traditional debates in metaphysics can be understood using the model of metalinguistic negotiation – as involved in *using* the terms as a way of pragmatically negotiating how – or sometimes whether – certain words or concepts *ought* to be used. There is no need, of course, for the deflationist to hold that *all* metaphysical debates fit this model: the deflationist is free to treat other legitimate metaphysical work as engaged in more directly descriptive conceptual work, or to dismiss still other debates and positions as based on confusions. Nonetheless, the idea of metalinguistic negotiation – and of pragmatic conceptual work more generally – can be used to *broaden* the options available to the deflationist in giving an account of what metaphysics has done and can legitimately do.

For example, in core metaphysical debates such as debates about what art is or what the conditions for personal identity are, the disputants can often be seen as using a term as a way of negotiating how it *should* be used, given its function. John Locke, for example, argues for a consciousness-based view of personal identity in part by noting that 'person' is a 'forensic term, appropriating actions and their merit, and so belongs only to intelligent agents, capable of a law, and happiness, and misery' (1964: 220). But, he argues, we are only rightly punished for actions we can attribute to our same consciousness, and so personal identity is to be measured by a continuity of consciousness, not of body. 'In this personal identity is founded all the right and justice of reward and punishment' (ibid.: 216). Locke is well aware that this might not mirror how we *actually* think of persons, or of rightful punishment – but he is not put off by that; he is more interested in how we *should* use the term in order that it fulfil its forensic function. The idea that 'person' is a 'forensic term' is an insight that, more recently, Lynne Baker uses in motivating her view that '*person* is a moral category', so that a person cannot be identified with the mere body of which she is constituted (Baker 2000: 8). Baker similarly appeals to what 'matters to and about us' – namely our first-person perspective – in arguing that persons should not be identified with our bodies, and that only by acknowledging the importance of the first-person perspective to personhood can we employ a concept of personhood that can bear the needed weight of attributing moral and rational agency (ibid.: 147–8). In short, we can see certain views in this area – expressed in the object language, as views about what persons are – as pragmatically pressing for views about how we *should* use the term 'person', driven (explicitly or tacitly) by views about what we need the concept of *person* to do for us: to capture what is important to us, to be usable in attributions of responsibility and agency, and so on.

On a different topic, consider David Davies, who argues that a work of art (of any type) is really a 'performance that specifies a focus of appreciation' (Davies 2004: 146). On this view, Mary Cassatt's *The Boating Party* is not a work on canvas, hanging on the walls of the National Gallery of Art, but rather a performance undertaken by Cassatt in 1893–4. To critics who would say that this is just false – even a category mistake – given a conceptual analysis of 'work of painting', Davies argues that what we want out of an ontology of art is a view that coheres with our critical practices – 'for the purposes of the philosophy of art, an artwork is whatever functions as the unit of criticism and appreciation' (ibid.: 188) – or rather, with those critical practices we *ought* to have:

It is not our actual practice as it stands that is to serve as the tribunal against which ontologies of art are to be assessed … but, rather, a theoretical representation of the norms that *should* govern the judgments that critics make concerning 'the ways in which works are to be judged and appreciated'.
(Ibid.: 143)

He goes on to argue that our appreciative interest in art (often) is and (always) should be interest in 'a generative performance whereby a focus of appreciation is specified' (ibid.: 199), giving us reason to accept that works of art are performances rather than products, in order to fulfill the function the term 'artwork' has in philosophy of art.[9]

Let us revisit the question 'What can we do, then, when we do metaphysics?' If we uphold the deflationist's demystifying standards, one thing we can legitimately do, as we have already seen, is to engage in descriptive conceptual analysis – combined sometimes with empirical work. But now we can go much further. For even deflationists needn't hold that a metaphysician's work should be limited to *descriptive* conceptual work; it can also involve (and *has* often involved) *prescriptive* conceptual work. And this conceptual work may be conducted in the object language – not by discussing how 'person' is or should be used, but by discussing what *persons are*. The extent of the relevant negotiations involved in the pragmatic work may vary greatly – whether it simply involves pressing for one way of precisifying a vague term (or a term that is indeterminate in some of its areas of application), or involves advocating more substantial changes in the ways a term is to be used – or indeed whether it is to be used at all. When (following the pattern of metalinguistic negotiation) disputants press their views by *using* the contested terms themselves (in the object language), they are likely to express their views in metaphysical terms, as views about when two individuals count as the same person, or about whether there is free will. But such uses of terms may serve not to describe surprising metaphysical discoveries (or to report obvious facts), but rather to advocate views about how the terms are *to be* used, on pragmatic grounds – for example, that such changes in the ways our terms are to be used would better enable them to fulfill their function. Such proposals – if made explicit – would also presuppose a kind of descriptive analysis of the *function* the term serves, so that one could thereby more clearly see that the proposed change in practice would better fulfill that function. Thus, so far, we can say that on this model the metaphysician may engage in descriptive conceptual analysis, descriptive functional analysis, and normative conceptual analysis (often driven by the descriptive functional analysis). In each case, these may also be profitably combined with empirical work.

For it is often an empirical matter whether the changes advocated will actually enable the term to better fulfill its function. Moreover, technological and empirical changes in the world often challenge the boundaries of our concepts, forcing us to make new conceptual choices or reevaluate old ones (consider debates about whether persons can survive replacements of various parts with artificial substitutes, or about what the identity conditions are for works of internet art).

But this still is not all that metaphysics can do – metaphysicians needn't be limited to recommending that we alter the way our terms are to be used so that they can better fulfill their *actual* functions. More deeply, some recommendations may (whether tacitly or explicitly) involve suggestions that the *function* of the term itself be changed; or that the term and its traditional function be dropped altogether. Foucaultian critiques often suggest that the function of our terms is different from what we might have thought – for example, that the function of 'madness' is not so much to serve as a medical diagnostic description as to serve as a means of social control and marginalization. Those convinced by such critiques will have good reason to reject terms like 'madness' – a move that might itself be expressed in the object language as the view that there is no such thing as madness (or that this is not a natural kind). This kind of normative functional analysis has also played a crucial role in work on race. Sally Haslanger, for example, has developed a social constructionist understanding of race, according to which races should be identified with racialized groups, where 'a group is racialized if and only if its members are socially positioned as subordinate or privileged along some dimension … and the group is "marked" as a target for this treatment by observed or imagined bodily features presumed to be evidence of ancestral links to a certain geographical region' (Haslanger 2012: 384). Whether or not this matches anyone's current or past concept of race is beside the point. For the goal, according to Haslanger, is to engage in what she calls 'ameliorative' conceptual analysis, asking 'What is the point of having the concept in question …? What concept (if any) would do the work best?' (ibid.: 386). The function of older race concepts might have been to falsely legitimate differential treatments of certain groups of individuals by presuming to track a 'racial essence' predictive of behaviour or abilities. But we can reject that function and recommend a new function for racial terms, enabling us to diagnose the source of illusions about race and motivate social change (ibid.: 385). In this way, we may engage not only in descriptive work in conceptual and functional analysis but also in *normative* work at both the conceptual and functional levels.

A PRAGMATIC ARGUMENT FOR THIS CONCEPTION OF METAPHYSICS

The work of this paper can be seen (in a kind of dialectical bootstrapping) as itself engaged in a kind of negotiation for how to understand the work of metaphysics: that we (deflationists) should treat the work of metaphysics as including pragmatic conceptual work. For, as I have argued, this preserves core continuities with traditional work and methods of argumentation in metaphysics. Moreover, as I shall now argue, it also brings about important pragmatic advantages.

What is the function of the concept of metaphysics? Plausibly, the concept functions to pick out a historical tradition of work, and also to identify it as a distinct area of enquiry, capable of contributing to human knowledge – an area we can work in and that is worthwhile to pursue. To do this, it is desirable for our concept of metaphysics to preserve continuities with historical work (both with *what* was done and *how* it was done), and to mark out an area of enquiry that is neither 'killed' by rivalry with the sciences,[10] nor so difficult that it should lead us to sceptically abandon the project, and that is potentially worthwhile.

Broadening the conceptualist approach to include both descriptive and prescriptive conceptual work at the levels of both meaning and function can preserve the virtues of the traditional conceptualist approach in these areas while avoiding its perceived difficulties. The expanded conceptualist approach retains the epistemic advantages of conceptualism over heavyweight metaphysics, for it still demystifies the methods of metaphysics by appealing to nothing more mysterious than empirical and conceptual work (now including under that both descriptive and normative conceptual work).[11]

The expanded conceptualist approach also, like the traditional conceptualist approach, avoids the problem of a rivalry with science. In fact, it does even better at responding to the threat of a rivalry with science. For we can still appeal to a division of labour, with the natural sciences focused primarily on empirical work, and metaphysics on conceptual. But thinking of metaphysical work as engaged in analysing meanings raises threat of another rivalry. When a young Ryle suggested to his tutor H. J. Paton that the proper role of philosophy lies in analysing meanings, Paton reportedly replied 'Ah, Ryle, how *exactly* do you distinguish between philosophy and lexicography?' (Ryle 1970: 6). By expanding conceptual work to include the normative as well as the descriptive, we can more clearly distinguish metaphysical work from the work linguists or psychologists do in discerning what rules our terms or concepts actually do follow. By bringing out the normative side of metaphysical work we can also appeal to a task that is widely accepted as something the natural sciences, taken alone, are ill suited to do. In answering Hawking's claim that 'philosophy is dead' since its questions are better answered by the sciences, we can then point to the important role philosophy can and does play in a wide range of normative areas.

The expanded conceptualist approach also has the virtue of accounting for the felt depth and importance of metaphysics. For we are not left thinking of metaphysics as engaged only in resolving shallow parochial issues about our language or conceptual scheme. Even where metaphysical disputes are engaged in conceptual negotiation, they are not properly thought of as merely verbal disputes, trivial, or just 'about words'. When we say 'a person at time 1 is only identical with a person at time 2 if there is a continuity of consciousness', for example, the literal semantic content is world-orientated (not about our language or concepts). While the pragmatic content is about how (or whether) the relevant terms ought to be used, the significance of that choice is again worldly – for example, to do with how we are to assign praise, blame, and punishment. In short, the conceptual choices we negotiate for in expressing metaphysical views are not merely verbal issues – they matter because what we call 'art', or a 'person', or a 'free action', has a deep and significant impact on our way of life.

Finally, the expanded conceptualist approach can do a better job than the traditional conceptualist approach of accounting for the presence of apparently intractable disagreements in metaphysics. For even if we can easily settle the 'internal' questions, difficult questions remain that involve normative disputes about how our terms or concepts should work, what rules they should follow, and what purposes they should serve. Moreover, the concepts at issue in classic metaphysical disputes are among those most central to our lives – concepts such as *person*, *art*, and *freedom*. How we (ought to) use these concepts is tied to deep issues about what we ought to value in art, when we ought to hold one another responsible, feel guilt and resentment, and so on. The difficulty and depth of such disputes then shouldn't be surprising – for it is symptomatic of the difficulties of working out and reconciling differences in our normative views about what we should value, how we should live, and what we should do.

Now some might think this counts as little progress. For resolving normative issues is itself notoriously difficult. Thus the move from thinking of metaphysical debates as epistemically metaphysical, to thinking of them as implicitly normative, might be thought to take us out of the frying pan into the fire.[12]

But the challenge here was not to *resolve* the debates (that we can do simply enough at the internal level), but rather to account for why the metaphysical debates have been so persistent, why they *seem* so irresoluble and intractable, and why they might nonetheless be worthwhile. And the idea here is that we can account for the apparent irresolubility of metaphysical debates by seeing the deep normative element that may be involved in them, leaving them as hard to resolve as many other pragmatic and normative questions. There is, however, an important twist here: seeing metaphysical debates as very difficult matters of discovering hidden facts that are 'epistemically metaphysical' might well lead to scepticism, thinking that such facts are forever opaque to us so that we may as well give up trying, and engage our efforts elsewhere. But if we see the difficulty of many metaphysical questions as instead manifesting the difficulties in addressing deep *normative* questions, we shall be much less inclined to think that the right – or even an acceptable – response is just to give up. And we shall be better able to see why – at least in many, central cases – working on them is important, and not at all pointless or a waste of time.

CONCLUSION

Deflationary metaontological approaches are clearly advantageous over their heavyweight counterparts in their ability to demystify the epistemology of metaphysics, avoid worries about rivalry with science, and avoid falling into a kind of sceptical torpor that might arise from thinking we may never discover the answers to our metaphysical questions. Yet deflating metaphysics by thinking of it as fundamentally conceptual work threatens to make metaphysical work *too* easy, leaving it unable to account for the depth and persistence of debates in metaphysics. I have argued here, however, that more options remain for the deflationist than are commonly acknowledged. For metaphysical work may include not just *descriptive* work in conceptual analysis or functional analysis, but also *prescriptive* work in determining what concepts we should have, how they should work, and what functions they should serve. Such a broadened conceptualist account of what we can do when we do metaphysics has promise of preserving the advantages of traditional conceptualist views, while also giving us a clearly improved account of why disagreements in metaphysics tend to persist, why they are important (and not just shallow verbal matters), and why it would be a mistake to simply give up work on them. Even if we retain the deflationary standpoint and appeal to nothing more than conceptual and empirical work, we can allow that there is plenty of useful and important work to do, when we do metaphysics.

NOTES

1 Conceptual analysis has of course been challenged by those suspicious of analyticity and all related notions, impressed by semantic externalism, or working in experimental philosophy. For defences of analyticity see (Boghossian 1996), (Thomasson 2007a: Ch. 2), and (Thomasson 2015: Ch. 7). Defences of conceptualist methods against Quinean attacks and externalism may be found in (Jackson 1998). For a defence of conceptualist methods against attacks from experimental philosophy, see (Thomasson 2012).

2 This is of course a contentious approach to the modal questions of metaphysics, but it is one I have argued for at length elsewhere (Thomasson 2007b; 2013) and the concern here is not to argue for this sort of conceptualist approach, but rather to show ways in which it can and should be broadened.

3 See Chapter 1 of (Thomasson 2015) for discussion of Carnap's distinction and its relation to the easy ontological approach.

4 In Chapter 2 of *Language, Truth and Logic*, Ayer gives a classic defence of the view that philosophy consists in analysis, and argues that 'the majority of those who are commonly supposed to have been great philosophers were primarily ... analysts' (Ayer 1952: 52). For a brief historical overview, see (Thomasson 2015: 4–13).

5 Matti Eklund (2015) makes a related argument that philosophy should be seen not as conceptual analysis but as 'conceptual engineering'. His motivations are a bit different – arising from the thought that our extant concepts might not be the 'best conceptual tools for describing and theorizing about the relevant aspects of reality'. Instead, he argues we should engage in conceptual engineering, where he thinks of this as a matter of studying 'what concept best plays the theoretical role of our concept [e.g.] of knowledge and what features this concept has' (Eklund 2015: 376). Much of this may be compatible with what I say above. But (in line with functional pluralism) I want to leave open that the functions of our concepts need not always be seen as aiming to describe and theorize about aspects of reality, and we need not always be concerned (merely) with a theoretical role.

6 The notion of pragmatic conceptual work relied on here, however, is broader than the Carnapian notion of conceptual engineering, to the extent that the latter is taken to focus on explication, in the sense of replacing a vague concept (typically of ordinary language) by a more precise one for use in science. That is one sort of pragmatic conceptual work, but I want to leave room for other sorts, aiming to serve a variety of scientific, social, moral, or other purposes.

7 In (Thomasson 2016), I argue that the verbal disputes model is not the best way for deflationists to conceive of metaphysical debates.

8 The waterboarding case is discussed in (Plunkett and Sundell 2013). See also mention of the other cases of metalinguistic negotiation in (Thomasson 2016).

9 Unfortunately there is not space for other examples here. Elsewhere (Thomasson 2016) I suggest how other metaphysical debates, for example about the persistence conditions for works of art, identity conditions for works of music, the existence of free will or of races, may be understood on this model.

10 Karen Bennett also identifies as two constraints on a proper characterization of metaphysics that it 'must to some extent respect the actual practices of actual metaphysicians' and 'must go some distance towards distinguishing it from science' (Bennett 2015: §4), parallel to the first two desirable features identified above.

11 For those who worry that the epistemology of normative facts introduces new mysteries, see below.

12 Of course if one were a heavyweight realist about normative facts, this might raise parallel epistemic issues. But the metaontological deflationist is unlikely to ally herself with that position, and plenty of alternative options remain, for example in the Blackburn/Gibbard tradition. (Moreover, even those who are heavyweight realists about the moral facts might find less plausible the idea that there are normative facts to be discovered about what conceptual scheme we should adopt for various purposes.)

7 Armchair Metaphysics Revisited

The Three Grades of Involvement in Conceptual Analysis[1]

1. PREAMBLE

Atomic theory gives an account of the nature of the chair I am sitting on. According to that account, my chair is a 'gappy' object. It is made up of items that are very widely spaced, comparatively speaking. Should I conclude that my chair is not solid? It depends on what is meant by 'solid'. If 'solid' means being everywhere dense, the answer is yes. If 'solid' means resisting the intrusion of other objects (including my body, in this case), the answer is no. The answer is no, because atomic theory *explains* how the gappy objects it postulates are able to resist intrusion by other gappy objects in terms of the nature of the bonds between the atoms that make up my chair. Or, to say all this in the language of concepts, the answer depends on the correct analysis of the concept of solidity, where by the concept of solidity I mean what it takes for something to be solid. (When mathematicians explain the concept of a prime number, they tell us what it takes to be a prime number.) If the correct analysis of the concept of solidity is in terms of being everywhere dense, atomic theory implies that my chair is not solid; if the correct analysis is resisting intrusion by other objects, atomic theory is consistent with my chair being solid.

This simple example tells us that there has to be a place for conceptual analysis in speculative cosmology. It would not be sensible to discuss the implications of atomic theory for whether or not we should say that my chair is solid, while refusing to discuss what it takes for 'solid' to apply to something, or, equivalently, the right analysis of the concept of solidity. We have here, in fact, a case where what to say about how things are in one set of terms (in terms of 'solid') given an account in another set of terms (those of the atomic theory) depends on a question about the correct analysis of a concept (of solidity).

However, our example invites an obvious question: are there more interesting examples? Who cares much about the correct analysis of the concept of solidity? We might, after all, define solidity$_1$ as being everywhere dense, and solidity$_2$ as resisting intrusion. We could then say that atomic theory implies that my chair is not solid$_1$ and is solid$_2$, and finesse the question of what to say in terms of our actual concept of solidity. The answer to this obvious question is that there are more interesting examples. The reason why turns on two facts. One is the importance of *a priori* determined properties in our explanatory theories; the other is the importance of having words for these properties and being able to think about them. I now turn to spelling this out.

2. THE VALUE OF *A PRIORI* DETERMINED PROPERTIES

When we seek to explain and predict, often a crucial step is finding the right *a priori* determined properties for the task at hand. Economists worry about housing price bubbles. When they address this worry, they ask themselves questions like: Is the ratio between average house prices and average incomes higher or lower now than before the last housing bubble? How does the average rent to average house price ratio in the country under investigation compare to the average rent to average house price ratio in other countries? These properties – the ratios – are *a priori* determined by the underlying facts about the economies the economists are studying. What the economists are looking for are the right *a priori* determined properties to draw on when seeking to explain and predict housing price bubbles.

Here are some more examples. If you are interested in explaining and predicting the rolling behaviour of solid objects, whether or not they are spherical is highly relevant, and whether or not they are spherical is *a priori* determined by the location of the particles that make them up. Physicists have found that the value of $\Sigma_i 1/2m_i \cdot v_i^2$, for a system of i particles, is good for predicting and explaining the behaviour of the system over time, and that value is *a priori* determined by individual facts about the particles. Again, if one is interested in predicting and explaining the flotation properties of objects, the result of dividing mass by volume – density – is especially relevant, and density is *a priori* determined by mass and volume.[2]

What we have in these examples are illustrations of how *a priori* determined properties can be of value. Of course – but I find from experience that the point needs emphasizing – in giving the example of $\Sigma_i 1/2m_i.v_i^2$, I am not saying that 'The kinetic energy of a system of i particles = $\Sigma_i 1/2m_i.v_i^2$' is *a priori* true. It is in fact false. I am saying that the property specified by the term on the right of the equals sign is *a priori* determined by facts about the masses and velocities of the particles, and is a property which is good for predicting and explaining the behaviour of the particles as a whole, although not as good as once thought, especially when the velocities are high.

Why do I say that these properties – the examples of the previous few paragraphs – are of *a priori* determined properties? In each case, given the relevant information about the determining properties, there is no need to carry out an experiment to settle whether or not they are possessed. Take, for instance, the housing bubble example. Given full information about individual house prices, arithmetic plus an understanding of the concept of an average is enough to tell one what the average house price is, and the same goes for rents and incomes. The final step to finding the ratios is then an exercise in division. Of course, there are other ways of finding the ratios – for instance, asking experts who have already done the calculations, which is a kind of experiment. But, in principle, the ratios are available from the relevant data – the data concerning the determining properties – without doing experiments. The same goes for all the examples, and for the examples to come. (We return to this point in §4 and §6.)

You now have before you the first grade of involvement in conceptual analysis – it is the thesis that *a priori* determined properties can be important for explanation and prediction. There is, I should emphasize, no mystery as to why *a priori* determined properties can be important. When we latch onto the right one or ones for the task at hand, what we do is find the crucial commonality in an otherwise diverse body of information; we find the patterns in the data that are good for predicting and explaining. Objects that differ in masses and volumes but are alike in the result of dividing their masses by their volumes are alike in flotation properties; moreover, the extent to which they differ in the results of dividing masses by volumes tracks the extent to which they differ in flotation properties. Likewise for our other examples.

In the foregoing paragraphs, I have talked of properties. This might invite a concern about whether I am presuming a controversial position in analytic ontology. However, the notion of property that is at work in this essay is the one tied to ways things are or might be, not the one tied to controversial views about the relationship between particulars and universals, and whether or not there are fundamental joints in nature. When economists say, as it might be, that there are three features of the current situation in China that are a cause for concern, it would be misguided for philosophers who are nominalists rather than realists in the debate over particulars and universals to object that work in analytic ontology casts doubt on what the economists are saying. The economists may be wrong, but not for that reason.

The second and third grades of involvement concern our ability, or lack of ability, first, to talk and think about the properties that are *a priori* determined, and, second, to articulate the way in which these properties are *a priori* determined. As we will see, there are cases where we have a word that we understand for an *a priori* determined property and are able to believe that something has the property, but are unable to articulate the way in which the property is *a priori* determined, and in particular the properties that do the *a priori* determining. We know how to do the articulation job for density: it is mass divided by volume; likewise, we know the equation for average house prices. But there are, as we will see, cases where this cannot be done. That's the second grade of involvement.

The third grade of involvement in conceptual analysis is what we have just observed is possible for density and average house prices. They are the cases where we can write down *a priori* true bi-conditionals of the form 'X is so and so if and only if X is such and such, thus and so and ...', where so and so is the determined property, and such and such, thus and so and ... are the determining properties. These are the cases where we can provide the bi-conditionals so often sought after when doing traditional conceptual analysis, and are, of course, what many think of when they think of conceptual analysis, be their thoughts friendly or unfriendly ones. We will sometimes call the third grade, the full monty.

3. THE SECOND GRADE OF INVOLVEMENT: AN EASY CASE

There are, as I say above, cases where we can say and believe that X has some property P that is *a priori* determined by further properties of X but we cannot articulate the properties that are doing the *a priori* determining. We may have some idea of which properties they might be, but cannot go close to giving chapter and verse.

Here is a case of a kind that I owe to a discussion many years ago with Steve Yablo. He should not be held responsible for the use I make of it.[3] John Doe is shown many closed plane figures. Some are ellipses, some are not – they are triangles, somewhat distorted circles that aren't ellipses, and so on. He is told which figures are such that 'is an ellipse' is the correct word in English for them. He is not told the famous formula and in fact does not know it.[4] After a time, we may suppose, Doe becomes very good at discriminating ellipses from non-ellipses, and uses the word 'ellipse' for a figure X just when it is an ellipse (unless the light is especially bad or there's some local distortion effect, etc.). He is able to reliably recognize ellipses. Indeed, certain shapes will look elliptical to him in much the way that certain sentences look grammatical to us.

There are two questions we need to address. One is what Doe *believes* about X when he uses 'is an ellipse' to describe X. The other is what Doe *says* about how X is when he uses 'is an ellipse' to describe X. The first is a question in the philosophy of mind, the second a question in the philosophy of language. Let's start with the question in the philosophy of mind. When X looks thus and so to one, one is in a state that represents that X is thus and so. This means that a belief about X essentially based on how it looks to one is a belief about X's nature, not a belief about one's own nature or about words. It follows that Doe's belief about X is a belief about X's nature and, in particular, about X's shape. But, in that case, what belief could that be other than that X is an ellipse, for that is the shape in question? Presumably, Doe will also believes that 'ellipse' is the right word for X's shape, and that X induces in him a certain distinctive state. But they are different beliefs. And now we have, in addition, an answer to the question in the philosophy of language. If what he believes is that X is an ellipse – where this is a belief about X's shape and not about words or about his own state – then surely what he says about how X is when he uses 'is an ellipse' for X is none other than that it is an ellipse.[5] For that's what he believes and seeks to convey about X when he uses the word to characterize X.

The upshot is that our case is one of the second grade of involvement in conceptual analysis. Doe can say and believe that X is an ellipse, meaning just what we mean by 'ellipse' and believing just what we believe when we believe something to be an ellipse, but cannot provide the familiar account of what it is about a figure that *a priori* determines that it is an ellipse. For consider:

X is an ellipse if and only if X is a locus of points in a plane such that the sum of the distances to fixed points, a, b, is a constant.

Despite the fact that he can say and believe that X is an ellipse, and, most likely, knows that being an ellipse is *a priori* determined by some pattern or other in the locations of the points that make up the figures he recognizes as ellipses, he cannot spell things out as we just have. As we might say it, he knows *that* being an ellipse is *a priori* determined by the locations of the points in some way susceptible of formulation, but doesn't know the *how* of it.

Here is a more everyday example of the same phenomenon. You and I can read writing in the Roman alphabet. This requires the ability to recognize the commonality, the pattern, which each handwritten token of any given individual letter of that alphabet exemplifies. Each written token of, say, 'g' needs to look alike – we have to see them *as* 'g's – despite their many differences. But we, the folk, cannot articulate the pattern. There is a formula to be found that will articulate the pattern, but finding it is a research project, not something known by the folk.

4. HOW WIDESPREAD IS THE SECOND GRADE OF INVOLVEMENT?

Many, myself included, hold what are sometimes called 'no further fact' views of, for example, personal identity and knowledge.[6] Take the question as to whether or not person, A, who enters the teletransporter is identical with person, B, who exits the teletransporter.[7] No further fact theorists hold that the answer to this question is determined by how things are in ways other than the very way in question. Some theorists focus on memory continuities and dependencies, some on psychological continuities more widely construed, some on the role of a single brain in underpinning those continuities, some give having the same body a special role, some focus on one combination or other of factors like these, and so it goes. Despite all the disagreement, our theorists are united in holding that what determines the answer lies in how things are in regard to some list of relevant factors, none of which is whether or not A is the same person as B *per se*.

Likewise, many philosophers are no further fact theorists about knowledge. They think that knowledge is a matter of some suitable combination of belief, reliability, justification, truth, non-defeasibility, not being right or justified by accident, properly ignoring certain alternatives, tracking the truth, and so on. They think it would be misguided to think of knowledge as some kind of extra ingredient to throw into the melting pot. Maybe we need more or different ingredients (though truth will surely be needed and, many insist, belief), and perhaps we need new insights into how to assemble the ingredients to get knowledge, but knowledge as such isn't one of the ingredients.

What is more, plausibly the passage from the ingredients to whether or not we have a case of knowledge is *a priori*. That's the insight behind the phrase 'no further fact'. If the passage from the ingredients to something's being or not being a case of knowledge were *a posteriori*, that could only be because there was some additional piece of information that one needed in order to settle whether or not some case was indeed a case of knowledge. It would tell us that we did not, after all, have all the ingredients, or that we have assembled them wrongly. If there is nothing more that is relevant, then there is nothing more that is relevant. An experiment would be beside the point. The same goes for the case of personal identity. No further fact theorists of personal identity are committed to holding that the passage from the right ingredients obtaining in some case or other to that case's being a case of personal identity is *a priori*.

Here I should highlight the difference from what many believe about the relationship between the water way things are and the H_2O way they are. These theorists hold that the water way things are necessitates, and is necessitated by, the H_2O way, and may also want to say that being H_2O is, in consequence, not a further fact over and above being water. But it is a further fact in the relevant sense. No-one thinks that there is no further information to collect on the subject of whether or not there is H_2O at some location than whether or not there is water at that location, and conversely. If that were true, the famous experiments carried out during the rise of modern chemistry would have been otiose. The no further fact views of knowledge and personal identity we are talking about are *inter alia* views about the kinds of information that might possibly be relevant to settling whether or not some case is one of knowledge or of personal identity.

Despite this, we all know how hard it is to find a counter-example immune bi-conditional linking 'S knows that P' to something of the form 'P, S believes that P, and ...'. And the same is true for personal identity. Knowledge and personal identity are two prime examples where philosophers have found it very difficult to find generally accepted analyses; they are cases where the third grade of involvement in conceptual analysis seems a bit like the end of the rainbow.

This invites an obvious thought. Should no further fact theorists about personal identity and knowledge hold that personal identity and knowledge are cases of the second grade of involvement in conceptual analysis but without the third grade? For we have beliefs about whether or not someone before us now is or is not the same person as the person we met last week, and beliefs about what is or is not known. What is more, we report these beliefs using words we understand. But maybe, runs the thought, the trouble we have had in articulating exactly how the relevant ingredients come together to make up personal identity and knowledge – the trouble we have had in achieving the third grade of involvement in conceptual analysis for knowledge and personal identity – lies in the fact that, although there is an *a priori* determined property in both cases, our situation is like Doe's in the previous section. We can recognize the property for both personal identity and knowledge, and, in doing this, are recognizing a property that is *a priori* determined without remainder by some suitable set of determining properties (the ingredients), but we cannot articulate how the ingredients do the determining.

Despite its initial appeal, I think we should reject this suggestion. One reason is an obvious difference between our situation and Doe's. We often form justified opinions about whether or not some case is or isn't a case of knowledge, or is or isn't a case of being the same person as, from written and verbal descriptions of cases. If that were not true, there would little point in writing articles and giving talks on knowledge and personal identity. Whereas Doe is exercising a perceptual recognitional capacity.

The second reason is that the suggestion would not in fact explain all the trouble we have had in finding generally acceptable bi-conditionals for personal identity and knowledge. Although Doe cannot articulate the determining property of the shapes he uses 'ellipse' for, he could come to. If he is smart enough and is given some help in the way of geometry lessons, he will come to know that

> X is an ellipse if and only if X is a locus of points in a plane such that the sum of the distances to fixed points, a, b, is a constant

is (*a priori*) true. When this happens, the matter will be settled. He will have reached the third grade of involvement in conceptual analysis for being an ellipse. He can regard the matter as done and dusted. This makes the point that the case of Doe is a case of ignorance, not of apparently interminable wrangling. Indeed, if his case were the model for thinking of our situation with respect to personal identity and knowledge, we should look forward with confidence to reaching general agreement after the needed spadework. After all, it took some spadework to find the correct filling after 'if and only if' in

> $n_1, n_2, n_3,$ ... fails to converge if and only if ...

but we got there. (I mean some logicians and mathematicians got there and we piggy-backed on their work.) So, it might be suggested, we should expect similar success for knowledge and personal identity in due course. Now perhaps this was the right attitude to take once upon a time. But not in 2016, in my view. (For those two examples. I am not endorsing pessimism across the board.) Too many smart people have come to too many different views over too many years about the right way to articulate the *a priori* determining properties for knowledge and personal identity for optimism to remain a viable option.

To solve our puzzle, I think we need to take a step back and ask what, exactly, is going on when philosophers disagree about the correct account of knowledge or personal identity. I will make the key points for the case of knowledge but it will, I trust, be obvious how to extend them to personal identity and indeed to many other cases.[8]

5. WHAT ARE THE RELIABILIST ABOUT KNOWLEDGE AND THE GETTIER HOLDOUT DISAGREEING ABOUT?

Let RTB be someone convinced that knowledge is reliably acquired true belief.

Let JTB be someone who resists the message of Gettier cases (Gettier 1963); JTB sticks to the traditional view that knowledge is justified, true belief.

It is obvious that RTB and JTB are disagreeing. But over what, exactly? Over the nature of a certain property – knowledge – would seem to be the obvious answer. But it would be a bad mistake to hold that there is a 'third' property, knowledge, such that RTB says it is reliably acquired true belief and JTB says it is justified true belief. There is no third property whose nature they disagree about. There are, according to them, just two serious contenders to be knowledge: reliably acquired true belief and justified true belief. What then does RTB think that JTB has got wrong? RTB thinks that knowledge is reliably acquired true belief. Is it *that* property JTB is wrong about, according to RTB? Of course not. RTB doesn't think that JTB thinks that reliably acquired true belief is the same property as justified true belief. RTB thinks that JTB has gone wrong but not to *that* extent. And what does JTB think that RTB has got wrong? JTB thinks that knowledge is justified true belief. Is it *that* property RTB is wrong about, according to JTB? Of course not. JTB doesn't think that RTB thinks that justified true belief is the same property as reliably acquired true belief. JTB thinks that RTB has gone wrong but not to *that* extent.

What then are they disagreeing about? One answer might be the pattern in epistemic situations that English speakers use the term 'knowledge' for. Now JTB and RTB may well disagree about that, and this would explain why they, and participants in the debate over the analysis of knowledge more generally, hold that intuitions about cases described in English are relevant.[9] But there is a further issue on the table, as was well understood back in the days when justified true belief, with the odd tweak or two, was the leading contender for an analysis of knowledge. The further issue is which pattern in epistemic situations is the one of most importance for one or another theoretical purpose, which corresponds, more or less, to what speakers of English have in mind when they use the term 'knowledge'.[10] From this perspective, two things happened when Gettier cases became well known in the analytical philosophy community: one was that members of that community realized that their own usage of 'knowledge' did not pick out justified true belief; the other was that they realized that had that been the way they used 'knowledge', they ought to make a change in their usage. We do not want to use a term with the kind of positive connotations associated with 'knowledge' to cover the kind of 'getting things right by a lucky fluke' cases that Gettier drew to our attention.

But now there is an obvious explanation for the failure to converge on a single analysis-cum-definition of knowledge. Epistemic situations are complex. Even a passing acquaintance with Kahneman and Tversky's work tells us that we make mistakes, get confused, and need guidance.[11] We should not expect there to be a single pattern, roughly corresponding to our usage of the word 'knowledge', that cries out to be codified, to be turned into an example of the third grade of involvement in conceptual analysis. Saying this is perfectly consistent with holding that Gettier cases tell us that justified true belief was a mistake. Allowing that complexity and confusion on the part of speakers of a natural language means that our usage may underdetermine a single best candidate[12] to be the pattern out of those we gesture at when we use the term 'knowledge' *is* consistent with our usage ruling out some candidates as viable ones. Also, I am not supporting admitting an unprincipled profusion of subscripted candidate concepts of knowledge, which would allow us to agree with almost every suggestion ever offered by way of an analysis of knowledge by holding that each suggestion gets knowledge$_i$ right, for some i or other.[13] But I see no reason why there should not be a modest number of equally viable candidates, each serving a different worthwhile purpose in epistemology. The explanation for the seemingly interminable wrangling would then be that we are mistakenly striving to find one concept – one pattern, that is – to do the job of, as it might be, two concepts.

Are there, however, cases where we might expect to be able to settle on one answer, rather than acknowledging a number of equally good candidates, each serving different, related purposes? In a number of cases in logic and mathematics, the answer seems to be yes. In other cases, the answer is also yes, but by virtue of stipulation, examples being the stipulative definitions of vixen and of sibling – we stipulate that 'vixen' means 'female fox', and 'is a sibling of' means 'has a parent in common with'. Let me close this section by noting a more controversial example: proper names. Is there a single account to be had of the conditions under which a proper name, N, refers to x? Well of course the answer is going to depend on what you mean by a proper name (for example, do so-called descriptive names count?), and on what you mean by 'refers'. But the great utility of proper names in facilitating the passing on of information about particular objects – cities, people, houses, race horses, and so on – strongly suggests that there is a single pattern that unites names with their putative bearers: it will be whatever it takes to play that important role. Thus, as 'Paris' stands to Paris, so 'Berlin' stands to Berlin, and 'Tony Blair' stands to Tony Blair, and so on, and, in each case, the way the name stands to its bearer is what is needed to play that important role. The challenge for philosophers of language is to articulate the pattern, to specify the pattern in words, and I think we can say this much: one or another version of the causal theory has to be correct. For surely information transmission has to involve causation.[14]

6. WHY IS CONCEPTUAL ANALYSIS IMPORTANT?

I started by distinguishing three grades of involvement in conceptual analysis. That gives us three questions to answer: Why is the first grade important? Why is the second grade important? Why is the third grade important?

The answer to the first question is straightforward. The first grade is nothing more than the acknowledgement that *a priori* determined properties can be important for explanation and prediction. It is hard to see how one could quarrel with that. Does anyone doubt the utility of averages and of density, to name two of the examples we gave earlier? Of course, a sceptic about the *a priori* might object that there are no *a priori* determined properties. I think that would be a mistake, as I said earlier, in §2, but notice that what is important for the examples of averages, density, and the rest is that the properties that are so useful are obtained by operations on data, not by collecting new data. Sometimes the operations are exercises in arithmetic, as in the case of averages and calculating $\sum_i 1/2m_i.v_i^2$, sometimes the operations are exercises in conjoining as in the vixen case, and so on. For *our* purposes, being *a priori* could just mean that. We are distinguishing the legwork that delivers the data, on the one hand, from the operations on the data in the search for the properties that are important when we seek to make good use of the data, on the other. The first grade of involvement is essentially the recognition of the importance of the second part of the process.

What about the second grade? Once one sees the importance of *a priori* determined properties, one can hardly quarrel with the importance of being able to talk and think about them. Averages can be important, and, consequently, so can being able to think and talk about them. Indeed, our examples were just as much an illustration of that as they were of the importance of the *a priori* determined properties themselves. Our examples were one and all of cases where we can think and talk about the *a priori* determined properties in question – as they had to be in order to be available as illustrations. But what about the possibility of being able to think and talk about the properties without being able to articulate how they are determined, the distinctive feature of the second grade of involvement in the absence of the third grade? Well it happens. That's what we learn from the case where Doe thinks, on occasion, that something is an ellipse, and can say that it is by using the word 'ellipse', without being able to articulate the determining property. So we need to inventory it. We saw, however, that the hope that it might be the key to explaining the notorious failure to converge on a single, agreed analysis of knowledge is likely a mistake. (And I suggested, without detailing the point, that the same is true in the case of personal identity.)

Why is the third grade important?[15] At one level, one can hardly doubt its importance. If *a priori* determined properties are important and, in consequence, thinking and talking about them is important (as we say above, averages and density wouldn't be of much use to us if we couldn't think and talk about them), how could articulating the way the properties are *a priori* determined be unimportant? Should we rejoice in ignorance? Were the founders of modern logic and mathematics wasting their time when they spelt out – analysed – key concepts like convergence, completeness, and the gradient of a curve? Obviously not. However, what I want to emphasize in the final section are two additional advantages – one epistemological, the other metaphysical – of the third grade of involvement.

7. THE EPISTEMOLOGICAL AND METAPHYSICAL PAYOFFS FROM THE THIRD GRADE OF INVOLVEMENT

Let's start with the epistemological payoff. Often we need the third grade, the full monty, in respect to some property P in order to say, with justification, whether or not P is instantiated. Take Doe. He is able to tell whether or not a closed figure is an ellipse by looking, but most of us need to use our knowledge of how to articulate the pattern (along with a measuring device). We need the third grade, even if he does not.

Here's a second example. In order to show that the real numbers are non-denumerable, we need to articulate what it takes to be non-denumerable, the concept of being non-denumerable. Once that is done, we are in a position to follow Cantor's proof. Without the third grade of involvement in conceptual analysis for being non-denumerable, we could not show that the reals are non-denumerable (uncountable). I doubt if these two examples will be found very contentious, but here are two cases that may be.

Why do we believe that gases have temperatures, volumes, and pressures? The answer lies in the way gases behave, a way that is captured in the famous laws of the thermodynamic theory of gases. However, we know from the kinetic theory of gases that gas behaviour can be fully explained in terms of certain atomic and molecular properties of gases. We know that gases are aggregations of very loosely bound atoms or molecules and, in virtue of this fact, have various atomic and molecular kinetic energy properties. We also know that these kinetic properties explain fully the behaviour we explain in terms of temperature, pressure, and volume. Why, in that case, don't we conclude that gases lack the properties of temperature, pressure, and volume? Why don't we say that the old explanations have been superseded by the new ones (which of course do a much better job of explaining a number of important details – what is special about absolute zero, for example). You might appeal to simplicity here. It is simpler to suppose that, for example, temperature = mean atomic or molecular kinetic energy – one property is simpler than two – and that, given that identity, anything explained by mean kinetic energy is also explained by temperature, and conversely. However, that would be a misunderstanding. There is no lack of simplicity in the sceptical position. The sceptical position is not that gases have two properties instead of one. It is that they have one, namely, mean atomic or molecular kinetic energy, but do not have temperature.

I think that there is only way to refute the sceptical position. It is to argue that categorizations in terms of the properties of the thermodynamic theory of gases are categorizations in terms of functional roles. The terms 'temperature', 'pressure', and 'volume' pick out functional patterns. We know how to articulate those patterns – that's what the laws of the thermodynamic theory in fact do – and when we do this, we have the third grade of conceptual analysis for the case, for example, of temperature. X is at so and so a temperature if and only if X has the property playing such and such a functional role. We then resist scepticism via the following argument:

> X is at so and so a temperature if and only if X has the property playing such and such a functional role. (Example of the third grade of conceptual analysis.)
> X has the property playing such and such a functional role. (Having thus and so a level of mean atomic or molecular kinetic is discovered to do just that.)
> *Ergo*, X is at so and so a temperature.

Here is my second example. I suggested earlier that perhaps the right way to understand why we have failed to converge on a single analysis of knowledge is that there is no single concept. Sometime in the future we will come to a consensus about how to analyse the, let us say, two different but related concepts, where 'analyse' here is meant in the full monty sense. None will, in my opinion and the opinion of many, be justified true belief. My hunch is that one concept will be something like true belief arrived at through a reliable process. But let's set aside the question of what the winners might look like and ask instead why it would be good to have winners, which is of course exactly the question of why it would be good to have the third grade of involvement in the case of knowledge – the full monty – for each of the two concepts.

It would be good to have winners because it would allow us to address a certain sceptical worry about knowledge. I do not mean scepticism in the traditional sense, the sense directed at what if anything is known. I mean sceptical worries about which creatures know things – sceptical worries concerning *who* knows things, not *what* they might know. I am confident that the table in front of me knows nothing. I am confident that the person in front of me knows many things. What explains the difference? Part of the answer is that the table does very little that is interesting by way of interacting with its environment, whereas the person does plenty. But what, exactly, am I entitled to infer from all the interesting interactions of the person in front of me? Leaving aside all sorts of qualifications and refinements, I think that the answer to this question lies in Daniel Dennett's notion of the intentional stance, shorn of its instrumentalist leanings (Dennett 1971). But what we get from this notion is an account of what the subject believes and desires. No doubt I will also have an opinion about whether the beliefs are true, what evidence the subject might have for them, the causal origins of the beliefs and the evidence for them, the role, if any, of chance in the whole set up, and so on, where 'and so on' is intended to cover the many considerations that appear in the debates over the analysis of knowledge. But how might I move from this body of evidence to the conclusion that the person in front of me knows something? My evidence simply supports that they have beliefs of so and so a kind (plus various desires, of course). What could warrant taking the extra step?

Timothy Williamson argues that the hypothesis that a subject knows something explains more than the hypothesis that they believe something true (Williamson 2000). This might be thought to open the way for a best-explanation type defence of making the inference to the existence of knowledge. For example, he argues that knowledge is more persistent than belief; it takes more to dislodge it. Suppose he is right about this. Even so, it would not make the worry go away. Our question now becomes: why prefer the hypothesis that the subject knows ahead of the hypothesis that the subject truly and persistently believes?[16] The key point here, of course, has nothing to do with persistence as such. The key point is that it is hard to identify any special property of knowledge, that of being H say, that might play some explanatory role that would not equally be played by supposing the subject has a belief which has, among other properties, that of being H.

What would be nice about having winners in the case of knowledge is that it would allow us to address the sceptical worry in a principled way. With the full monty for knowledge, or maybe better, I have been suggesting, the full monty for knowledge$_1$ and knowledge$_2$, we could review the best hypothesis about what the person in front of me believes and whether or not it is true, the causal origin of their so believing, the available evidence and all the rest, and see whether or not it entails – given the two analyses of knowledge – that they know$_1$ or that they know$_2$.

Finally, what about the promised help with the metaphysics? We noted that the full monty for being an ellipse helps those of us who lack Doe's recognitional ability with respect to ellipses find out whether or not some closed plane figure is an ellipse. But the full monty does more than help with the epistemology. It tells us what it takes to be an ellipse, and in that sense helps with the metaphysics. When we ask how things have to be for there to be instances of ellipses, it gives us an informative answer: there need to be closed figures which are a locus of points in a plane such that the sum of the distances to fixed points, a, b, is a constant.

In the same way, the winners for knowledge we have just been talking about would tell us what it takes to be knowledge$_1$ and knowledge$_2$, as well as helping us reply to sceptics about one or other of the two varieties of knowledge. Likewise, when we observed above that the analysis (in the full monty sense) of being non-denumerable is crucial for showing that the reals are non-denumerable, we made the point by noting that the analysis tells us what it takes to be non-denumerable. That is to say, the epistemology and the metaphysics came as a package deal from our having an analysis in the fullest sense.

I know that some will respond to what I have just said by insisting that conceptual analysis cannot tell us about the metaphysics and epistemology of, say, knowledge, perhaps adding that, in their view, knowledge is a natural kind.[17] Conceptual analysis tells us about concepts, not properties or natural kinds. This is true but misses the point. When physicists introduced and explained the concept of a gravitational field (in moving away from thinking of gravity in terms of attraction between point masses), they did not create gravitational fields, obviously. What they did, rather, was to make it possible for us to think and talk about gravitational fields, and thereby to address, in principled ways, whether or not they exist, and what it takes for them to exist. A sensible discussion of the epistemology and metaphysics of gravitational fields requires, somewhere along the line, a grasp of the concept of a gravitational field. Why do I say 'somewhere along the line'? Well, some reasonably believe in gravitational fields in the absence of a full grasp of the concept. This is because they take the word of expert physicists that gravitational fields exist. But someone – *someone* – had better know what they are talking about. The same goes, I am saying, for, for instance, knowledge. And no-one will want to say, I trust, that the view that knowledge is a natural kind, in and of itself, addresses the epistemological question of whether and when we have knowledge. The luminiferous aether was postulated as a natural kind, but being so postulated did not save it from elimination.

So here is the story I have told you about the role of conceptual analysis in metaphysics in the sense of speculative cosmology. *A priori* determined properties are important for making sense of our world. They facilitate prediction and explanation. It follows that it is good for us to be able to talk and think about these properties. It further follows that it is good for us to be able to detail which properties do the *a priori* determining of some given property P, both because it is good to know more rather than less, and because the detailing (the full monty sense of conceptual analysis) allows us to address the epistemology and metaphysics of property P. A conceptual analysis of our concept of, say, being P is an account of what it takes to count as a P, so it is no surprise that it allows us to address the metaphysics and epistemology of being P.

NOTES

1 Apologies to Quine for the sub-title; thanks to the many who have discussed these issues with me since (Jackson 1994).

2 Often, the determining properties are, in some sense, more basic than the *a priori* determined property. But that need not be the case. For example, density, mass, and volume are inter-definable. I am indebted here to Lloyd Humberstone.

3 However, I think that what I go on to say is consistent with some, though not all, of what is said in (Yablo 2002).

4 Here we take the famous formula to *define* what it is to be an ellipse in order to ensure that satisfying the formula *a priori* determines being an ellipse.

5 Within a margin of error set by the extent to which perceptual representation is indeterminate.

6 To borrow, for example, Derek Parfit's way of expressing reductionist thoughts, see his (1984: Ch. 12).

7 A phrasing four-dimensionalists hold is potentially misleading. For them, the question is whether there is a person such that the temporal stage that enters and the temporal stage that exits are both parts of that person, but no matter here.

8 I discuss disagreements about motion and the implications for ethical theory in (Jackson forthcoming). See also (Lewis 1990).

9 Intuitions here should not be understood in some heavy-duty way, as referring to a special sense deployed when we do conceptual analysis. It is simply the deployment of a recognitional capacity that typically leads to belief – the capacity, for example, that we exercise when we recognize a sentence as grammatical. See (Jackson 2011), but the point has been made by many (and disputed by some). It is this sense of 'intuition' that figures in (Jackson 1998).

10 See, for example, (Ayer 1956).

11 See, for example, (Kahneman, Slovic and Tversky 1982).

12 To borrow a term from the personal identity debate, see, for example, (Nozick 1981).

13 For more on this, see (Jackson 2002).

14 However, I favour the version known as causal descriptivism, see, for example, (Kroon 1987), with an emphasis on information-preserving causal chains and centred content, see, for example, (Jackson 2010), rather than the account in (Kripke 1980).

15 Here and in what follows I revisit (Jackson 1994). The 'revisiting' is an exercise in setting the key ideas in a new context, although I insist that the context was always there in the background.

16 For more on this issue, see (Jackson 2002).

17 Thanks here to a reader for this volume for reminding me of the need to address this line of thought.

8   A Naturalistic Methodology

This paper presents and defends a naturalistic methodology for philosophy. In particular, an approach to epistemology is presented as a case study in how philosophy in general might be approached.

Questions about knowledge and justified belief have a long history, and the manner in which philosophers have attempted to answer these questions has varied dramatically. Within the analytical tradition, for example, various armchair approaches to issues within epistemology played a large role in the twentieth century, and they continue to be well represented even in current work. At the same time, a good deal of work in epistemology, at least from the time of Descartes to the present day, is bound up with views about the ways in which our minds actually function. Descartes was deeply committed to a wide range of views about the structure and normal functioning of the human mind, as were Locke, Hume, and Kant. Our understanding of human psychology, however, has progressed a great deal since that time, and any approach to epistemology today which, like Descartes, Locke, Hume, and Kant, attempts to present a view about knowledge and justification which is informed by an account of human psychology will need to come to terms with current work in the cognitive sciences. A view of just this sort is presented and defended here.

On this view, work in the cognitive sciences does not merely constrain our philosophical theorizing within epistemology. Rather, I argue that traditional philosophical questions about knowledge and justification are both clarified and answered by work in the cognitive sciences. The view that knowledge is a natural kind is defended, with an eye towards the issues about philosophical methodology which it illustrates.

I

Philosophers of mind have long been interested in the nature of mental states. There is a certain phenomenon with which we are richly familiar – namely, that we have beliefs, desires, intentions, sensations, and so on – and there are a variety of puzzling features of this phenomenon. What, for example, is the relation between these states and the various physical states of our bodies? On their face, these states don't seem as if they could possibly be nothing more than just physical states; but the alternative, that they are not physical states at all, is hardly unproblematic. So there is a puzzle. States of ourselves with which we are richly familiar seem, after just a few moments of reflection, to be utterly puzzling and problematic. How can we make sense of them? This is one of the points of entry into the complex web of issues that constitute the mind/body problem.

In epistemology, the very possibility of knowledge can seem problematic. Once again, there is a certain phenomenon with which we are richly familiar: there are a great many things which we know. We know our names and addresses; we know that the sun rises each morning and sets each evening; we know that water will quench our thirst, and that drinking battery acid would kill us. All of these bits of knowledge we have about the world seem to have their source in our various senses: without our eyes, ears, noses, and so on, it seems that knowledge of the world around us would be impossible. At the same time, the senses are not infallible. While they convey an accurate picture of the world to us often enough, they can also mislead us. So what reason do we have to trust the senses? To put the point only slightly differently, what reason is there to think that we are in a position to know anything about the world at all? One might try to show, by way of their track record, that the senses, while not infallible, are very reliable. Perhaps that is good enough for knowledge. But any such track record would need to be acquired, once again, by way of the senses, and this seems hopelessly circular. We are using the senses themselves to assure ourselves that the senses are reliable. This seems no better, on its face, than checking to see whether a thermometer is reliable by testing it against itself. But if we cannot do anything like this to test the reliability of our senses, then it seems we have no reason to trust them; and if we have no reason to trust them, then it seems that genuine knowledge is impossible. This is one of the points of entry into the various issues that constitute the problem of scepticism.

These familiar examples are not idiosyncratic; they are, in many ways, quite typical of philosophical problems. We begin with a familiar phenomenon, a phenomenon which is, indeed, so familiar as to be taken for granted in everyday life. But many such phenomena come to seem quite problematic after only a bit of reflection, and some of these seem, indeed, to grow still more problematic the more we try to make sense of them.

There are familiar strategies for dealing with such problems. There is eliminationism in philosophy of mind and scepticism in epistemology, views which would solve our problems by denying that the phenomena which raised the problems genuinely exist. There are attempts to domesticate the phenomena by showing that they are not as problematic as they originally seemed. And there are attempts to locate the mysteries, not in our (mis)understanding of the world, but in the world itself; the world, on such views, is not only far less simple than it seemed at first blush, but far less comprehensible than it seemed as well.

In every case, however, what we begin with is a certain phenomenon which we seek to understand. I belabour this point because I think that it has important implications for the methodology of philosophy. We are concerned in philosophy, first and foremost, with certain phenomena, not our concepts of those phenomena.[1] In philosophy of mind, we are concerned with understanding mental phenomena themselves, not our concepts of mental phenomena. In epistemology, we are concerned with knowledge itself, not our concept of knowledge. There is a seemingly familiar feature of the world which raises certain problems for us, and we seek a better understanding of the world so that we may either come to see that phenomenon as unproblematic; or see the world itself as fundamentally mysterious; or come to see that there really is no such phenomenon there at all.

Now in mathematics, it seems, we begin with a series of definitions, and then we draw out interesting consequences that follow from them.[2] Thus, for example, in geometry, Euclid began with definitions of *point*, and *line*, and *circle*, and so on, before drawing out interesting consequences of these definitions. And there are certainly many in philosophy who have seen this as a model for philosophical methodology as well. Roderick Chisholm, to take just one especially clear example, begins a work in epistemology by giving definitions of what it is for a proposition to be *counterbalanced* for an agent; for a proposition to be *probable* for an agent; for a proposition to be *beyond reasonable doubt* for an agent; and so on. He then goes on to draw out numerous consequences from these definitions.[3] If we see the targets of philosophical understanding as various worldly phenomena, however, then this method of beginning with definitions and working out their consequences seems particularly unpromising.

Thus, consider the attempt by various investigators in the seventeenth and eighteenth centuries to understand the phenomenon of combustion. Initially, combustion was thought to involve the presence of a certain substance, phlogiston, which was released into the air as combustion proceeded, but this view faced a number of difficulties when it was found that many substances actually gained, rather than lost, weight as they continued to burn. A number of solutions to this problem were tried on, including the suggestion that phlogiston has negative weight, but further experimental work led eventually to the discovery of oxygen by Lavoisier, and along with it, the modern understanding of the process of combustion.[4]

Now there would have been little point in beginning this investigation with definitions of the central terms of any proposed theory of combustion. A proper definition of the relevant terms, including 'combustion' itself, was, eventually, the result of successful theorizing, not something that could be provided in advance, at the start of the investigation. The investigation began with a certain familiar phenomenon, and the goal of that investigation was to understand precisely what that phenomenon amounted to. Of course, putative instances of the phenomenon could easily be enumerated, but any serious definition would have to await detailed experimentation and testing. Providing a definition was not a matter for stipulation; it was, instead, the product of extensive empirical investigation. This is not a feature peculiar to the investigation of the phenomenon of combustion. Rather, it is characteristic of investigations of worldly phenomena in general.

Similarly, I want to suggest, to the extent that we see philosophical investigations as beginning with the identification of a certain phenomenon which appears to be puzzling and which we seek to understand, we should not expect that we may begin by defining key terms and proceed to deduce a variety of consequences from them. Instead, we should expect that definitions of key terms will be among the outcomes of successful theorizing, something which we may provide once our theorizing has reached its conclusion, rather than at the outset of our investigation, before any serious engagement with the phenomenon has even begun.

What this means, in practice, is that philosophical investigations must involve empirical investigations. If we wish to understand the nature of mental states, as philosophers of mind clearly do, then an empirical investigation of mental phenomena is thereby called for. If we wish to understand the nature of knowledge, as epistemologists clearly do, then an empirical investigation of cognition is thereby called for. This can be accomplished, when philosophers have the training to carry out experimental work themselves, by having philosophers perform various experiments. Alternatively, it can be accomplished by having philosophers engage in a serious way with the experimental literature on such topics as mental phenomena in general, or cognition in particular. But on the view advocated here, one cannot adequately engage with the phenomena philosophers seek to understand without engaging with empirical work.

Before I proceed to explain how it is that this empirical engagement may serve as a source of philosophical understanding, it will be important to head off, or at least acknowledge the existence of, an obvious objection. Many philosophers do not accept the suggestion that empirical enquiry is very much a part of proper philosophical methodology, and a good deal of philosophical work has not adopted anything like this approach. The suggestion that philosophy should be conducted 'from the armchair' rather than 'from the laboratory' is widely defended, and even more widely acted upon.[5] It would be a mistake, I believe, to reject all of the work which seems to depend on an armchair methodology as utterly misguided and unilluminating. It will thus be necessary for the advocate of a naturalistic methodology to explain how it is that such armchair theorizing can prove fruitful.

I take up this challenge in a concluding section of this paper. The challenge can best be addressed, however, after the proposed empirical methodology has been elaborated and defended. I thus turn to an account of the naturalistic approach.

II

Let me begin with a description of two important epistemic phenomena: doxastic deliberation and memory.

Although most of our beliefs are acquired unselfconsciously, we do, at times, stop to deliberate about what to believe, and such doxastic deliberation has been the focus of a great deal of work in epistemology. Descartes' *Meditations* begins with a first-person account of the perspective of the doxastic deliberator, and this is used not only to motivate fundamental epistemological questions, but as a device, as well, for answering them. Nor is this peculiar to Descartes. The question of what one ought to believe is widely regarded as utterly central to epistemology, and the first-person perspective on that question – the perspective of the doxastic deliberator – is widely seen as crucial to answering the question. It is safe to say that the phenomenon of doxastic deliberation is an important object of study in epistemological theorizing.

By the same token, the phenomenon of memory has served as an object of much epistemological theorizing. The extent to which memory serves as a source of knowledge and justification has been much discussed and disputed, as has its role in preserving content, justification, and knowledge. Memory seems to be crucially involved, as well, in the process of reasoning. It is thus unsurprising that it is universally recognized as an important epistemological phenomenon.

When epistemologists engage in theorizing about these phenomena, it is not at all uncommon to adopt an armchair perspective. Rather than engage in, or engage with, empirical theorizing about these matters, many philosophers simply adopt the first-person perspective, that is, the perspective of the deliberator or the individual who remembers or seeks to remember. There is, of course, an extensive empirical literature on these topics, however, and it is worth considering how the first-person perspective compares with that of the experimental investigator, and what the relationship is between the accounts which result from these different perspectives.[6]

Thus, if we stop to reflect on a belief which we already possess, in order to question its epistemological status, we may introspect in order to determine why it is that we have that particular belief. Often enough, our reasons for belief will seem to present themselves directly to consciousness. We seem to be able to tell, merely by introspecting, what the reasons are for which we hold the belief in question. These reasons will typically amount to a relatively small number of beliefs which jointly constitute an argument in favour of the belief we seek to evaluate. The beliefs which seem to constitute our reasons for belief are, in the typical case, beliefs we held prior to forming the belief under consideration. Thus, for example, if I ask myself why it is that I believe a particular candidate is likely to win a certain election, introspection may reveal that, only a few days earlier, I heard a report on the radio discussing this very issue, presenting what I took to be a strong case in favour of the claim that this candidate would win, and that was why I came to accept that particular conclusion. After determining the reasons for which I believe a particular claim, I may stop to evaluate the strength of those reasons, and then, in light of that evaluation, either continue to believe as I did before or, should the evaluation of my reasons prove less favourable, give up the belief which I held unreflectively. Engaging in this process of reflective self-examination seems to result in beliefs which are more accurate, on the whole, than beliefs unreflectively acquired.

The first-person perspective on deliberation presents a vivid picture, to be sure, of the various steps in the deliberative process. An experimental examination of doxastic deliberation presents a very different account, however.[7] We do not have direct access, by way of introspection, to the processes by which our beliefs are produced. Instead, a process of theory construction occurs, unavailable to consciousness, when we reflect on the source of our beliefs. This process can, at times, give us a vaguely accurate reconstruction of the process by which a belief has been formed, but it may also, in a wide range of cases, result in confabulation, giving us a wildly inaccurate view of the source of our beliefs. There are a variety of different processes which go to work when we reflect on the source of beliefs we hold which serve to further entrench these beliefs, producing a greater confidence in the reflective agent, without, thereby, improving reliability. The processes which in fact go to work when we reflect are utterly different than they seem to the deliberating agent.

By the same token, the phenomenon of memory is, in fact, nothing like what it seems from the first-person perspective. When one remembers an event, it seems that one is able to bring forth, from mental storage, an account of that event in either propositional or imagistic form which was placed in storage at the time the event was perceived. In fact, however, the processes of storage and retrieval both involve a great deal of construction and reconstruction. More than this, the first-person perspective on memory leaves out entirely the fundamentally important process of encoding. Memory does not involve the passive storage and retrieval process which the first-person perspective seems to present. It is, instead, shot through with inference at every stage.[8]

These two examples illustrate the ways in which the first-person perspective on various mental phenomena gives us thoroughly misleading views of matters central to epistemological theorizing. If our approach to epistemology is to engage in armchair theorizing about these topics, beginning with our first-person perspective on our own mental lives and leaving no room for correction by experimental work in these areas, then it is clear that the views we end up with will be thoroughly divorced from the very phenomena we sought to understand.

Philosophers have sometimes stressed that a philosophical approach to topics addressed by empirical scientists, while it involves a common subject-matter with scientific investigations, as in the examples given above of deliberation and memory, also involves asking a different set of questions about those subjects. Philosophers often ask normative questions of a kind which experimental scientists leave unaddressed. Even if we suppose that this is so, however, it should be clear that we cannot profitably address normative questions about, for example, deliberation and memory, if we thoroughly misunderstand what those phenomena amount to. However different the focus of philosophical questions may be from that of the questions which psychologists ask about these phenomena, they are, in the end, questions about the very same phenomena. We philosophers must have an accurate view of the phenomena we seek to ask questions about if our investigations are to result in any genuine understanding. As these examples make clear, however, an armchair approach to philosophical theorizing is not well suited to gaining such understanding. Only the empirical investigation of these phenomena will provide the kind of accurate account which is needed.

III

There has been a good deal of discussion, of late, about the extent to which our intuitions about various phenomena of philosophical interest are reliable.[9] Those who wish to defend armchair methods in philosophy seek to defend the reliability of intuition because, to the extent that they defend a method which treats our intuitions as playing the same role in philosophical theorizing which observation plays in scientific theorizing, they are thereby committed to the claim that our intuitions are reliable. It is certainly true that, if it can be shown that our intuitions about hypothetical cases are unreliable, and armchair theorizing uses such intuitions in the very same manner as scientific theorizing uses observation, then armchair theorizing is thereby undermined. It is important to recognize, however, that even if our intuitions about hypothetical cases should be reliable, this is very far from sufficient for defending armchair methods.

First, even if our intuitions about hypothetical cases were reliable, so long as they are less than perfectly reliable, there will still be a need for the kind of correction which only empirical enquiry can provide.[10] A single reliable source of information about some phenomenon does not make other sources of information unnecessary. Rather, the most accurate picture is inevitably presented by making use of multiple reliable sources, and this assures the importance of empirical input to philosophical theorizing.

Second, my suggestion that philosophical enquiry begins with the identification of a phenomenon of philosophical interest itself presupposes that we have at least roughly reliable recognitional capacities. We must be able to pick out certain phenomena as worthy of study, and this requires that we are able to pick out at least many instances of those phenomena. At the same time, it is important to note that the ability reliably to recognize many instances of a phenomenon does not in any way entail that the characterizations we would give of that phenomenon prior to empirical investigation are themselves accurate. As the examples of deliberation and memory illustrate, we may certainly recognize instances of these phenomena quite reliably while simultaneously holding extremely inaccurate views about what these phenomena consist of. Armchair theorizing about these phenomena, even if it begins with accurate classificatory judgements about individual cases, will not be sufficient for getting at the truth.[11] If it were, psychological theorizing would not require empirical enquiry.

The debate about the reliability of intuitions about hypothetical cases, or the reliability of our pretheoretical classificatory judgements, important as it is, thus should not be understood as offering a potential defence of armchair methods in philosophy. Whatever the final verdict on the reliability of intuition, empirical input to philosophical theorizing is absolutely essential if our philosophical theories are adequately to engage with the phenomena we seek to understand.

IV

My claim that philosophical enquiry involves the investigation of various phenomena brings with it one further commitment: the objects of philosophical investigation have a certain theoretical unity to them.[12] Perhaps this can best be illustrated by way of the literature responding to the Gettier Problem.[13]

Numerous attempts were made, famously, to articulate some fourth condition which, when added to justified, true belief, would yield knowledge. As these became more and more baroque, observers divided into roughly three groups. Some, of course, simply redoubled their efforts to discover the Great White Whale of epistemology, the elusive fourth condition. Others suggested that the failure of so many to discover such a condition should be viewed as evidence that no such non-trivially statable condition exists.[14] Still others, however, suspected that, if knowledge should turn out to have truth conditions as baroque and seemingly gerrymandered as much of the literature on the Gettier Problem seemed to reveal, then the very idea of knowledge was, in virtue of that fact, far less interesting than had initially been supposed.[15] It is this last reaction which I wish to endorse, and which the idea that the subjects of philosophical theorizing are phenomena is meant to capture.

There are a number of different ways in which this idea of theoretical unity might be played out. Certainly one of the more demanding, and metaphysically ambitious, ideas in this area is that the objects of philosophical investigation might be natural kinds. Such a view would straightforwardly account for not only the possibility of a gap between pretheoretical conceptions of philosophical subjects, such as deliberation and memory, and the facts about these subjects; it would also give reason for thinking that such a gap is more than just a bare possibility, since a theoretical understanding of natural kinds tends to be far removed from our common-sense views about them. If the objects of philosophical investigation are natural kinds, then the need for an empirical approach to philosophical subjects is obvious.

But philosophical subjects need not be natural kinds in order to have theoretical unity. One might think that philosophical subjects generally, or at least some of them, are socially constructed kinds rather than natural kinds.[16] One might reasonably think that the standards for knowledge, for example, are not something that exist independently of us and which we discover, in the way, for example, that we discover the structure of DNA. They are, instead, on this view, something that we impose upon the world.

It is important to recognize, however, that even on the view that the targets of (at least some) philosophical theorizing are socially constructed kinds, empirical investigation will still be called for in coming to understand them.[17] Thus, consider the case of knowledge. Let us suppose, for the sake of argument, that knowledge is a socially constructed kind because the standards for knowledge are something which we impose upon the world rather than discover in it. Even so, what the standards are which we impose is a complex issue for social scientific investigation. If we think of the standards as imposed by a community, as is typical of this sort of view, then there is no reason to think that any individuals need have privileged access to what those standards are. Members of a community have a wide variety of relationships to the standards which govern that community. Some may have intimate knowledge of those standards; others may be largely ignorant of them. Some may be quite responsive to community standards even without having much explicit knowledge of them; others may fail not only to have explicit knowledge of community standards but fail to be very responsive to those standards as well. Understanding community standards, and thus the socially constructed kinds which embody those standards, is an empirical project for the social sciences. So on the view that the targets of philosophical theorizing include socially constructed kinds, empirical investigation will be called for no less than on the view these targets are natural kinds.

There are, perhaps, other ways in which the idea of theoretical unity might be played out. Certainly, there are many philosophers who make no explicit commitment either to a view of the objects of philosophical theorizing as natural kinds or as socially constructed kinds. Nevertheless, it is not uncommon to suggest that philosophical accounts should, in some sense or other, be explanatory. Timothy Williamson's Knowledge First approach to epistemology (Williamson 2000), for example, puts the explanatory role of knowledge at its centre. While Williamson focuses on common-sense explanations in everyday contexts rather than scientific explanations, these explanations are, nonetheless, straightforwardly empirical. More than this, commonsensical as they are, they are nevertheless subject, as all such explanations are, to correction by further scientific investigation.

The idea then that the subject matter of philosophical investigations concerns worldly phenomena brings with it a commitment to the relevance of the kinds of empirical investigation characteristic of the sciences. Once we see philosophy as engaging with subjects that have some theoretical unity to them, the conclusion that empirical work is relevant to philosophical theorizing becomes impossible to avoid.

V

I do not wish to rest content, however, with the conclusion that philosophical subjects have some theoretical unity to them. I wish to argue that, at least in the case of epistemology, there is reason to think that the objects of philosophical investigation are natural kinds.[18]

Consider, then, the case of knowledge. One might reasonably think that it is belief, rather than knowledge, which is most directly implicated in the explanation of behaviour. Thus, for example, although we might *say* that the reason Mary went to the shop is because she knew that it was open and she could buy what she wanted there, Mary would have gone to the shop even if she didn't know those things just as long as she believed them. Knowledge entails belief, but it seems that it is belief which does the explanatory work here rather than any of the requirements for knowledge which go beyond it.

Even if this is true in the case of explanations of individual acts,[19] there is reason to think that knowledge itself nevertheless plays an important explanatory role. Thus, when cognitive ethologists investigate the cognitive capacities of various species, they are interested in how it is that a given species is able to successfully negotiate its environment. It is typical, in these investigations, to take an evolutionary approach, as is absolutely central to any biological investigation.[20] Cognitive capacities are regarded, in the normal case, as evolutionary adaptations, allowing species to respond to the informational demands of their environments. Creatures who inhabit complex environments need cognitive capacities to be able to reliably pick up information about their environments if they are to satisfy their biologically given needs. What this means is that an object of theoretical investigation here is the reliable capacity to acquire true belief, and true beliefs which are the product of such reliable capacities are thus deeply implicated in the explanation of successful behaviour. Since the evolutionary processes which are responsible for the shaping and retention of such cognitive capacities are sensitive to the regular success or failure of behaviour in satisfying biologically given needs, true belief reliably acquired plays an important explanatory role in these theories.

Unsurprisingly, investigators working in this area refer to these true beliefs which are reliably acquired as knowledge. The following remarks, by Louis Herman and Palmer Morrel-Samuels, are utterly typical:

Receptive competencies support knowledge acquisition, the basic building blocks of an intelligent system. In turn, knowledge and knowledge-acquiring abilities contribute vitally to the success of the individual in its natural world, especially if that world is socially and ecologically complex.

(Herman and Morrel-Samuels 1990: 283)

There is thus a notion of knowledge which plays an explanatory role within a body of scientific theory, and knowledge seems here to be identified with reliably produced true belief. 'Knowledge' is thus a theoretical term, embedded in a successful scientific theory, implicated in the explanation of successful behaviour. Knowledge in this sense is not a socially constructed kind; it is, instead, a natural kind: something we discover in the world, rather than something we project upon it.

Just as terms such as 'water' and 'dog' were widely used long before they were successfully embedded in scientific theories, we may view common-sense talk of knowledge in much the same way. We were able to identify samples of water as such, and dogs as well, long before a scientific account was available which made plain just what it is that makes something water or a dog. Scientific talk of chemical kinds, and biological species, are not divorced from our everyday usage. Instead, our everyday usage succeeded in latching on to certain natural kinds, even before we had a theoretical understanding of the nature of those kinds.[21] So too, I would argue, with 'knowledge'. We have a tolerably accurate recognitional capacity for cases of knowledge, and it is this that allowed for the successful introduction of a term which latched on to a natural kind even before a theoretical understanding of the nature of knowledge was available. Once the term was embedded in a successful scientific theory, we were able, thereby, to understand just what knowledge is. The investigation of knowledge is thus viewed as an empirical enterprise. It is the successful embedding of the term in a scientific theory which allows for a proper understanding of the nature of knowledge.

Viewing knowledge in this way allows us to see epistemology as an empirical enterprise with a methodology no different from the sciences. This kind of approach has proven to be extremely productive in the philosophy of mind, where empirically informed work has largely taken over the field in the past twenty-five years. There is no doubt that the viability of such an approach needs to be examined on a case by case basis, but I have purposely chosen epistemology as my parade case because epistemology has been widely thought to be susceptible to armchair methods. If epistemology can be shown to deal with natural kinds and thus require engagement with empirical science, it may well be that many other fields within philosophy are susceptible to such treatment as well. There is a good deal of empirically influenced work being done even in ethics,[22] so I think it is fair to say that the limitations of such an approach have yet to be fully understood.

It is important, as well, to reiterate a point made briefly above. Although I have argued that knowledge is properly understood as a natural kind, the case for the relevance of empirical methods to philosophical questions is not dependent on viewing the objects of philosophical theorizing as natural kinds. Many will wish to deny that knowledge is a natural kind, and even among those who would not disagree about knowledge, the suggestion that all areas of philosophical investigation are properly regarded as natural kinds will seem, at best, premature. But even if we regard other areas of philosophical investigation as ones which deal with socially constructed kinds rather than natural kinds, the case for an empirically engaged approach, as I've argued, remains equally strong. If the objects of philosophical investigation are theoretically unified, rather than mere arbitrary collections, engagement with empirical work seems inevitable.

VI

I have been arguing that proper methodology in philosophy requires engagement with empirical work. It should be clear, however, that a good deal of work in philosophy seems to employ armchair methods which do not have the requisite empirical engagement. This presents a problem for my view. I must either argue that work which avoids empirical engagement is thoroughly misguided and of no value, or, alternatively, that work which seems to have been conducted independently of empirical work is, in fact, suitably engaged in the requisite way. On its face, neither of these alternatives seems terribly plausible.

It would be absurd, on my view, simply to dismiss all armchair philosophy as misguided and unilluminating. Much as I am concerned to defend the importance of empirical work for philosophical progress, I have myself learned a great deal from philosophers who make no obvious use of empirical work, and I would regard it as the height of arrogance to suggest that all such work is of no value. At the same time, I do think that there are certainly areas within philosophy where armchair methods have been responsible for losing touch with the very phenomena philosophers have sought to study.

Rather than focus on these problematic areas, I wish to argue that apparently armchair methods do, in fact, make use of empirical information to a far greater extent than is often realized. While

I do not believe that the armchair approach makes sufficient use of available empirical information, and so I will not be taking back any of the criticism of armchair methods which I have made above, I do believe that it is important to explain how illuminating philosophical work could have arisen from the armchair.

Let me begin with an example. I have made use, above, of a causal or historical account of reference, and one might think that this is precisely the sort of product of armchair methods in philosophy which my commitment to empirical engagement should make me suspicious of. Kripke, famously, proudly trumpets his commitment to a method which relies on intuition:

> Some philosophers think that something's having intuitive content is very inconclusive evidence in favor of it. I think it is very heavy evidence in favor of anything, myself. I really don't know, in a way, what more conclusive evidence one can have in favor of anything.
>
> (Kripke 1980: 42)

There is no doubt that Kripke sees himself as a practitioner of armchair methods. At the same time, Putnam, whose work on reference and natural kinds is also quite central in this literature, would certainly not see himself as a practitioner of armchair methods, deeply reliant, as they are, on intuitions about cases.

Putnam's work on reference and natural kinds arose out of his attempt to develop a post-positivist philosophy of science. He was responding, not only to the positivists but to the work of such philosophers as Kuhn (1970) and Feyerabend (1975), who argued that scientists with fundamentally opposing theories, as in the case of the dispute between Newton and Einstein over the nature of mass, were not actually talking about the same thing; indeed, on the views of Feyerabend and Kuhn, sameness of reference across fundamentally opposing theories is impossible. Putnam rightly saw this as seriously problematic, for it failed to account for the fact that the best explanation for the increased instrumental success of later theories would have to appeal to their ability to correct mistakes in earlier views. What was needed in order to allow for the possibility of communication across deep theoretical divides, such as the divide between Newton and Einstein, was an account of reference which allowed for sameness of reference even in the face of such fundamental disagreement. This was Putnam's motivation for the causal or historical theory.[23]

Seen in this light, it is clear that Putnam is not simply trying to account for our intuitions about hypothetical cases, but rather that he sees himself, rightly, as offering an empirical theory, based on an inference to the best explanation. The history of science is filled with examples of theories which improve on their predecessors, either by making more accurate predictions or by making predictions over a broader range of phenomena, or both. This is, as Putnam emphasized, a typical feature of later theories in mature sciences. The best explanation of this feature of scientific theorizing must allow for conflicting theorists to disagree about a common subject matter, and this, in turn, requires an account of reference which does not make it depend on the descriptions which the individual theorists would offer if asked to characterize the subject of their investigations. Putnam's work is thus not an example of armchair methods in philosophy. It is, instead, precisely the sort of empirical theorizing which I have been advocating.

It is worth pointing out that, when we sit down in the armchair in order to engage in philosophical contemplation, all our prior beliefs, whatever their source, may influence our theorizing. And this means that armchair methods will often bring empirical information to bear. It is for this reason that the results of armchair theorizing cannot be viewed as automatically *a priori*. More than this, the starting points for much armchair theorizing, which many would characterize as 'intuitions', may themselves, in many cases, be the product of empirical input and subconscious theorizing. What armchair methods exclude, however, is explicit appeals to elaborate empirical experimentation.

From my perspective, this serves to explain both the successes and the failures of armchair methods. There are certainly areas of enquiry where, to a first approximation, all the empirical input which is needed is easily available to any tolerably alert and thoughtful individual. If one wants to know what pencils are, for example, no extensive experimental investigation will be called for, since experience with pencils is so ubiquitous, and what pencils are is obvious to anyone who has used them. Of course, this does not make the knowledge we have about pencils any less empirical, even though it can be obtained from the armchair. Its accessibility from the armchair is just a product of our experience prior to sitting down.

By the same token, there are lots of subjects where one is unlikely to have adequate experience for accurate judgement without extensive and explicit exposure to empirical theorizing. Some of these involve subjects where one will likely have no opinion at all without the requisite empirical input. Those untutored in quantum mechanics are unlikely to have views about the implications of Bell's Theorem should they engage in armchair theorizing about the nature of the physical world. More interesting, and more threatening to philosophical theorizing, however, are cases where one is likely to have views about a certain subject matter even apart from explicit exposure to the results of experimental work, but those untutored thoughts are likely to be inaccurate. My examples of views about deliberation and memory are of exactly this sort.

In those cases where further empirical investigation is unlikely to overturn our untutored views about some subject matter, armchair theorizing based on such untutored views may be extremely illuminating. There are, after all, lots of consequences of obvious truths which are themselves anything but obvious. But the real problem here, of course, is that we cannot so easily tell, in advance, where untutored views are likely to be overthrown or where further empirical work may lead to a radical revision in our understanding of some phenomenon. Epistemology and philosophy of mind have, I believe, proven to be rich with phenomena that are badly misunderstood without extensive input from the sciences. What this suggests is not that armchair theorizing can never prove illuminating, but rather that, without some empirical check on such theorizing, armchair results should be viewed, at best, as only tentative. In some areas, where a great deal is known about the ways in which untutored views are likely to be inaccurate, armchair theorizing is just bad practice.

VII

Some have sought to distinguish philosophy from the sciences by way of its methods. On such a view, philosophy, unlike the empirical sciences, is an armchair enquiry; it needs no input of the kind which is typical in the systematic empirical work characteristic of the sciences. I have argued that no such view of philosophy can be maintained.[24] Armchair approaches to many areas of philosophy are likely to go badly astray, losing contact with the very phenomena they seek to illuminate. The methodology of philosophy must involve input from the sciences if it is to engage properly with its subject matter.

NOTES

1 I have argued for this at length in the case of epistemology in (Kornblith 1998) and (Kornblith 2002). Timothy Williamson has also made much of this point. See (Williamson 2000) and (Williamson 2007).

2 I don't actually think that this is an accurate account of methodology in mathematics, but arguing against this familiar view would take me too far afield from the subject of this paper. For a view of mathematical methodology which I find more congenial, see (Kitcher 1983).

3 See, for example, (Chisholm 1989).

4 This important episode in the history of science has been discussed on many occasions in the philosophy of science literature. For an extremely brief account, see (Hempel 1966: 29–30); for a more detailed account, see (Kitcher 1978); the discussion of the phlogiston case appears on 529–36. An important collection of papers is contained in (Conant 1950).

5 For a sampling of such defences, see a number of the essays in (Haug 2014).

6 I have discussed this in (Kornblith 2014); (Kornblith forthcoming); and, in far more detail, in (Kornblith 2012).

7 See, for example, (Gopnik 1993); (Kunda 1999: Ch. 10); (Nisbett and Wilson 1977); (Wilson 2002).

8 See, for example, (Baddeley, Eysenck, and Anderson 2009); (Eichenbaum 2008); (Lieberman 2011).

9 Thus, see, for example, many of the papers collected in (Haug 2014); but also (Goldman 2007); Nagel 2012); (Shieber 2012); (Stich 2013); (Swain, Alexander and Weinberg 2008); (Wright 2010).

10 Almost everyone who defends armchair methods in philosophy allows that intuition is not perfectly reliable. George Bealer argues, however, that intuition, properly understood, stands in no need of correction by science, and that it offers greater support for philosophical claims than any support which science could offer. See (Bealer 1998). At the same time, Bealer allows that it is an open question as to whether human beings are even capable of having the sorts of intuitions which he describes. This acknowledgement certainly compromises Bealer's account of the significance of intuition, in his preferred sense, for the actual practice of philosophy.

11 I have discussed this in further detail in (Kornblith 2014).

12 For a particularly valuable discussion of the notion of a phenomenon in philosophy of science, see (Bogen and Woodward 1988).

13 For an illuminating review of this literature, see (Shope 1983).

14 (Williamson 2000) is the most detailed working out of this idea.

15 I remember Louis Loeb making exactly this suggestion at a Spring Colloquium at the University of Michigan in 1997. Stephen Stich expresses a similar sentiment in (Stich 1990: 3). Alvin Goldman's insistence that an account of knowledge must be explanatory (Goldman 1992a: 106) seems to be an expression of much the same idea.

16 Thus, for example, Alvin Goldman remarks, 'Whatever one thinks about justice or consciousness as possible natural kinds, it is dubious that knowledge or justificational status are natural kinds' (Goldman 1992b: 144). The idea that knowledge is a socially constructed kind has been suggested by Barry Barnes, David Bloor, Robert Brandom, John Haugeland, Martin Kusch, Michael Williams, and Stephen Woolgar, among others. See (Barnes 1977); (Brandom 1994); (Haugeland 1998); (Kusch 2002); (Williams 2004); (Woolgar 1988).

17 I have discussed this issue in some detail in (Kornblith 2006). I have discussed the ways in which semantic issues, metaphysical issues, and epistemological issues having to do with kinds need to be kept separate in (Kornblith 2007).

18 I have argued for this position in detail in (Kornblith 2002).

19 Williamson argues that this is not correct, and even here, knowledge may explain features of such behaviour which belief cannot. See (Williamson 2000).

20 See, for example, (Alcock 2013); (Shettleworth 2010).

21 Here I simply endorse the approach to these issues found in Putnam and Kripke. See (Putnam 1975b); (Kripke 1980).

22 See, for example, (Doris and the Moral Psychology Research Group 2010).

23 One sees this quite clearly when one looks at Putnam's papers on reference in the context of his other work, not only in philosophy of science, but also on philosophy of mind. Thus, see his papers in (Putnam 1975a), as well as those in (Putnam 1975b).

24 Timothy Williamson defends a similar claim, arguing against what he calls 'philosophical exceptionalism', although, at the same time, he presents his work as a defence of armchair methods. Thus, he remarks, 'One main theme of this book is that the common assumption of philosophical exceptionalism is false' (Williamson 2007: 3). Just a few pages later, however, he comments, 'this book is a defense of armchair philosophy' (ibid.: 7) I have discussed this tension in Williamson's work in (Kornblith 2009).

9 What is Negative Experimental Philosophy Good For?

My objective here is to make a case for the positive philosophical contribution of the 'negative programme' in experimental philosophy, and head off a few common misconceptions about it along the way. To do so, I first need to say a bit about what experimental philosophy ('x-phi') is, and what in particular is its negative programme.

I take x-phi to be constituted most broadly by a thesis, and a research motivation as a clear consequence of it. The thesis: philosophical practice has substantially deeper empirical commitments than generally presupposed, in our explicitly stated theories but also in our methods, our practices with our evidential sources, and our modes of inference. The research motivation, accordingly, is for us philosophers to take those commitments seriously, and to evaluate where they are – or are not – adequately fulfilled. Perhaps we do so working on our own, or perhaps in interdisciplinary collaborations, but either way, we experimental philosophers are motivated by a desire to play a direct role in taking on this methodological responsibility.

These empirical commitments of philosophical practice are broad and heterogeneous; therefore, so too are the specific research projects that experimental philosophers are engaged in. Some work in x-phi directly engages with theories that have explicit empirical content, such as Joshua Knobe's work (2010) on human nature, or Nina Strohminger and Shaun Nichols' (2014) research on the psychological basis for attributions of personal identity over time, or Eric Schwitzgebel and Joshua Rust's (2014) investigation of the question, whether training in philosophical ethics actually produces morally better behaviour. I take such work to be both plainly philosophical, and also with obvious empirical commitments, and as such it requires no sales pitch from me here.

But other work – and perhaps this is what most philosophers have in mind when they think about x-phi – addresses specifically a tacit empirical commitment, one embedded not in a theoretical claim but in a method. This is the 'method of cases': most typically, we consider a vignette, and find ourselves strongly inclined towards a verdict about it that is salient to a philosophical theory under discussion – whether the behaviour of someone appearing in the story is or isn't a freely chosen action, or what some speaker refers to with their words, or what is or isn't a morally permissible course of action for an agent, and so on. These verdicts then serve as evidence for or against various competitor theories of the target philosophical topic.[1]

I take it that this practice itself will be familiar to most readers, yet its empirical commitments, while typically left unstated and unexamined, are actually rather substantial. For example, in order for the verdicts to serve as evidence for or against competitor theories, they must themselves be broadly independent of those theories; if our minds arrive at those verdicts only by consulting our already-preferred theories, then the verdicts cannot themselves count as further evidence for those theories.[2] Moreover, however our minds arrive at those verdicts, it must not be done in a manner that is too sensitive to factors that do not actually track the relevant philosophical truths. For, suppose that our verdicts about what is or is not knowledge are overly influenced by factors that do not themselves track what knowledge really is (or, depending on your preferred way of framing philosophical theories, what is really part of our concept KNOWLEDGE). Then the verdicts, to the extent they are so influenced, will lead us away from the correct epistemological theory, not towards it. These commitments are only rarely addressed or even acknowledged, and in one sense, there is a good reason to leave them tacit – the analytic philosopher's traditional tools of the trade are simply inadequate to engage with them. But in another sense, this silence is methodologically rather dangerous. For if these commitments should turn out to be unsatisfied, then the verdicts relied upon in the method of cases would in fact be of much less evidential value than is assumed in our practice. No one expects these commitments to be *perfectly* fulfilled – everyone expects some epistemically malign influence of wishful thinking here or a bit of unconscious bias there – but if they are substantially false, then this philosophical practice will be in trouble.

Philosophers have thus looked to exploit our own minds as tolerably-good-albeit-imperfect trackers of the contours of those categories. We have among our many cognitive competences, a capacity to confront a situation, in real life or hypothetically, and, independently of any general theory of the target domain, to register the presence or absence in that situation of knowledge, agency, moral permissibility, and so on. These are standardly called 'intuitions' but that has become a somewhat contentious piece of terminology, so instead I will refer to this general capacity as our 'human philosophical instruments' ('HPI'), and the deliverances regarding such cases as 'HPI verdicts'. I would emphasize that the central questions here about the empirical presuppositions of the method of cases, stand largely independent from any particular psychological or epistemological theory about the what and how of the HPI verdicts.

The method of cases is so prominent in analytic practice, and at the same time has such substantial yet under-attended empirical presuppositions – and thus it has proved a highly enticing topic for experimental philosophers. Indeed, by my estimate the great bulk of experimental philosophy work today aims to do some combination of challenging the method of cases and participating in it, by probing for potential failures of the empirical commitments of the method, and where possible, correcting for them.

These two different dimensions of engagement with the method of cases – documenting its empirical failures, and compensating for them – underwrite the now-standard distinction of 'negative programme' and 'positive programme' x-phi.[3] Despite these differences in emphasis, though, I want to make plain how these two different kinds of projects actually complement each other. The names suggest that they pull in opposite directions, but in fact they more resemble two distinct but non-conflicting perspectives on the same object. Both address the quality of philosophical signal readily available to creatures like us. The positive programme seeks primarily to extract the signal that is already there in the HPI; the negative, to point out areas where perhaps we are mistaking just what the content of that signal may be, or where sometimes maybe there is no real signal to be found. While it is consistent with these formulations that some sort of negative programme could *in principle* hold that there is no signal whatsoever to be found in the HPI anywhere, nonetheless I do not think that view has many, even any, proponents. (I will argue in a moment that such a view would be self-undermining anyhow.) And the negative project need not – and should not – be at all committed to any radical thesis of the overall unreliability of HPI. Attributing such a radical commitment to negative x-phi is an unfortunately common misunderstanding, even among philosophers who are sympathetic to x-phi on the whole, and despite frequent and explicit disavowals by negative programme researchers.[4]

It is surely accurate, however, to say that the negative programme aims in part to show that those instruments are *less* reliable than current philosophical practice seems to presume. But I must caution that that characterization does not exhaust the philosophical relevance of that work. For that would leave out a further positive expectation that we can also use those results to improve those human philosophical instruments – or, more likely, to improve our practices in deploying such instruments to inform our philosophizing. And that such improvement is possible is itself a shared commitment between positive and negative x-phi: were no improvement in our current armchair practices needed or possible, then there would be little point in positive x-phi, either.

In terms of the general, on-balance reliability of the human philosophical instruments, the armchair practitioner, the positive x-phi researcher, and the negative x-phi researcher are in broad agreement. All acknowledge that the HPI may get matters right on a very wide class of cases, while recognizing that they make their share of mistakes as well. Even high-church rationalists like BonJour (1998) and Bealer (1998) openly affirm the fallibility of HPI (described under the terms 'rational insight' and 'intuition', respectively). The disagreements, though deep, are not amenable to any easy gloss in terms of reliability. The question of to what extent one should trust an apparent source of evidence goes well beyond the basic question of its alethic batting average (Weinberg forthcoming; Alexander and Weinberg 2014).

It is important for negative programme researchers to foreswear any such global unreliability thesis, that HPI has on balance a low yield of accurate verdicts, because there is simply no way to get to such a conclusion on the basis of the sort of data we have. X-phi studies can show, at best, that some sources of error may exist in the HPI. But they simply cannot hope to show what the ratio of accurate to inaccurate HPI verdicts might be, because we do not have any way whatsoever at this time of estimating what the first of those two quantities might be. Grant *arguendo* that some of the x-phi studies show that some frighteningly large number of HPI verdicts may be misled by order effects and what-not – even so, the overall cardinality of actually-ever-produced HPI verdicts, let alone the number of in-principle-producible ones, surely dwarfs the number of ones impugned by those studies. So the negative restrictionists have not typically been committed to any sort of large-scale unreliability claim.[5]

I. THE RESTRICTIONIST CHALLENGE: ARMCHAIR PHILOSOPHY IS SICK, WITH A BAD CASE OF ARMCHAIR PSYCHOLOGY

Now, philosophers have so often taken the negative programme to be so radical, that the reader may worry that either I am practising a bit of defensive retroactive revisionism, or that the ballyhoo over the 'x-phi movement' has been mere false advertising. I will happily acknowledge that some of the hoopla that accompanied x-phi in its early years involved some mischaracterizations, most particularly whenever it was suggested that x-phi was meant to replace armchair practices altogether. No x-phi practitioner ever suggested *that*, but it was a common misunderstanding nonetheless. Putting that hullabaloo-induced confusion aside, though, *some* sort of charge of radicalism may fairly be lodged here, to which the negative programmers should cop. My point is that this radicalism cannot be theorized well in terms of any radical view about the HPI themselves, to the effect that they are wildly unreliable. Rather, what is radical here must be understood in terms of how well we can use the HPI *if we wish to deploy only those methodological resources available from the armchair*. The rallying image of x-phi is not a human brain on fire, after all, but an armchair. (I think perhaps some philosophers have simply identified the armchair with intuitions themselves, such that to reject the former is *ipso facto* to reject the latter, but that strikes me as bizarre and, er, counterintuitive.)

What is being rejected even more specifically is any optimistic estimation of our armchair capacity to detect just where the HPI may go awry. Again, no full-blown unreliability claim is needed, even about our armchair error-detection capacities. There are of course a great many things some humans can do spectacularly well from the armchair, such as mathematics. Even our capacity for armchair psychologizing can be pretty impressive, as Jerry Fodor and Daniel Dennett among others have emphasized. But high baseline reliability is nonetheless consistent with inadequacy to perform some particular bit of epistemic work.

I won't spend much time here offering a theory of the armchair. But just as it is important not to identify the armchair with the HPI themselves, so too in these debates must one avoid thinking of it in terms of the pure *a priori*. For defenders of the armchair clearly include all sorts of interpersonal interactions; quotidian, commonsensical, contingent facts; knowledge of the history of philosophy; and even the history of science, as legitimate resources for philosophical deliberation (Nolan 2015; Weinberg 2015). It's enough here to just stipulate a negative definition, along the lines usefully floated by Williamson: 'thinking, without any special interaction with the world beyond the chair, such as measurement, observation or experiment would typically involve' (Williamson 2007: 1). 'Observation' is perhaps a bit ambiguous, in that we may wonder if it ought include what one could, as it were, spot without standing up, but for our purposes here let us grant whatever resources we can to the armchair. Let us define the methodological situation of the armchairs simply as: whatever resources we have without making any substantial reliance on scientific methods.[6] I will use the term *'cathedra'* for the set of philosophical practices trying to use the HPI in an armchair-restricted way, and 'cathedrists' are those who either engage in that practice and/or defend it.

We can now formulate the negative programme's 'Restrictionist Challenge' to the *cathedra* in what might be called its classical form, as originally developed in places like Alexander and Weinberg (2007) and Alexander (2012). The Challenge, in a nutshell, is that the evidence of the HPI's susceptibility to error makes live the hypothesis that the *cathedra* lacks resources adequate to the requirements of philosophical enquiry. Cathedrists must then figure out how to meet that Challenge, by some combination of demonstrating that the HPI are not as susceptible to error as had been thought; supplementing their methods to correct for these possible errors; or restricting their methods so as to avoid more error-prone situations. (It is this last possibility that gives the Restrictionist Challenge its name, but to be clear, the Challenge itself does not really make any case for one line of response over another; more on this in section III.) For the Challenge to get off the ground, three distinct lines of evidence must combine together:

1. a body of empirical evidence of some pattern π of HPI sensitivity to some set of factors;
2. a metaphilosophical claim that π diverges from the relevant philosophical truths. Usually this divergence is a matter of sensitivity to irrelevant factors, such as order or font or personality of the intuiter, but in principle it could also involve a lack of sensitivity to factors that should matter;[7]
3. an abductive argument from the observation of π in the sample to the predicted occurrence of π in the professional population.

The sort of evidence that falls under 1. is, I think, what most people think of as typical of negative programme experimental work. There is at least suggestive evidence, that HPI verdicts can vary with factors of the presentation of the vignette, but not part of its content, such as order (Swain *et al.*, Liao *et al.*), or the type of font that the text is presented in (Weinberg *et al.* 2012); various factors that are based on the content of the target vignette, such as first-person vs. third person (Tobia *et al.*), affect (Nichols and Knobe), moral valence of a proposition considered as known or not (Buckwalter and Beebe); and psychological distance[8] (Weigel); and aspects of the individual rendering the verdict, such as personality type (Feltz and Cokely) or ethnicity (Machery *et al.*). Although a few famous results have not replicated (see in particular Kim and Yuan 2015 on Weinberg *et al.* 2001), nonetheless many other of these results have been replicated and extended. To illustrate: if one considers just the first four negative programme results that were published – demographic variation of knowledge attributions (Weinberg *et al.* 2001); demographic variation of referential attributions (Machery *et al.* 2004); order effects on knowledge attributions (Swain *et al.* 2008); and variation of free will judgements by personality type (Feltz and Cokely 2009) – then while the first has failed to replicate, the other three have proved robust (see, e.g., Machery *et al.* 2015; Wright 2010; Schultz *et al.* 2011).

Regarding 2., I take it that philosophers will agree that the factors just discussed are not generally truth-tracking ones. Whether someone has acted freely or not does not depend on whether their behaviour takes place in a few days or a few years; whether someone has knowledge or not does not depend on whether the proposition in question has any particular moral valence; the correct moral verdict on a 'loop' trolley case does not depend on which other cases have been recently considered. Even if there is not a complete consensus in this regard, nonetheless, given the contours of the results reported thus far I will take the second strand required by the Restrictionist Challenge to be mostly uncontroversial.

As for 3., several philosophers have launched what has come to be known as the 'expertise defence' designed precisely to block this piece of the Challenge (e.g., Hales, Ludwig, Williamson). I cannot get into the details here,[9] but will simply make two observations about it. First, this defence is not really one that it is wise to attempt from the armchair. For it comes down to a very particular sort of empirical claim, to the effect that the various sorts of training or experience or demographic filtering that shape the professional population manage to shield that resulting population from the effects described above and their ilk. From the armchair, one can present it as a plausible hypothesis – but not any better than that. Second, the empirical work that has been done thus far on the professional philosopher population has generally disconfirmed the defence, and thereby supported the inference required in part 3 of the Restrictionist Challenge (e.g., Schulz *et al.* 2011; Tobia *et al.* 2013; Schwitzgebel and Cushman 2015).

I cannot attempt to canvass here all the responses to the Restrictionist Challenge.[10] My purpose has been, rather, to clarify what those three interlocking strands are that together weave the Restrictionist Challenge, such that they are not obviously dismissible, but must be reckoned with. The three strands together pose a challenge by providing substantial empirical evidence that there is a very live threat of unexpected error in the HPI verdicts that cathedrist practice so often relies upon. Given this body of evidence that the HPI verdicts that we want to use as evidence face a live threat of unexpected, hitherto-undetected, and as-yet-undelimited errors, the ball goes into the cathedrists' court to propose possible responses. This is the Challenge that they are confronted with: how are they to handle, mitigate, escape, avoid, compensate for, or otherwise live with this threat of error? It is an invitation to the philosophical community to take stock of this problem, and devise approaches to it, which could then themselves be evaluated both hypothetically and, hopefully, in some sort of implemented practice.

II. REFINING THE CHALLENGE

Instead of pursuing such constructive approaches, however, cathedrists too often have fallen back on a response that is something of a cross between charges of scepticism, and a 'what, me worry?' shrug: hey, so what if intuitions are fallible? After all, everything this side of the *cogito* is fallible! Science certainly makes its share of mistakes, as do our most everyday sorts of epistemic resources, like vision. If the challenge were to give us reason to panic about HPI, then it gives us reason to do so across the board. So, hey, philosophy is hard, we make mistakes, and when we do, we come up with new arguments and try again harder. What's so bad about that?[11]

Although this response is not particularly constructive, it is nonetheless not obviously wrong. It is fair to ask the restrictionist how their proposed Challenge does or does not afflict the everyday and the scientific as well. And thus restrictionists who are dissatisfied with this response face a dilemma: how big a threat of error should they say the Challenge poses? Go with full-blown unreliability, and they have a hard uphill climb to show that so strong a claim is true, or even moderately well-evidenced. But go with a weaker standard, like mere fallibility, and it can look as though the armchair may be threatened by it only to the extent that all human epistemic activity is.

Thus, yet a fourth strand must be interwoven into the restrictionist web, to ensnare cathedrist practices while allowing ordinary epistemic activities and scientific research to pass through, more or less intact. A key idea here is that the danger posed by a threat of error for some epistemic practice is proportional to the demandingness of the standards in that practice, and inversely proportional to the availability and efficacy of other resources to detect, correct for, or quarantine such errors. In general, how dangerous a mistake is for you depends on how much is riding on your getting it right, and how well you can make it up if you get it wrong in the first place. This is just the research methodology version of that piece of everyday wisdom. We are concerned here not so much with practical or ethical dangers of error, but the threat of having our inquiries sent off in misleading directions. And different modes of enquiry may vary in terms of just how bad such a threat may be, should those modes impose varying degrees of *epistemic demandingness*.

This is the term Jennifer Nado introduces to theorize a key difference across various modes of enquiry, in terms of just how high a degree of reliability they might require for their proper operation. She argues that philosophical enquiry can be highly demanding, when it trades in various sorts of exceptionless universals. Philosophical inferences are much more demanding than everyday sorts of cognitive activity, and as such, they impose a normative requirement for a much higher degree of freedom from error than those that govern the epistemic practices of our ordinary lives. She offers the following illustration:

Consider a group of ten objects, a, b, c … j, and two properties, F and G. Now consider a subject who possesses a 'folk theory' devoted solely to those objects and their properties, on the basis of which the subject makes judgements regarding the applicability of F and G to the objects in the group. Suppose that, by means of this folk theory, our subject produces the judgements Fa, Fb, Fc … Fj, and the judgements Ga, Gb, Gc … Gj. Finally, suppose that in actuality, ~Fa and ~Gb – all other judgements are correct. Out of twenty judgements, the subject has made eighteen correctly – she is, then, a reasonably reliable judger of F-hood and of G-hood on the cases to which her folk theory applies. We would likely say that it is epistemically permissible for the subject to rely on such judgements in normal contexts.

Suppose, however, that our subject is a philosopher; further, suppose her to be concerned with the nature of F-hood and of G-hood. Our subject might then come to hold certain theoretical claims about the nature of F-hood and G-hood on the basis of those initial classificatory judgements. She might, for instance, infer that everything … is F, that everything is G, and that if something is F then it is G. She would be wrong on all counts. The example is simple, but it shows that a certain principle – that the general reliability of one's classificatory judgements directly entails the general success of one's theory-building – is clearly false. Generating an accurate theory is highly epistemically demanding; an otherwise respectable source of evidence may not suffice.

(Nado 2015: 213–14)

So when we operate under the demanding standards of philosophical research, we may need to operate under more error-intolerant norms than in our ordinary lives, without in any way needing to think of our ordinary practices as anything close to fully unreliable.

Let me emphasize how non-sceptical this point is. The demands of methodological responsibility can require us to forsake some particular source of evidence, in some context and for some purposes, even when that source has a reasonably high baseline reliability, and even when it might be adequately trustworthy for other contexts and purposes. For an intra-scientific illustration, consider the use of litmus paper to measure pH. It would be preposterous to say that standard litmus paper pH indicators are out-and-out unreliable as a measure of pH. For many purposes, even many scientific purposes, they work just fine. But the use of such colour-based indicators is nonetheless susceptible to sorts of errors that render them insufficiently trustworthy when the scientific purposes in question become more demanding. A few minutes' easy googling returns many discussions like the following:

The paper turns a different color depending upon the pH of the solution. It provides a very coarse measurement of pH – it is fine for making simple determinations, but it is too coarse a measurement for allowing comparisons between sampling dates or stations.[12]

In addition to variations of demandingness thereby imposing varying standards of error-tolerance, restrictionists have also observed that not all evidentiary practices are equal when it comes to the resources their practitioners may deploy to mitigate whatever risk of error they may face. In Weinberg (2007), I used the term *hopefulness* for the resources available to those using an evidentiary practice to detect, correct, and/or quarantine any errors that may arise in their deployment of that practice. Note that hopefulness is not reliability: the latter pertains to how often a source gets things right, and the former to what happens when it gets things wrong. Whenever some method lacks the specific hopefulness resources needed for at least some kinds of errors that we have real, positive reasons to suspect may afflict our use of that practice, then, would-be practitioners of that method have grounds for concern, even if their method is on balance highly reliable. We might have all sorts of excellent tools for managing some sorts of error, but if some other important sorts of mistake can pass by them unnoticed and untouched, then we still have a problem.

Concerns about the limitations on armchair-available psychological resources come to the fore here. Even as the epistemic demandingness of philosophical inferences rises, our resources for satisfying those demands by detecting and correcting for errors is rather more impoverished than we may have thought – precisely because many of the sorts of errors that HPI turns out to be susceptible to, are ones that lie outside of the capacity of the armchair to do a sufficiently good job of monitoring. The sorts of effects that negative x-phi has been documenting are simply not of a sort that by and large can be either detected or controlled for within the constraints of the *cathedra*.

First, demographic variation may be invisible, because an individual philosopher may only exchange HPI verdicts with a fairly homogenous group of fellow philosophers (given, e.g., the relative dearth of Anglophone philosophers who are not of white/European background, and for that matter, the great number of non-Anglophone philosophers who generally lie outside such conversations); and because some dimensions of demographic variation may be highly difficult to discern without the assistance of various instruments of the social sciences (such as personality type, though of course extreme cases will by their nature be detectable as such).

Second, the large range of subtle, unconscious effects will likewise by their very nature be invisible to introspection or unsystematic observation. In addition, philosophers up until now have not been particularly adept at even hypothesizing such effects for consideration, let alone detecting where they may be in play. Perhaps that is something that could change as more philosophers become better acquainted with the relevant scientific literatures.

But I suspect it is more likely that such acquaintance would lead them to a greater appreciation of the need for the more discerning methods of the sciences, to determine truly where such effects afflict HPI.

To recap: we now have a steadily growing body of evidence that the HPI are susceptible to a wide class of subtle errors that we cannot do a particularly good job of picking up on, if we allow ourselves only armchair psychological resources.

At *this* stage of the game, it ill behoves cathedrists to continue digging in and ducking the Challenge. If we are to continue relying on HPI, we must instead amend our philosophical practices to take these risks of error seriously. As noted above, doing so may require liberating our philosophical practices from the self-imposed cathedrist limitations. Practitioners must remember that 'armchair intuitions' contains two distinct terms, and the former may yet be abandoned to the flames while attempting to place the latter on a safer, more hopeful footing with the sciences' help. More gently: since the armchair is defined negatively, to give it up is in no way to abandon what one was doing inside it in the first place, but rather to supplement those activities with further epistemic resources.

III. A BRIEF BUT SPIRITED REJECTION OF SOME UNFORTUNATE RECENT CALUMNIES

One sometimes hears x-phi, especially the negative programme, characterized as committed to an unpalatable scepticism about the HPI, or even to a more general scepticism; alternatively, it is sometimes pilloried as merely a form of philosophy-hating scientism. Yet I hope the preceding sections demonstrate that those charges are patently inaccurate. For we do not need any thesis to the effect that HPI are on the whole evidentially bankrupt. Rather, we are committed to the claim that our unaided resources are inadequate for telling where the HPI may go off track. This is not scepticism, but just a realistic and informed view of the limits of armchair psychology. And we are not imposing any sort of unreasonably high demands on our use of HPI that would fail on analogy with our ordinary epistemic lives, or with the sciences: our ordinary epistemic lives are rightly held on the whole to a lower standard, and the sciences generally can meet those standards where cathedrist practice cannot – not least of all because the sciences make ample use of the sorts of tools of hopefulness that cannot be reached from the armchair.

As for the charge of scientistic philosophy-phobia, well, critiquing a philosophical practice for a susceptibility to error, and advocating reforms, is a time-honoured philosophical activity in its own right, including such figures as Descartes, Hume, Kant, the pragmatists, the logical positivists, and Austin. I am of course not claiming that any work by the restrictionists makes them into Humes reborn. My point, simply, is that offering these sorts of arguments in no way entails either scientism or being a self-hating philosopher. The restrictionists are calling for constructive revisions to, and augmentation of, current philosophical practice. They are not at all calling for the dismantling of philosophy, to be replaced by some scientific ersatz.

There is perhaps some interesting similarity between the Restrictionist Challenge and Descartes' deployment of hyperbolic scepticism as a tool for enquiry. For both are motivated by the discovery that our cognitive lives are more shot through with error than we had expected. Both strive to identify the worrisome cognitions, and then make a novel application of philosophical tools to restore confidence to those that deserve it, and prevent further mischief from those that do not. But they diverge sharply regarding the standards for flagging something as epistemically worrisome. For Descartes, famously, the merely conceivable possibility of error sufficed to place beliefs into suspension; for the restrictionist, error possibilities must be live and empirically attested. As a consequence, Descartes ultimately did not really have the resources he needed in order to pull back from his nosedive of doubt, with too much called into question and not enough resources left over to recall them to trustworthiness. The Restrictionist Challenge faces no such worry. The sorts of concerns that its empirical methods raise can be addressed by those same methods.

IV. GOING POSITIVE BY GOING NEGATIVE?

Yet such methodological contributions may seem purely, and problematically, negative. Where x-phi can show that our case verdicts are in fact untroubled, despite perhaps initial appearances to the contrary, then that is a constructive result: we can retain it as a meaningful piece of evidence as was perhaps originally reported from the armchair. And where x-phi of a positive sort allows us to discern such evidence better than we could from the armchair, then that is a clear methodological benefit. But when the negative experimental philosopher achieves a result that tells us to pull a particular case from circulation, then it can seem as though we have taken a step backwards. We thought we had a bit of evidence in the neighbourhood of that case to help us choose between competing theories, and now (*ex hypothesi*) we do not. Pulling us out of a blind alley is perhaps a way of being constructive, but that is not the same as steering us towards a more correct path. *Usefully* negative, but still *only* negative.

Yet such an impression of the limits of negative x-phi may well be mistaken. In many places, the problem for philosophy has been having too many cases to capture, not too few! It's not like trying to figure out an underlying causal mechanism, where you may start out without any good hypotheses, and may need tremendous amounts of data just to start building a plausible set of theoretical options. Enquiry into the nature of philosophically interesting kinds, such as knowledge or agency, is rarely, probably never, of that sort. Rather, in philosophy we usually have plenty of good hypotheses, each of which has a small number of sticking points. If you find that you have removed the sticking points for one, but not its competitors, then voilà! Progress! It is a mistake to think that the only way philosophy can progress is by having a larger set of case verdicts, principles, and so on, and then devising, in a feat of philosophical cleverness, some systematic way to capture them all in one fell swoop. When we can neutralize some bit of evidence as only apparently having bearing on our theories, that too may be a path of progress. We already do something like this in 'explaining away' intuitions that are unfriendly sticking points for our preferred theories (Ichikawa 2010). Negative x-phi thus reveals that more cases merit such a treatment than we may have suspected; provides better tools for bringing to light good candidates for such a discounting; and, hopefully, resolves such suspicions where possible.

One might have hoped that x-phi could move philosophy forward with dazzling new discoveries that we could not achieve from the armchair. Yet, I suspect that the way x-phi will help move the philosophical ball down the field will be in this rather more limited, and negative way. Pretty much any pattern in the HPI that is strong enough to be worth taking seriously as a guide to philosophical truth, will be so strong that it would very likely have been observed already from the armchair. We should not look too much to positive x-phi to produce brand-new pieces of philosophical evidence to base our theories upon, then, so much as to help us do quality control on the set of HPI products we already have before us, and to thresh out which are wheat and which are mere chaff.

Progress by *via negativa* can take several different forms. To illustrate, let me briefly discuss three such modes of negative philosophical progress here.

First, two theories may be in competitive equipoise, one having greater simplicity but the other cleaving more closely to the HPI. Here, dissolving a few of those case verdicts may disrupt the balance and tilt the scales firmly in favour of the first theory. For example, Buckwalter (forthcoming) reviews the evidence for epistemic contextualism, in terms of how the folk report their verdicts across a range of different scenarios and experimental conditions. Contextualism predicts that various conversational contours can shift the standards required for the attribution of knowledge, such as just what is at stake for the potential attributor of knowledge, whereas invariantism makes no such predictions. It is precisely to capture those shifting standards that contextualists look to introduce a contextual parameter into their model of knowledge, one lacking in the invariantist model. Buckwalter examines the extant literature, and determines that the results are, at best, 'mixed': many studies find no such patterning, while others do find it, albeit in a fairly weak form. Suppose that this part of his evaluation is right, and that as far as the observed patterning in the attribution data is concerned, then, neither contextualism nor invariantism really gain any support. On the model I am suggesting here, we should consider that state of play to be substantially in the invariantist's favour, because of the greater simplicity of their theory of knowledge.[13]

Second, sometimes we will progress by coming to a firmer realization that different members of a set of competing theories must each be reckoned as containing some key philosophical truths, and that the space of competitors must be upended and reconfigured. Nichols *et al.* (forthcoming) uncovered similarly complicated results regarding verdicts about reference. Their results indicate that, depending on context, sometimes natural kind terms operate in a manner consistent with a causal-historical semantics, and sometimes with a descriptivist semantics. They theorize this contextual instability in terms of an 'ambiguity theory of reference', positing that kind terms are ambiguous in much the same way that terms like 'bank' are ambiguous. The authors accurately observe that this idea 'runs against just about everything in the literature'.[14] If HPI verdicts about reference can no longer serve their earlier role in helping us choose between causal-historical and descriptivist theories, then on the one hand, that is a starkly negative result. On the other hand, it puts into play a whole new class of theories worthy of philosophical exploration.

For a third example of going positive by going negative, negative findings may bring theoretical options into view that had been misleadingly shuttered by their inconsistency with what had *seemed* an incontrovertible set of verdicts. For decades now, the power of the Gettier cases has kept Gettier-inconsistent theories almost entirely off the table of theoretical options in the theory of knowledge, with a small number of interesting exceptions (Sartwell 1991; Hetherington 2012). Perhaps this has been due in part to epistemologically dubious factors such as an enforcement of conformity, and 'thought-experimenter bias', as Turri suggests (Turri 2016). But even supposing that the reports are sincere and widespread, it nonetheless appears that verdicts about such cases are surprisingly susceptible to various non-truth-tracking effects like the influence of the moral valence of the target proposition (e.g., Beebe and Shea 2013; Turri 2016); as well as framing effects (Machery *et al.* forthcoming-a); and they show some patterning in terms of how different groups respond to different versions of Gettier cases (Machery *et al.* forthcoming-b). Our Gettier verdicts have been shown thus far on the whole to display rather more noise than our verdicts about more paradigm cases of knowledge or non-knowledge (Weinberg forthcoming). Although the evidence points clearly towards the existence of some element of human psychology that can pick up on Gettier-type structures, and will often in their presence produce a diminished attribution of knowledge, nonetheless the substantial quirks of this 'Gettier effect' indicate that we should take seriously the possibility that it is really just noise, and ought not be included in our best theories about the nature of knowledge. I argue that the status of the Gettier effect ought be treated as an open question, and the virtues of Gettier-insensitive theories of knowledge need to be given a closer evaluation. The re-opening of such theoretical possibilities is itself a form of progress, when such possibilities had been closed out upon insufficient grounds in the first place.

V. WHAT CAN THE VIA NEGATIVA GET US THAT WE COULD NOT GET FOR OURSELVES?

But might we not have expected, nonetheless, that all these forms of progress could be attained by philosophers residing safely within the *cathedra*? These sorts of activities are, after all, hardly unknown to philosophical practice. For example, here is David Papineau, on the nature of philosophy:

Go back to the idea ... that philosophy is characteristically concerned with theoretical tangles. We find our thinking pulled in opposite directions and cannot see how to resolve the tension. Often part of our predicament is that we don't know what *assumptions* are directing our thinking. We end up with conflicting judgments, but are unclear about what led us there. In such cases thought-experiments can bring the *implicit principles* behind our conflicting judgments to the surface. They make it clear what *intuitive general assumptions* are governing our thinking and so allow us to subject these assumptions to explicit examination.

(Papineau 2009: 22–3, emphases mine)

Even if negative x-phi can count as providing some sort of philosophical progress, isn't *this* sort of philosophical progress better and more substantial? It is, in its way, negative: some of these assumptions, once subjected to that 'explicit examination', will turn out to be unworthy of further endorsement. And the verdicts that these rejected assumptions had enabled will also fall by the wayside. Yet we end up in a position of both greater insight into our (previous) philosophical commitments, and a firmer grasp of *why* the view we might now less equivocally endorse merits that endorsement. Negative x-phi offers no such intellectually satisfying conclusions. Moreover, uncovering hidden assumptions is exactly the sort of thing we might well expect to be able to do from our armchairs, in part because the space of such principles will be delimitable by considering what might at least seem to make sense for beings like us to assume. The set of hypotheses for armchair-detangling tend to be ones that have at least some *prima facie* plausibility in their own right.

This is an attractive story for philosophy, yet unfortunately negative x-phi teaches that many philosophical 'tangles' will simply not derive from anything so respectable, or so rationally discernible, as principle-like assumptions. Rather, philosophical tangles might be spawned in rather more shallow waters of our minds, like an order or framing or context effect. Or they may lie outside the view from the *cathedra*, such as when different linguistic constructions' subtle and unconsciously encoded patterns of frequency of use lead to unconscious inferences that are not commonsensical in themselves (Fischer *et al.* 2015). Or the tangle might emerge not even within any one individual at all, but across them, along various sorts of demographic lines. Papineau's armchair-friendly tangles may deserve to be unwound and unravelled, with their entwining threads perhaps each worthy of philosophical examination in their own light. Yet when they arise from the rather more unprincipled psychological sources that the negative programme traffics in, such philosophical puzzles do not deserve to be solved, only dissolved. The knots of such tangles ought to receive a more Gordian treatment, and experimental philosophy helps sharpen the requisite blades.

In fact, what is a methodological virtue when we are trying to decide hidden principles, instead threatens to be a troublesome vice when we must seek more oddball distorting factors in our cognition. We philosophers have a professionally trained bias towards claims that make sense, that are at least plausible candidates for enthymemes and are worthy of some extended examination and consideration. Those are the sorts of things one can do some philosophy on. But non-rational biases, the short-circuiting of unconscious heuristics, the quirky influences of factors that lie beyond any plausible rationalizing story – *these* are not generally going to occur to philosophers on a Papineauvian project. Our education and experience perhaps cultivates in us a keener sensitivity to one sort of unconscious cognition, but at the cost of a diminished capacity to notice or theorize in terms of other sorts. I conjecture that we philosophers suffer a bit of *déformation professionnelle*. It turns out to be very hard to turn oneself into a finely crafted instrument that can perform some specific set of tasks with great discrimination and puissance, without thereby rendering oneself at the same time rather a clunker when it comes to still other tasks, tasks no less subtle and wonderful in their own right but for which now one is utterly ill-suited.

It is not just the effects of our training on our minds that can lead us astray. When our best philosophical practices come into contact with the various sorts of unconscious effects and biases, it can lead to an intensified problem of 'myside bias'. With no malice aforethought, we can find ourselves unintentionally designing our thought-experiments so that they skew our verdicts in favour of our preferred results. When we construct a thought experiment to serve as input to HPI, we make dozens upon dozens of seemingly minor and insubstantial decisions about how we would like to phrase, frame, and style the case. Yet this is one of the key lessons of negative x-phi: we just do not know what are innocent factors that can be left up to personal preference and aesthetics, and what may have an inadvertent effect on the outcome.

Alexander and colleagues (in prep.)[15] examined the epistemological literature on peer disagreement, which is a particularly HPI-intensive corner of the literature, and from which they thus had no trouble extracting a large set of vignettes that had been actively deployed. Presenting these vignettes to a large group of participants, they found that on the whole they showed no predilection one way or another between 'conciliatory' and 'steadfast' views. That is, the set of verdicts in their totality did not incline one way or another on the question of whether or not, when confronted with a peer whose judgement diverges from one's own, one ought to adjust one's credences in their direction at least somewhat. While that finding by itself is perhaps a useful negative instrumentist result, suggesting that these verdicts may not be of a sort to be trusted in determining which epistemological theories to adopt, it gets more interesting from there. For they have evidence not just that these HPI verdicts may not be trustworthy, but also that we philosophers may be less trustworthy than we might have hoped in how we try to solicit such verdicts.

The researchers found an array of differences between cases that would systematically tilt their participants' responses either towards a conciliatory or steadfast verdict, and these tilts matched closely the direction in which the original authors of the vignettes claimed that the verdicts would go. Presenting a vignette with a forced-choice question ('Should you give your friend's diagnosis equal weight and think that it is no more likely that you are right than that your friend is right, or should you continue to prefer your own diagnosis?') would incline their participants towards more conciliationist reports; and indeed, conciliationist philosophers tended to use forced-choice frames in their articles. Scalar questions ('How confident should you be that your diagnosis is correct now that you know that your friend disagrees with you?') produce more steadfast answers, and the epistemologists who favoured a steadfast approach to the puzzle preferentially used that framing. Similarly, it seems that steadfastness proponents have tended to construct their thought-experiments framed in first-person instead of third-person terms; to include more highly affective stories (such as involving heinous crimes) instead of emotionally more inert ones (such as performing a calculation on a restaurant check); and to select matters of disagreement for which there may be ready-to-hand methods for resolving the disagreement. *Mutatis mutandis* fans of conciliationism tend to make the opposite choices.

According to this study, philosophers are in one sense designing their vignettes in just the right way to get what they want. But it raises the worry that in another, deeper sense, they are perhaps designing them in exactly the wrong way: they may be creating situations where they are unlikely to find out if their theories are false. Because they are unaware of the ways in which these subtle factors can influence their HPI verdicts, they may be producing merely an illusion of evidence for their preferred views. Surely good philosophical practice requires that we construct our vignettes cleverly, with careful attention to detail, and an eye towards the results we seek to produce. Yet in the absence of the kind of insight the negative programme can provide, this sort of craftsmanship can lead not to a closer attainment of philosophical truth, but to the epistemically disastrous juxtaposition of our own desires between ourselves and that truth. This sort of bias is notoriously hard to defuse in the first place (e.g., Stanovich and West 2007), yet without negative x-phi's help, we philosophers would perhaps be doomed to aggravate it for ourselves by dint of our own cleverness.

Give the human mind a bit of slack, a bit of free space to repackage or reframe what it is thinking, and it turns out that unconsciously and even against our own express wishes, the mind will exploit any such ambiguity to distort its view into a picture more pleasing to itself. Many good experimental practices are designed to assist with just this problem. Some scientific norms serve to diminish the amount of cognitive wiggle room in the first place, such as by operationalizing key variables or using instruments (like pH meters!) to reduce ambiguity. Other norms, like deploying double-blind procedures, steer us clear of bias by not letting the mind know which way it should want to twist what it sees. It seems that one element of future philosophical progress may be for philosophers to learn similarly how to avoid letting their minds play tricks on them. I titled this last section with the question: what can negative x-phi do for us that we cannot do for ourselves? I close with the answer: it can help us philosophers to get out of our own way.[16]

NOTES

1 This characterization is broadly shared by both friends and opponents of the method. See, for example, (Bealer 1998); (Pust 2000); (Weinberg et al. 2001); (Nagel 2012).

2 See, for example, (Talbot 2013).

3 One caveat: the term 'positive programme' has typically been taken to include also the kind of explicitly empirical philosophical investigations I briefly mentioned and set aside earlier.

4 See, for example, (Knobe 2016) and (Boyd and Nagel 2014) for examples of such mischaracterization; and (Swain et al. 2008) and (Weinberg 2007) for such disavowals.

5 (Machery 2011) is committed to one for a subset of HPI verdicts, but this problem afflicts even his more targeted attempt to raise concerns framed in terms of reliability.

6 The 'substantial' is a simply a hedge to keep various funny sorts of cases from making trouble here, like, what if I can only follow my proofs because I have had high-tech ophthalmological surgery, would that make my logic non-armchair? In short: no.

7 See (Sunstein 2005) for examples of problematic intuitive insensitivity in the moral domain.

8 For example, whether an event being evaluated is described as happening 'in a few days' or 'in a few years' from the current time of the evaluator.

9 But see (Machery 2012); (Nado 2014); (Alexander 2016); and (Buckwalter forthcoming).

10 The response in (Bengson 2013) is particularly worthy of attention, though see (Alexander and Weinberg 2014).

11 For example, (Sosa 2007); (Williamson 2007); (Horne and Livengood 2015).

12 http://www.ecy.wa.gov/programs/wq/plants/management/joysmanual/4ph.html. See also, for example, http://en.wikipedia.org/wiki/PH_indicator

13 See also Gerken (ms) for similar arguments about how the evidence for stakes effects on knowledge attribution is insufficiently robust to merit our crediting it as tracking a real aspect of knowledge.

14 Nichols , S., N. Pinillos, and R. Mallon 2016, p. 160

15 J. Alexander, D. Betz, C. Gonnerman, and J. Waterman (in prep.) 'Framing how we think about disagreement'.

16 Thanks especially to Joshua Alexander and anonymous referees from the publisher for many useful comments on earlier drafts.

Part III

Between Analysis and the Continent

10 Life-changing Metaphysics

Rational Anthropology and its Kantian Methodology

The field of philosophy ... can be brought down to the following questions:

1. *What can I know?*
2. *What ought I to do?*
3. *What may I hope?*
4. *What is the human being?*

... The last [question] is the most necessary but also the hardest.

(Kant *JL* 9: 25)[1]

Enlightenment is the human being's emergence from his own self-incurred immaturity. Immaturity is the inability to make use of one's own understanding without direction from another. This immaturity is *self-incurred* when its cause lies not in lack of understanding but in lack of resolution and courage to use it without direction from another. *Sapere aude!* Have the courage to use your *own* understanding! is thus the motto of Enlightenment.

(Kant *WE* 8: 35)

[T]wo things fill the mind with ever new and increasing admiration and reverence (*Ehrfurcht*), the more often and more steadily one reflects on them: *the starry heavens above me and the moral law within me.* I do not need to search for them and merely conjecture them as though they were veiled in obscurity or in the transcendent region beyond my horizon; I see them before me and connect them immediately with the consciousness of my existence.

(Kant *CPrR* 5: 161–2)

Here there is no place that does not see you. You must change your life.

(Rilke)[2]

I. INTRODUCTION

I think that authentic philosophy is what I call *rational anthropology*. Rational anthropology, in turn, is a philosophically *liberationist* – that is, an ethically, religiously, and politically *radical* re-working of Kant's Critical theoretical and practical philosophy in a contemporary context.

The Kantian methodology of rational anthropology contains six basic theses:

(i) that there is *no deep difference* between philosophy and the history of philosophy;

(ii) that there is a fundamental distinction between (a) *works of philosophy*, and (b) philosophical *theories*, such that the category of philosophical works is essentially wider and more inclusive than the category of philosophical theories – and more generally, that philosophical theorizing is only one way of creating and presenting authentic philosophy;

(iii) that theories in *real metaphysics* are possible, by reverse-engineering theories of manifest reality from phenomenologically self-evident insights about the primitive fact of purposive, living, essentially embodied, conscious, intentional, caring, rational, and moral human experience;

(iv) that real metaphysical theoretical explanation is a form of philosophical *abduction*, that is, 'inference to the best explanation', that I call *transcendental explanation*;

(v) that the primary aim of authentic philosophy is *to change one's own life*, with a further, ultimate aim of *changing the world* through free, existentially authentic, morally principled action, hence all philosophy is liberationist, with radical ethical, religious, and political aims, or what I call, collectively, *radical enlightenment*; and finally

(vi) that what I call *transcendental idealism for sensibility*, when fused with a Kantian aesthetics of the beautiful and sublime in external nature and a Kantian self-evident phenomenology of 'reverence' (*Ehrfurcht*) for external nature and human nature, jointly provide a transcendental explanation for radical enlightenment.

In sections 3–7, I will briefly unpack and defend the six basic theses of rational anthropology. But before I do that, I want to contrast its philosophical methodology with other contemporary alternatives.

2. RATIONAL ANTHROPOLOGY VS. ANALYTIC METAPHYSICS, THE STANDARD PICTURE, AND SCIENTIFIC NATURALISM

Rational anthropology is committed to what I call *real, human-faced*, or *anthropocentric metaphysics*. Real metaphysics in this sense starts with the primitive, irreducible fact of purposive, living, essentially embodied, conscious, intentional, caring, rational, and moral human experience, and then reverse-engineers its basic metaphysical theses and explanations in order to conform strictly to all and only what is *phenomenologically self-evident* in human experience.

Real metaphysics therefore rejects the idea of any theoretically fully meaningful, non-paradoxical ontic commitment or cognitive access to non-apparent, non-manifest, 'really real' entities that are constituted by intrinsic non-relational properties, that is, to 'noumena' or 'things-in-themselves' (see Hanna 2016a). Such entities are logically, conceptually, or 'weakly metaphysically' possible, but strictly unknowable by minded animals like us, both as to their nature, and as to their actual existence or non-existence. In this sense, real metaphysics is *methodologically* eliminativist about noumena. Therefore, real metaphysics rejects all *noumenal realist metaphysics*, including contemporary *Analytic metaphysics*.[3]

In the first half of the twentieth century, the new and revolutionary anti-(neo)Kantian, anti-(neo)Hegelian philosophical programmes were Gottlob Frege's and Bertrand Russell's *logicism*, G. E. Moore's *Platonic atomism*, and the 'linguistic turn' initiated by Wittgenstein's *Tractatus*, which yielded The Vienna Circle's *logical empiricism*, and finally its nemesis, W. V. O. Quine's critique of the analytic-synthetic distinction (see Hanna 2001). Logical empiricism also produced a domestic reaction, *ordinary language philosophy*. Powered by the work of H. P. Grice and Peter Strawson, ordinary language philosophy became *conceptual analysis*. In turn, Strawson created a new 'connective', that is, holistic, version of conceptual analysis, that also constituted a 'descriptive metaphysics' (see Strawson 1959; 1992). Strawson's connective conceptual analysis gradually fused with John Rawls' holistic method of 'reflective equilibrium' and Noam Chomsky's psycholinguistic appeals to intuitions-as-evidence, and ultimately became the current *Standard Picture* of mainstream analytic philosophical methodology (see, e.g., Jackson 1998).

Coexisting in mainstream contemporary philosophy alongside the Standard Picture, is also the classical Lockean idea that philosophy should be an 'underlabourer' for the natural sciences, especially as this idea was developed in the second half of the twentieth century by Quine and Wilfrid Sellars, as the reductive or eliminativist, physicalist, and scientistic doctrine of *scientific naturalism*, and again in the early twenty-first century in even more sophisticated versions, as 'experimental philosophy', a.k.a. 'X-Phi', and the doctrine of *second philosophy* (see, e.g., Quine 1969; Sellars 1963; Maddy 2007).

From the standpoint of rational anthropology and its real metaphysics, what is fundamentally wrong with the Standard Picture is its intellectualist, coherentist reliance on networks of potentially empty, non-substantive *concepts* (see also Unger 2014), and above all, its avoidance of the sensible, essentially non-conceptual side of human experience and human cognition, which alone connects it directly to what is manifestly real (see Hanna 2015a: esp. Chs 1–3).

Correspondingly, what is wrong with scientific naturalism/X-Phi/ second philosophy is its reduction or elimination of the primitive, irreducible fact of human experience (see Hanna and Maiese 2009).

Rational anthropology and its Kantian methodology are all about *the rational human condition*, and not all about noumenal entities, coherent networks of concepts, or fundamentally physical, essentially non-mental, facts.

3. PHILOSOPHY AND ITS HISTORY: NO DEEP DIFFERENCE

In freely going back and forth between Kant's philosophy and contemporary philosophy, I am applying the following strong metaphilosophical principle that I call *The No-Deep-Difference Thesis*:

There is no fundamental difference in philosophical content between the history of philosophy and contemporary philosophy.

In other words, in doing contemporary philosophy one is thereby directly engaging with the history of philosophy, and in doing the history of philosophy one is thereby directly engaging with contemporary philosophy. And in authentic philosophy, there is no serious distinction to be drawn between the two.

What I mean by The No-Deep-Difference Thesis is that every authentic philosophical work is a logically governed attempt to say something comprehensive, illuminating, and necessarily (or at least universally) true about the rational human condition and our deepest values, including our relationships to each other and to the larger natural and abstract worlds that surround us, and that in order to convey this basic content it does not matter at all *when* the work was created or *when* the work is interpreted.

If I am right about this thesis, then it cuts three ways: *first*, it means that everything in the history of philosophy also belongs substantively to contemporary philosophy; *second*, it means that everything in contemporary philosophy also belongs substantively to the history of philosophy; and *third*, it means that Quine was completely wrong when he (reportedly – there seems to be no published source for this) wickedly and wittily said that there are two kinds of philosophers: those who are interested in the history of philosophy, and those who are interested in philosophy. In fact, there is really only one kind of authentic philosopher, and whether s/he likes it or not, s/he should be deeply interested in the history of philosophy.

The sub-discipline called 'History of Philosophy' is philosophy, as philosophical as it gets, and all philosophy is also History of Philosophy, as historical as it gets. Those who on the contrary are Deep Differentists must hold that History of Philosophy is at best an enterprise in historical scholarship with a superficial philosophical inflection, but *not* philosophy as such, and that philosophy in effect always begins anew, from argumentative Ground Zero, with every new philosophical work that is created. This *metaphilosophical occasionalism* seems to me not only very implausible as a way of thinking about the relation between philosophy and its own history, but also apt to trivialize and undermine the very practice of authentic philosophy itself.

4. WORKS OF PHILOSOPHY VS. PHILOSOPHICAL THEORIES: PRESENTATIONAL HYLOMORPHISM AND POLYMORPHISM

In the *Critique of the Power of Judgment*, Kant says that there are '**aesthetic idea**[s]', by which he means:

[a] representation of the imagination that occasions much thinking though without it being possible for any determinate thought, i.e., **concept**, to be adequate to it, which, consequently, no language fully attains or can make intelligible ..., [and] [o]ne readily sees that it is the counterpart (pendant) of an idea of reason, which is, conversely, a concept to which no intuition (representation of the imagination) can be adequate.

(Kant *CPJ* 5: 314)

In other words, an aesthetic idea is a non-empirical, metaphysical representation, like an 'idea of pure reason', but also *non*-discursive and *non*-conceptual, hence linguistically *inexpressible* by means of concepts, propositions, or Fregean 'thoughts', precisely to the extent that it is a product of human sensible imagination. Kant himself does not make this point, but I think that the doctrine of aesthetic ideas has profound meta-philosophical implications: *philosophy need not necessarily be theoretically expressed*. Correspondingly, as I mentioned above, I think that there is a fundamental distinction between (i) works of philosophy and (ii) philosophical theories, such that the category of 'philosophical works' is essentially wider and more inclusive than the category of philosophical theories – and more generally, philosophical theorizing is only one way of creating and presenting philosophy, as important as it is.

The aim of philosophical theories, according to rational anthropology, is to provide philosophical explanations that lead to essential, synoptic insights about the rational human condition, guided by the norms of propositional truth and logical consistency, by means of conceptual construction and conceptual reasoning. A similarly open-minded conception of philosophical theorizing, in the tradition of connective conceptual analysis, was developed by Robert Nozick in his influential book, *Philosophical Explanations* (1981). But I think that Nozick's conception is still too much in the grip of the deeply wrongheaded, scientistic idea that all philosophy *must* be modelled on natural science, mathematics, or logic.

According to rational anthropology, the aim of philosophical works, *as such*, is to present insights about the rational human condition and the larger world around us, with synoptic scope, and *a priori*/necessary character, tracking categorical normativity and our highest values, with the ultimate goal of radical enlightenment. But this can be achieved even without concepts, propositions, arguments, or theories, in an essentially non-conceptual way, by presenting imagery, pictures, structures, and so on, that have strictly universal and strongly modal implications, and categorically normative force. These essentially non-conceptual insights could *also* be called 'truths', if we use the term 'truth' sufficiently broadly – as in 'the truth shall set you free'. My basic point is that philosophy should be as much aimed at being *inspiring and visionary*, as it is at being *argumentative and explanatory*.

Pivoting on that basic point, here is a proposal for five disjunctively necessary, individually minimally sufficient, and collectively fully sufficient criteria for something *W* – where *W* is a 'work', any intentional human product, whether an object (material or intentional), or performance – to count as a 'work of philosophy' –

(i) *W* provides a philosophical theory or a visionary worldview (or both);

(ii) *W* negatively or positively engages with earlier or contemporary philosophical ideas;

(iii) *W* expresses and follows a philosophical method;

(iv) *W* contains an explicit or implicit 'philosophy of philosophy', a metaphilosophy;

(v) *W* deals with some topic or topics germane to the rational human condition, within a maximally broad range of issues, encompassing epistemology, metaphysics, ethics, history, culture, society, politics, aesthetics, art, formal and natural science, religion, and so-on.[4]

Given how I defined the term 'work', by my use of the term 'works' in the phrase 'works of philosophy', I mean something as broad as its use in 'works of art'. So there is no assumption or presupposition whatsoever here that works of philosophy must be *written or spoken texts*, although obviously many or most works of philosophy have been and are written or spoken texts. Correspondingly, I want to put forward two extremely important metaphilosophical theses of rational anthropology:

(i) the thesis of *presentational hylomorphism* in works of philosophy (PHWP), and
(ii) the thesis of *presentational polymorphism* in works of philosophy (PPWP).

PHWP says:

There is an essential connection, and in particular, an essential *complementarity*, between the presentational form (*morphê*) of philosophical works and their philosophical content (*hyle*).

'Content' here is *cognitive-semantic content*, but this content can be either (i) conceptual, or (ii) essentially non-conceptual (see Unger 2014), and also it can be either (iii) theoretical content, or (iv) non-theoretical content, including, aesthetic/artistic, affective/ emotive, pragmatic, moral, political, or religious content. Also, (i) and (ii) cross-cut with (iii) and (iv). Hence there can be conceptual content that is either theoretical or non-theoretical, and there can be essentially non-conceptual content that is either theoretical or non-theoretical.

The *first* thing that PHWP implies, is the intimate connection between truly creative, ground-breaking works of philosophy, and truly creative, original forms of literary and spoken philosophical expression. Thus Socrates created philosophical works entirely by conversation; Plato did it by writing dialogues; Aristotle did it by presenting (it seems) nothing but lectures; Descartes wrote meditations; Locke and Hume wrote treatises; Kant wrote the Critiques; Kierkegaard wrote strange pseudonymous books; Nietzsche wrote poetry and aphorisms; Wittgenstein wrote the *Tractatus* and the *Philosophical Investigations*, both of them completely original, completely different, and equally uncategorizable, and so on.

The *second* thing that PHWP implies is that since all works of written and spoken philosophy are essentially connected to their literary style and expressive vehicles, then it is a mistake to impose a needlessly restrictive stylistic and expressive straight-jacket on works of philosophy, for example, the standard professional 'journal essay', '200+ page book', and 'philosophy talk'.

And a *third* thing that PHWP implies is that since the standard view of philosophical content in the Analytic tradition – whether as logical analysis, linguistic analysis, conceptual analysis, Analytic metaphysics, or scientific naturalism – is that the content of philosophy is exclusively conceptual and theoretical, then recognizing the essential non-conceptuality and non-theoreticality of philosophical content, completely opens up the way we should be thinking about works of philosophy, in three ways.

First, all written and spoken philosophy is in fact shot through with imagery, poetry, rhetorical devices, and speech-acts of various kinds. *Second*, philosophy need not necessarily be presented (exclusively) in written or spoken form. There could be works of philosophy that are cinematic, diagrammed or drawn, painted, photographed, musical (instrumental or voiced), sculpted, performed like dances or plays, and so on, and so on, and perhaps above all, mixed works combining written or spoken forms of presentation and one or more non-linguistic forms or vehicles. *Third*, if philosophical content is as apt to be essentially non-conceptual or non-theoretical as it is to be conceptual or theoretical, then there are vast realms of philosophical meaning that very few philosophers, even the most brilliant and great ones, have ever even attempted to explore.

Therefore, in full view of PHWP, we also have PPWP:

Philosophy can be expressed in any presentational format whatsoever, provided it satisfies PHWP.

From the standpoint of rational anthropology, and looking towards the philosophy of the future, this is a truly exciting thesis.

5. RATIONAL ANTHROPOLOGY AND REAL METAPHYSICS

Kant discovered the metaphysics of *transcendental idealism* between the publication of his seminal proto-Critical essay of

1768, 'Concerning the Ground of the Ultimate Differentiation of Directions in Space', and 1772. Indeed, the philosophical implications of the 'Directions in Space' essay almost certainly triggered the major proto-Critical philosophical breakthrough that Kant famously reports when he says in one of the *Reflexionen* that 'the year '69 gave me great light' (*R* 5037, 18: 69). More precisely, what Kant had discovered between 1768 and 1772 is what I have called *transcendental idealism for sensibility* (see also Hanna 2016b). In 1772, Kant told Marcus Herz that if the human mind conformed to the world, whether phenomenal or noumenal, then *a priori* knowledge would be impossible (*PC* 10, 130–1), but by 1770, Kant already also held that *a priori* knowledge of the phenomenal world is actual and therefore really possible in mathematics, hence the phenomenal world must conform to the non-empirical sensible structure of the human mind, and more specifically must conform to our *a priori* representations of space and time, since that is what makes mathematics really possible (*ID* 2: 398–406).

So transcendental idealism for sensibility says that the apparent or phenomenal world fundamentally conforms to the essentially non-conceptual *a priori* forms of human sensibility, our representations of space and time. Kant worked out explicit proofs for transcendental idealism for sensibility in the Inaugural Dissertation and again in the Transcendental Aesthetic in the first *Critique*. The simplest version of the proof, provided in the Transcendental Aesthetic, goes like this:

(1)   Space and time are either (i) things in themselves, (ii) properties of/relations between things in themselves, or (iii) transcendentally ideal.

(2)   If space and time were either things in themselves or properties of/relations between things in themselves, then *a priori* mathematical knowledge would be impossible.

(3)   But mathematical knowledge is actual, via our pure intuitions of space and time, and therefore really possible.

(4)   Therefore, space and time are transcendentally ideal.

(Kant CPR A 23/B37–8, A38–41/B55–8)

In a nutshell, then, Kant's thesis of transcendental idealism says that the basic structure of the apparent or phenomenal world necessarily conforms to the pure or non-empirical (hence *a priori*) structure of human cognition, and not the converse (*CPR* B xvi–xviii). Or in other words, Kant is saying that the phenomenal world fundamentally conforms to the *a priori* structure of the human mind, and it is also *not* the case that the human mind fundamentally conforms to the phenomenal world, or indeed to any non-apparent or *noumenal* world. So if Kant is correct, then he is saying that the world in which we live, move, and have our being (by which I mean the phenomenal natural and social world of our ordinary human existence) is fundamentally dependent on *our* minded nature, and not the converse. If transcendental idealism is true, then we cannot be inherently alienated from the world we are trying to know, as global epistemic sceptics claim, and human knowledge – not only *a priori* knowledge, but also *a posteriori* knowledge – is therefore really possible (Hanna 2015a: esp. Chs 3 and 6–8).

According to rational anthropology and Kant alike, *real*, or transcendental idealist, metaphysics must be evidentially grounded on human experience. Or otherwise put, real metaphysics reverse-engineers its basic metaphysical theses and explanations in order to conform strictly to all and only what is *phenomenologically self-evident* in human experience. By 'phenomenologically self-evident' I mean this:

A claim C is phenomenologically self-evident for a rational human subject S if and only if (i) S's belief in C relies on directly given conscious or self-conscious manifest evidence about human experience, and (ii) C's denial is either logically or conceptually self-contradictory (i.e., a Kantian analytic self-contradiction), really metaphysically impossible (i.e., it is a Kantian synthetic a priori impossibility), or pragmatically self-stultifying for S (i.e., it is what Kant calls 'a contradiction in willing' in the *Groundwork*).

This leads directly to what I call *the criterion of phenomenological adequacy for metaphysical theories*:

A metaphysical theory is phenomenologically adequate if and only if it is evidentially grounded on all and only phenomenologically self-evident theses.

By this criterion, contemporary Analytic metaphysics is clearly phenomenologically *inadequate*, so is classical noumenal metaphysics more generally, and so is scientific naturalism, whereas by sharp contrast, Kant's metaphysics of transcendental idealism is, arguably, fully phenomenologically adequate.

In the B Preface to first *Critique*, Kant notes that radically unlike seventeenth- and eighteenth-century *meta*physics, seventeenth- and eighteenth-century *physics* entered the 'highway of science' (*Heeresweg der Wissenschaft*) by virtue of a 'sudden revolution in the way of thought' (Kant *CPR* Bxii). This thought-revolution consisted in shifting from the empiricist idea that our rational human *a priori* knowledge of necessary or essential properties of objects is somehow derived by Baconian induction from individual or collective samples, to the idea that *a priori* knowledge is generated by *self-knowledge* of the spontaneous cognitive activity of human theoretical reason in non-empirically introducing formal features into its mental representations of objects. With that basic thought in place, Kant's philosophy of physics smoothly transitions into his real metaphysics. Here is his basic line of argument.

Manifest material or physical nature is rationally comprehensible via natural scientific investigation, and thereby knowable *a posteriori*, only to the extent that it is governed according to principles or laws that have the epistemic, modal, non-sensory, purposive, and normative properties of necessary *a priori* truths, but are nevertheless also *empirical*, in that these principles and laws bind together apparent, phenomenal, or manifest material or physical objects and states-of-affairs that are themselves actual-world bound, and contingent. Indeed, it is precisely the principle-governedness or causal-law-governedness of manifest actual-world bound, contingent material or physical nature that makes it *objective*, and therefore a proper subject for the authentic objective *a priori* science of physics. So, odd as it might at first seem, even an *empirical* science like physics is an authentic science only and precisely to the extent that it has a *non-empirical* foundation that of course includes both logic and mathematics, but also extends *beyond* the purely logico-mathematical part of its foundation into the necessary and objectual *a priori* law-governed *causal* connections between actual-world bound, contingent manifest material things and states-of-affairs.

Now the causal natures of these manifest material things and states-of-affairs are knowable *a posteriori* in all their specificity by means of experimental investigations that involve not only Baconian (i.e., simple colligative, descriptive, and generalizing) induction but also another method only partially anticipated by Bacon, namely what I will call *Kantian abduction*, or Kantian *inference-to-the-best-explanation*. The theory of Kantian abduction is developed by Kant during both his Critical period and also his post-Critical period, in his scattered and all-too-brief remarks on 'the method of those who study nature' (*CPR* Bxviii–Bxix n.), 'the empirical affinity of the manifold' (*CPR* A113–14), 'empirical laws' or 'particular laws' (*CPR* A127–8 and B163–5; *Prol* 4: 318–22), and also under the rubrics of what he calls the 'regulative use of the ideas of pure reason', the 'hypothetical use of reason' and 'reflective judgment' (*CPR* A642–68/B670–96; *CPJ* 20: 211–17, 5: 179–81).

In any case Kantian abduction, as exemplified in the B Preface by Galileo, Torricelli, and Stahl, is not itself *merely* an empirical or *a posteriori* method, but in fact systematically closes the epistemic and semantic gap between empirical/*a posteriori* generalizations and non-empirical/*a priori* principles and causal natural laws. It does *not* do so, however, by what classical Logical Empiricist philosophy of science calls *the hypothetico-deductive method*, according to which general propositions about the material or physical world, originally derived by induction, are laid down, more or less arbitrarily, like extra axioms added to first-order classical logic, and then particular propositions about empirical consequences deduced from these axioms, which in turn are tested by observations. For such a procedure would be unable to distinguish between, on the one hand, inductive hypotheses that are *noumenal*, and therefore humanly unknowable and anthropocentrically meaningless, and, on the other hand, humanly knowable *empirically meaningful* hypotheses that are specifically grounded on the objectively valid and objectively real metaphysics of rational human experience, transcendental idealism.

By sharp contrast to the hypothetico-deductive method, then, Kantian abduction does *not* operate by induction + analytic stipulation + deduction + observation, but instead operates by *synthetic a priori 'counterfactual', or subjunctive conditional, reasoning*. Thus, according to the Kantian real modal semantics of counterfactual conditionals that I am using, a conditional proposition of the form,

$P \mathbin{\square\!\!\rightarrow} Q$

which in English says 'If if P *were* the case, then Q *would be* the case', and is therefore a counterfactual or subjunctive conditional proposition, is true if and only if:

Given the smallest restricted class of logically possible worlds, each member of which has the same basic transcendental structure as the apparent or manifest actual natural world, that is, *the class of humanly experienceable worlds*, and is also consistent with the truth of P, then, in every member of this class, the truth of P synthetically necessitates the truth of Q.

Granting this truth-definition, then according to Kantian abduction, natural science advances inferentially from:

(i) the complete set of schematized synthetic *a priori* Principles of the Pure Understanding, which, in turn, collectively specify the basic transcendental structure of the apparent or manifest actual natural world, and thereby determine the smallest restricted class of logically possible worlds, that is, *the class of humanly experienceable worlds*, each member of which has the same basic transcendental structure as the manifest actual natural world, and is also consistent with the truth of some general empirical natural causal law proposition P,

together with

(ii) P, which is partially derived by induction, but which also specifically reflects the creative and imaginative insight (a.k.a. the 'genius') of the individual natural scientist who formulates P, in whom '[genius] gives the rule to **nature**' (*CPJ* 5: 308), and which is postulated as the hypothetical antecedent of a subjunctive conditional of the form,

If, given the schematized Principles of Pure Understanding, P *were* true in the experienceable worlds W_1, W_2, W_3.... W_n,

to

(iii) a synthetically *a priori* entailed proposition Q in all those experienceable worlds, as the consequent of that same subjunctive conditional of the form,

... then Q *would be* true in the experienceable worlds W1, W2, W3 ... Wn,

then

(iv)   compares and contrasts that synthetic *a priori* counterfactual or subjunctive conditional implication Q with what is supplied by direct observational evidence in the actual world,

and then

(v)   also compares and contrasts the physical explanation provided by the counterfactual or subjunctive conditional P $\Box \to$ Q with all the other relevant possible sufficiently good physical explanations of the same actual apparent, phenomenal, or manifest natural facts, thus ruling out the worry that the explanation provided by P $\Box \to$ Q is only 'the best of a bad lot', and not the best *overall* explanation,

and then

(vi)   asserts the general proposition P as the true synthetic *a priori* representation of a natural causal law governing dynamic interactions and processes in the apparent or manifest actual natural world, by Kantian inference-to-the-best-explanation (see also Douven 2011; Lipton 1991).

Correspondingly, much later in the first *Critique*, we learn that philosophical reasoning, and more specifically metaphysical reasoning, is (i) inherently conceptual and *a priori*, like logic, but at the same time, (ii) synthetic *a priori*, objective, and objectively valid, like mathematics and physics, yet also (iii) non-constructive, unlike mathematics, and also (iv) not the direct result of *empirical* reasoning constrained by abduction or inference-to-the-best-explanation, unlike natural science or physics, nevertheless also at the same time (v) *non-empirically* abductive, and also necessarily *indirectly* related to abductive empirical reasoning in natural science, via what Kant calls *transcendental deduction* (*CPR* Axvi–xvii, A84–92/B116–24) and *transcendental proof* (*CPR* A782–94/B810–22).

In this way, Kant thinks that there is a deep analogy between the kind of *experimental* reasoning that natural scientists like Galileo, Torricelli, and Stahl engage in, and his own *abductive counterfactual* approach to philosophical reasoning via transcendental idealism.

But Kant's analogical appeal to the experimental reasoning of Galileo, Torricelli, and Stahl isolates only the *first* phase of a Kantian abduction, which adds a hypothetical antecedent general empirical natural causal law proposition P – which is derived by induction, together with the creative and imaginative insight of some individual natural scientist, in whom '[genius] gives the rule to **nature**' (*CPJ* 5: 308) – to the complete set of schematized synthetic *a priori* Principles of the Pure Understanding. These Principles, in turn, collectively specify the basic transcendental structure of the apparent, phenomenal, or manifest actual natural world, and thereby determine the smallest restricted class of logically possible worlds, that is, the class of experienceable worlds, each member of which has the same basic transcendental structure as the manifest actual natural world, and is also consistent with the truth of P. Then Kantian abduction completes its first stage by advancing, via the subjunctive synthetic *a priori* conditional $P \mathbin{\square\!\!\rightarrow} Q$, to the truth of Q. By contrast to this first phase of reasoning, however, the *experimental* phase in Kantian abduction isolates the *second* phase of reasoning, in which the truth of Q is tested against the manifest facts of the natural world. In the *third* phase of a Kantian abduction, it is inferred that, amongst all the good possible *natural scientific or physical* explanations of Q, P yields the best physical explanation of Q. And then in the fourth and final phase of a Kantian abduction, it is inferred that, amongst all the good possible *meta*physical explanations of Q, the complete set of schematized synthetic *a priori* Principles of the Pure Understanding, together with P, together with transcendental idealism, yields the best possible metaphysical explanation of Q, namely *the transcendental explanation*, or 'transcendental proof', of Q. Furthermore, transcendental idealism, by being a real metaphysics of *human experience*, satisfies the phenomenological criterion of adequacy for metaphysical theories. So every Kantian *natural scientific abduction, via counterfactuals* is also, at least potentially, the basis of a Kantian *real metaphysical abduction, via transcendental proof* (*CPR* Bxii n.).

6. RATIONAL ANTHROPOLOGY AND RADICAL ENLIGHTENMENT

In the eleventh of his *Theses on Feuerbach*, Marx wrote that 'philosophers have only *interpreted* the world in different ways; the point is to *change* it'. I completely agree with him that the ultimate aim of philosophy is to change the world, not merely interpret it. So Marx and I are both *philosophical liberationists*: that is, we both believe that philosophy should have radical political implications. But I also sharply disagree with him, insofar as I think that the primary aim of philosophy, now understood as rational anthropology, and its practices of synoptic reflection, writing, teaching, and public conversation, is *to change our lives*. Then, and only then, can we act upon the world in the *right* way.

Ironically, although perhaps altogether understandably, in view of the very real risks of political and religious dissent and unorthodoxy in eighteenth-century Europe, Kant's own political theory, as formulated in the *Metaphysics of Morals*, part 1, the *Rechtslehre* is sharply out of step with the central ideas of his own moral philosophy (see Hanna 2016c). The *Rechtslehre*, in fact, presents a fairly run-of-the-mill and explicitly anti-revolutionary, hence politically mainstream and safe, version of classical individualist liberalism, in the social-contract tradition of Hobbes, Locke, Grotius, and Rousseau, plus constitutional monarchy and/or parliamentarianism, plus a peace-securing internationalism.

But emphatically on the contrary, I think that a highly original, politically radical, and if not revolutionary, then at least robustly State-resistant, State-subversive, and even outright civilly disobedient *cosmopolitan*, *existentialist* version of *anarchism* that I call *existential Kantian cosmopolitan anarchism* (see Hanna and Chapman 2016) very naturally flows from Kantian ethics (see Hanna 2015b), Kantian philosophy of religion, and Kantian political anthropology. Roughly, the idea is that if we take Kant's famous injunction *to have the moral courage to use your own understanding*, and apply this morally courageous act not merely to 'the public use of reason' (that is, to intellectual activity, writing, and speech or self-expression in the broad sense of 'free speech'), but also to our individual choices, our individual agency, our shared social life, and especially to what Kant quite misleadingly calls 'the private use of reason' (that is, to our social lives as functional role-players, or functionaries, within the State, including, e.g., citizenship or public office), then the result is existential Kantian cosmopolitan anarchism. Then and only then, in my opinion, can we understand the last sentence of 'What is Enlightenment?' as it truly ought to be understood, namely as formulating a vision of Kantian 'maximalist' or *radical* enlightenment (Fleischacker 2013: 7):

When nature has unwrapped, from under this hard shell [of the 'crooked timber of humanity' (*IUH* 8: 23)], the seed for which she cares most tenderly, namely the propensity and calling to *think* freely, the latter gradually works back upon the mentality of the people (which thereby gradually becomes capable of *freedom* in acting) and eventually even upon the principles of *government*, which finds it profitable to itself to treat the human being, *who is now more than a machine*, in keeping with his dignity.

(*WE* 8: 41–2)

To be sure, neither the term 'existentialism' nor the term 'anarchism'[5] existed until the nineteenth and twentieth centuries. But insofar as existentialism was substantially anticipated by certain lines of thought in Pascal's seventeenth century writings (see Clarke 2012: esp. §6), and insofar as the very idea of cosmopolitanism was already a well-established notion in political philosophy by the time Kant came to write about it (see Kleingeld and Brown 2013: esp. §1), and insofar as philosophical and political anarchism, as a radical political thesis and doctrine, was substantially anticipated by certain lines of thought in Rousseau's and William Godwin's eighteenth century writings (see Bertram 2012: esp. §3.1; and Philp 2013: esp. §3), it is clear that Kant belongs to an emergent existential cosmopolitan anarchist tradition in seventeenth- and eighteenth-century philosophy. In any case, insofar as it is at once existentialist, Kantian, cosmopolitan, and philosophically and politically anarchist, rational anthropology in its life-changing aspect constitutes a fundamental project in Kantian radical enlightenment.

I fully realize that even when it has been helpfully reduced to a philosophical label, 'existential Kantian cosmopolitan anarchism' is still rather a mouthful. So what, more precisely, do I mean by it?

1. By *existential* (see also, e.g., Crowell 2012),[6] I mean the primitive motivational, or 'internalist', normative ground of the

philosophical and political doctrine I want to defend, which is the fundamental, innate need we have for a wholehearted, freely-willed life *not essentially based* on egoistic, hedonistic, or consequentialist (e.g., utilitarian) interests, a.k.a. *the desire for self-transcendence*, while at the same time fully assuming the natural presence – a.k.a. the *facticity* – of all such instrumental interests in our 'human, all too human' lives. In a word, the existential ideal of a rational human wholehearted autonomous life is the ideal of *authenticity*.

2. By *Kantian*, I mean the primitive objective, or 'externalist', normative ground of the philosophical and political doctrine I want to defend, which is the recognition that the fundamental, innate need we have for a wholehearted, freely willed, non-egoistic, non-hedonistic, non-consequentialist life, which I call *the desire for self-transcendence*, can be sufficiently rationally justified only in so far as it is also a life of *principled authenticity*, by which I mean *principled wholehearted autonomy*, or having *a good will* in Kant's sense, guided by respect for the dignity of all real persons,[7] under the Categorical Imperative.

3. By *cosmopolitan* (see also Kleingeld and Brown 2013: esp. §2), I mean that this philosophical and political doctrine recognizes States (e.g., nation-States) as actual brute past and contemporary facts, but also requires our choosing and acting in such a way that we reject in thought, and perhaps also reject and resist in words and/ or actions, any immoral commands, limitations, restrictions, and prejudices present in any contemporary States, especially including the one (or ones, in my case, Canada and the USA) we happen to be citizens or members of, and regard ourselves instead as citizens or members of a single moral world-community of real persons, The Real Realm of Ends.

4. Finally, by *anarchism* (see also Kropotkin 1910; Bookchin 1995), I mean that this philosophical thesis and political doctrine fully recognizes that there is no adequate rational justification for political authority, and correspondingly also no adequate rational justification for the existence of States or any other State-like institutions. Here is a very short version of the Kantian argument for philosophical anarchism:

Because there is no adequate rational justification, according to the set of basic Kantian moral principles, for an individual real person's, or any group

of real persons', immorally commanding other people and coercing them
to obey those commands as a duty, yet the very idea of political authority
entails that special groups of people within States or State-like institutions,
namely governments, have not only the power to coerce, but also the right
to command other people and to coerce them to obey those commands as a
duty, even when the commands and/or coercion are immoral, then it follows
that there is no adequate rational justification for political authority, States,
or any other State-like institutions – therefore, philosophical anarchism
is true.

Or in other and even fewer words:

Human *governments* have no moral right to do to other people what *real
human persons* have no moral right to do to other people, according to
the set of basic Kantian moral principles; yet *all* human governments
falsely claim this supposed moral right; hence philosophical anarchism
is true.

According to existential Kantian cosmopolitan anarchism, the
sole adequate rational justification for the continued existence of any
aspects or proper parts of *actual contemporary* States or other State-
like institutions, is that they fully satisfy the moral requirements
under 1., 2., and 3. Otherwise, resistance, subversion, or even outright
civil disobedience – strictly constrained, however, by using at most
minimal sufficiently effective, last resort, defensive, preventive, and
protective moral force – is at the very least permissible, and possibly
also required. In any case, we are morally obligated to *reject* and *exit*
the State and other State-like institutions, in order to create and
belong to a real-world cosmopolitan universal ethical community,
in a post-State world. That is existential Kantian cosmopolitan
political anarchism.

7. FROM (TRANSCENDENTAL) AESTHETICS TO RADICAL ENLIGHTENMENT

According to rational anthropology, Kantian transcendental
idealism for sensibility, when taken together with some central
claims of Kantian aesthetics and some self-evident Kantian
phenomenology, jointly provide a transcendental explanation
for radical enlightenment. The argument for this claim fuses the

Transcendental Aesthetic of the first *Critique* with a Kantian aesthetics of the beautiful and the sublime in external nature in the third *Critique* and a Kantian self-evident phenomenology of our experience of 'reverence' (*Ehrfurcht*) for external nature and human nature in the second *Critique*. In turn, the argument has four basic steps.

Step 1. Given the truth of transcendental idealism for sensibility, then we can take fully seriously the sensibility-grounded, essentially non-conceptual evidence provided by the aesthetic experience of the beautiful in nature outside us, as veridically tracking natural purposive form, without a purpose, in a way that is inherently *disinterested* and therefore *divorced from all possible self-interest* (*CPJ* 5: 204–11). In short, the experience of the beautiful shows us that beautiful nature outside us *cannot be and ought not to be regarded or treated purely instrumentally*, that is, merely as a means, or exploited.

Step 2. Given the truth of transcendental idealism for sensibility, and the experience of the beautiful in nature, then we can *also* take fully seriously the Romantic/natural-religious/natural-theological reverential experience of what Kant calls 'the mathematically sublime in nature', for example, 'the starry heavens above me'. Now since, according to Kant, via the human experience of the mathematically sublime in nature, external nature is thereby experienced as having a specific character and normative value that is expressible only as a *transcendently* infinite, *transfinite*, or *non-denumerably infinite*, quantity, it follows that external nature inherently cannot reduced to any denumerable quantity, no matter how great (*CPJ* 5: 244–60). Hence external nature, experienced as mathematically sublime, *cannot have a 'market price' and is experienced as beyond price, or priceless*, since all 'market prices', or exchangeable economic values (say, monetary values) 'related to general human interests and needs' (*GMM* 4: 434), are expressible only as denumerable (natural number, rational number) quantities, even infinite ones. Otherwise put, the specific character and normative value of external nature, experienced as mathematically sublime, inherently transcends any economic calculus.

Step 3. Steps 1 and 2 jointly entail *the proto-dignity of external nature*. External nature is not itself a real person, and therefore does not have dignity *per se*. Nevertheless, external nature, as beautiful and sublime, *inherently cannot* (without eco-disaster) and *inherently ought not* (without moral scandal) be merely exploited, merely bought or sold, or otherwise treated as a mere capitalist resource or commodity (a.k.a. 'commodified').

Step 4. *But human nature belongs to external nature.* Therefore, transcendental idealism for sensibility, plus the self-evident phenomenology of our reverential experience of beauty/ sublimity in external nature ('the starry heavens above me'), plus our equally reverential experience of respect for the autonomous dignity of human nature ('the moral law within me'), *transcendentally prove* that external nature is the metaphysical ground of all real human persons and their autonomous dignity.

8.CONCLUSION

In shorthand format, the Kantian philosophical methodology of rational anthropology consists of:

(i)   The No-Deep-Difference Thesis,
(ii) The Theses of Presentational Hylomorphism and Polymorphism for Works of Philosophy,
(iii) The Criterion of Phenomenological Adequacy for Metaphysical Theories,
(iv) transcendental idealism for sensibility and Kantian abduction,
(v)   Kantian radical enlightenment, and finally
(vi) the Kantian (transcendental) aesthetics of external nature and the self-evident phenomenology of our reverence for external nature and human nature.

The real metaphysics of transcendental idealism, plus the self-evident phenomenology of aesthetic and natural-reverential human experience, yields a life-changing radical politics. So rational anthropology is life-changing metaphysics.

Socrates said 'know thyself'. Rational anthropology says: 'know the world by knowing yourself; then change your life; and then change the world too'.

ABBREVIATIONS

CPJ	*Critique of the Power of Judgment.*
CPR	*Critique of Pure Reason.*
CPrR	*Critique of Practical Reason.*
GMM	*Groundwork of the Metaphysics of Morals.*
ID	'On the Form and Principles of the Sensible and Intelligible World (Inaugural Dissertation)'.
IUH	'Idea for a Universal History with a Cosmopolitan Aim'.
JL	'The Jäsche Logic'.
PC	*Immanuel Kant: Correspondence.*
Prol	*Prolegomena to Any Future Metaphysics.*
WE	'An Answer to the Question: "What is Enlightenment?"'

NOTES

1 For convenience, throughout this essay I cite Kant's works in parentheses. The citations include both an abbreviation of the English title and the corresponding volume and page numbers in the standard 'Akademie' edition of Kant's works: *Kants gesammelte Schriften*, edited by the Königlich Preussischen (now Deutschen) Akademie der Wissenschaften (Berlin: G. Reimer [now de Gruyter], 1902). For references to the first *Critique*, I follow the common practice of giving page numbers from the A (1781) and B (1787) German editions only. Because the Akademie edition contains only the B edition of the first *Critique*, I have also consulted the following German composite edition: *Kritik der reinen Vernunft*, ed. W. Weischedel, Immanuel Kant Werkausgabe III (Frankfurt: Suhrkamp, 1968). For references to Kant's *Reflexionen*, that is, entries in *Kants handschriftliche Nachlaß* – which I abbreviate as '*R*' – I give the entry number in addition to the Akademie volume and page numbers. The translations from the *Reflexionen* are my own. I generally follow the standard English translations of Kant's works, but have occasionally modified them where appropriate.
2 'Archaic Torso of Apollo', trans. S. Mitchell, lines 13–14.
3 The leading figures of Analytic metaphysics include David Lewis, David Chalmers, Kit Fine, Ted Sider, and Timothy Williamson; and some of its canonical texts are (Lewis 1986), (Sider 2011), (Chalmers 2012), and (Williamson 2013).

4 I'm extremely grateful to Otto Paans for proposing this basic list of criteria in e-mail discussion.

5 As opposed to 'anarchy', popularly meaning 'pandemonium, social-political chaos, and/or universal moral nihilism', which has been around since at least the mid-eighteenth century – including Kant's own use of 'anarchy' at *CPR* Aix, Percy Shelley's radical poem, *The Masque of Anarchy*, and so on.

6 For an extended response to the classical 'formalism', 'rigorism', and 'universalism' worries about Kantian ethics, see (Hanna 2015b: esp. Chs 1–2).

7 By 'real person', I mean *an essentially embodied person*, or a rational minded animal, as opposed to either disembodied persons (e.g., souls) or collective persons (e.g., business corporations). On essential embodiment, see, for example, (Hanna and Maiese 2009). And for a general theory of real personhood, see Hanna 2015c: Chs 6–7).

11 Collingwood's Idealist Metaontology

Between Therapy and Armchair Science

INTRODUCTION

In recent discussions the traditional conception of philosophy as an *a priori* armchair activity, and with it the view that philosophy has an autonomous domain of enquiry, has come under attack from two fronts. On the one hand naturalists and experimental philosophers have questioned the idea that philosophy can deliver ontological truths from the proverbial armchair.[1] On the other hand another attack has also gained more prominence: the claim that disputes in metaphysics are 'futile and interminable pseudo-theoretical arguments' because the disagreements on which they are premised are merely verbal.[2] This is a view which is commonly traced back to Carnap, who is often hailed as the champion of deflationary/ sceptical approaches towards ontology (Carnap 1950).

To illustrate what a merely verbal dispute is one may compare the following two cases. Consider on the one hand two persons disagreeing about whether something is a mug or a glass. If, on closer examination, one established that the first person used the term 'mug' to mean a ceramic drinking vessel whilst the other used the term to mean any drinking vessel with a handle, there would not seem to be anything substantive at stake in their disagreement. In spite of appearances to the contrary the disagreement is not ontological; it is not about the way things are but about what linguistic conventions to adopt. Such a disagreement is no more profound than that between an Englishman who says, this is an eggplant, and a Frenchman who rebuts, 'Ceci n'est pas une eggplant, c'est une aubergine' (see Hirsch 2011c and Manley 2009). Consider on the other hand the disagreement between two persons over whether a certain celestial body is a moon or a planet. Even if, on reflection, one established that the two persons have different linguistic conventions (one person has a moon-exclusive concept of a planet whilst the other person's concept of a planet includes both bodies which orbit around a star and bodies which orbit around another celestial body), the dispute would not, as a result of this discovery, be unmasked as *purely* verbal. For whether we call a celestial body which revolves around another one a planet or a moon is a matter of linguistic convention, but whether the Moon revolves around the sun or around Earth is not. Altering our linguistic conventions does not, after all, change the orbits of celestial bodies any more than naming something an aubergine or an eggplant determines whether it is a fruit or a berry.

For some philosophers ontological disputes are more like the planet/moon case than the mug/glass case because what is at stake is not mere linguistic codification. The participants in these debates are trying to determine what the nature of reality is like. Even if in ontological disputes, the matter must be decided *a priori* or from the proverbial armchair rather than empirically, there is something at stake between the disputants other than the adoption of certain linguistic conventions. Although metaphysical disputes are, in some crucial respects, unlike that between the persons with the moon-inclusive and moon-exclusive concept of a planet, the participants in ontological debates are not disagreeing merely about nomenclature; they are disagreeing about the nature of things.

For others ontological disputes are merely verbal and thus more like the mug/glass case rather than the planet/moon one. There really is nothing substantive at stake. If the participants could see past their linguistic conventions, the disputes would dissolve because they are ultimately very trivial linguistic disputes. It is arguably because of its therapeutic implications that the view that (at least some) philosophical disputes are verbal – and the philosophical disagreements on which they are based amount to much ado about nothing – has attracted attention. For if *all* philosophical disagreements were merely verbal, then it would seem to follow that there are no genuine philosophical problems and that philosophy lacks an autonomous domain of enquiry.[3] As a result, as Eklund has recently put it, the contemporary metaontological debate has focused on 'whether ontological questions, questions about what there is, are genuine questions deep enough to be worthy of philosophical attention, or whether rather some skeptical or deflationary view on ontology which takes ontological questions somehow to be not genuine or else somehow shallow is correct' (Eklund 2013: 229).

The proposal advanced here mobilizes some of the arguments which have been used to deflate ontological disputes in contemporary analytical metaphysics, *but* it reaches a rather different conclusion about the role and character of philosophical analysis; it argues that there are philosophical disagreements which are substantive even if they are *not* ontologically deep. The underlying assumption that this paper sets out to challenge is that if a philosophical dispute is not ontologically deep then it *must* be merely verbal and, accordingly, trivial. Conversely, the key assumption that this paper sets out to defend is that there are substantive disagreements which are not ontologically deep and that these substantive yet not ontologically deep disputes express the structure of philosophical problems.[4] This view is, if not explicitly stated, implicit in the work of R. G. Collingwood whose metaphilosophical position occupies an intermediate space between armchair ontology and therapeutic philosophy. Yet, one might ask: why is it necessary to carve out an intermediate space between therapy and armchair metaphysics? In the latter half of the twentieth century mainstream philosophy has witnessed a U-turn away from ordinary language philosophy and an ontological backlash against the linguistic turn which has resulted in the return of robust armchair metaphysics.[5] The reasons for the return of 'serious' metaphysics[6] to the philosophical mainstream are very complex, nonetheless it is perhaps fair to say that many philosophers have grown weary of the view, rightly or wrongly associated with Wittgenstein, that philosophy is a kind of illness of which they need to be cured (see Hutto 2003; 2009). Whether or not this is a mere caricature, this image of philosophy's task has stuck, and left many dissatisfied with the anti-intellectualism implicit in the suggestion that engaging in theoretical pursuits generates conceptual confusion rather than leading to greater clarity of thought. The need to articulate an intermediate space between armchair metaphysics and therapeutic philosophy arises precisely from the need to do justice to the view that there is something for philosophy to do, even if it is neither to compete with science in determining what there is, nor to clear up the muddles into which philosophers have got themselves.

Is the existence of ordinary macroscopic objects such as tables and chairs threatened by the scientific discovery that the ultimate structure of reality as revealed by our best scientific theories is quite different from how it is envisaged by the everyday classification of objects in accordance with their functional properties? Can there be tables and chairs as well as molecules? Some philosophers have argued that if the ultimate structure of reality as revealed by our best scientific theories is quite different from how it is presented by the everyday classification of objects in accordance with their functional properties, then this is very bad news indeed for middle-sized dry goods (see Austin 1962: 8); it is not possible for there to be *both* ordinary macroscopic objects such as tables, baseballs and so on *and* the corpuscles, molecules/atoms which make them up (see, e.g., Merricks 2000; Unger 1979a, 1979b; van Inwagen 1990). The ensuing nihilism or eliminativism about everyday objects is very radical because it presupposes that ordinary people are systematically mistaken in their statements concerning ordinary objects such as tables and chairs. It is not simply that they are occasionally wrong in believing that there is a cat on the mat or a cup on the table, but that they are mistaken about the existence of ordinary macroscopic objects as a matter of *a priori* necessity (see Hirsch 2011: 183).

In a bid to save the manifest image from this onslaught Eli Hirsch has argued that there is no correct use of the existential quantifier 'there exists ...' The ontological commitments of common sense and those of a scientifically inspired metaphysics are at loggerheads only if a) the ultimate structure of reality as revealed by our best scientific theories is quite different from how it is envisaged by the everyday classification of objects in accordance with their functional properties, *and most crucially* b) if there is only one correct use of the existential quantifier. Only if these two premises are conjoined does any conflict between the manifest and the scientific image arise. Thus if the tacitly presupposed premise of quantifier invariance is removed then questions which appeared very deep and profound are revealed to be trivial: 'If whenever you make an existential claim in metaphysics you are tacitly or unconsciously assuming that the claim has to be couched in terms of a quantificational apparatus that is the uniquely right one – the one that God would use – then this assumption is likely to lead you to futile and interminable pseudo-theoretical arguments' (Hirsch 2011b: 82). 'Serious' ontologists associate the correct use of the existential quantifier with a technical rather than the everyday use of words: 'Metaphysical realists are afflicted with a kind of hyper-theoreticalness' (ibid.) to which they are driven by their rejection of quantifier variance. Remove the assumption of quantifier invariance and you also remove the bias towards the ontological picture associated with the technical/scientific use of terms.

A slightly different argument in defence of the manifest image has been put forward by Amie Thomasson. Like Hirsch, Thomasson argues that there is no contest between the ontology of natural science and that of common sense. But rather than appeal to quantifier variance Thomasson argues that metaphysical disputes arise when it is expected that existence questions could be answered independently of linguistic frameworks which provide rules for the use of words.[7] For Thomasson the claims and debates of serious metaphysicians about existence (especially about what 'things' or 'objects' exist) and about explanatory exclusion are often attempts to answer existence questions in which the relevant terms are used without frame-level conditions of application (see Thomasson 2007, 2009). Just as anyone who knows that there is a left hand glove and a right hand glove also knows (by analytic entailment) that there is a pair of gloves, likewise anyone who knows 'that there are molecules arranged baseballwise' knows (by analytic entailment) 'that there is a baseball'. And just as anyone who grasps the analytic entailments between the claims 'there is a left hand glove and a right and glove' and 'there is a pair of gloves' would not say 'there is a right hand glove, a left hand glove *and* a pair of gloves', likewise anyone who grasps the analytic entailments between the claims 'there are molecules arranged baseballwise' and 'there is a baseball' should not say 'there are molecules arranged baseballwise *and* there is a baseball'. These conversational prohibitions undermine the idea that it is necessary to eliminate ordinary macroscopic objects in order to avoid causal rivalry between scientific and common-sense explanations. For, if it is illegitimate to conjoin the claims 'there is a baseball *and* there are atoms arranged baseballwise', it is also illegitimate to conjoin the claims 'the shattering of the window was caused by the baseball *and* by the atoms arranged baseballwise' (see Thomasson 2007: Ch.1). Making such analytic entailments explicit defuses the problem of explanatory exclusion and eases the pressures that have driven contemporary metaphysicians to advocate a kind of nihilism. Once we correctly grasp the grammar of certain expressions the apparent conflict between scientific and common-sense explanations simply evaporates.

Both Hirsch and Thomasson are adamant that their position should not be confused with a form of linguistic idealism. A commitment to quantifier variance or to a claim that existence claims are meaningless when they are advanced without any reference to frame-level conditions of application does not entail that language creates or constitutes the world (see Hirsch 2011b: 72; Thomasson 2007: 187; Thomasson 2001). In the following I want to explore a deflationary strategy which is friendly to the proposals advanced by advocates of a shallow or easy approach to ontology but which is developed within the idealist tradition, has less of a therapeutic flavour and takes conceptual analysis to have a very robust, even if not robustly metaphysical, role.

In contemporary metaphysics 'idealism' is mostly identified with an ontological claim concerning the constitution of reality and the causal powers of the mind to bring reality into existence.[8] But there is a different strand of idealism according to which to be an idealist is to take a stand on the conditions of meaningfulness rather than on the constitution of reality. This form of (conceptual) idealism informed the work of philosophers such as R. G. Collingwood and underpins the view which is defended here, namely that philosophical problems are substantive and yet not ontologically deep.

SUBSTANTIVE YET NOT ONTOLOGICALLY DEEP PHILOSOPHICAL PROBLEMS

Substantive yet not ontologically deep philosophical disagreements arise when we deploy not just different concepts but also different conceptions of reality. Whilst such disagreements are not metaphysically deep, as serious ontologists would claim, they are not merely verbal either, as some deflationary approaches to disputes in contemporary analytical metaphysics typically imply. Consider, for example, the disagreement between causalists and anti-causalists in the philosophy of action.[9] Causalists maintain that all events are causally explained and that since, given the assumption of the causal closure of the physical, nothing escapes the nomological net, actions too are (covert) events to be explained causally: they are events with a particular type of causal history, one that is internal (a brain process) rather than external. Anti-causalists, by contrast, maintain that to explain an action is *not* to explain it causally but to understand it rationally as an expression of thought or by invoking a practical argument which explains the action in the hermeneutic rather than the causal sense of 'explain'. The 'serious' ontologists on either side of this divide would argue that a revision of our ontological commitments follows from a methodological endorsement of either causalism or anti-causalism. Much as the nihilist would claim that there are no ordinary objects, the causalist would claim that there are no actions, at least if by actions one means something that has an irreducibly non-causal explanation. Causalists may not demand any linguistic reform as a result of the ontological commitments entailed by the endorsement of their preferred conceptual framework, but since their view is that what really/genuinely/truly rather than apparently exists are (nomologically connected) events, strictly speaking there are no such things as actions, at least not in the sense of action espoused by the anti-causalist. So whilst we may, outside the philosopher's study, be allowed to speak with the vulgar, any talk about actions is at best a *façon de parler*.

On the proposal advanced here the causalist and the anti-causalist are disagreeing about the categorial framework that is normative for practitioners of the natural and the human sciences. The disagreement between the causalist and the anti-causalist is thus *not* ontologically deep. Yet it is not merely verbal either. In a purely verbal dispute, such as the aubergine/eggplant example, there is nothing substantive at stake other than terminological convention. But there is something substantive at stake between the causalist and the anti-causalist when they assert or deny '*this* is an action'. When causalists speak about actions they simply use the term to qualify the type of event that is being described; for the causalist the term action denotes a species of the category event in the way in which 'Siamese' qualifies the genus 'cat'. For anti-causalists, by contrast, action is a category *sui generis* that is logically or conceptually independent of the concept of event. The causalist and the anti-causalist are therefore disagreeing about whether the concepts of 'action' and 'event' are or are not concepts *sui generis* and whether the mode of enquiry which is concerned with actions is an autonomous discipline. For the anti-causalist to use the term action in the causalist sense would be tantamount to admitting that the form of enquiry which is concerned with actions is a branch of the mode of enquiry that is concerned with events, just as cardiology is a branch of medicine that specializes in the heart and the diseases which affect it. And this would be to make a mockery of the human science's claim to autonomy.[10]

For the 'serious' metaphysician what is at stake in the causalist/ anti-causalist debate is whether or not there is something that has the properties actions have according to the anti-causalist, and this is why the debate is substantive, not trivial. On the approach advocated here the debate between the causalist and the anti-causalist is substantive *not* because it is ontologically deep (in the sense in which the serious metaphysician requires it to be in order for the dispute not to be merely verbal), but because what is at stake is whether the concept of action is or is not a category *sui generis* and thus whether or not the study of human action is a branch of natural science rather than an autonomous form of enquiry with its own distinctive subject matter. Since on this proposal the concept of action and event are analytically independent *sui generis* categories, the dispute between the causalist and the anti-causalist cannot be deflated by claiming that anybody who states 'there is an action' ought to accept 'there is an event' in the manner in which anybody who accepts 'there is a house' ought to accept 'there is a building'. In other words, the dispute between the causalist and the anti-causalist cannot be deflated by showing that anti-causalists have a limited or partial grasp of the concept of action and were they to have a complete grasp of this concept they would see that 'there is an action' entails 'there is an event', much as someone with a full grasp of the concept of a triangle would be able to see that the Pythagorean theorem is entailed by it. The claim that the human and the natural sciences have different *explananda* is premised not on a (fallacious) argument from ignorance, but on the view that the concept of action and event do *not* stand to one another as the species to the genus.[11] Substantive but non-ontologically deep disagreements arise when logically independent categories come into contact and clash and a decision must be made concerning which categorial structure to apply. The task of philosophy is precisely that of locating these logical or conceptual joints. And this occurs when the *sui generis* nature of certain concepts is acknowledged.

Whilst this view has much in common with deflationary approaches to disputes in contemporary analytical metaphysics, it does not share the suspicion of technical terms that seems to be implicit in some attempts to dissolve philosophical problems by appealing to ordinary language use. For technical terms and distinctions are sometimes needed precisely to denote the *sui generis* categories at the joints of our conceptual map. Technical philosophical terms do not necessarily lead us astray into endless pseudo-theoretical disputes. Instead of muddying our thinking they help to clarify it. Many philosophers have found it necessary to use technical terms to bring into view the articulations of our conceptual framework. Heidegger's distinction between the present-at-hand and the ready-to-hand is one such case (Heidegger 1927). The distinction is not between hammers and nails on the one hand and wood and iron molecules on the other, as a botanist might distinguish between two kinds of plant or two species of the same plant, but between the conceptions of reality within which objects are revealed either as utensils or as objects of scientific investigation. Philosophy finds the hinges on the doors which open up onto different world views. The role of conceptual analysis in metaphysics is to open up doors onto different aspects of reality without removing the mechanism which will allow the doors to reopen onto the conception of reality which one needed to shut out in order to view things from a different perspective. Philosophy oils the hinges of the doors that open onto different conceptions of reality thus preventing the mechanism from getting stuck in one world view.

PHILOSOPHY OPENS DOORS ONTO DIFFERENT
CONCEPTIONS OF REALITY

This conception of the role and character of philosophical analysis is implicit in the idealism of R. G. Collingwood, a form of idealism which is conceptual, not ontological. In The *Idea of History* (1993 [1946]) Collingwood sought to isolate a technical sense of the term action (*res gestae*) from the everyday use of the word. In its everyday use the term action denotes anything that a human being does ranging from knee-jerk reactions to voluntary movements as well as fully fledged intentional actions. In the technical sense of *res gestae*, actions denote the autonomous domain of enquiry of history understood as a hermeneutic discipline.[12]

Actions in the sense of *res gestae* are thus 'not the actions, in the widest sense of that word, which are done by animals of the species called human; they are actions in another sense of the same word, equally familiar but narrower, actions done by reasonable agents in pursuit of ends determined by their reason' (Collingwood 1999: 46). Action (in the sense of *res gestae*), is therefore a term of art which denotes rational actions. Isolating this technical sense of the term action from its everyday use is necessary to bring to the fore a joint in our conceptual system which enables us to articulate the distinction between a conception of reality as a system of nomologically interconnected *events* and as a system of intelligible (rational) *actions*. This joint is invisible. Not only is it partially obscured by the way in which the term action is used in ordinary speech, where it is deployed to denote both intentional action and involuntary bodily movements. It is invisible also because the distinction between (rationally intelligible) actions and (nomologically connected) events, very much like Heidegger's distinction between the *ready-to hand* and the *present-at-hand*, denotes not a sorting of objects into different empirical classes, but refers rather to the conceptions of reality that are entailed by the methodological assumptions and practices which govern different forms of enquiry. Were the distinction between (rationally intelligible) actions and (nomologically connected) events not made, history, here understood as a *Geisteswissenschaft*, would have no subject matter of its own. History acquires its autonomy from the natural sciences when the category of action is understood as a concept *sui generis* that is analytically independent of, and irreducible to, that of (nomologically connected) events. In other words, history gains its autonomy from the natural sciences *not* by being granted authority over a subset of events such as wars, revolutions, *coup d'états*, treasons, and so on, but when it is acknowledged as investigating reality under a different categorial framework, qua *res gestae*.

For Collingwood the conflict between the causalist and the anti-causalist is best understood as a conflict between the methodological practices which govern different forms of enquiry and the conception of reality that is entailed by them. Yet there is no suggestion here that – because the dispute between the causalist and the anti-causalist concerns the methodological practices which govern different forms of enquiry rather than the nature of things – the disagreement is, for this very reason, *merely* verbal. In a purely verbal dispute the participants in the discussion are talking past each other. Were they to adopt the language of their opponent, they would acknowledge that there is no genuine disagreement, just different linguistic conventions.[13] But this does not appear to be how things are in the case of the dispute between causalists and anti-causalists. The participants in the causalist/anti-causalist debate cannot agree that what the other is saying is true in the language of their opponent without undermining the categorial framework which underpins their own conception of reality. Such an option is unavailable in the case of the dispute between causalists and anti-causalists because the distinction between actions (in the technical sense) and events captures a joint in our conceptual framework which does not enable us to keep the door open on both world views simultaneously. The idea that philosophy uncovers such invisible joints and that the doors which it opens must be closed on one view in order to be opened on another is probably best understood by considering Collingwood's discussion of absolute presuppositions.[14]

METAPHYSICS WITHOUT DEEP ONTOLOGY: THE PHILOSOPHER AS A JEDI KNIGHT

In *An Essay on Metaphysics* (1998 [1940]) Collingwood claims that different forms of enquiry are governed by different absolute presuppositions which determine the kind of 'why' questions and 'because' answers that one can reasonably expect when engaging in those forms of enquiry. He illustrates the point by saying that history (understood as a hermeneutic science) and the practical and the theoretical sciences of nature absolutely presuppose different senses of causation. For example, in what Collingwood calls the practical sciences of nature, sciences such as medicine and engineering, a cause is an 'event or state of things by producing or preventing which we can produce or prevent that whose cause it is said to be' (Collingwood 1998: 296–7). No self-respecting car mechanic, doctor, or engineer, could operate without presupposing that this sense of causation captures what it means to provide an explanation. For without presupposing that nature can be manipulated to produce certain results (wind to generate electricity; vaccines to prevent illnesses) their form of enquiry would not be possible. Different practitioners presuppose different senses of causation. In what he calls the theoretical sciences of nature, such as physics, the sense of causation is deterministic and abstracts from human purposes. Thus, a cause is not a handle that can be manipulated to obtain certain desired effects but an unconditional antecedent condition such that if the cause obtains the effect will follow. By contrast since the subject matter of history is actions, a cause in historical explanation is not an antecedent condition but a motive which conceptually entails the action that it explains. Explanations of actions relieve us of our puzzlement by showing us what the point of acting in a particular way is.

The practitioners of these forms of enquiry cannot deny the sense of causation which governs their form of enquiry without undermining the enquiry itself. Without rational explanations there would be no actions (in the technical sense of *res gestae*), and thus no distinctive subject matter for historical enquiry. Without a conception of causes as handles which can be turned to produce or prevent certain effects, there would no practical sciences of nature. This is not to say that the proposition 'there are no such things as causes' on the handle conception of causation cannot be formulated in plain English, since the sentence is grammatically correct. Nor does this mean that the proposition cannot be denied by someone who adopts a different explanatory framework. A physicist can deny that causes (in the sense used by the car mechanic and the engineer) exist but what it is not possible to do is to deny the presuppositions which govern one's form of enquiry and make true or false claims which rely on the methodological assumptions on which they are premised. So it cannot be truly asserted that ingesting vitamin C helps preventing colds unless one presupposes the handle conception of causation. And Collingwood would argue it makes no sense to ask whether the presupposition itself is true or false because the presupposition provides, as Thomasson might say, the 'frame-level conditions of application' within which doctors, mechanics and engineers can pursue their lines of investigation.[15] Yet, although many of Collingwood's claims could be rephrased by casting them in terms of a commitment to the view that the *explananda* of any form of enquiry cannot be identified without any reference to linguistic frameworks, there is no suggestion that philosophical disputes are therefore merely verbal, as the standard characterization of the contemporary metaontological debate would seem to imply.[16]

The ontology that Collingwood develops is at once both *more egalitarian* than 'serious' metaphysics and *more esoteric* than the kind of ontology which is inspired by the tradition of ordinary language philosophy that goes back to Austin and Ryle. The contrast between esoteric and egalitarian metaphysics has been recently introduced by Hofweber to distinguish between the view that 'the questions in the domain of metaphysics are expressed in ordinary, everyday terms, accessible to all' (egalitarian metaphysics) and the view that the claims of metaphysics are articulated in a technical terminology that is known to the professional ontologist only (esoteric metaphysics) (Hofweber 2009: 266–7). Revisionary metaphysicians and their critics in the contemporary ontological debate appear to fall on one or the other side of this divide. For the former there is a privileged use of the existential quantifier that is associated with technical terms as employed by the trained ontologist; for the latter, on the other hand, the everyday use of language provides a much needed antidote against the hypertheoretical tendencies of revisionary metaphysicians which are to be opposed precisely by acquiescing in ordinary usage (see Hirsch 2011b: 83).

The categories of Collingwood's metaphysics are more esoteric than those found in the tradition of ordinary language philosophy because, as we have seen, the concept of action, in the technical philosophical sense, is a concept *sui generis* that defines the autonomous domain of enquiry of history understood as a *Geisteswissenschaft*. This technical meaning partially overlaps, but does not coincide with the everyday use of the term. The categories of (rationally intelligible) actions and (nomologically connected) events are, in a tradition that goes back to Kant, to be associated with forms of judgement. The categories of Collingwood's metaphysics will thus be as many as the forms of inference. Whilst establishing such a list will be hard (Kant has often been castigated for getting it wrong or for erroneously presuming he had provided a complete list), it seems clear that whatever this list might be it is unlikely to be very long. This approach to metaphysical questions does not exemplify 'a shopping list approach' (Jackson 1998: Ch. 1) to ontology, an approach which provides a long list of the various kinds of things which exist. Collingwood is not so much defending the existence of middle-sized dry goods such as tins of tuna fish, baked beans and such like, as vindicating the kind of world view within which objects can be revealed in a particular way. In the tradition of Kantian metaphysics, rather than that of ordinary language philosophy, he is concerned not with middle-sized dry goods but with the nature of the judgements which are at work in various domains of experience, theoretical, practical, aesthetic, and so on. The categories of his metaphysics are determined by the form of the inference we adopt. The philosophical concept of action is neither a Platonic form nor an empirical class but the *explanandum* of that form of enquiry which makes sense of what happens by appealing to practical arguments where the 'thing' explained is the result of a train of thought. To put it differently: method determines subject matter: the categories of Collingwood's metaphysics are therefore the correlatives of forms of explanation.

Collingwood's metaphysics is also more egalitarian than revisionary metaphysics. Although the categories of his metaphysics are not the ordinary objects of common-sense ontology, they are not completely alien to the ordinary person either. As he says, actions in the sense of *res gestae* 'are actions in another sense of the same word, *equally familiar but narrower*, [my emphasis] actions done by reasonable agents in pursuit of ends determined by their reason'. Philosophical investigations, unlike empirical ones, do not teach us something completely new. On learning that the cranberry bush is a subgenus of the genus *vaccinium*, in the plant family *ericacae*, whose botanical name is *viburnum trilobum*, one finds out something completely new. Scientific classifications may even be genuinely surprising. Biological taxonomies based on DNA, for example, have overthrown traditional ideas of how organisms are related. On the other hand the philosopher who alerts us to the fact that there is a sense of action that is *sui generis* and irreducible to the concept of (nomologically connected) event 'does not ... bring us to know things of which we were simply ignorant, but brings us to know in a different way things which we already knew in some way' (Collingwood 2005: 161).

How does this conception of the nature of philosophical analysis sit in the current debate concerning the role of conceptual analysis in metaphysics? On the one hand the kind of conceptual analysis advocated here does not uncover any truths because it advances no first order claims but only claims of a second order concerning the presuppositions of knowledge. As such this form of conceptual analysis does not compete with the special sciences. It cannot, and indeed does not aim to tell us, whether Caesar won the battle at Pharsalus, or whether fire has the power to melt wax. On the other hand, this kind of conceptual analysis does not concede that philosophy should play second fiddle to any of the special sciences. It sees philosophy as an epistemologically first science whose role is to uncover the tacit presuppositions that are constitutive of first order enquiries. As such it differs not only from the Quineian conception of philosophy, which sees it as continuous with natural science, but also from the view of the role of conceptual analysis in metaphysics which has been advocated by Frank Jackson, according to which the role of conceptual analysis is 'that of addressing the question of what to say about matters described in one set of terms *given* a story about matters in another set of terms' (Jackson 1998: 44). For, on the kind of conceptual analysis defended here, any *given* story about how matters are described in one explanatory context depends on the presuppositions that govern that form of enquiry, which is precisely the task of philosophical analysis to make explicit. Thus, although this conception of philosophical analysis does not compete with the special sciences (for it advances no claims at first order level) it does conflict with a particular second order philosophical view according to which the method of the natural sciences enjoys ontological priority over that of other disciplines so that the role of philosophy would be, for example, to find how mind fits in the natural world given a story about the world articulated in terms of the explanatory framework of physics. Since, on Collingwood's conception of the role of philosophical analysis the explanatory framework of the *Geisteswissenschaften* discloses reality as action, in the technical and *sui generis* sense of the *res gestae*, there is nothing that can be said about actions starting from the explanatory framework of the natural sciences. For if we wish to speak about actions in this sense, we have to do so from within the set of presuppositions that are normative within a different explanatory framework.

The serious ontologist might still complain that, in spite of the robust role allocated to philosophical analysis this is yet another deflationary strategy and that insisting the dispute between causalists and anti-causalists is not merely verbal does not suffice to make it substantive. For the dispute to be substantive it would have to be settled by establishing what there really is in some presuppositionless sense of being. Collingwood does deny that the conflict is ontological in the sense of 'ontological' required by the serious metaphysician. For once it is acknowledged that the human and the natural sciences have different *explananda*, and that there is no *explanandum* for God, the conflict is somehow deflated since it is no longer construed as being about whether reality (in some presuppositionless sense of the term) can be both causally and rationally ordered, but about whether reality can be simultaneously *described* as being both causally and rationally ordered. But there is also a sense in which Collingwood's approach is not straightforwardly deflationary. First, were it not for the fact that the term ontology has been so successfully hijacked by the revisionary metaphysician one would be tempted to say that there are plenty of serious ontological claims and distinctions being made here, and that since such ontological claims and distinctions do not map straightforwardly onto common-sense ontological claims and distinctions, the metaphysics of which they are part is not straightforwardly descriptive either. Second, although he denies the conflict is ontological (in the sense of ontology espoused by the revisionary metaphysician), he does hold that there is a genuine conceptual tension between the explanatory practices of the human and the natural sciences even if the tension is not in the things, but in the way in which we represent them. He denies both that philosophical problems are ontologically deep and that rejecting the traditional construal of philosophical disputes as ontologically deep entails that philosophical disputes are therefore merely verbal. His conceptual idealism, unlike the more robust ontological idealism endorsed by his (British idealist) predecessors, combines the critique of the traditional conception of metaphysics that one finds in the tradition of pragmatism and in particular in the Carnap of 'Empiricism, Semantics and Ontology' with a renewed commitment to the value of philosophy as providing a second-order reflection on the methodological principles which govern the first order disciplines (see D'Oro 2015). The task of the philosopher is not to get rid of the tensions between different forms of world disclosure in the manner of the revisionary metaphysician (for example, by reducing or eliminating the mental, or by denying that there are any aesthetic properties strictly speaking). Nor is it to denounce the tensions between the manifest and the scientific image as somewhat fake, but to allow them to be by exposing the multi-faceted character of reality. The role of the philosopher, like that of the Jedi knight, is to keep order in the universe by restoring balance to the force when the scales tip too heavily on one side.[17]

NOTES

1 For a survey of recent methodological debates see (Haug 2014).

2 Disagreements between endurantists and perdurantists in the philosophy of time as well as those between mereologists and anti-mereologists about how many objects there are, are often cited as cases in point. See Hirsch 2011a: 68–9, 81–4, 221–4, 220–33).

3 To be fair Eli Hirsch does not argue that *all* ontological disagreements are verbal (see Hirsch 2009: 253).

4 Some philosophical disagreements may indeed be purely verbal and, by implication, trivial. The view that I defend here is that there are disagreements that are not trivial even if they are not ontologically deep. In fact since merely verbal disagreements are not real, but only apparent disagreements, the claim that there are disagreements which are not ontologically deep, and yet not merely verbal, is a precondition for there being (genuine) conceptual disputes.

5 See, for example, (Heil 2003; Devitt 2010; and Sider 2011). For a critical response to this ontological backlash see (Price 2009).

6 I am using the adjective 'serious' to denote the conception of ontology as independent of semantics and epistemology that has become prominent in the last part of the twentieth century. On this view about the true nature of ontological enquiry metaphysics of a Kantian type is not serious metaphysics. On this see (Heil 2003: Ch. 1; and Lowe 1998: Ch. 1).

7 Thomasson outlines the differences between her approach and Hirsch's in (Thomasson 2015: 48).

8 A notable exception is (Rescher 1973).

9 For a recent survey of the causalist/anti-causalist debate see (D'Oro and Sandis 2013).

10 For an in depth account of Collingwood's defence of the autonomy of the human sciences see (D'Oro 2011 and 2012).

11 The objection that the argument for dualism is an argument from ignorance was first raised by Arnauld in his fourth objection to the Cartesian *Meditations*. Arnauld argued that Descartes was led to the conclusion that the mind and the body are really distinct by his false belief that there is no relation of analytic entailment between the concept of the mind and that of the body. When Descartes asserted that the concepts of mind and body are logically or analytically independent of one another he committed a fallacy similar to the person who fails to see that the Pythagorean theorem is covertly entailed by the concept of a triangle. Descartes retorted that his argument was not an argument from ignorance because the concepts of mind and body are genuinely distinct and that what is genuinely conceptually distinct can also exist apart metaphysically. The form of idealism defended here, being purely conceptual, does not presuppose the further Cartesian premise that conceivability entails metaphysical possibility and thus that conceptual dualism entails ontological or substance dualism.

12 Collingwood's claim was appropriated and developed in the 1950s and 60s by W. H., Dray who argued that action explanations are rational explanations which are distinct in kind, not merely in degree from the explanation of events, which is causal/nomological. Dray defended Collingwood's view against Mill's claim that the study of action differs only in degree from the study of events, a view which was revived by (Hempel 1942). See (Dray 1957; 1963) and (D'Oro 2012).

13 Hirsch describes merely verbal disputes as follows: 'In my view, an issue in ontology (or elsewhere) is "merely verbal" in the sense of reducing to a linguistic choice only if the following condition is satisfied: Each side can plausibly interpret the other side as speaking a language in which the latter's asserted sentences are true' (Hirsch 2009: 221).

14 It should be noted that for Collingwood the *Geistes/Naturwissenschaften* distinction captures the distinction between the study of actions and the study of events. The distinction, as he draws it, is one between a normative study of the mind and a descriptive study of nature (see D'Oro and Sandis 2013).

15 For a more detailed discussion of Collingwood's account of absolute presuppositions see (D'Oro 2002).

16 Thomasson has recently distanced herself from the view that conceptual disputes are properly thought of as 'merely verbal'. See 'What can we do, when we do metaphysics?' in this collection.

17 This analogy was suggested to me by Nicholas Heath.

12 Pragmatism and the Limits of Metaphilosophy

I. PRELUDE: A PUZZLE ABOUT METAPHILOSOPHY

Enduring movements in the history of philosophy often owe their influence not to their core doctrines, but rather to the distinctive vision of philosophy they embody. Indeed, one might say of such movements – think of the varied traditions associated with the Stoics, Descartes, Hume, Kant, Hegel, the positivists, the existentialists, and beyond – that they are *primarily* conceptions of *what philosophy is*. A conception of what philosophy is – a *metaphilosophy*, as I'll call it – coordinates ideas about philosophical method, the nature of philosophical problems, and the limits of philosophy. In other words, a metaphilosophy tells us not only *how to do* philosophy but also *what philosophy can do*, what we *can expect* from philosophy. A metaphilosophy hence often distinguishes genuine philosophical problems from pseudo-problems and nonsense; it also typically demarcates genuine philosophical problems from those genuine problems that reside within the purview of some other kind of enquiry, such a natural science, psychology, and history. It is tempting to conclude that although we tend to think of the history of philosophy as a series of debates concerning truth, goodness, knowledge, being, meaning, and beauty, it is actually an ongoing clash among metaphilosophies.

Though tempting, this conclusion should be resisted, at least for the time being. This is because it is as yet unclear how metaphilosophical clashes are to be resolved, or even addressed. Which area of enquiry is suited to adjudicate conflicts over what philosophy is? Must there be a meta-metaphilosophy? But then wouldn't we also require a fourth tier to address conflicts at the meta-meta level? Then a fifth, sixth, and seventh? This proliferation of 'meta' discourses about philosophy looks well worth avoiding. A further cause for resistance lies in the fact that the very idea of a clash among metaphilosophies is opaque. Why regard, say, the Cartesian dualist and the eliminative materialist as embroiled in a metaphilosophical clash at all? Why not say instead that they *are engaged in entirely different enterprises* and be done with it? Why posit something over which they are in dispute? The fact that it is not clear how there could be an adjudication of metaphilosophical clashes may be marshalled as a consideration in favour of the idea that opposing schools normally identified as philosophical do *not* promote different *conceptions* of philosophy, but instead embrace distinctive *concepts* that each calls 'philosophy', and so ultimately do not even *clash* at all, but only speak past each other.

To be sure, that is a dispiriting result. I presume that we should aspire to preserve the idea that proponents of different philosophical schools may nonetheless *disagree* about first-order philosophical issues. But if we accept the idea that first-order disputes are merely proxies for metaphilosophical clashes, then the ground upon which even first-order disagreement could proceed begins to dissolve. At the very least, then, the conclusion that all philosophical disputes ultimately bottom-out in metaphilosophical differences looks premature. Many would go further to say that it should be repelled to the last.

This all-too-brisk sketch is meant only to highlight a general puzzle about metaphilosophy. It seems undeniable that different philosophical traditions embrace their own distinctive metaphilosophies, and that these metaphilosophical commitments often drive their first-order philosophical views. Consequently, one familiar way of *diagnosing* first-order philosophical disputes is to ascend to the metaphilosophical plane, where the disputants' different methodological commitments can be laid bare and examined. But once this point is acknowledged, it is difficult to sustain another seemingly undeniable thought, namely, that different philosophical schools genuinely *disagree* about first-order philosophical matters. Put otherwise, metaphilosophical ascent seeks to dissolve first-order philosophical disagreements by relocating them to the metaphilosophical level. However, there is no progress in this manoeuvre, as it is hard to make sense of the very idea of a *metaphilosophical* disagreement. One wonders *what* exactly such purported disagreements are *about*, and thus it is difficult to see how they could be resolved. Again, metaphilosophical disputes look like paradigmatic pseudo-disputes, cases where the disputants use the same words only to talk past each other.

The puzzle, then, can be posed as a *metaphilosophical antinomy*. On the one hand, we seek to accommodate the thought that first-order philosophical programmes are manifestations of metaphilosophical stances; on the other, we want to preserve the thought that genuine philosophical disagreement is possible. One obvious and promising response to the antinomy is to deny that the tie between metaphilosophical and first-order commitments is as tight as has been supposed thus far. One must, that is, constrain the role that metaphilosophy plays in explaining first-order philosophical commitments. This is achieved by leaving open the conceptual space for first-order philosophical views that are *not* the product of, or fully explicable by, a background metaphilosophy. This, in turn, would countenance the possibility of first-order philosophical disputes that are *not* resolvable by means of metaphilosophical ascent. If this tempering of metaphilosophy is unachievable – if first-order philosophical disputes *simply are* clashes among divergent metaphilosophies – then there's an obvious sense in which the enterprise of philosophy is imperilled.

A central aim of this essay is to call attention to the ways in which pragmatism, in both its classical and some of its current varieties, invites an especially potent version of the metaphilosophical antinomy just described. The following section provides a survey of the place of metaphilosophy in the classical pragmatists; it will be shown that the progression from Peirce to James and Dewey manifests an increasingly robust role for metaphilosophy, and this 'metaphilosophical creep' (as I'll call it) is naturally accompanied by increasing pressure to confront the antinomy. In response to this pressure, more recent pragmatisms have faced a dilemma of either abandoning the robust metaphilosophical commitments central to Deweyan pragmatism, or more fully embracing them and adopting an 'end of philosophy' programme. I shall argue that an 'end of philosophy' stance is pragmatically unappealing. My positive task, undertaken in the final section of this essay, is to provide a pragmatist strategy for constraining pragmatism's pernicious metaphilosophical impulses. What emerges is a conception of pragmatism as metaphilosophically *minimalist*.

2. PRAGMATISM AND THE PROBLEM OF METAPHILOSOPHICAL CREEP

Pragmatism has never been a unified philosophical school. Its founding trio – Charles Peirce, William James, and John Dewey – disagreed sharply about fundamental issues regarding truth, meaning, knowledge, existence, and value. Yet there are philosophical threads and shared concerns by which one can tie Peirce, James, and Dewey together – along with a long subsequent cast of philosophers – into a common, though loose, idiom. In other work I have told the story of pragmatism's disorderly founding and development, and will not rehearse it here.[1] At present, it is important to stress that from its inception, pragmatism has been unusually overt in its metaphilosophical orientation. Whereas other philosophical trends typically frontload their first-order philosophical doctrines and leave their metaphilosophy implicit, pragmatists have tended to place their metaphilosophical agenda at centre stage.

The *overtness* of pragmatism's metaphilosophical programme is evident in the fact that its inaugurating documents – Peirce's 'How to Make our Ideas Clear' and 'The Fixation of Belief', and James' 'Philosophical Conceptions and Practical Results' – are explicitly *methodological* works, aimed expressly at initiating a new way forward for philosophy. As with the first-order issues, one finds considerable disagreement among the classical pragmatists concerning the precise contours of pragmatism's conception of philosophy. Again, as the details are well known the following sketch will suffice.

For Peirce, pragmatism is fundamentally a *semantic* programme, a way of making ideas clear, that culminates in a maxim for discerning the meanings of 'hard words and abstract concepts' (CP5: 464).[2] According to an early formulation, the pragmatic maxim is as follows:

Consider what effects, that might conceivably have practical bearings, we conceive the object of our conception to have. Then our conception of these effects is the whole of our conception of the object.

(Ibid.: 402)

There are many respects in which this statement is itself less than clear, but the details of Perice's multiple attempts to improve on it need not detain us.[3] The point at present is that, with this maxim, Peirce gives expression to a central motif of pragmatism, namely, that ideas are tools-in-the-making whose significance consists in how they direct human action.[4] According to Peirce, then, pragmatism is more a rule for conducting enquiry than a philosophical doctrine or position. It is the claim that in order to get a firm grip on an idea or concept, one must look to how it is *used*, the role it plays in guiding action (ibid.: 416). However, as it is a semantic principle, the pragmatic maxim also has a metaphilosophical bite: it proposes a criterion for meaningfulness, thereby enabling inquirers to identify 'make believes' (ibid.) and clear the path of enquiry of nonsense and pseudo-questions. In this way, Peirce sounds another enduring theme which pragmatism shares with several other late nineteenth- and twentieth-century philosophical trends, namely, a commitment to empiricism and an accompanying distrust of metaphysics.[5] Echoing a common empiricist sentiment, Peirce said that pragmatism serves to leave philosophy with a 'series of problems capable of investigation by the observational methods of the true sciences' (ibid.: 423).

Though it has much in common with familiar brands of verificationism, the pragmatic maxim embodies a less militant stance than is found in, say, the logical positivists.[6] To be sure, Peirce regarded certain longstanding metaphysical disputes as nonsensical and thus disposable, but he nevertheless regarded many of the traditional problems to be legitimate. In these cases, the pragmatic maxim is claimed to provide a means by which philosophers could make progress towards their resolution. Contrast Peirce's attitude towards the medieval dispute concerning transubstantiation with the same period's debates concerning nominalism. Both are *metaphysical* disputes, yet whereas Peirce regards the former as 'senseless jargon' (ibid.: 401), he takes the latter to be a philosophical debate of the utmost import, one admitting of a resolution in the course of properly conducted enquiry.[7]

The details of Peirce's pragmatism are complicated, and there is certainly a lot more to say. The important point here is that Peirce took pragmatism as a methodological prescription for doing philosophy, a tool to apply to philosophical problems that would help philosophy progress. Crucially, Peirce did not propose pragmatism as a collection of philosophical *results*. Although he did hold that pragmatism could expose certain alleged philosophical problems as nonsense, he also thought that the legitimate philosophical problems were to be addressed by means of ongoing enquiry.

Matters are markedly different in the case of James. Although he seems to have taken himself to be merely popularizing Peirce's maxim, James actually radically transformed it. In 'Philosophical Conceptions and Practical Results' and his later *Pragmatism* lecture, 'The Present Dilemma in Philosophy', James deploys a version of the pragmatic maxim that is not a semantic device, but a strategy for *diagnosing* – and ultimately *settling* – longstanding metaphysical disputes by identifying first-order philosophical positions with underlying *psychological* temperaments (James 1977: 363, 374). To see how this works, consider one of James' favourite examples. He holds that although materialism and spiritualism present themselves as opposed first-order theses, they are actually expressions of two distinct psychological tendencies (ibid.: 393). The former is the proposal that the cosmos is doomed to end in 'utter final wreck and tragedy' (ibid.: 398); the latter is the view that there is ground for hope that there is an 'eternal moral order' (ibid.: 398). When materialism and spiritualism are psychologized in these ways, the dispute between them is no longer recognizably *philosophical* at all. On James' view, what divides materialists and spiritualists is no matter of fact or principle; rather, they embody conflicting psychological dispositions, and their philosophical pronouncements are expressions of those tendencies. Ultimately, then, on James' analysis materialists and spiritualists do not really *disagree* about anything. They are driven by their psychologies to assert philosophical positions that *appear to be* opposed, but, once subjected to the proper pragmatic clarification, in fact just express two different attitudes towards the world. According to James, the supposedly metaphysical debate between materialism and spiritualism thus collapses into 'insignificance' (ibid.: 379).

And so it is for the whole of philosophy. James contends that all of the grand philosophical debates are the epiphenomena of the more fundamental psychological rift between the 'tender minded' and the 'tough minded' psychological types (ibid.: 365). And here is where Jamesian pragmatism purports to make its most vital contribution. The 'dilemma' James sees lies in the fact that so few of us are purely 'tender' or 'tough' in temperament; rather, we are mixed psychologically, yearning for certain elements of both options that traditional philosophy has to offer (ibid.: 366). The trouble is that traditional philosophy presents itself as a series of exclusive disjunctions: spiritualism *or* materialism; rationalism *or* empiricism; principles *or* facts; monism *or* pluralism; and so on. Consequently, philosophy as a discipline strikes most as alien, disconnected, and divorced from the travails of life (ibid.: 369).

Pragmatism is James' remedy. By translating seemingly intractable metaphysical disputes into expressions of divergent psychological tendencies, James ensures that philosophy will resonate with everyday life. And, moreover, once such disputes are pragmatically translated, they admit of almost instant and clear resolutions. For example, James holds that once the debate between spiritualism and materialism is pragmatically reformulated into psychological terms, it becomes clear that spiritualism is the superior doctrine. We simply *cannot live* with the materialist proposition; materialism is psychologically *incommodious* (ibid.: 397). And, according to James, this counts decisively in favour of spiritualism, for 'the whole function of philosophy ought to be to find out what definite difference it will make to you and me, at definite instants of our life, if this world-formula or that world-formula be the true one' (ibid.: 379).

We see, then, that James' pragmatism isn't directed towards rooting out nonsense and guiding philosophical enquiry in more productive ways. It is rather aimed at disclosing the *significance* of philosophical claims and resolving philosophical disputes. This contrast with Peirce is most evident in James' treatment of the issue of transubstantiation. Recall that Peirce regarded the doctrine of transubstantiation as a paradigmatic example of metaphysical nonsense. According to James, it is not only not nonsense but one of the most important philosophical issues in currency (ibid.: 392). This is because, on James' analysis, the doctrine of transubstantiation has nothing to do with the metaphysical categories of substance and accident; rather, the doctrine is the claim that we can 'feed on the substance of divinity' (ibid.: 392). And, James holds, the need to feel such an intimate connection with the divine is 'one of the deepest' in our psyches (ibid.: 354).

Notice here the metaphilosophical commitments driving the Jamesian programme. First, there is the idea that first-order philosophical positions express psychological temperaments rather than state judgements about the world. Then there is the further claim that the *meaning* of first-order philosophical positions is exhausted by the psychological temperaments that they express. And finally there is the idea that philosophical disputes are to be resolved in favour of whichever position is attached to the psychological temperament that strikes the individual thinker as most attractive or useful. What emerges, then, is a conception of philosophy as a kind of intellectual therapy, a way of finding one's place in the cosmos, and making oneself at home in the world.

Whatever its attractions, James' metaphilosophy must grapple with the metaphilosophical antinomy. James claims that his pragmatism is a method of 'settling metaphysical disputes that otherwise might be interminable' (ibid.: 377). But that is not quite accurate. Jamesian pragmatism rather *re-describes* traditionally opposed philosophical positions so that they are no longer things that could stand in philosophical opposition to each other. Recall that on the Jamesian analysis, the materialist and spiritualist simply express different attitudes about the future of the universe (ibid.: 397). Thus the very idea of a philosophical disagreement is jettisoned. Now again, this may strike some as unobjectionable. Perhaps there is too much philosophical disputation that seems interminable, and maybe philosophy's traditional debates are indeed too divorced from everyday concerns. The trouble is that one might share James' general aspiration to lay traditional debates to rest in a way that renders philosophy more relevant to everyday life, and yet *reject* the particulars of James' metaphilosophy. In other words, one could reject the Jamesian thesis that first-order philosophical positions are expressions of psychological tendencies and yet nonetheless embrace the aspiration to make philosophy more relevant and less tedious.[8]

The problem, then, is that James' pragmatism provides no way forward in addressing the *metaphilosophical* disputes that his treatment of first-order philosophical claims will naturally occasion. In fact, it is not clear how James even could make sense of such disputes. One might ask whether James' metaphilosophical strategy of re-describing all philosophical disputes as psychological differences is *itself* merely an expression of psychological temperament. If so, then pragmatism offers no lasting resolution of any purported dispute, it merely relocates them to a plane where it is even less obvious how to proceed. The result is simply an impasse.

Could that be the point? James might allege that, properly understood, philosophies are not things over which people should disagree. One instead should simply adopt one's own preferred philosophy and get on with life, leaving others the same latitude to proceed in their own ways. James appears to voice this kind of thought on occasion (ibid.: 644–5), and, again, some may find this an attractive vision of philosophy. The trouble, however, is that in its effort to bring 'peace' (ibid.: 349) and harmonize (ibid.: 386), Jamesian pragmatism also insulates the individual philosopher from critique. That is once one's philosophical positions are reinterpreted in the psychologizing way James recommends, all criticism can be dismissed as merely the expression of alternative psychological tendencies. And the same must be said of the Jamesian pragmatist's critical manoeuvres against non-pragmatist philosophies. On Jamesian grounds, these, too, amount only to the Jamesian giving voice to her own attitudes, expressing that she has intellectual needs that differ from the non-pragmatist's. In the end, not only are philosophical disagreements jettisoned, but the very idea of philosophical *engagement* – sharing and fielding criticisms of our fellow philosophers' ideas, learning from the philosophical views of others, refining our thoughts in the face of objections – also goes by the board. This is an unfortunate result, especially for a philosophical idiom that often prides itself on being experimental, progressive, fallibilist, and anti-dogmatic.

One can read Dewey's pragmatism as an attempt to avoid the implications of James' psychologized metaphilosophy. In Dewey, one finds a return to certain Peircean themes: there is an explicit emphasis on enquiry and the corresponding aspiration to model philosophy on the experimental sciences. However, one also finds in Dewey a far more robust critique of traditional philosophy than is found in either Peirce or James. Whereas Peirce regarded traditional philosophers as insufficiently trained in successful methods of enquiry, and James saw the tradition as helplessly detached from real life, Dewey proposes a *sociological critique* of traditional philosophy. Philosophy, Dewey alleges, is always the cultural site where traditional values and new science clash (MW12: 89).[9] Accordingly, as traditional philosophy is the product of pre-modern, non-democratic, and hierarchical cultural forms, it has been – unwittingly – the intellectual business by which traditional social and moral norms were guarded from the encroachment of new knowledge. Put otherwise, Dewey contends that although traditional philosophy has presented itself as a disinterested examination of eternal verities and perennial problems, it actually has served the sociological function of protecting the interests and values of privileged cultural and economic groups (ibid.: 94). It does this by erecting dualisms of varying kinds – mind and body, reason and experience, knowledge and opinion, reality and appearance – that place the traditional values beyond the reach of scientific and empirical examination (MW12: 92; LW4: 195).

What Dewey calls for, then, is neither a new method for doing philosophy nor a new way to resolve traditional philosophical problems, but a wholesale *reconstruction* of philosophy. A reconstructed philosophy will embrace overtly the role that philosophy has traditionally played covertly and 'unconsciously'; it will present itself as the social mediator between inherited moral tradition and scientific progress (MW12: 94). Yet, as it is self-avowedly the product of modern social forms, reconstructed philosophy will openly function as a *democratic* force, employing the methods of experimental enquiry in the service of democracy (LW13: 168).

Consequently, philosophy reconstructed along Deweyan lines does not aspire to address traditional problems, not even in the dissolving way that James proposed.[10] Proper philosophy rather 'gets over' (MW4: 14) those problems, discards them as 'chaff' (LW1: 4), and takes up the wholly new problems deriving from the interface of contemporary democracy and modern science. Although his radical vision prescribes a full break with traditional philosophy, Dewey understandably devoted much of his career to combating the reflexes and habits bequeathed by philosophy's history. Consequently, in Dewey one finds an even greater role for metaphilosophy than it is assigned in the work of his pragmatist predecessors. One might say that for Dewey metaphilosophy plays the role of *first philosophy* – it is that set of issues that must be examined and settled before progress in any other area of philosophy can commence.

This is why one finds in Dewey's major writings so much preparatory spadework. Before Dewey is able to spell out his positive views, he first must dispose of what he regards as the bad accretions inherited from philosophy's past. Admittedly, the spectacle is often exhilarating, sometimes even liberating: the stifling constraints of implicit presuppositions are exposed and cast off, and new possibilities are brought into view. Crucially, all of this is accomplished by means of a single and relatively simple line of metaphilosophical critique. As Dewey holds that traditional philosophy is the covert attempt to insulate inherited values from the encroachment of modern science, he also holds that the standard problems are entirely the products of the dualisms mentioned above. Taking as the decisive philosophical lesson from Darwinism that continuity and change (rather than disjuncture and fixity) are the fundamental facts (MW4: 3), Dewey declares these dualisms false; he concludes that the problems they generate can be simply discarded, not as meaningless or irrelevant, but as *obsolete* and *unfit* for our attention (MW4: 12–13; MW10: 46).

With the decks cleared in this way, Dewey then proceeds as if his brand of pragmatism were the only viable philosophy available. Accordingly, Dewey's positive programme is not advanced by means of arguments, but rather by way of dense reportage. In a similar fashion, his engagements with his real-time critics tend to be evasive rather than direct; one gets the impression that Dewey takes every purported criticism to be instead a *detraction*, a stubborn or wilful misunderstanding to be handled rather than a challenge to be met (Misak 2013: 137). This is Dewey at his most frustrating, but this mode of interaction is precisely what one should expect from a philosopher committed to a metaphilosophy that regards every philosophical perspective other than his own to be defunct. On the Deweyan metaphilosophy, there is, indeed, no *philosophical* debate to be engaged, but only diagnoses of others' confusion and obstinacy.

In this way, then, Deweyan pragmatism faces many of the same difficulties invited by James' view. Where all potential criticisms are dismissed with a metaphilosophical gesture, the very idea of a philosophical debate dissolves, as does the possibility of refinement in the face of objections and challenges. Again, this is not an encouraging implication for a philosophy that describes itself as experimentalist and fallibilist.

But Dewey's pragmatism occasions a further kind of difficulty that is more troubling still. As was mentioned above, the case Dewey presents for his positive views typically depends upon the success of his metaphilosophical dismissal of the philosophical alternatives. That is, the reason Dewey provides for adopting his variety of pragmatism is *comparative*; he argues that alternatives are nonviable and that his experimentalism is 'the only way ... by which one can freely accept the standpoint and conclusions of modern science ... and yet maintain cherished values, provided they are critically clarified and reinforced' (LW1: 4). The only case Dewey offers for his view, then, is that it's really the only game in town.

A contrast with James is instructive. Recall that for James, philosophical disputes are actually manifestations of clashes between different psychological temperaments. This requires James to acknowledge that there could be some for whom pragmatism is simply dissatisfying. He must recognize the possibility that there could be others who really are tender-minded (or tough-minded); to these individuals, pragmatism offers nothing, and thus James must conclude that for them pragmatism is useless and therefore *false*. Accordingly, James must allow that there could be individuals who are correct to reject pragmatism. Dewey's *socialized* metaphilosophy does not permit this; for him, the rejection of pragmatism is a refusal to accept what Dewey regards as a core truth about philosophy itself, namely, that philosophy is not and never has been in the business of impartial investigation of perennial problems, but has always been the cultural site where traditional values and scientific progress clash. Non-pragmatist philosophies are accordingly benighted or in denial about themselves. Again, according to Dewey, only his brand of pragmatism can perform the required integration of modern democratic values with contemporary science; and, indeed, his pragmatism is the only philosophy that is consistent with science.

As it turned out, Dewey was mistaken on this score. In the latter decade of Dewey's career and in the years shortly following his death, there emerged new versions of the non-pragmatist views that Dewey took himself decisively to have undermined, and these new views all claimed formidable scientific credentials. Chomsky's (1957) nativism is an obvious case in point, but one could also look to the increasingly sophisticated versions of utilitarianism developed by social choice theorists employing the tools of the behavioural sciences. Within a decade of Dewey's death, one finds refurbished versions of epistemic foundationalism, Kantian ethics, and even a dualism of mental and physical properties that are broadly compatible with naturalism and contemporary science. These developments could hardly be dismissed as 'chaff' (LW1: 4). Hence the case for Deweyanism could not be made strictly on the basis of a simple metaphilosophical lesson drawn from Darwin. However, the Deweyan programme had little else to proffer in its favour. In fact, the entire enterprise of reconstructing philosophy along Deweyan lines relied on the premise that traditional views – including concept nativism and property dualism – could not be articulated in scientifically respectable ways. Alas, this premise proved false. The metaphilosophical edifice upon which Deweyan pragmatism had been built turned out to be unsound.

By the close of Dewey's career, pragmatism was in crisis. If discernably pragmatist first-order theses were to be maintained, pragmatist philosophers would have to devise first-order arguments in their favour, and thus give up the Deweyan idea that non-pragmatist views could be swept away at the metaphilosophical level. The task of preserving pragmatism as a philosophical idiom was taken up by several of the mid-century giants of American philosophy, including C. I. Lewis, Nelson Goodman, Wilfrid Sellars, and W. V. O. Quine. In their work, one finds clear continuities with the classical idiom; for example, there is the insistence that meaning and action are inexorably entwined, the suspicion that traditional metaphysical disputes are ill-formed, the abiding interest in aligning philosophy with current science, and much else. But there is also in their work a concerted effort to engage directly with their non-pragmatist opposition, to show that pragmatism can hold its own on the first-order issues.

Of course, one of the unsurprising outcomes of this approach is that the mid-century pragmatists needed to concede some ground. For instance, Lewis was quick to recognize the need to reintroduce the *a priori* (1923), Quine had to countenance classes as abstract objects (1960: 266ff.), Sellars saw fit to theorize intentionality and related mental phenomena (1956), and all were compelled to take decisive stands on modal logics. And, also unsurprisingly, the mid-century pragmatists disagreed sharply, and often publicly, over first-order issues. These disagreements, along with the absence of the encompassing metaphilosophical motifs familiar from the days of Dewey, gave to many onlookers the sense that pragmatism had been abandoned. It was left to late twentieth-century pragmatists such as Susan Haack (1993), Issac Levi (1991), Christopher Hookway (2000), Nicholas Rescher (1992), Cheryl Misak (1991), and Huw Price (2011) to draw explicit ties from the mid-century articulations of first-order positions back to classical pragmatism.

The neo-pragmatism of Richard Rorty represents a strikingly different reaction to the crisis brought on by Dewey's metaphilosophical overreach (Rorty 1979; 1982; 1989). Rather than follow the mid-century pragmatists in trying to defend first-order pragmatist theses in the absence of the Deweyan metaphilosophical architecture, Rorty retrieves the diagnostic elements of Dewey's metaphilosophy and combines it with the therapeutic bent of Jamesian pragmatism. What emerges is an explicit rejection of much of Dewey's *positive* programme; Rorty dismisses Dewey's attempts to rehabilitate empiricism and to theorize enquiry (Rorty 1982: 77–85). In fact, Rorty overtly jettisons the very ideas of a *philosophical* problem and a *philosophical* method altogether (ibid.: xxxix).[11] One might say that Rorty *doubles-down* on the metaphilosophical programme inaugurated by Dewey. What emerges is an end-of-philosophy proposal, with a Jamesian twist. According to Rorty, we are to abandon philosophy and turn our efforts to something else, namely, poetic conversation aimed at re-describing our bourgeois and ethnocentric aspirations in attractive, reassuring, and inspiring ways (Rorty 1989: 196f.).

Rorty's brand of pragmatism has been the target of extensive critique, both on the part of pragmatists and others, and I will not survey these debates here.[12] Rorty's significance at present lies in his unabashed embrace of pragmatism's creeping metaphilosophy. In Rorty, one finds an even more extreme metaphilosophy than Dewey's; for Rorty, metaphilosophy isn't merely first-philosophy, it's all the philosophy there could be. Rorty then concludes that, as there could be no *meta*philosophy without a first-order discipline of philosophy, the only thing left for philosophers to do, given their distinctive training, is to tell the tale of philosophy's ultimate disintegration. With that story told, the philosopher joins the ranks of 'all-purpose intellectuals' (Rorty 1982: xxxix) offering social commentary that no longer poses as anything other than interesting chatter.

The foregoing survey of pragmatism's trajectory is admittedly highly selective, and much more detail would need to be provided in order for it to stand as a viable account of pragmatism's history.[13] Thus far, I have aimed only to suggest that the trajectory of pragmatism is marked by a struggle regarding the scope of metaphilosophy. The progression from Peirce to James and Dewey is characterized by a creeping metaphilosophical tendency. Peirce originally proposed a semantic rule for philosophical enquiry that was transformed by James into a method for re-describing traditional philosophical problems as expressions of psychological differences; Dewey expanded pragmatism further into a full-bore metaphilosophical platform, a comprehensive second-order vision that fixes first-order philosophical views and so ultimately treats all purportedly philosophical disputes as metaphilosophical impasses.

Pragmatists working in Dewey's wake faced the dilemma of either abandoning the bloated metaphilosophical elements that had become central to pragmatism since Dewey, or embracing them even more completely. I have suggested that neither horn is comfortable. The former threatens to lose the distinctiveness of pragmatism; the latter abandons philosophy entirely.

3. PRAGMATISM AS METAPHILOSOPHICAL MINIMALISM

The task is to devise a way to preserve a distinctively pragmatist trajectory while rejecting the problematic metaphilosophical commitments associated especially with Jamesian and Deweyan varieties of pragmatism. The natural place to look is Peirce. Although treatments of Peirce's pragmatism – including the one I offered above – tend to fix on the pragmatic maxim as Peirce's core methodological insight, there is I believe a deeper idea that gives rise to the maxim. To be specific, from his earliest writings, Peirce is keen to reject the idea of a natural 'order of analysis' in philosophy, and he also rejects the corresponding idea that there is a first philosophy. Accordingly, the maxim offers an action-guiding conception of meaning that does not rely upon any particular ontological inventory, and similarly does not employ the familiar categories of *substance, accident, predicate*, and the like. Peircean pragmatism is, one might say, the attempt to provide a workable conception of philosophical enquiry in the absence of settled answers to longstanding philosophical questions concerning what there is.

The point is subtle, but important. Since at least Aristotle, philosophers have tended to think that certain philosophical issues are conceptually dependent upon others. On the standard Aristotelian hierarchy, for example, all other philosophical issues are conceptually dependent upon the fundamental metaphysical questions concerning *being qua being*. According to this scheme, metaphysics is first philosophy, and a properly structured philosophical perspective would need to first settle its metaphysics before any views in the other areas of philosophical enquiry could be stably established. Alternatives to the Aristotelian hierarchy are easy to find in the history of philosophy. For example, Descartes is commonly read as proposing that epistemology (rather than metaphysics) is first philosophy. The details of these views are not important at present. What is to be emphasized is that views of this kind do not only assert that there is a natural order of philosophical analysis, and thus a proper order in which philosophers should take up their questions; it also fixes a scheme of *conceptual priority* among areas of philosophical enquiry. It holds that, if, say, metaphysics is first philosophy, then in cases where one's metaphysics clashes with one's epistemology, the latter must be reformulated to fit the former. Views of this kind, then, show us not only how to build a philosophical system but also how to fit our philosophical pieces together.

Pragmatism, in its Peircean variety at least, rejects this traditional picture. It denies that there is a natural order of analysis and a corresponding scheme of conceptual priority among philosophical results. One could say that the pragmatist therefore embraces a kind of *holism* about philosophical enquiry, where the aim is not to build a system with the results of some ordained 'first' area of philosophy as its foundation, but rather to 'understand how things in the broadest possible sense of the term hang together in the broadest possible sense of the term', as Sellars famously put it (Sellars 1963: 1). According to this holist view, the conceptual relations between the different philosophical areas are *themselves* matters to be worked out in the course of continuing enquiry, and it is consequently *conceptually* possible that well established results in, say, moral philosophy should provide the basis upon which our metaphysics is revised. The objective in the meantime is to propose a way for philosophers to pursue whatever enquiries they may wish, without prejudging the substantive conclusions such inquiries will reach. In a nutshell, the aspiration is precisely what Peirce held it to be: to keep open the way of enquiry (CP1: 135). And what is required in order to do so is an all-purpose conception of how to enquire that does not itself presuppose or fix particular answers to ongoing philosophical disputes. In other words, the pragmatist should seek to devise a conception of enquiry that is *neutral* among contending first-order positions; it should leave philosophical debates just as they are, and recommend a way in which the disputants could make progress. Understood in this way, pragmatism's metaphilosophy is *minimalist*.

That very rough Peircean-Sellarsian depiction is acceptable as far as it goes. Importantly, as a minimalist metaphilosophy, it offers a way of skirting the metaphilosophical antinomy. On the view I've sketched, pragmatism is a two-part metaphilosophical programme. First, it offers a methodological prescription for conducting philosophical enquiry according to which, roughly, the content and meaning of a concept is, at least in part, a matter of the role that concept plays in human practice. Second, it rejects the traditional idea that there is a natural order of philosophical analysis, a 'first philosophy' upon whose content the rest of philosophy relies. The absolutely crucial thing is to avoid what I've been calling metaphilosophical creep; pragmatists must resist the tendency to propose this minimalist metaphilosophy as a first philosophy. Pragmatist metaphilosophical minimalism rather must be regarded as itself a tentative *modus operandi*, rather than a prescription for a full-scale reconstruction of philosophy.

The way to eschew metaphilosophical creep is to foreground a distinction that has been well articulated recently by Huw Price between *active* and *passive* rejection (Price 2011: 258). The pragmatist *passively* rejects the metaphilosophical claim that there is a natural order of analysis; that is to say, the pragmatist simply declines to affirm it. But the pragmatist need not go so far as to actively affirm its contrary in her 'theoretical voice', as Price puts it (ibid.). The pragmatist is banking on her metaphilosophical prescription proving most fruitful, but recognizes that this, too, is little more than a hypothesis, a prediction concerning what will emerge in the course of enquiry. It therefore cannot serve as a theoretical standpoint from which to dismiss alternative philosophical programmes, including those committed to the hierarchical conception of philosophy's structure.

This is not to say that the pragmatist cannot offer criticisms of those alternatives. To be sure, pragmatist metaphilosophical minimalism can offer *internal* critiques of those metaphilosophies; as pragmatists have long argued, such views look circular and question-begging. The point here is to avoid presupposing one's own metaphilosophical views when criticizing another's. Similarly, pragmatist minimalists can devise forceful criticisms of hegemonic metaphilosophical programmes that – like Dewey's – aspire to police the discipline of philosophy according to their own methodological commitments. Here, too, those arguments can be cast as *internal* criticisms; metaphilosophies are fragile things, and there is as yet no metaphilosophy so well established as to be fit to police all of the others.

One important implication of this conception of pragmatism's metaphilosophy is that it presents pragmatism as *exclusively* a second-order idiom. After all, if pragmatism is indeed the combination of a methodological suggestion for philosophical enquiry with a holistic view of the relations among different compartments of philosophy, then it looks as if pragmatism *itself* proffers no *distinctive* first-order results. To be sure, the pragmatist's first-order commitments will tend to be empiricist and naturalist; but this is because these commitments look to her the most promising given the current state of enquiry. She must concede that new findings and unexpected results could compel her to adopt first-order views of a quite different stripe. More importantly, on the picture I've proposed, the pragmatist must recognize that at present there is a broad range of first-order philosophical views that are consistent with well-ordered enquiry and yet not consistent with each other. The pragmatist thus must recognize that there are pragmatist-compatible options on all sides of many standing philosophical debates. Accordingly, those disputes must be pursued on non-metaphilosophical terrain. This requires the pragmatist to acknowledge that her current first-order commitments are still only hypotheses that could readily be defeated in the course of enquiry, and that defeat could come from a position she is presently disposed to regard as non-pragmatist.

The minimalist metaphilosophy I've proposed for pragmatism hence looks to be a minimalist conception of pragmatism itself. Pragmatism emerges as a methodological suggestion that has an empiricist and naturalist bent, but ultimately is compatible with almost any first-order view. Accordingly, in debates regarding first-order issues, there will be no distinctively *pragmatist* view. In fact, according to the position I'm proposing, the very idea of a *pragmatist* first-order view is strained; with pragmatism understood as a minimalist metaphilosophy, there are only pragmatist *considerations*, appeals to pragmatist methodological ideas about how to conduct enquiry into a given subject-matter. To be sure, in some cases, minimalist pragmatism can press severe criticisms of first-order views that seem to be lacking support in human enquiry and experience. That is, minimalist pragmatism still has claws. Still, what pragmatism cannot be on this minimalist picture is a *philosophy* unto itself. To put matters succinctly, on the minimalist version, pragmatism is at most a *way* of arriving at and holding one's first-order philosophical views, whatever they may be.

There is no doubt that some pragmatists will regard this as objectionable; and some may go so far as to regard it as a *reductio* of the position I've sketched here. For those invested in the classical conceptions of pragmatism offered by James and Dewey, it is crucial to retain the idea that pragmatism is at once a metaphilosophical stance *and* a first-order programme. I have indicated above why I think this double-duty conception is problematic. But a further consideration in favour of the minimalist view now presents itself. However important the first-order contributions of Peirce, James, Dewey, and the others may be, it is nonetheless important to retain an idea central to the classical pragmatists that, as a forward-looking philosophy, pragmatism envisions a philosophical future that is better than philosophy's past and present. It seems to me that this means that pragmatists have to not only invite but try to occasion the development of philosophical views – at the first-order and beyond – that are better than their own.[14]

NOTES

1 See (Talisse 2007: Ch. 1) and (Talisse 2012: Ch. 3) for details. See also (Talisse and Aikin 2008).

2 Citations to Peirce's work refer to the *Collected* Papers and will follow the standard convention: (CP volume number: paragraph number).

3 See (Misak 2013: 29ff.) and (Hookway 2012: Ch. 9) for discussion.

4 Hilary Putnam expresses this sentiment nicely when he characterizes pragmatism as the 'insistence of the supremacy of the agent point of view' (Putnam 1987: 70). Robert Brandom characterizes this insistence as 'fundamental pragmatism' (Brandom 2011: 65–7).

5 See (Misak 1995) for a sustained study of the several varieties of late nineteenth- and twentieth-century empiricism.

6 Here I follow (Misak 2013: 17ff.) in holding that the pragmatic maxim is compatible with a cognitivist conception of value judgements.

7 See (Forster 2011) for a comprehensive examination of Peirce's engagements with the debates regarding nominalism.

8 One struggles to find an example of a philosophical tradition that stands in favour of irrelevance and tedium. Charges of philosophical irrelevance and tedium are always second- or third-personal, insults directed at one's philosophical opposition. As such the aspiration to make philosophy more 'relevant' and less 'tedious' is by itself vacuous. Philosophical idioms disagree about what relevance is, and what level of precision is called for.

9 Citations to Dewey's work will refer to the *Collected Works* and will follow the standard convention: (CW volume: page number).

10 Dewey criticizes James for assigning to pragmatism the task of resolving traditional philosophy's debates; according to Dewey, pragmatism shouldn't bother with problems that it has not generated (MW4: 109). See (Talisse 2007: 10–11) for discussion.

11 Rorty also expels Peirce from the pragmatist trajectory, claiming his only contributions were to have 'given it a name, and to have stimulated James' (Rorty 1982: 161).

12 See especially (Haack 1993: Ch. 9); (Price 2003); and (Talisse 2001) for pragmatist critiques of Rorty.

13 (Misak 2013) begins to tell the fuller story. See also (Burke 2013).

14 I would like to thank Scott Aikin, Diana Heney, D. Micah Hester, Cheryl Misak, and Luke Semrau for comments on an early draft of this essay.

13 On Metaphysical Quietism and Everyday Life

The dogmatism into which we fall so easily in doing philosophy.

(Wittgenstein 1958: §131)

Metaphysical quietism threatens the projects of contemporary metaphysics, projects to which a large number of people have devoted their lives and energies; and it leaves many philosophers with the impression that the work of philosophy, so conceived, is entirely destructive – say, an end-of-philosophy stance. They feel it is unworthy of the aspirations and achievements of traditional philosophy, despite the fact that there is no consensus about what these achievements are.[1]

Famously advocated by Wittgenstein, and championed in recent times by John McDowell and Richard Rorty, metaphysical quietism has been castigated by Crispin Wright – who is, in this respect, representative of many contemporary Anglo-American philosophers – as 'an explanation-proscribing view of philosophy' that is 'far too unclear about its methods and objectives' (Wright 2001: 373, 221).[2]

In this paper I would like to address these concerns about the methods and objectives of metaphysical quietism. For this purpose I shall defend it against three objections: 1) Does quietism simply refuse to answer legitimate problems? 2) Is quietism self-refuting, a theoretical position masquerading as a way of avoiding choosing sides in theoretical debates? 3) Is quietism a pessimistic, unambitious philosophy or, more radically, a self-destructive stratagem that aims for an end of philosophy? I take it that this last objection is the most powerful. In what follows I want to work towards a response to it inspired by Wittgenstein's teaching.

Although the first two objections are relatively easy to answer, I shall argue that the critics of quietism are right to see a problem in its wider significance, at least as it is portrayed in the work of leading contemporary quietists, Rorty and McDowell. Wittgenstein provides a way of defusing this objection. In his philosophical practice, metaphysical quietism addresses itself to a fundamental feature of the human condition, not merely a problem of a certain class of professional philosophers. If metaphysical thinking is a ubiquitous distorting influence on human intellectual and practical activity then the persistent effort to find an alternative way of thinking can be cast in a positive light as a form of enlightenment and self-overcoming – a vital aspect of living a reflective life free (to the extent that one can be free) from powerful illusions and fixations to which we are repeatedly drawn.

DEFINING PHILOSOPHICAL QUIETISM

In its original use for a form of heterodox Roman Catholic theology, 'quietism' referred to a withdrawal from worldly affairs and intellectual activity together with a doctrine of self-annihilation. Religious quietists held that through the constant contemplation of God one could overcome the self and merge with Him.[3] Quietism in philosophy, however, has a wholly different meaning.

At a minimum, quietism in philosophy refers to a non-doctrinal non-constructive mode of philosophizing. It is not a philosophical doctrine, as its name perhaps suggests, but a *method* of philosophizing that aims at ridding oneself of philosophical doctrine in one region of thought or another. Its earliest form is ancient Pyrrhonian scepticism. The Pyrrhonist cultivated dialectical skills to show that the reasons for any proposition p are cancelled out by the equally plausible reasons for not-p. In this way they avoided making *any* unqualified assertions at all about what is true and what not (see Sextus Empiricus 1994). By way of this intellectual discipline they arrived at a detached state of mind termed *ataraxia* on all matters of reflective concern including, but not limited to, philosophical doctrines or theories.

As a quietist, without doctrine, the Pyrrhonian is careful to avoid making assertions about the conclusions of her arguments or the practical benefits of her therapy unless carefully qualified as statements about how things strike her at a certain time, without any general implications for others or herself at other times. As Sextus Empiricus puts it, 'We report descriptively on each item according to how it appears to us at the time' (Sextus Empiricus 1994: 3). If coherent this represents a truly global philosophical quietism. Since it is based on a failure of reason to authorize *any* proposition we might call it *aporetic quietism*.

Quietism in contemporary philosophy comes in different versions, which are differentiated by their targets. One can be a quietist about a specific philosophical issue (e.g., external world scepticism), a philosophical concept (e.g., correspondence Truth, God) or an entire philosophical discourse (e.g., religious discourse). For example, a quietist about God refuses to think that the concept of God plays any substantial metaphysical role (e.g., as creator of the universe, or ultimate source of moral goodness). This may reveal itself as a refusal to use the term altogether, or just a refusal to do so in the context of metaphysical theorizing. The quietist is not denying that God exists, for that would be a kind of negative metaphysical claim; rather, she eschews a metaphysical response altogether by refusing to either assert or deny the existence of God. Why? Perhaps she does not consider there to be any sufficient reason to believe one way or another; or she might not find the idea of the Christian God (fully) intelligible; or she might not see any genuine point in endorsing theism or atheism. Such a person may, however, continue to use the term in ordinary (non-metaphysical) contexts but its meaning or point would then have to be explained. A quietist might even eschew religious discourse altogether in so far as she felt that its significance in any context inevitably presupposed metaphysical commitments of various sorts (e.g., to God as a supernatural being, to an immortal soul).

The most influential modern quietist is Ludwig Wittgenstein whose advocacy of *metaphysical quietism* serves as the model or inspiration for current forms of this method of philosophizing (e.g., John McDowell, Huw Price, Richard Rorty). In the *Tractatus* Wittgenstein writes, 'Philosophy is not a body of doctrine but an activity. A philosophical work consists essentially in elucidations'

(Wittgenstein 1961: 4.112). This theme is continued in the *Investigations*: 'Philosophy simply puts everything before us, and neither explains nor deduces anything' (Wittgenstein 1958: §126). It is this Wittgensteinian version of quietism as addressed specifically to metaphysical doctrines that I shall be defending in this paper.[4] For convenience I shall, henceforth, simply refer to it as 'quietism' – adding qualifications as needed.

In contrast to Pyrrhonian aporetic quietism, Wittgenstein's version is a form of *semantic quietism*.[5] It is a method based on suspicion of the *intelligibility* of metaphysical 'problems' and their 'solutions'. A quietist of this kind engages in the delicate art of *scrutinizing the problems themselves* – rather than working on answers to them – to avoid having to take a stand in metaphysical debates about which theory (say, which form of realism or anti-realism) is best.[6] The immediate aim of the quietist in the region of philosophical thought to which it applies is not to debate metaphysical doctrines, which are seen as semantically dubious (non-truth-apt, non-explanatory, etc.), but to attempt to get along without them.[7]

Schematically, a quietist is a philosopher who sees that there can be no point in attempting to answer a problem that is unclear or confused or that does not hang together sufficiently well with everything else we believe about the world. In short, quietists adopt a sceptical attitude to metaphysical problems themselves. The philosophical task is to examine their legitimacy based on a close philosophical scrutiny of the problems and their presuppositions or motivations. Once suspicious of the intelligibility or coherence of a problem, the quietist engages in philosophy in order to earn the right to free herself of any obligation to go in search of an answer to it.

The most fully explicit example of quietist therapy in contemporary philosophy is McDowell's *Mind and World* (2nd edn 1996) which deals with the Cartesian sceptical problematic of a metaphysical gap between mind (reason) and world (nature). The task, as McDowell sees it, 'is diagnosis, with a view to a cure' (McDowell 1996: xvi). He sees modern scepticism (e.g., the problem of the external world), as well as constructive programmes in epistemology (especially the battle between foundationalism and coherentism) as inchoate expressions of an underlying philosophical 'anxiety' about how it is possible that we can have thoughts with *any* empirical content at all.

As a quietist, McDowell does not attempt to answer this how-possible question but, rather, to diagnose and neutralize the source of its power. This he traces to a restrictive scientific naturalism, which understands sense experience – part of our natural animal endowment – by locating it within the realm of law-governed phenomena studied by the sciences. His 'cure' takes the form of an alternative way of thinking about human nature that allows us to see experience as playing a rational role in belief formation and revision.[8] The problem of the relation of mind and world is not answered but made to appear less 'urgent' (ibid.: 176–8).[9] If successful, we come to see that we suffered from the *illusion* of imagining there was a gap between subject and object.

We also might want to recognize a third category of quietist best represented by Richard Rorty. He is what we might call a *pragmatic quietist* because he refuses to accept Wittgenstein's view of metaphysics as 'unobvious nonsense' (Wittgenstein 1958: §464) a troubling claim I shall discuss below, preferring to question not the intelligibility of metaphysical problems but their pragmatic *fruitlessness*. Rorty does not accept 'nonsense' or 'conceptual puzzlement' as worthwhile terms of criticism in philosophy, preferring pragmatist alternatives such as 'useless' and 'unprofitable'. This has seemed to some to leave the traditional problems intact, since use and fruitfulness are, to some extent, in the eye of the beholder.[10] But I shall leave discussion of pragmatic quietism for another occasion.

What is more important for present purposes is to note that recent discussions of quietism, pro and con, have lost sight of the fact that the two most important forms of quietism in the history of philosophy, Pyrrhonian aporetic quietism and Wittgensteinian semantic quietism, were both practised as a way of life. Quietism is best understood, I shall argue, as a form of reflection with an ultimately *ethical* goal in the ancient Greek sense of 'ethics', which concerns how to live a complete human life well. This theme will emerge in due course.

THREE OBJECTIONS

Let us now consider three objections that have been raised against quietist methodology:

1. Does Quietism Simply Refuse to Answer Legitimate Questions?

The first problem is that quietism might seem to involve neglecting genuine problems. If a real problem confronts one how can it possibly help to leave it unaddressed? This is a common complaint against Wittgenstein's methodological remarks, even though his complex literary strategies can seem to lend encouragement to metaphysicians – prompting some to see an inconsistency between his philosophizing and his avowed method of philosophy. But this apparent inconsistency is *merely* apparent and is, in fact, a consequence of his commitment to quietist therapy.[11]

A key aspect of this therapy is to attempt to accurately express various forms of metaphysical thinking *as it strikes the one gripped by it*, in order to bring about a shock of recognition on the part of the one whose thinking it is. Once this is achieved the thinking is exposed to interrogation, which may reveal that what first presented itself as genuine thought is, under examination, only the illusion of thought. To practice quietism, therefore, requires giving up the philosophical dogma that if something *seems* to make sense then it *does* make sense.

Since he is diagnosing his own confusions, Wittgenstein traces the intricate twists and turns of his own thoughts by employing unresolved voices of temptation and correction, of doubt and the silencing of doubt, and so on. This serves to instil an appreciation of the way metaphysical thinking arises from 'the immensely manifold connections' (Wittgenstein 1993: 133) between concepts of different kinds employed in different language-games. It also allows a reader to see their own metaphysical thinking expressed there. But one is not supposed to stop at that point. One is supposed to find in Wittgenstein's cues, hints, and examples the resources to subject one's own metaphysical thinking to sceptical scrutiny – a step that is, it seems, often missing from his readers.

The apparent weakness of quietist methodology is that one cannot be told to give up metaphysical thinking. Successful treatment requires that one undergoes something like a conversion experience. But since the basis of the therapy is reflecting on one's own mastery of language (and so, of course, on the reality that language is about) this anti-authoritarianism is also a strength in so far as it is an appeal to something familiar or common or everyday. Like the coming to consciousness of a repressed emotion in psychoanalytic therapy, one has to come to see the emptiness of metaphysical assertion for oneself by comparing metaphysical language 'on holiday' with ordinary language that is 'doing work' (Wittgenstein 1958: §38, §132). This requires self-transformation: a coming to see for oneself not just that such and such metaphysical 'thinking' falls apart under critical examination but also that the attempt to theorize in this way loses its charm.[12] That is the rationale behind Wittgenstein's remark, 'I should not like my writing to spare other people the trouble of thinking' (ibid.: §4).

A crucial part of the success of the quietist method, then, depends on convincing oneself that what first presented itself, in philosophizing, as a clear problem (that already points to the possibility of a solution) is really a *conceptual puzzle*, that is, a confusion or difficulty in understanding that has the misleading form of a problem. It changes its aspect from being a *problem*, which we think we perfectly well understand, to a *puzzlement*, which poses serious semantic difficulties of comprehension. '[Philosophical] difficulties', Wittgenstein muses, 'as long as they are seen as *problems*, are tantalizing and appear insoluble' (Wittgenstein 1969a: 46, italics added).

It is, then, no part of quietist methodology to turn away from a legitimate problem in philosophy. The quietist is sceptical that the alleged 'problem' is a genuine problem. To satisfyingly exorcize this perplexity is to diagnose its source and to provide an alternative way of thinking in which it does not present itself as a problem requiring an answer.

Andy Hamilton, considering scepticism about the external world, misses this key transformation in the nature of the problem by remarking, '"Quietism" suggests a turning to other issues, recognizing that scepticism is intractable' (Hamilton 2014: 277). But it is not, as Hamilton implies, that the 'problem' is too difficult to solve but that a conceptual confusion is cleared up so that the 'problem' is made to '*completely* disappear' (Wittgenstein 1958: §133). This remark can only appear in the right light if we make a distinction between a *generic conception* of a philosophical problem (say, external world scepticism) and *specific forms* of this problem (e.g., external world scepticism as it appears in the *Meditations*).

Wittgenstein's therapy is *only* addressed to *specific forms* of philosophical problem: to particular plights of mind and the forms of words that express them. What are made to disappear are these specific forms of the problem not the generic problem, which often recurs in different guises interminably. Wittgenstein likens work in philosophy to the attempt to address '(finite) cross strips' rather than '(infinite) longitudinal strips' of paper; that is, he sees himself as treating specific expressions of problems that re-occur in different forms indefinitely (Wittgenstein 1967: §447).[13]

2. Is Quietism Self-Refuting?

A second and perhaps more serious problem for the quietist is that of self-refutation. How can the quietist argue against metaphysical theorizing without that very argument being understood, in spite of itself, as *another* metaphysical theory? Isn't the denial of theory simply a negative theory? Charles Larmore, in commenting on *Mind and World*, puts it like this:[14]

Wittgensteinian quietism has been enormously influential, despite the inescapable paradox that manifestly lies at its heart. For how, we must ask, can showing up the mistaken assumptions underlying some philosophical problem amount to anything other than putting better views in their place? And must not these views be of a similar scope and thus provide the makings of a positive theory of the phenomena in question?

(Larmore 2002: 194)

McDowell replies:

This talk of mistaken assumptions might make Larmore's point look stronger than it is. Superstitions and confusions are not theories, to be replaced with better theories. To remind oneself of what is obvious, or would be if it were not for philosophy, is quite different from putting forward a substantive view.

(McDowell 2002: 294)

McDowell's first point is that, according to the quietist, a traditional philosophical 'problem' is a matter of 'superstitions and confusions', *not* a genuine problem, so its removal is not to be thought of as engaging in a constructive theoretical enterprise. As Wittgenstein teaches, we do not require a philosophical theory of, say, confusion or nonsense in order to show that certain statements are confused or nonsensical. All we need is our ordinary sense of what makes sense and our ordinary capacity to explain what we mean when.[15]

Wittgenstein writes:

My aim is: to teach you to pass from a piece of disguised nonsense to something that is patent nonsense.

(Wittgenstein 1958: §464)

One reason philosophers have not found themselves at all sympathetic to this statement is the sense that Wittgenstein is relying on a very unobvious theory of 'grammar'; one that is not apparent to ordinary masters of the language.[16] Another is that the term 'nonsense' seems a hard, even outrageous, term of abuse. So, let us address some possible misreadings of Wittgenstein's use of 'nonsense' as a term of criticism in philosophy as well as the question of grammar:[17]

1. To repeat, Wittgenstein has no strict theory of nonsense, unlike Carnap and other logical positivists who appeal to a verificationist theory of meaning. Wittgenstein's technique of investigating the sense of various utterances by trying them out in (mostly) imagined contexts relies on nothing more or less than the capacities that any master of a language possesses: an ability to judge what makes sense when, of how to project words into new or further or different contexts of use.

2. What is being called 'nonsense' is a person's *use* of language, a particular speech act. On Wittgenstein's view, a piece of language considered in isolation is neither intelligible nor nonsensical unless or until it is inserted back into a speech context in 'the stream of life' (Wittgenstein 1967: §173). So, as a term of criticism, 'nonsense' is not directed at a given statement as such but at a *particular employment* of it on a certain occasion. We should be careful not to be fooled by the fact that we may quite easily be able to *imagine* a legitimate use for the words in question; or that we may find it relatively easy to *give* them one (Wittgenstein 1969b: §622).

3. When Wittgenstein castigates a particular employment of language as nonsense ('when language goes on holiday', Wittgenstein 1958: §38) he does so for an open-ended variety of reasons and purposes, for example, because it is: i) pointless because, say, uninformative; or ii) wavering between quite different logical functions, for example it may be presented as if it is both a rule and an empirical claim; or iii) involves terms whose use has yet to be settled, and so on. He never denies that there are many differences between the nonsense utterance, 'Fuzzle, muzzle, wuzzle' and a metaphysical thesis such as, 'Causally isolated possible worlds exist'.[18]

4. In sharp contrast to logical positivists, Wittgenstein is not concerned with policing what makes sense and what doesn't. For him it's not a matter of telling us what we can and can't say according to established rules of meaningful discourse.[19] He is better understood as teaching, 'Say what you like so long as you can explain what you mean by reference to our common language.' A guiding idea is that metaphysical uses of language, when fully thought through, go to pieces and that we can demonstrate that they do so.

5. It is a central part of Wittgenstein's technique to elicit a kind of self-recognition on the part of the metaphysician, or the metaphysician in each of us. In a similar manner to psychoanalytic therapy, the one gripped by the problem must be led to see that it is she *herself* that has suffered from, say, an illusion of meaning if the therapy is to be successful.

It is also important to see that the quietist need not be understood as having no theories at all, for the term 'theory' is flexible enough to cover *any* view, account, or position offered in a philosophical context. On such a broad understanding Wittgenstein has a theory (or theories) about how metaphysics arises, for example: it may be a matter of reading features of our mode of representation into the world; or of taking certain pictures we associate with words to dictate a certain application; or confusing a conceptual with an empirical question. The quietist is not inconsistent in having theories in *this* sense since they are not metaphysical in character. Self-refutation would require his self-consciously endorsing a *metaphysical* theory.[20]

In Wittgenstein's own practice, there is an important contrast between recalling the common criteria on the basis of which we apply concepts to things – which he calls a description of the logic of language or 'grammar' – and substantial philosophical theories. He remarks, 'We must do away with all *explanation* and description alone must take its place' (Wittgenstein 1958: §109).[21] Wittgenstein wants to call on his reader to first test the *sense* of metaphysical pronouncements against the ordinary uses of the terms that occur in them, that is cases in which we can say what work language is actually doing. Again, this requires no worked out theory of 'grammar'. Rather what counts as 'grammar' is *negotiated* through one's investigations of the sense of propositions. In Moore's 'Notes' of Wittgenstein's lectures from the 1930s there is the highly illuminating phrase 'the grammar of that discussion' which reveals how flexible the notion of 'grammar' is supposed to be (Moore 1955: 17).

Similarly, to clear away 'superstitions and confusions' by recalling 'what is obvious' is not to propose a philosophical theory of the obvious. As Wittgenstein puts it, 'The work of the philosopher consists in assembling reminders for a particular purpose' (Wittgenstein 1958: §127). For example, sign-posts point the way to those who understand them; or we can point to one and the same object to teach a child the meaning of terms for its shape and its colour. These are not philosophical theses; they are statements of the obvious. But while they would not be news to most people, they can help one in the grip of philosophical confusions about what it is to follow a rule, or what is achieved by ostension.

In McDowell's presentation the quietist relies for conviction on 'truisms' (McDowell 2002: 27), which suggests an element of dogmatism that is entirely lacking in Wittgenstein's writings. McDowell seems to assume that there will be agreement with him about what is obvious or truistic unless we've been perverted by philosophy. But, how does he know *that*? Wittgenstein avoids the term 'truism', preferring to speak of 'everyday' or 'ordinary' uses of language:[22]

What *we* do is bring words back from their metaphysical to their everyday use.

(Wittgenstein 1958: §116)

'Everyday', in Wittgenstein, means non-metaphysical, not what is usual or statistically likely or non-technical. If metaphysics is something whose discovery requires careful investigation then, for the same reason, so does the everyday – which is, perhaps surprisingly, not simply available or 'given' to reflective consciousness in the way that we might have supposed. It is also worth observing that a scientific report or a legal document written in highly abstruse language are examples of ordinary language in Wittgenstein's sense despite the fact that they are technical employments of language.[23]

In recounting what 'we' *can* say, or how 'we' *can* project concepts into new or imagined contexts, Wittgenstein is not assuming or predicting agreement – as, say, G. E. Moore does in regard to his 'common sense propositions' – he is *searching* for it.[24] The 'we' is problematic, raising the question of who else, if anyone, grants that we speak for them in our projections. The 'can' contrasts with the metaphysical 'cannot' or 'must'. And though there must be *some* 'agreement in judgments' (ibid.: §242) if we are to find each other intelligible, what is primarily in focus is agreement in 'possibilities of phenomena' (ibid.: §90).

As Rorty's writings make clear, quietists face the following dilemma: if they use ordinary non-philosophical locutions then there is a danger of failing to make contact with the targets of their therapy; but if they employ philosophical language then it will almost inevitably embody philosophical assumptions that the quietist has no wish to endorse.[25] Wittgenstein chooses the first horn of the dilemma. His text involves almost no explicit reference to traditional philosophical doctrines or theories so his readers face the difficulty of trying to connect his remarks to them.[26] McDowell chooses the second horn of the dilemma, and does his best to defuse the sense that there is anything metaphysically contentious in his philosophically weighty statements of what is (supposedly) obvious.[27]

3. Is Quietism a Defeatist, Unambitious Conception of Philosophy?

The third and most important difficulty for quietism is given voice to by Crispin Wright:

According to Wittgenstein, the limit of our philosophical ambition should be to recognize the assumptions we are making in falling into philosophical difficulty, and to see our way clear to accepting, by whatever means, that nothing forces us to make them. It is, for Wittgenstein, the very craving for legitimizing explanations of features of our talk about mind, or rules, or mathematics that leads us into hopeless puzzles about the status – the epistemology and ontology – of those discourses. Philosophical treatment is wanted not to solve these puzzles but to undermine them.

(Wright 2001: 43–4)

If quietism simply undermines philosophical puzzles then it would seem to be, as Wright intimates, disappointingly negative and unambitious. The very natural urge to explain seems to find no expression in what Wright castigates as 'an explanation-proscribing view of philosophy' (ibid.: 45).[28]

Wittgenstein worried about this aspect of his quietist vision, remarking:

Where does this investigation get its importance from, given that it seems only to destroy everything interesting: that is, all that is great and important? (As it were, all the buildings, leaving behind only bits of stone and rubble.).

He responds:

But what we are destroying are only houses of cards, and we are clearing up the ground of language on which they stood.

(Wittgenstein 1958: §118)

But demolishing metaphysical *Luftgebaude* (literally, *aircastles*) and 'clear[ing] up the ground of language' that gave a specious support to them can appear underwhelming, especially when compared to the grand explanatory ambitions of metaphysicians. Of course, one might observe that these ambitions have never been realized; but, in philosophy, hope springs eternal. Whence the importance of quietism?

Rorty and McDowell seem to suggest that *only in so far* as one is gripped by traditional (say, Platonic or Kantian) metaphysical problems and the search for solutions to them and, *furthermore*, is suspicious of these 'problems' and 'solutions', *only then* will one find value in quietism. Its significance lies in entitling such a person to turn towards more profitable or more urgent matters. The trouble is that this answer does nothing to dislodge the unfortunate impression that quietism is addressed *only* to disenchanted academic metaphysicians.

Wittgenstein's much more ambitious answer depends on extending the scope of quietist therapy to *all* human thought, including self-reflection, ethics, and politics. In a letter to Norman Malcolm he remarks:

> what is the use of studying philosophy if all it does for you is to enable you to talk with some plausibility about some abstruse questions of logic, etc., & if it does not improve your thinking about **the important questions of everyday life**, if it does not make you more conscientious than any ... journalist in the use of the DANGEROUS phrases such people use for their own ends. You see I know that it's difficult to think well about 'certainty', 'probability', 'perception', etc. But it is, if possible, still more difficult to think, or *try* to think, really honestly about your life & other people's lives. And the trouble is that thinking about these things is *not thrilling*, but often downright nasty. And when it is nasty then it's *most* important.
>
> (Malcolm 2001: 35, bold added)

What is of particular interest in the present context is that Wittgenstein sees a connection between studying 'abstruse questions of logic' (i.e. the logic of language or 'grammar') and the aim to improve one's thinking 'about the important questions of everyday life'. In other words, the grammatical investigations that aim to bring words back from their metaphysical to their everyday use are supposed to be no less applicable to ethics and politics and other vital concerns.[29]

The present suggestion is that Rorty and McDowell do not do justice to the depth of the human attachment to metaphysical modes of thought. Rorty quixotically speaks of a 'post-philosophical culture' (Rorty 1982: xli) as if it is clear that we *could* have a culture whose ethics, politics, and social life is free from metaphysics. And McDowell seems to exclude such things as 'reflection about the requirements of justice or the proper shape for a political community' (McDowell 2009: 367) from the scope of quietist therapy. In both cases there is a failure to acknowledge that metaphysical thinking can and does characterize ethical, social, and political reflection no less than reflections about, say, the mind, propositions, science, mathematics, and God.

The key to understanding the wider relevance of Wittgenstein's quietism is to see that the urge to metaphysical thinking is *ubiquitous* in human thought, extending well beyond abstruse questions of logic (or 'grammar') into the realm of everyday thought and talk. For this reason quietist therapy (in an extended sense) is urgently needed in considering the important questions of everyday life. At least this is so if we are of the view that the universal and absolute 'explanations' of metaphysics are spurious and insulated from empirical criticism. And, of course, any such criticism must be based on the detailed working-through of particular metaphysical pronouncements.

EXTENDING THE SCOPE OF QUIETISM THERAPY

To make these initial steps towards an answer to the third objection clearer we must say more about what metaphysics is and the naturalness of the urge to metaphysical thinking. We have so far skirted a key question: if the target of quietism is metaphysics then how do we know what to *count* as metaphysics? Numerous commentators on Wittgenstein's philosophy would have us understand metaphysics as a family resemblance term, so that a range of different, variously related, activities count as engaging in metaphysics. For example, *essentialism*, the idea that there is something common to all things that fall under a concept, is a paradigm metaphysical commitment. Or, to give another well-known example, *realism about universals*, the idea that there are abstract properties that are actually or potentially instanced by many different concrete things at various times and places. Or *theism*, the commitment to the existence of the God of the Judeo-Christian tradition often characterized as omnipotent, omniscient, and omnipresent.

The trouble with this characterization of metaphysics is that everything resembles everything else in indefinitely many ways. The very idea of family resemblance – an analogy with 'the various resemblances between members of a family... that overlap and criss-cross' (Wittgenstein 1958: §67) – provides insufficient guidance as to *which* resemblances are at issue. So the appeal to family resemblance does not solve the problem of demarcating the metaphysical or, indeed, even giving us a useful criterion for a candidate metaphysical claim.[30] So I propose that we characterize metaphysics in a way that abstracts from matters of content as far as possible and instead look to its distinctive method of enquiry and the distinctive stance or attitude that the metaphysician adopts towards his or her putative discoveries.

It would be widely agreed in philosophy that metaphysics is a non-empirical or *a priori* study of reality distinct from mathematics and formal logic. As it is often put, it is a study of the 'nature' or 'essence' or 'deep structure' of reality. One does *not* answer metaphysical questions by way of empirical research in the form of, say, scientific enquiry. Put otherwise, metaphysics is insensitive to empirical research; it is based only on what is acceptable to *a priori* reason. The contrast with mathematics is particularly instructive. Although both mathematics and metaphysics are produced *a priori* (say, without dependence on controlled experiments or systematic observations of the empirical world), mathematics is, by rational consensus, applicable to the world through its incorporation into the sciences. The same cannot be said for metaphysics. Even those who claim that science inevitably has metaphysical commitments do not agree about what these are.

It is the non-empirical *a priori* character of metaphysical enquiry together with the fact that it is a mode of reasoning distinct from mathematical or logical proof that has led to unresolvable disagreements. As Albert Einstein remarks, 'Time and again the passion for understanding has led to the *illusion* that man is able to comprehend the objective world rationally by pure thought without any empirical foundations – in short, by metaphysics' (Einstein 1950: 13, emphasis added).[31] And as the history of philosophy clearly demonstrates, metaphysical systems differ considerably amongst themselves, without being resolvable by further appeals to reason. C. S. Peirce acutely observes:

> [The *a priori* method of metaphysics] makes of inquiry something similar to the development of taste; but taste, unfortunately, is always more or less a matter of fashion and accordingly metaphysicians have never come to any fixed agreement.
>
> (Pierce 1955: 16–17)

Kant, using a more combative metaphor, famously spoke of metaphysics as 'the battlefield of these endless controversies' (Kant

1998: A *vii*) – an intellectual war that, in spite of his best efforts, his own critique was unable to quell.

Let me, then, characterize metaphysics in terms that connect it to our everyday thinking. We can put it like this: metaphysics is a commitment to ***dogma*** by which I shall mean *claims about reality whose truth is taken to be authoritatively established independently of the empirical.* This is a refinement of the everyday sense of the term which is: 'laying down of principles by an authority as incontrovertibly true' [OED]. Metaphysics aims to arrive at fixed and universal 'truths' whose independence of the empirical comes in two main forms: 1) independence of empirical grounding, there being no empirical criteria for the application of the concept at issue;[32] and/or 2) an insensitivity to, or being too remote from, the evidential bearing of observation and experiment.[33] Sensitivity to the empirical does not require direct confirmation through observation or experiment, of course. As Quine argues, it is enough to be part of a system (e.g., physics) which, as a whole, does justice to the empirical data. For instance, the quasi-necessary framework principles of physics such as Riemannian geometry are not confirmed or verified by observation or experiment. Nonetheless, as Putnam explains, they are still sensitive to the empirical in the attenuated sense that a revision of a framework principle can be rationally required by empirical discoveries (Putnam 1975: 88). It is characteristic of metaphysics that no empirical discovery ever rationally requires its revision.

With this understanding of metaphysics-as-*dogma* in place we can distinguish the sophisticated and systematic *academic metaphysics* characteristic of professional philosophers (e.g., Armstrong's theory of universals, Lewis' theory of possible worlds, Danto's essentialist conception of art) from the relatively unsophisticated and unsystematic *everyday metaphysics* characteristic of everyday life, an example of which we shall consider shortly. The suggestion is that *both* count as kinds of metaphysical thinking, whether systematic or not, whether sophisticated or not. Metaphysics, to repeat, is *dogmatism* – the familiar term that I am using for the human tendency to hold fixed convictions about how things are whilst lacking a proper sensitivity to the empirical.

Instead of casting the quietist as requiring a mysterious skill of discerning esoteric metaphysical thinking in the manifold topics of human reflection, she need only have a suspicion of the disengagement of some thinking from a proper sensitivity to the empirical. This is the incentive to philosophical reflection. What, then, is a proper sensitivity to the empirical? In some cases it is relatively easy to say what this comes to. The current controversy over the metaphysical status of string theory in physics concerns whether it has *any* empirical consequences, however remote, that can be confirmed or disconfirmed.[34] In other cases we can say relatively easily what a proper sensitivity to the empirical is *not*, for example, basing a general claim on only a few examples, and thereafter not being open to revision on the basis of further or future experience. But many cases where one suspects *dogmatism* are not so straightforward and require philosophical investigation.[35] There is no all-purpose test for *dogmatism* so we need to investigate case by case whether a claim suspected of being *dogmatic* does or does not 'hang together with our whole system of [empirical belief and] verification', as Wittgenstein puts it (Wittgenstein 1969b: §279).

THE EVERYDAY IMPORTANCE OF QUIETISM

With the preceding understanding of metaphysics we can now explain the wider practical significance of quietism in Wittgenstein's teaching. It is important to see that quietism is not merely aimed at systematic metaphysical theorizing of the sort engaged in by academic metaphysicians. Quietism bears on **any** *dogmatic* thinking in any region of our lives including our ethical and political lives. Indeed in ethics and politics one is tempted to use such thinking 'for their own ends', as Wittgenstein puts it. Here there is the possibility of imposing invidious distinctions between oneself and others for self-aggrandisement, condescension, control, consolation, and so on; and that is why examining such thinking 'is not *thrilling* but often downright nasty'. Metaphysical thinking in an academic setting may have a charm or grandeur but in the realm of ethics and social life it is often *nasty* – so something bound up with self-deception and avoidance.

If this is on the right track then we can now counter the suggestion that quietism is a pessimistic or unambitious philosophy. If, as recorded history suggests, the tendency to *dogmatism* is a central and enduring feature of human nature then the importance of quietism is ultimately a product of the significance of overcoming the metaphysical fixities – false 'necessities', arbitrary absolutizations – that distort our thinking about the world and each other and to which we are all too susceptible.

Let me give an example of everyday metaphysics for illustration. To *stereotype* people, in the pejorative sense, is to hold *dogmatic* (metaphysical) views about people which often take the form of disparaging generalities regarding race, sex, religion, age, and so on.[36] These typically have the form 'All x's are y's' where the term 'x' refers to some social category and 'y' to a rich evaluative expression, for example, stupid, ignorant, immature, terrorist. Such claims may superficially look like empirical generalities garnered from experience – they have the form of such – but they actually function as quasi-necessities in so far as they play an unquestioned foundational or presuppositional role in one's thinking. To the extent that they are insensitive to empirical confirmation or disconfirmation, such thinking is not open to serious empirical challenge. It thus qualifies as metaphysical in the expanded sense we are considering. Like religious true believers – another form of metaphysics – people who engage in dogmatic ethical or political stereotyping may have various strategies for maintaining their *dogmas* (i.e., metaphysical claims) in the face of reasonable criticism. For instance, one may treat contrary evidence as 'the exception that proves the rule' thus seeming to deal with it rationally whilst, in fact, setting it aside.

Consider the recent case of a man at a town hall meeting in America shouting, 'All Muslims are terrorists.'[37] It seems clear that this is meant as a *dogma* rather than an over-hasty empirical generalization. Would it be withdrawn if we pointed to the many Muslims who have committed no terrorist act and so on? Presumably not. He is using a metaphysicalization of the term 'terrorist' to indicate that Americans like himself are on the side of good, Muslims on the side of evil. Quietist therapy in such a case is not a matter of taking sides in the debate over whether the *dogma* in question is true or false. Work is first needed to expose the conceptual confusion. It consists in revealing this *dogma* as a *dogma*, demonstrating its insensitivity to the empirical despite its outward appearance of being an empirical claim; exposing the distortion in the use of the concept 'terrorist'. The aim is to reveal to the one who uttered it, that this claim actually expresses an essentialist prejudice, not an empirical truth. That may be all the therapy that is needed; or perhaps work will be required to undermine a commitment to essentialism about race. The therapy is successful only when the one who uttered the problematic remark comes to their senses and withdraws it.

As we have seen, metaphysics includes the *a priori* claims of traditional philosophy that are, in principle, not decidable by appeal to empirical criteria or evidence. But it also covers everyday claims that are, through various intellectual subterfuges, quarantined from empirical disconfirmation or that lack empirically distinguishable criteria (e.g., the belief in reincarnation). Here human psychology, especially latent animosities and psychological self-defence mechanisms, has an important bearing on the motivation to metaphysical thinking. The indignant man in the town hall meeting may hide the nature of his thinking from himself and others by self-deceptively blurring empirical and conceptual considerations because it is emotionally convenient.[38] This is an aspect of the nastiness that Wittgenstein refers to in the quote above. Quietist therapy is directed, in the first instance, at exposing and criticizing the empirical insensitivity of metaphysical thought and so the distortion of everyday language that ensues[39] – the details of which will take as many different forms as there are different kinds of metaphysical thinking.[40]

A key insight of Wittgenstein's quietism, which helps to explain its power, is the thought that we *all* tend to suffer from what Kant called 'dogmatic slumber' (Kant 1950: 4:260) in *every* area of intellectual or practical enquiry. Metaphysics-as-*dogmatism* is here pictured by Kant as a disengagement from reality, a dream of reality. One tends to think immediately of religious fanaticism, the beliefs of cult followers, and devotees of astrology. But there are many more mundane examples apart from social stereotyping, for example, consider the belief that mothers exhibit an inimitable kindness towards their children (one supposed not to be possible for fathers), a dogma used to strip fathers of custody in divorce cases. Thus I cannot fully agree with Nigel Pleasants when he writes, 'Wittgenstein's deconstruction of pseudo-explanations is merely the prolegomenon to thinking about urgent social, political and ethical issues' (Pleasants 1999: 182). On the contrary, a large part of the difficulty in thinking honestly *about* social, political, and ethical issues is to diagnose and root out metaphysical pseudo-explanations.

Wittgenstein's conception of the human chimes with Plato's vision of us as self-deluded, taking shadows on a wall for realities and struggling indefinitely to see reality for what it is. But, unlike Plato, Wittgenstein teaches us that we can make our home in the cave, by the only light we have, firelight. Imagining or pretending that there is another super-light – in Plato's image the light of the sun – is *the* fundamental illusion of metaphysics. Since the urge to metaphysical thinking is a mark of the human throughout history, quietism is not an end-of-philosophy philosophy. Nor is it a defeatist philosophy. If metaphysics constantly binds and fixes us making movement impossible, then quietism plays the role of persistently attempting to untie the tethers that hold us, freeing us to confront new possibilities of human life as well as the practical problems arising from the 'crooked timber' of human psychology.[41]

NOTES

1 For a trenchant expression of this view see Hilary Putnam's criticism of the end-of-philosophy stance in (Putnam 2012: 65–6).

2 It is partly for this reason that many readers of Wittgenstein do not take his methodological remarks seriously, mining his texts for what appear to be inchoate expressions of metaphysical commitment. Mostly, analytic philosophers have *not wanted* to see Wittgenstein as a metaphysical quietist despite his unambiguous non-doctrinal intentions (Wittgenstein 1958: §§109–33). Many pass over the methodological remarks in silence, reading him as propounding metaphysical theses, including the picture theory of representation (e.g., David Pears), radical conventionalism (Michael Dummett), quasi-realism (Blackburn), meaning-scepticism (Saul Kripke), and a use-theory of meaning (Paul Horwich), and so on. I shall not endeavour to criticize these misreadings here; only to note their almost complete refusal to take Wittgenstein at his word.

3 The tradition arises from the teachings of Miguel de Molinos in the seventeenth century. Patricia Ward writes: 'Quietism emphasized the abandonment of self to God, annihilation of the will in union with God, pure love, and a form of inner prayer' (Ward 1995: 107).

4 Although Wittgenstein is a metaphysical quietist, it is arguable that he practices a more global quietism. I leave consideration of this matter to another occasion.

5 While I am sympathetic to a good deal of David Stern's fine discussion of what he calls Wittgenstein's 'Pyrrhonism about philosophy' it is misleading to straightforwardly identify Wittgenstein with Pyrrhonism. For one thing, it misses the difference between aporetic and semantic quietism: Pyrrhonians do not question the sense of philosophical

claims, but only their all-things-considered rational support. See (Stern 2004: 168–70).

6 Andy Hamilton (Hamilton 2014: 278) wrongly supposes quietists cannot engage in philosophical argument. Rather, what they cannot do is to argue for a *metaphysical* thesis. But other uses of argument are available, for example *reductio ad absurdum*, arguing for a non-metaphysical thesis.

7 Famous semantic quietists in the history modern philosophy include Hume and Carnap. One might also include Kant at least in his attitude towards traditional or speculative metaphysics and the dialectical illusions to which it gives rise.

8 One might well raise the question whether this strategy is consistent with quietist therapy given that McDowell's way of thinking about (conceptualized) experience is highly controversial and draws heavily on substantial theoretical insights of Sellars, Davidson, and especially Kant. There is not space to explore this issue in the present context.

9 Wittgenstein demands something stronger than this: that the problem should be made to '*completely* disappear' (Wittgenstein 1958: §133).

10 McDowell, for one, has charged Rorty with not doing enough to avoid the charge of indifferentism rather than taking the preferred path of 'exorcism' (McDowell 1996: 142, fn 17).

11 For example, Felicia Ackerman sees Wittgenstein as simply confused about his own method (Ackerman 1992). Simon Blackburn is representative of a kind of middle position in saying that 'Wittgenstein seems to leave unfinished business' (Blackburn 1993: 589), as if Wittgenstein was engaged in metaphysical speculation that, for idiosyncratic reasons, he was unable to complete.

12 Part of this charm is, no doubt, rhetorical. It is a feature of the great metaphysical systems that no matter how sophisticated they become their core tenets are simply stated in a few words (e.g., 'Forms are immutable', 'God exists', 'Nothing exists but physical objects') and so give the false appearance of being relatively easily graspable by the human mind.

13 See (Macarthur 2014) for further discussion.

14 Similarly, Wright remarks: 'The paradox is that while, like all "deflationists", Wittgenstein needs to impress us of the illegitimacy of more traditional aspirations, *argument* for that is hard to foresee if it is not of the very coin which he is declaring to be counterfeit' (Wright 2001: 372).

15 For an elaboration of this vision of what we ordinarily mean when, see (Cavell 1969).

16 This is essentially Putnam's criticism of Wittgenstein in 'Wittgenstein: Pro and Con' in (Putnam 2012).

17 Putnam's recent criticism is, arguably, based on misunderstanding Wittgenstein's use of the term 'nonsense'. See 'Wittgenstein: Pro and Con' in (Putnam 2012).

18 (Wittgenstein 1958: §499). The example is drawn from David Lewis's 'realism' about possible worlds.

19 Contrast here the reading of Wittgenstein as a sort of 'nonsense policeman' inspired by Peter Hacker (Hacker 1996).

20 Metaphysical quietism is compatible with philosophical theory, even explanatory philosophical theory, so long as the latter is non-metaphysical. An example is Huw Price (Price 2011) who combines metaphysical quietism with a subject naturalist explanatory programme for concepts (e.g., truth) and speech acts (e.g., assertion). Many philosophers, including Crispin Wright (Wright 2001: 373), seem to have missed that quietism need not be global. For a recent example of this oversight see Hamilton (Hamilton 2014: 278).

21 The italics matter: it would be a mistake to read Wittgenstein as denying that philosophers can provide, say, explanations of meaning.

22 Wittgenstein does not appeal to truisms to secure the agreement of his readers. He uses the term only once in the *Investigations* in the phrase 'the form of a truism' (Wittgenstein 1958: §95).

23 However, Wittgenstein does tend to focus on ordinary non-technical uses of language (e.g., 'table', 'lamp', 'door') in his grammatical investigations. Consider (Wittgenstein 1958: §104).

24 Here I rely on Cavell's interpretation of Wittgenstein's philosophy in (Cavell 1979).

25 See (Rorty 1982: xiv).

26 Warren Goldfarb, in his Harvard seminars on Wittgenstein, argues that Wittgenstein is trying to discover the very first step ('the decisive move') into the full-blown metaphysical picture, something Goldfarb calls 'a proto-philosophical picture'. This might involve nothing more than a false emphasis, or insistence.

27 For instance, McDowell is perfectly happy to subscribe to what he calls 'naturalized platonism' understood as 'the idea … that the dictates of reason are there anyway, whether or not one's eyes are opened to them; that is what happens in a proper upbringing' (McDowell 1996: 91). Is naturalized platonism constructive philosophy, as it appears to be? Not at all, McDowell replies, 'the phrase serves only as shorthand for a "reminder", an attempt to recall our thinking from running in grooves that make it look as if we need constructive philosophy' (*ibid*.: 95). But not everyone will be convinced. Indeed McDowell acknowledges, 'It is true that much of what I put forward in my own person does not sound like reminders of what is merely obvious' (McDowell, in Smith 2002: 294).

28 A similar sentiment is expressed by both Blackburn (Blackburn 1993) and Robert Brandom (Brandom 1994: 29–30).

29 This remark is addressed to Malcolm in a letter in which Wittgenstein explains why he broke off friendly relations with Malcolm for a period of five years! I discuss this remark and the original incident that provoked it in detail in a forthcoming paper (Macarthur forthcoming).

30 I do not take this to be a problem for Wittgenstein's own use of the notion of family resemblance, namely, as a counter-picture to the picture of a word having a logical essence.

31 Of course the difficulty in drawing the distinction between science and metaphysics is, in part, that science is often (highly) speculative *before* it is experimentally confirmed (e.g., the general theory of relativity, or the postulation of the Higgs Boson).

32 Putnam has written, 'there is a conceptual connection between grasping an empirical concept and being able to grasp a perceptually justified application of that concept' (Putnam 1995: 295). Putnam mentions some qualifications such as that the ability in question might require testimony and expert judgement but this does not affect the main point, which is, 'the interdependence of our grasp of truth-claims and our grasp of verification' (*ibid.*: 305), that is empirical grounds of concept application.

33 I shall not consider here how to extend this understanding of *dogma* to the relatively *a priori* fields of mathematics and logic. One possibility would be to include the idea of being insensitive to what Putnam has referred to as 'quasi-empirical methods' in mathematics and logic: 'By "quasi-empirical" methods I mean methods that are analogous to the methods of the physical sciences except that the singular statements which are "generalized by induction", used to test "theories", etc., are themselves the product of proof or calculation rather than being "observation reports" in the usual sense' (Putnam 1975: 62).

34 In a debate on string theory the science writers Jim Baggott and Mike Duff ask, 'Should a theory that makes no predictions be regarded as scientific?' (2013).

35 An important theme of Putnam's work is the difficulty of drawing a line between the metaphysical and genuine science at least in the distant reaches of scientific theorizing. Unlike him, I do not think this means that we must say science is inevitably committed to a metaphysics. Rather, I take it to show that it takes philosophical work to constantly draw and redraw the line between legitimate science and metaphysics.

36 This is consistent with the definition of the term in psychology. A stereotype is 'a fixed, overgeneralized belief about a particular group or class of people' (Cardwell 1996).

37 See http://metro.co.uk/2015/11/20/man-shouts-all-muslims-are-terrorists-towards-muslim-speaker-at-town-hall-meeting-5514908/

38 Wittgenstein remarks, 'Philosophical investigations: conceptual investigations. The essential thing about metaphysics: it obliterates the distinction between factual and conceptual investigations' (Wittgenstein 1967: §458).

39 We can speak of giving a concept such as terrorist a 'metaphysical emphasis' (Wittgenstein 1969b: §482) by dogmatically treating it as having a fixed meaning which lacks a proper sensitivity to our actual use of the term 'terrorist' in our linguistic practices.

40 Wittgenstein remarks, 'People are deeply imbedded in philosophical, i.e., grammatical confusions. And to free them presupposes pulling them out of the immensely manifold connections they are caught up in' (Wittgenstein 1993: 133).

41 Kant writes, 'Out of the crooked timber of humanity no straight thing was ever made' (Kant 2007: 8.23; 113). I have altered the translation slightly. I'd like to thank the editors of this volume, Giuseppina D'Oro and Søren Overgaard, as well as Robert Dunn, Andy Hamilton, Gavin Kitching, and Talia Morag for comments on early drafts of this paper.

14 The Metaphilosophy of the Analytic–Continental Divide

From History to Hope

The prospect of yet another paper on the analytic–continental divide will fill many readers with despair. The current consensus seems to be that the distinction between 'analytic' and 'continental' philosophy no longer merits serious attention – if it ever did. According to many recent commentators,[1] any attempt to draw a line, no matter how blurry, between these camps is bound to fail. No matter what one proposes as the distinguishing feature of continental philosophy – a subject matter, a method, a writing style, or anything else – it is easy to find paradigmatically 'analytic' thinkers who display this feature and paradigmatically 'continental' thinkers who do not. Nor is the problem solved by replacing an 'essentialist' approach to this distinction with one that looks only for family resemblances.[2] No matter how many resemblances we identify between particular thinkers, it is hard to see how they could justify dividing philosophy into these particular camps. After all, 'analysis' sounds like an activity, 'the continent' like a place, and as Bernard Williams memorably put it, opposing the two is like dividing 'cars into front-wheel drive and Japanese' (Williams 2003: 23). Given how difficult it is to make sense of this distinction, it is easy to see why more and more philosophers either ignore the divide or actively try to bridge it. Surely, we might think, the wisest thing is to follow their lead? Surely we should just stop talking about the analytic–continental divide, and strive to be, in Hilary Putnam's phrase, 'philosophers without an adjective' (Putnam 1997: 203)?

As attractive as the ideal of 'philosophers without an adjective' is, I suspect it is too early to abandon these particular adjectives. For one thing, the idea of an analytic–continental divide still plays some role in contemporary philosophy, though a less important one than it did twenty or thirty years ago. It still has a certain institutional reality, inasmuch as courses in 'continental philosophy' continue to be taught and scholars continue to list the phrase on their CVs. More importantly, it is easy to overstate how much cross-pollination there is between paradigmatically 'analytic' and 'continental' work. Donald Davidson is often cited as an example of a philosopher influential on both sides of the divide, but as James Chase and Jack Reynolds point out, this obscures the fact that 'the early Donald Davidson is a major presence in the analytic tradition and the late Davidson is not' (Chase and Reynolds 2011: 5). And there is a deeper reason to think we cannot yet put the analytic–continental divide behind us. Those who are sceptical of this divide often argue that it is not enough to ignore it. We must, they say, actively bridge it, actively undermine the divide by drawing on work from both sides of it whenever possible.[3] But we cannot bridge a divide without knowing what we are bridging. In order to take steps to put the analytic–continental divide behind us, we must have some idea of what sort of divide it was once supposed to be. If our understanding of the divide is deficient, then our attempts to move past it will be deficient as well.

I say all of this because I believe that in one important respect, our understanding of the divide *is* deficient. Most commentators take for granted that if there were a significant analytic–continental divide, it would be a *first-order* divide: a difference in how philosophers in these camps handle some first-order matter. This matter might be a topic of interest to both camps, or a thesis endorsed by both, or a common influence, or any number of other things. But it would be something like an answer to a specific question or a solution to a concrete problem. Thus Samuel Wheeler tries to undermine the divide by claiming that 'Jacques Derrida and Donald Davidson are both right about a number of central topics' (Wheeler 2000: 1) – notably, their denial that there is a 'magic language' that does not need to be interpreted (ibid.: 3). From Wheeler's perspective, the question of whether Derrida and Davidson are the same sort of philosopher just is the question of whether they agree on this and other 'central topics'. Similarly, Lee Braver argues that a promising way to 'end the dispute' between analytic and continental philosophy is to recognize that 'there is at least one important topic shared by both'

(Braver 2007: 4): an anti-realist metaphysics that originates in Kant's first *Critique* and resurfaces in Heidegger and Derrida as well as in Putnam, Dummett, and others. Like Wheeler, Braver apparently assumes that the only thing that could bridge the analytic–continental divide is agreement on some first-order topic. Perhaps an assumption like this is one reason many philosophers think the analytic–continental divide does not merit serious attention. If it were purely a divide about first-order topics, then bridging it would be straightforward. We would simply find philosophers on both sides of the divide who agree about the topics in question, and that would be the end of the matter.

But what if the analytic–continental divide were primarily a higher-order divide – a divide in *metaphilosophy*? What if philosophers on opposing sides of the divide were distinguished not by their stance on some first-order issue, but by their conceptions of what philosophy is? In that case, bridging the divide would be more difficult. We could not make it go away by showing that Derrida and Davidson agree about magical languages or that Heidegger and Putnam share an anti-realist metaphysics. Two philosophers might agree about any number of first-order issues but have significantly different views about philosophy's nature. In these circumstances, bridging the divide would be a matter of showing that philosophers thought to be on different sides of it actually agree significantly about metaphilosophical issues. That would be much more difficult, not only because metaphilosophical issues are typically broader in scope than first-order ones, but because it is relatively rare for philosophers to make their metaphilosophies fully explicit – which is partly why Colin McGinn calls metaphilosophy 'the most undeveloped part' of the field (McGinn 2002: 199).

This thorny issue is precisely the one I want to explore here. I want to explore the possibility that the analytic–continental divide is best understood as a metaphilosophical divide, and that bridging the divide requires us to find metaphilosophical common ground on both sides of it. Of course, showing that many or most of the disputes between 'analytic' and 'continental' philosophers have really been about metaphilosophy would be an enormous undertaking, and space does not permit me even to start it here. I will focus instead on the more positive, bridge-building side of this issue – or more specifically, on one example of such bridge-building. I will try to show what it might look like to move past the analytic–continental divide after reconceiving it as a metaphilosophical divide. My strategy for doing so will be to argue that a pair of philosophers usually placed on opposite sides of this divide – Paul Ricoeur and Richard Rorty – share a commitment to two substantive and unusual metaphilosophical principles. One is what I will call a *metaphilosophy of historicity*: a commitment to what Charles Taylor calls 'the historical thesis about philosophy' (Taylor 1984: 18).[4] Roughly stated, this is the view that 'philosophy and the history of philosophy are one', such that 'you cannot do the first without also doing the second' (ibid.: 17). The other is what I will a call a *metaphilosophy of hope*: a belief that philosophy is a *melioristic* enterprise constituted by the drive to 'make a better future' (Koopman 2009: 17).[5] These principles are so distinctive, and so far-reaching in their consequences, that from a metaphilosophical perspective, Ricoeur and Rorty have much more in common with each other than either does with many philosophers usually placed on the same side of the analytic–continental divide. Insights of this sort, I argue, are exactly what we need if we are to have any chance of moving beyond the divide for good.

My decision to focus on Rorty and Ricoeur is a controversial one. Rorty, it might be objected, is no mainstream analytic philosopher. He may have begun his career as one, but he grew increasingly 'dubious about analytic philosophy as disciplinary matrix' (Rorty 2007: 126), and by the late 1970s, he was calling himself a pragmatist rather than an analytic philosopher. But two points need to be stressed here. First, even if Rorty's shift from analytic philosophy to pragmatism was as complete as he sometimes claimed – and some argue that it was not[6] – there is no reason to see these movements as antithetical. Rorty's pragmatism is not that of Peirce or Dewey. It is a *neo*-pragmatism or *analytic* pragmatism, a pragmatism that has taken the linguistic turn and learned decisive lessons from analytic philosophy. Second, while Rorty rejects many of the doctrines often associated with analytic philosophy, this does not preclude placing him on the analytic side of the analytic–continental divide. Philosophical movements, I assume, are ill-defined things without essences, and all of the 'analytical' doctrines rejected by Rorty are also rejected by many paradigmatically analytic philosophers. He denies that philosophy has a distinctive method called conceptual analysis, but so does Timothy Williamson (2007: 10–15). He is sceptical about progress in philosophy, but so is Colin McGinn (1993: 10). That Rorty rejects these doctrines does not preclude placing him on the 'analytic' side of the analytic–continental divide. A similar point can be made about Ricoeur. His work is extraordinarily difficult to pigeonhole: it draws on analytic philosophy as well as the traditions of personalism, phenomenology, and philosophical hermeneutics, and it is suspicious of the paradigmatically 'continental' movements of deconstruction and post-structuralism. All that this shows, however, is that Ricoeur is not *merely* or *exclusively* a continental philosopher, and that it is possible to categorize him in other ways as well. But no one would claim that 'analytic' and 'continental' are the *only* groups into which philosophers can be sorted. Belonging to one of these groups is compatible with belonging to many others as well.

I

Let me explain what I mean by a metaphilosophy of historicity and of hope. By 'metaphilosophy', I mean simply what Timothy Williamson (2007) calls 'the philosophy of philosophy'[7] – the branch of philosophy that examines philosophy itself. This is obviously an enormous domain. In their *Introduction to Metaphilosophy*, Overgaard, Gilbert, and Burwood divide metaphilosophy into no fewer than seven distinct enquiries, including the questions of whether philosophy progresses and of how it relates to the humanities and the natural sciences (Overgaard, Gilbert, and Burwood 2013). I will focus on three metaphilosophical questions that I consider particularly central. First is the question of 'how philosophy is to be done' (ibid.: 14). This is chiefly a question about the *methods* philosophers should use, but it is more than that, because among other things, it involves reflection on the *data* to which these methods are applied.[8] The second question concerns the *standards* that govern philosophical work. Work on this topic asks what makes some contributions to philosophy more successful than others, and 'what serious lapses from these standards would disqualify something from counting as philosophy at all' (ibid.: 15). Third is the matter of philosophy's *goals*: the question of what the enterprise aims at and of 'what sort of results we can expect from it' (ibid.). As open-ended as these questions are, they are a different sort of question than the first-order questions to which most philosophers devote most of their energy. They are more sweeping, in that the way we answer them has consequences for nearly everything else philosophers do. My views about qualia or distributive justice might not have any implications for my views about how philosophy should be done, but my views about the latter question have clear and dramatic implications for my views about the former. The second-order questions are also more reflexive, in that they aim at a certain kind of self-awareness – not just an answer to some concrete question, but an understanding of what we are *doing* when we ask such questions.[9] This is not to say that it is always easy to distinguish first-order and second-order questions, or that the answers to first-order questions never bear on second-order ones. But just as the questions asked by biologists typically look different from the questions asked by philosophers of biology, the questions posed in the philosophy of philosophy typically look different from those posed in garden-variety first-order philosophy – hard cases notwithstanding.

My claim is that Rorty and Ricoeur share a metaphilosophy in that their views about the methods, standards, and goals of philosophy overlap significantly. They share a metaphilosophy of historicity in that their answers to all three questions make essential reference to philosophy's dependence on its past. First, their views about how philosophy should be done involve the past. Both Rorty and Ricoeur see philosophy as an essentially historical undertaking. Part of what philosophers must do as they go about their work is engage with the history of philosophy in a certain way. To the extent that they do not do so, their work is deficient. Second, their conceptions of the standards that apply to philosophical work make essential reference to the past. For both thinkers, part of what makes some philosophical work more successful than others is the way and the degree to which it engages with the history of philosophy. Third, Rorty and Ricoeur understand the goal of philosophy in a way that makes essential reference to the history of the discipline. Part (though not all) of the point of doing original philosophical work is to attain a deepened understanding of our historical situation, a better sense of where we stand in a historical development.

Rorty and Ricoeur also share a metaphilosophy of hope. They see philosophy as a melioristic enterprise as well as an historical one, an enterprise constituted by the drive to build a better future. This metaphilosophical outlook, however, is not based on a warranted belief that philosophy actually is building a better future. For both, this better future is an object of hope, a practical presupposition we adopt in the absence of evidence. The hope for a better future is essential to Rorty's and Ricoeur's conceptions of philosophy. Both think it informs the matter of how philosophy should be done. They think philosophers should work in ways that actively contribute to this better future that is hoped for rather than justifiably believed in. They also think that part of what makes some contributions to philosophy better than others is the way they contribute to this hoped-for future. Finally, they believe that the attempt to build a better future is a major part of the point of philosophy. We cannot understand philosophy's methods, standards, or goals without making reference to the attempt to realize a hoped-for future.

The metaphilosophies of historicity and hope might seem to be in tension, since one nudges philosophers towards the past, the other towards the future. But they are actually complementary. A better future is presumably one in which some of the problems we now face have been solved or ameliorated. Moving towards a better future thus requires that we have some idea of what is problematic about our current situation. Understanding current problems, however, often requires a grasp of their history, since serious and complex problems have often become so through lengthy temporal developments. More importantly, problematic features of a situation can go unnoticed, and when they do, it can be much more difficult to solve them. Problems need to be identified, and as Koopman argues, one strategy for doing so is to engage in genealogical reflection on 'the way in which certain of our practices, beliefs, and conceptions have become severely problematic sources of tension' (Koopman 2009: 220). Identifying problems can involve *problematizing* these practices, beliefs, and conceptions, in the light of their histories. At the same time, when we try to understand the past, we invariably do so in the light of our current situation and projects. We cannot learn anything about the past unless we have some way of focusing our attention on it, some way of discerning which parts of the past are relevant to us and which are not. This focus comes from our current projects.

What we notice in the past is typically a function of what we wish to do with it. But these projects are future-orientated: they aim to bring about something that does not currently obtain, something we *hope* to realize. So it makes perfect sense for the metaphilosophies of historicity and hope to appear together.

II

Let me turn to the roles that historicity and hope play in Rorty's metaphilosophy. To explicate Rorty's views on these matters, I will focus on his 1984 essay 'The Historiography of Philosophy: Four Genres'. This remarkable essay presents itself as an exercise in categorization: an attempt to delineate a number of activities that go by the name of 'history of philosophy'. Rorty sets out to explain how these activities are related, arguing that they do not compete: that we can engage in all of them, but that we should do so separately. But in the course of the essay, Rorty's focus shifts, giving way to a wide-ranging account of philosophical practice. The account turns on the idea that the practice of philosophy is a highly specific *conversational* practice, and that its conversational logic imposes on it a requirement to engage with its past. Even more remarkably, this requirement to engage with the past itself turns out to rest on a certain orientation towards the future – an orientation of hope. Philosophy's conversational nature rests on a metaphilosophy of historicity, and that metaphilosophy of historicity in turn implies a metaphilosophy of hope.

The starting point of Rorty's essay is the observation that the phrase 'history of philosophy' does not always name the same thing. It can refer to four different things, so when we speak of studying the history of philosophy, we can have four different activities in mind. One is 'rational reconstruction', or the attempt to treat past philosophers 'as contemporaries, as colleagues with whom one can exchange views' (Rorty 1984: 49). In rational reconstruction, the philosopher starts with a question of contemporary interest, and studies past thinkers to learn how they answered it – or how they *would* have answered it, if they did not pose it explicitly. Jonathan Bennett's readings of the British empiricists and Peter Strawson's reading of Kant are good examples of rational reconstruction. Their danger is a tendency towards anachronism – towards 'beating texts into the shape of propositions currently being debated in the philosophical journals' (ibid.). Rorty's second genre is 'historical reconstruction' (ibid.), or the attempt to understand past thinkers 'in their own terms'. Historical reconstruction tries to 'recreate the intellectual scene in which the dead lived their lives' (ibid.: 50). It does not force past thinkers to have views on issues of current concern. It attributes to them only views they could be brought to accept as a correct description of what they thought. But while it avoids anachronism, it runs the risk of antiquarianism: of getting so wrapped up in what dead philosophers meant that it fails to ask whether their views are true or their questions worth asking.

Rorty goes on to describe two less familiar ways of engaging with philosophy's past. One is the 'big', 'sweeping' histories written by Hegel, Heidegger, and their ilk (ibid.: 56). These histories do not try to understand past thinkers in their own terms, but also do not apply their work to contemporary questions. They work 'at the level of problematics rather than of solutions to problems' (ibid.: 57). They describe how contemporary philosophers came to be in the situation they currently occupy: which larger forces have led them to have the concerns, standards, and values they now have. Hegel's purpose in tracing the development of freedom, and Heidegger's purpose in narrating the history of Being, is 'to give plausibility to a certain image of philosophy' (ibid.), by revealing that image to be the outcome of a meaningful development. Rorty calls this third genre *Geistesgeschichte*. Its aim is 'to justify the historian and his friends in having the sort of philosophical concerns they have – in taking philosophy to be what they take it to be' (ibid.). *Geistesgeschichte* tries to show that the historian is justified in thinking that certain questions and not others are the genuinely philosophical ones. It is therefore an exercise in 'canon formation' (ibid.: 58). Rorty's fourth genre, and the one he considers most dubious, is 'doxography' (ibid.: 61). Doxography tries to summarize what all important past thinkers have said about the 'central problems of philosophy' (ibid.: 62). It is 'exemplified by books which start from Thales or Descartes and wind up with some figure roughly contemporary with the author, ticking off what various figures traditionally called "philosophers" had to say about problems traditionally called "philosophical"' (ibid.: 61–2). Works in this genre inspire 'boredom and despair' because their authors 'know in advance what most of the chapter headings are going to be' (ibid.: 62) – which figures they will discuss, and which questions those figures will be made to weigh in on. They are, however, 'continually embarrassed by the failure of even the most salient and unskippable figures to discuss some of those concerns' (ibid.: 65).

Rorty does not claim that philosophers must engage in every one of these genres. They need not do doxography; in fact, they should not. 'We should', he argues, 'just stop trying to write books called *A History of Philosophy* which begin with Thales and end with, say, Wittgenstein' (ibid.). As for rational and historical reconstruction, we *can* engage in them, if doing so serves our purposes in a given context. However, there is no reason to think they are the only way of serving any given purpose, so there is little reason to consider them necessary. But things are different with *Geistesgeschichte*. Rorty argues that we do need big, sweeping stories that define canons and thereby justify our own standpoints. At times he suggests this is because of a psychological need for heroes – for 'mountain peaks to look towards' (ibid.: 73). But he also suggests there is a deeper reason – a reason he articulates by saying that 'the *Geisteshistoriker* ... puts the philosopher in his place' (ibid.: 61). The reason is that the term 'philosophy' has an important honorific sense. When I call a question philosophical, one of the things I mean is that I consider it so fundamental that I think all thinkers ought to have grappled with it.[10] The activity of honouring questions in this way seems to demand a role for history. Composing *Geistesgeschichte* is a conversational activity, an activity in which I address claims to others – either actual or potential conversation partners. As a good Sellarsian, Rorty thinks that to make a claim is to commit oneself to defending it: to be willing to justify the claim by giving reasons. Justification, Rorty tells us, is a matter of solidarity – of 'getting as much intersubjective agreement as you can manage' (Rorty 1999: 15). But two kinds of agreement are relevant here. The more obvious kind is first-order agreement about a particular claim being justified. You and I attain solidarity in this sense once we accept the same claim about evolution or quarks or some other topic. The less obvious kind is agreement about standards of justification: about *how one goes about* defending a claim about evolution or quarks or whatever. For you and I to have a conversation at all, we must agree substantially about these standards of justification. They vary from field to field, from community to community. They can and do change. Nevertheless, philosophical conversations clearly aim at solidarity, and solidarity is not just a matter of agreement about some first-order topic. It also involves substantial agreement about how the conversation should proceed.

This need for agreement about conversational protocols seems to be the reason Rorty says that 'the *Geisteshistoriker* ... puts the philosopher in his place'. He claims the way we justify a philosophical outlook – including our view of how to justify a philosophical outlook – is to invoke a sweeping history that shows how that outlook developed and why it is reasonable for us to occupy it. By taking part in a philosophical conversation, therefore, I commit myself to telling (or at least gesturing towards) a *Geistesgeschichte* that would make my view of philosophy look reasonable. And by taking part in a philosophical conversation *with you*, I commit myself to telling (or gesturing towards) largely *the same* story you would tell to defend *your* outlook. Most of the time, I make this commitment very unreflectively, by sharing with you some vague sense of what some of the canonical examples of philosophical conversation are – a sense you and I will have obtained by reading some of the same books, having similar educations, and so on. If I were forced to articulate this sense explicitly, I might fare poorly, and the history I would narrate might be very thin. The point, however, is not what I actually do in the course of a conversation, but what I *commit* myself to doing by taking part in one. For you and I to converse philosophically – even in an honorific sense of 'philosophical' – we must to some degree share a philosophical canon. And canon formation is the business of *Geistesgeschichte*.

This dependence on *Geistesgeschichte* is the reason I have described Rorty as having a metaphilosophy of historicity. He accepts a version of the historical thesis about philosophy, but a very precise version. He does not think philosophy is historical in the sense that philosophers must engage in rational reconstructions of past arguments, or in historical reconstructions of the contexts of those arguments. Those activities are specialized instruments useful for highly specific purposes. But Rorty does think philosophy is essentially historical in the sense that it is a highly specific conversational practice that takes place against the backdrop of some *Geistesgeschichte* or other. Philosophy is, so to speak, a conversational game, and whenever it is played, some *Geistesgeschichte* or other provides the rules of that game. These canon-forming stories furnish participants with an understanding of how the game is to be played. When we take part in a philosophical exchange, you and I implicitly agree to proceed in a manner exemplified by figures in whatever canon you and I share. *Geistesgeschichte* also furnish us with standards. By conversing philosophically, you and I implicitly accept some understanding of what better and worse philosophical conversations would look like – again, an understanding exemplified by the figures we agree to be canonical. This lets us recognize when the conversation is succeeding and when it is not. Finally, we implicitly agree on the point of the conversation, or on what a satisfactory outcome would be. We do not need total agreement on any of these matters, but we need some agreement on all of them. Suppose that you and I agree that Kant is a canonical philosopher, but I think Frege is one and you do not, while you think Deleuze is one and I do not. This might be enough to get the conversation going, provided I do not start invoking Fregean understandings of the method, standards, and goals that govern our conversation, and you do not start invoking Deleuzian ones. There is always a chance the conversation will break down. But when it succeeds, it succeeds because of our shared understanding of how this particular game is played – a shared understanding provided by the canon-forming stories that loom over us as we converse.

But the past is not the only temporal dimension to bear on this conversational practice. The future bears on it as well, and that is why I have described Rorty as endorsing a metaphilosophy of hope as well as a metaphilosophy of historicity. As we have seen, our dependence on history arises because once we have decided to engage in the conversational practice known as philosophy, we find ourselves bound by certain rules, simply because of the logic of this practice. But what leads us to engage in this practice in the first place? What justifies our decision to play this particular conversational game? Rorty's answer to this question turns on the future, and more specifically, on our *hopes* for the future. We engage in philosophy because we hope – not know, but hope – that doing so will advance 'the present needs of high culture' (Rorty 1984: 70). These hopes for the future explain why we form the canons we do. After all, canons of great thinkers are made rather than found. There are indefinitely many canons to make, and indefinitely many ways of revising them once they have been made. What justifies the construction of any particular canon is the problems it allows us to solve. But perhaps more importantly, the more we allow canons to proliferate, the more resources we will have for solving future, as yet unanticipated problems. For these reasons, Rorty thinks philosophers:

should be at liberty to seek out their own intellectual ancestors, without reference to a previously established canon of great dead philosophers. They should also be free to claim to have no ancestors at all ... We should welcome people who, like Reichenbach, wave Hegel aside. We should encourage people who are tempted to dismiss Aristotle as a biologist who got out of his depth, or Berkeley as an eccentric bishop, or Frege as an original logician with unjustified epistemological pretensions, or Moore as a charming amateur who never quite understood what the professionals were doing. They should be urged to try it, and to see what sort of historical story they can tell when these people are left out and some unfamiliar people are brought in.

(Ibid.: 67)

'Experimental' is the key word here. We need a proliferation of canons because canons are instruments that serve our purposes, and we cannot know in advance which ones will best serve our future purposes – or indeed which future purposes we will have. The only way to discover this is to 'try it, and to see'. Experimenting, however, does not mean refusing to back any candidates. We *need* canons; we cannot conduct philosophical conversations without them. All we can do is hope that the canon we favour will advance our purposes, and be willing to revise it as we go.

III

Now let me turn to Ricoeur. Like my discussion of Rorty, my discussion of Ricoeur will focus on a single text that gives a particularly clear presentation of his metaphilosophy: the essay 'Freedom in the Light of Hope'. Like Rorty's essay, this essay presents itself as having a modest goal: that of reflecting on a recent development in theology and asking whether it has a parallel in philosophy. As in Rorty's essay, however, the focus shifts and broadens, and Ricoeur ultimately gives a comprehensive account of the method, standards, and goal of philosophy. The notion of hope proves crucial to this account. Doing philosophy well, as Ricoeur understands it, involves orientating oneself hopefully towards the discipline's subject matter. This hopeful stance, however, turns out to commit the philosopher to a certain sort of engagement with the past. Rorty's metaphilosophy leads from history to hope; Ricoeur's leads from hope back to history.

The theological development with which Ricoeur is concerned is the 'eschatological interpretation [of] the Christian kerygma' instituted by Jürgen Moltmann, Johannes Weiss, and Albert Schweitzer (Ricoeur 1974: 404). According to this interpretation, Christianity's defining feature is its 'discourse on last things' – its conviction that the Christian God is 'the God who is coming' rather than 'the God of present manifestation' (ibid.). We misinterpret the Christian message if we see the coming of God as an historical event among others, a present that has not yet arrived but eventually will. The coming of God must rather be seen as a horizon that is never present, a horizon that opens a new experience of time and a new stance towards the divine. This new stance should be characterized as one of hope. To believe in the God of eschatology is not to seek a 'pledge of all divine presence in the present world' (ibid.: 406), or to see creation as a temporal reflection of an eternal order. It is 'to enter into the movement of hope in resurrection from the dead, to attain the new creation *ex nihilo*, that is, beyond death' (ibid.). Ricoeur sees the eschatological interpretation as a radical break with the 'Hellenistic schemas' (ibid.) to which Christian doctrine has long been subject. The ' "He is coming" of Scripture must be opposed to the "It is" of the *Proem* of Parmenides' (ibid.: 407). The longstanding tendency to see religion's deep significance as metaphysical or epistemological must be opposed to 'the power of the possible and the disposition for being in a radical renewal' (ibid.: 408).

Ricoeur now asks whether this shift towards eschatology has an analogue in philosophy. What would be the philosophical equivalent of Moltmann's privileging of hope over knowledge and the future over presence? His answer is a form of Kantianism: specifically, the 'post-Hegelian Kantianism' (ibid.: 412) that he himself favours, and that he sees as the most promising way of doing philosophy in his own time. The defining feature of this Kantianism is that it renounces the ambition of acquiring definitive, systematic knowledge of the traditional objects of philosophical enquiry. Following Kant, Ricoeur calls these objects ideas of reason, and he insists that they are theoretically unknowable. He agrees with Kant about what these ideas are – self, world, and God – and he suggests that all philosophical enquiry is engaged with them in one way or another. But – again like Kant – he insists that renouncing the ambition to acquire theoretical knowledge of self, world, and God is not the same as ceasing to think about them. These ideas play crucial rules in regulating experience, so abandoning them is not an option. We must continue to think in terms of them, to relate particular episodes of experience to them. But we must do so without trying to know them theoretically.

'Post-Hegelian Kantianism' is Ricoeur's name for the enterprise of thinking regulatively about the Kantian ideas without trying to attain theoretical knowledge of them. What makes it 'post-Hegelian' is Ricoeur's conviction that Kant's own approach to the ideas is overly formalistic and lacking in content. Self, world, and God must be understood 'not in the abstraction of a separated form', but 'in the further constitution of concrete communities: family, economic collectivity, political community' (ibid.: 413). Hegel's great contribution to this enterprise is to have seen that failing to grasp the ideas in their historical concreteness leads to unsolvable tensions and dualisms. Ricoeur gives the following example:

> For my own part, I abandon the ethics of duty to the Hegelian critique without regrets: it would appear to me, indeed, to have been correctly characterized by Hegel as an abstract thought, as a thought of understanding. With the *Encyclopedia* and the *Philosophy of Right*, I willingly concede that formal 'morality' is simply a segment in a larger trajectory, that of the realization of freedom.
>
> (Ibid.)

To approach the ideas of reason in a post-Hegelian manner is above all to approach them dialectically: to try to overcome the oppositions they generate, to the extent that we can, by tracing the development of their concrete historical appearances. Doing so shows that what look like unbridgeable dualisms from the perspective of the understanding can be reconciled in the fullness of time through the mediation of concrete institutions. But what make this position a post-Hegelian *Kantianism* are its modest expectations about what this process can accomplish. No amount of dialectical mediation will overcome every tension in our understandings of self, world, and God. We must endeavour to make our understandings of these ideas as coherent as possible without ever claiming to know that they are fully coherent. In other words, we must proceed as if the ideas of reason have a certain character – maximal coherence – without turning that character into an object of theoretical comprehension. It must remain an object of hope. To philosophize as a post-Hegelian Kantian is therefore to be committed to the ultimate coherence of our understandings of self, world, and God – but *practically* committed. This commitment is a 'demand' or 'claim' (ibid.: 416) built into philosophical activity itself, not a conclusion to be reached by it.

It is clear that Ricoeur's defence of post-Hegelian Kantianism amounts to a comprehensive metaphilosophy. It is an elaborate account of how philosophy ought to be done, an account that spells out both the method philosophers should follow and the data to which this method should be applied. Philosophers should think dialectically: they should approach the objects of their enquiries as moments of fluid processes rather than static in-themselves. The data to which they should apply this procedure are the three Kantian ideas, apparently implicated, one way or another, in all philosophical enquiries. Ricoeur's account also articulates the standards that govern these efforts. Dialectical reflection on the ideas of reason is successful to the extent that it renders our understandings of these ideas more coherent – that is, helps overcome the tensions and contradictions displayed by these ideas. Finally, it specifies the goal that is pursued by this reflection. That goal is a maximally coherent understanding of the Kantian ideas, an understanding that is to be hoped for rather than believed on the basis of evidence. Philosophical reflection 'demands completeness; but it believes in the mode of expectation, of hope, in the existence of an order where the completeness can be actual' (ibid.: 420). This hope for completeness orientates the philosopher towards the future – not the future understood as something that will ever be made present, but a horizon that plays a role analogous to that of the God of eschatology. This hopeful stance towards the future, however, demands a role for the past as well. The Kantian ideas to which the philosopher responds with hope are ideas approached in a Hegelian way: not abstractions, but ideas manifested in a series of concrete historical forms. To approach these ideas dialectically is to trace the development of these historical forms. To make our understandings of them as coherent as possible is to see how later forms respond to problems and tensions in earlier ones. And to pursue the goal of maximal coherence here is to posit a satisfactory outcome to the historical development of which our current philosophizing is a part. For Ricoeur, then, philosophy is animated by hope, but a hope embedded in history – a hope that manifests itself in 'spontaneous restructurings of our philosophical memory' (ibid.: 413).

IV

This is obviously a very brief discussion of two extraordinarily complex thinkers. Nevertheless, the similarities in Rorty's and Ricoeur's metaphilosophies are striking. Both think we cannot adequately characterize philosophy's methods, standards, and goals without discussing the necessity of engaging with philosophy's past and orientating oneself hopefully towards the future. It would be interesting – and, I think, fairly straightforward – to show that this commitment to history and hope runs through both thinkers' larger bodies of work. But even those with no particular interest in Rorty or Ricoeur have much to learn from an engagement with their metaphilosophies. Let me close by sketching two lessons to be drawn from such an engagement.

The first concerns the future of the analytic–continental divide. The question of whether there are fundamentally different sorts of philosophy – an analytic kind and a continental kind – is obviously a metaphilosophical question of the highest importance. In one way, my discussion serves to undermine this divide. Its main lesson is that from the standpoint of metaphilosophy, Ricoeur and Rorty have more in common with each other than either does with most of the figures with whom they are usually grouped. But nothing in my discussion suggests that there is something wrong in principle with the practice of dividing philosophers into fundamentally opposed camps – not even into just two of them. If the analytic–continental divide, as usually understood, is dubious, it does not follow that we should abandon divides altogether and be philosophers without adjectives. We might instead conclude that the business of sorting philosophers into camps is simply much more complicated than we previously supposed, and that doing it well requires that we pay attention to unobvious metaphilosophical similarities as well as obvious first-order ones. Some philosophers interested in bridging the analytic–continental divide might see this complexity as cause for despair. I see it as reason for optimism. The more issues we must consider when dividing philosophers into groups, the more possible points of connection there are between the figures in any two groups. The more varied the terrain, the more sites there are for building bridges.

The second lesson concerns the importance of metaphilosophy – and the precise *ways* in which metaphilosophy matters. In my discussion of Rorty and Ricoeur, it quickly became apparent that we could not even start to determine what kind of philosophers they are without examining their metaphilosophical commitments – quite unorthodox commitments, as it turns out. To identify these commitments, it was necessary to engage with their writings on topics that were not obviously metaphilosophical or not only metaphilosophical. With Ricoeur, it was necessary to engage with his writings on the philosophical implications of a theological debate; with Rorty, it was necessary to examine his thoughts on the ambiguous phrase 'history of philosophy'. The lesson, it seems to me, is that understanding a philosopher's work can require us to understand her metaphilosophy, but that her metaphilosophy may be largely implicit and need to be unearthed. This is an especially important lesson at the current stage in the development of metaphilosophy. During the last decade, many who work in the field have taken up Williamson's slogan that they 'must do better' (Williamson 2007: 278). Often, however, doing metaphilosophy better is taken to be a matter of posing entirely new questions, or of posing old questions properly for the first time.[11] There is a bias here towards what Overgaard, Gilbert, and Burwood call 'explicit metaphilosophy' (Overgaard, Gilbert, and Burwood 2013: 11), as opposed to the 'implicit metaphilosophical views we can extract from contributions to other parts of philosophy'. I have nothing against explicit metaphilosophy, and I welcome the contributions of those who have taken up Williamson's slogan. But it would be a shame if the current emphasis on it led us to think that metaphilosophy must be explicit to deserve our attention. It is also important, I believe, to pay more attention to the implicit metaphilosophical commitments in familiar arguments, texts, and debates – commitments that cannot help but shape our understandings of first-order issues, but that often go unnoticed. Part of doing metaphilosophy better is noticing how central it has *always* been to the rest of philosophy. If this makes the field more messy, it also makes it more interesting. Doing metaphilosophy *better* also means doing *more*.

NOTES

1 See, for example, the essays in (Bell, Cutrofello, and Livingston 2015a).
2 On the distinction between 'essentialist' interpretations of the divide and interpretations based on family resemblances, see (Overgaard, Gilbert, and Burwood 2013: 112).
3 See, for example, the essays in (Prado 2003). For their part, Bell, Cutrofello, and Livingston reject the image of bridge-building, preferring that of 'two streams that, having a common origin and trajectory for much of their course, have recently diverged ... before converging once again' (Bell, Cutrofello, and Livingston 2015b: 3).
4 I discuss the historical thesis at greater length in (Piercey 2003), (Piercey 2009a), and (Piercey 2009b).
5 My understandings of historicity and hope are heavily indebted to (Koopman 2009). However, I use these notions in the service of a larger project than Koopman does: he uses them to characterize the pragmatist tradition, whereas I see them in the metaphilosophies of a wider range of thinkers.
6 See, for example, (Szubka 2010).
7 Williamson dislikes the term 'metaphilosophy' because he thinks it suggests an attempt to 'look down on philosophy from above, or beyond' – an attempt he rejects, on the grounds that 'the philosophy of philosophy is automatically part of philosophy' (Williamson 2007: ix). I agree that the philosophy of philosophy is automatically part of philosophy, but I do not think 'metaphilosophy' has the connotations Williamson thinks it does. So I use 'metaphilosophy' and 'philosophy of philosophy' interchangeably.
8 For an overview of questions that arise concerning the data of philosophy, see (Overgaard, Gilbert, and Burwood 2013: 70–104).
9 For a fuller discussion of this issue, see (Piercey 2010).
10 Rorty does not claim that it has *only* an honorific use; it also 'has an important descriptive use' (Rorty 1984: 58).
11 Williamson seems to encourage this interpretation when he writes: 'Philosophy has never been done for an extended period according to standards as high as those that are now already available, if only the profession will take them seriously to heart. None of us knows how far we can get by applying them systematically enough for long enough' (Williamson 2007: 291).

Part IV

Continental Perspectives

15 Phenomenological Method and the Achievement of Recognition

Who's Been Waiting for Phenomenology?

> As I said just now, Meno, you are a rascal. You now ask me if I can teach you, when I say there is no teaching but recollection, in order to show me up at once as contradicting myself.
>
> (Plato *Meno*: 81e–82a)

INSTRUCTION AND RECOGNITION

In the Preface to the *Tractatus*, Wittgenstein begins with the following speculation:

> Perhaps this book will be understood only by someone who has himself already had the thoughts that are expressed in it – or at least similar thoughts.
>
> (Wittgenstein 1963: 3)

Such an opening signals that the proper audience for the text is likely to be limited, as whatever thoughts the book expresses will be available only to those who have already had them. (Wittgenstein even says that 'its purpose would be achieved if it gave pleasure to one person who read and understood it' (ibid.).) For this reason, Wittgenstein adds in the subsequent sentence that the work 'is not a textbook' (ibid.). A textbook, these remarks suggest, would not depend for its comprehension on the reader *already* understanding or knowing what it seeks to impart; indeed, a textbook that did depend on such prior knowledge would be a dismal failure, as there would be no one for whom the textbook would really be of use. Those who had such prior knowledge would have no need of the book's instruction and those who did not could not be instructed, because they would not be able to understand what the book is trying to teach.

If the work Wittgenstein is introducing depends for its uptake on the reader already having the thoughts it expresses, then there would appear to be no one for whom the book would be of use. As with the failed textbook, the book would either be incomprehensible or be superfluous. Perhaps, however, these alternatives – incomprehensibility or superfluity – are too starkly posed. After all, a reader will not *know* that she has had the same – or similar – thoughts until she has worked through the book and finds herself comprehending what the work is trying to do. (There is no saying in advance just which readers are the ones that Wittgenstein singles out here in the Preface.) And one of the things the work might be understood as trying to do is just that, namely, calling the reader's attention to her having had just those – or similar – thoughts. The thoughts in question may have gone unnoticed or unappreciated and one goal of the work is to overcome that kind of neglect: by expressing something like those very thoughts, but perhaps in a clearer and more perspicuously organized way, the reader is not only *reminded* that she has had such thoughts, but now understands their import. Unlike a textbook, which seeks to impart some previously unknown *information*, a work of the kind Wittgenstein offers seeks instead to facilitate a kind of *recognition* on the part of the reader: by understanding the book, the reader thereby sees herself – her own thoughts – *in* the work.

PHENOMENOLOGY AND RECOGNITION

My aim in this paper is not to offer a reading of Wittgenstein's *Tractatus*. Rather, I began with a consideration of his opening remarks in the Preface because I think they are instructive for considering the notions of recognition and self-discovery as they appear in *phenomenology*. Far from being marginal or occasional themes in the development and practice of phenomenology, they are central to its self-conception. Consider, to cite another preface, Merleau-Ponty's bold declaration in *Phenomenology of Perception* that 'we shall find in ourselves, and nowhere else, the unity and true meaning of phenomenology' (Merleau-Ponty 1962: viii). He goes on to note that the kind of self-discovery essential for phenomenology bears upon readers' orientation towards, and reception of, texts in phenomenology:

> It is less a question of counting up quotations than of determining and expressing in concrete form this *phenomenology for ourselves* which has given a number of present-day readers the impression, on reading Husserl or Heidegger, not so much of encountering a new philosophy as of recognizing what they had been waiting for.
>
> (Ibid.)[1]

Immediately following this remark, Merleau-Ponty adds that 'phenomenology is accessible only through a phenomenological method' (ibid.). What this suggests is that the practice of phenomenology both relies upon and tries to effect this kind of recognition on the part of its audience. Both the comprehension and the confirmation of a phenomenological text depend upon readers recognizing in it 'what they had been waiting for'.

Although no text in phenomenology that I am aware of is structured in any way like Wittgenstein's highly idiosyncratic *Tractatus*, the crucial role of recognition in phenomenology nonetheless raises the question of whether there can be (straightforward) *textbooks* in phenomenology. If the kind of instruction a text in phenomenology imparts is something along the lines of enabling a kind of self-discovery – of bringing readers to the point of 'determining and expressing this *phenomenology for ourselves*' – then a successful work in phenomenology does not seek so much to convey a body of doctrine, a set of results that may now be transmitted from author to reader, as instruct or train the reader in a certain kind of *activity*. Any 'results' reported by a text in phenomenology will have little in the way of significance without the reader traversing the necessary steps to confirm them for herself. That confirmation is thus achieved – when it is – by the reader's actually *doing* phenomenology. Indeed, doing phenomenology is the key to understanding what a text in phenomenology has to say, as whatever insights it conveys can only be understood from within the perspective of phenomenology. What this suggests is that any work in phenomenology faces a considerable challenge in terms of comprehension: the work must encourage the reader to *do* phenomenology, even though just what phenomenology *is* will only become clear via the doing of it. The work thus relies upon the reader already having some inkling of what the work wants to convey so that the reader will indeed recognize – or come to recognize – the work as indeed what she 'had been waiting for'.

Following his invocation of Husserl and Heidegger in his remarks about the reception of phenomenology, I will explore the theme of recognition as it appears in these two illustrious predecessors of Merleau-Ponty. I will suggest that although the notion of recognition is crucial for Husserlian phenomenology, the possibility of its achievement is compromised by the extent of the gap between what Husserl refers to as the natural attitude and the perspective purportedly opened up by phenomenology. (By the 'natural attitude', Husserl means our ordinary way of being orientated towards, engaged with, the world around us, such that we understand ourselves to be materially and psychologically real beings located within a materially real world.)[2] One way of understanding Heidegger's conception of phenomenology is to see it as attempting to close that gap considerably. This is especially evident in some of his early lectures offered in the run-up to *Being and Time*. At the same time, despite these efforts, Heidegger's conception of phenomenology only transposes, rather than eliminates, the challenges for comprehension Husserlian phenomenology poses.

WAITING FOR PHENOMENOLOGY: HUSSERL

Merleau-Ponty's remark in the Preface to *Phenomenology of Perception* is an echo of sorts of a remark Husserl makes in the first volume of *Ideas*. There, in §62, Husserl refers to his newly emerging 'pure phenomenology' as 'the secret longing of the whole philosophy of modern times' (Husserl 1962: 166).[3] As Husserl sees it, everyone from Descartes and Locke to Hume and Kant would ultimately recognize phenomenology precisely as what they had been waiting for, as it would be the fulfilment of their ambitions, only in a clarified and rigorous manner.

Fred Kersten translates the German *Sehnsucht*, which Gibson aptly renders as *longing*, with *nostalgia*, which seems an odd choice in this context (see Husserl 1982: 142). That is, it is difficult to see how a group of philosophers – or all of modern philosophy – could be nostalgic for a view that is *yet to come*. On its own,

longing can be directed in either temporal direction. Nostalgia, by
contrast, although a kind of longing, would appear to be directed
only towards the past (although nostalgia's conception of the past
may be distorted in various ways or even outright false).[4] At the
time Descartes composed the *Meditations*, for example, Husserl's
phenomenology is nearly three centuries off in the future, and so it
is not clear how he could feel nostalgic for it. At the same time, it is
not as though he could *long* for it in a fully transparent way either,
but Husserl does not claim anything so ludicrous here. Notice that
he is careful to flag the longing in question as *secret*. What Husserl is
thus claiming here is that if one looks at what is driving all of these
modern philosophers, however diverse in many respects, it becomes
clear that they are all hankering (another translation of *Sehnsucht*)
after the kind of perspective and project laid out in phenomenology,
a kind of *absolute* foundation that is at the same time fully *critical*
with respect to what gets rendered in phenomenology as the *natural
attitude*. Viewed in retrospect, we can see the desire for such a
perspective coursing through all of modern philosophy starting with
Descartes' idea of First Philosophy, continuing through Locke's and
Hume's interest in ideas and the subjective realm more generally,
and reaching a crucial plateau in Kant's Copernican Turn. So what
Husserl is really claiming is that if all of these philosophers from
the past were *per impossibile* to be gathered together as an audience
for phenomenology, they would (he hopes) feel a kind of shock of
recognition; they would see phenomenology as indeed what they
had been waiting for and so as the fulfilment of a longing that their
own philosophical efforts failed really to satisfy.

Kersten's choice of 'nostalgia' is thus decidedly odd here, as it
seems to be almost a category mistake, and it is hard to know what
led him to choose it rather than the more straightforward 'longing'
that Gibson uses.[5] Although it is true that modern philosophy could
not long *explicitly* for phenomenology, the term still points in the
right direction, so to speak, whereas 'nostalgia' does not. I can only
speculate here, but perhaps what led Kersten to choose 'nostalgia'
rather than longing is a desire to indicate (rather awkwardly)
the way in which, for Husserl, the exciting new discoveries of
phenomenology are nonetheless a kind of *recovery* of something
lying hidden, but operative in a subterranean manner all along. In
other words, what modern philosophy was longing for was not to

reach or discover something new and different, but instead to *return* to something already there. Part of the secret of their longing is that it really is a kind of nostalgia.

We can get a sense of what I mean here by attending to some characteristic passages from Husserl's 1917 inaugural lecture at Freiburg im Breisgau (see Husserl 1981: 10–17). Early on, Husserl announces his intention to speak of 'pure phenomenology', with respect to both 'the intrinsic nature of its method and its subject matter' (Husserl 1981: 10). He goes on to note that this subject matter 'is *invisible* to naturally oriented points of view' (ibid., my emphasis). After spending several paragraphs delineating the notion of a phenomenon, the contrast between what is immanent and transcendent with respect to consciousness, and the character of sensuous givenness in perception, he returns to the contrast between the natural attitude and the phenomenological attitude and with it, the theme of invisibility. Summarizing the various 'processes' at work in the ordinary perceptual experience of an object, he notes:

The bestowing of each of these senses is carried out in consciousness and by virtue of definite series of flowing processes. *A person in the natural attitude, however, knows nothing of this.* He executes the acts of experiencing, referring, combining; but, while he is executing them, he is looking not toward them but rather in the direction of the objects he is conscious of.

(Ibid.: 13, my emphasis)

Despite being the executor of these various acts of experience, the person in the natural attitude is entirely unaware of the processes operative in them. These processes remain invisible, despite their being constitutive of the person's own conscious experience. Now, there is a sense in which an appeal to 'invisible processes' in experience is entirely unremarkable. If we consider experience from a causal point of view, for example, then it is unsurprising to learn that there are processes at work that are invisible to the one whose experience is being so considered. When I perceive my coffee cup, for example, all sorts of things are happening causally involving light rays, reflective surfaces, and the stimulation of my retina, along with a whole cascade of events in my nervous system. All of these processes are entirely invisible to me, despite their being crucial to my coffee cup's being seen by me at this particular moment.

But *this* sense of an invisible process cannot be what Husserl has in mind, since all of these processes are the subject matter of *hypotheses* that exceed what is – and can be – given in my experience of the coffee cup. Notice that Husserl says that when a person is in the natural attitude, 'he is not looking toward' the kinds of process he has in mind, 'but rather in the direction of the objects he is conscious of'. If we consider the kinds of causal process listed above, then there is really no direction that person can look in order to bring them into view.[6] The processes Husserl has in mind, by contrast, can come into view by the person's making a reflective turn away from the experienced objects towards the experience of them:

On the other hand, he can convert his natural attentional focus into the phenomenological reflective one; he can make the currently flowing consciousness and, thus, the infinitely multiform world of phenomena at large the theme of his fixating observations, descriptions, theoretical investigations – the investigations which, for short, we call 'phenomenological.'

(Husserl 1981: 14)

Phenomenological investigations are to be distinguished from other kinds of investigation one might undertake with respect to consciousness because the 'world of phenomena' revealed by reflection is something the subject whose experience it is can *recognize as* operative in her experience. Causal hypotheses, by contrast, are things such as a subject might come to *accept* about her experience, as, for example, well-confirmed, highly plausible, and so on, but there is nothing by way of confirmation of these hypotheses from within the first-person point of view.

What the person in the natural attitude 'knows nothing of' is what Husserl refers to in the discussion surrounding these passages as the *bestowing* of *sense* 'upon its own phenomena', which are the 'immanent' data of consciousness:

Within this widest concept of object, and specifically within the concept of individual object, *Objects* and *phenomena* stand in contrast with each other. Objects [*Objekte*], all natural objects, for example, are objects foreign to consciousness. Consciousness does, indeed, objectivate them and posit them as actual, yet the consciousness that experiences them and takes cognizance of them is so singularly astonishing that it bestows upon its own phenomena the sense of being appearances of Objects foreign to consciousness and knows these 'extrinsic' Objects through processes that take cognizance of their sense. Those objects that are neither conscious processes nor immanent constituents of conscious processes we therefore call Objects in the pregnant sense of the word.

(Ibid.: 13)

What I referred to above as the reflective turn away from the things we experience towards our experience of them directs our attention to these conscious processes. What we thereby find 'singularly astonishing' is that – and how – these immanent processes manage to present all of those objects ('Objects in the pregnant sense of the word') that are 'foreign to consciousness'. We come to appreciate the difference between the former and the latter in that the former (conscious processes) are 'multiform' and involve 'constantly changing immanent constituents' that are nonetheless 'construed referentially and causally' as being of or about 'real circumstances' (ibid.). 'The bestowing of each of these senses is carried out in consciousness and by virtue of definite series of flowing conscious processes' (ibid.). When I am only interested in taking a sip of coffee, I look towards my coffee cup and see it there, on my desk. I pay attention only to the cup and what it contains, but if I shift my attention, I come to notice that the cup is presented to me in a changing series of appearances: the shape of the cup is, as Husserl puts it, 'perspectivally silhouetted in definite ways', and I can similarly note the way the colour of the cup – a quality I see as constant – is given through sensuously altering shadings. What I take to be one stable object with stable properties is given through 'continuously flowing aspects' (ibid.). If I begin to inspect each of these 'aspects' as though they were snapshots, I will see how different in appearance they are: the stable and uniform colour of the cup is presented through appearances that are by no means uniform, but involve numerous variations in shading, replete with highlights, glare, shadows, and colour shifts caused by, among other things, variations in illumination and reflections of other neighbouring surfaces. I can gain some appreciation for this variation if I were to take a photograph of the cup from my current position and analyse the image in Photoshop: as I move the 'colour picker' tool around on the surface of the image, markedly different shades of colour would be selected. Being made aware of all this variation will have the feeling of discovery; by seeing my seeing of the object, I become aware of something altogether new and different. At the same time, however, I recognize that what I have discovered has been there all along, continuously happening in my perceptual experience of the world, but I am now struck – even astonished – by it in a way I had never been before.

I adduced these passages from Husserl's 1917 lecture as a way of probing Kersten's choice of 'nostalgia' to translate the original *Sehnsucht* in §62 of *Ideas*. Although the processes Husserl seeks to delineate are 'invisible' from the standpoint of the natural attitude, they are nonetheless *there to be seen* in a way that causal processes, for example, are not. In being led to such processes via reflection, I am being *led back* to something that I recognize as having been operative in my experience all along. That such 'sense bestowal' has been operative may help to account for how such recognition is even possible, but it still remains unclear how it can be longed for in the first place. What I mean here is that if such processes are indeed invisible from the standpoint of the natural attitude *as a whole*, then what motivates the search for them? Moreover, what really facilitates their recognition since the natural attitude presumably contains little in the way of resources for bringing such invisible processes to light?

Attention to Eugen Fink's *Sixth Cartesian Meditation* helps to bring these questions into sharper focus (Fink 1995).[7] Written by Husserl's last assistant as a continuation of his original five 'meditations' (Husserl 1973), this work is a radical reflection on phenomenological method, a 'phenomenology of phenomenology'. As such, Fink is especially sensitive to questions concerning the motivation to practise phenomenology, which begins with the performance of the phenomenological reduction. Doing so requires suspending or 'bracketing' all of the commitments and presuppositions making up the natural attitude.[8] Accordingly, Fink devotes considerable attention to questions concerning the kinds of discoveries the reduction makes possible and the difficulties that attend adequately reporting them. Fink takes seriously Husserl's talk of invisibility when it comes to the natural attitude's relation to the discoveries of phenomenology, so much so that the motivation to engage in phenomenology is not something that of itself belongs to the natural attitude: 'The self-reflection of the phenomenological reduction is not a radicality that is within human reach; it does not lie at all within the horizon of human possibilities' (Fink 1995: 32). Although Husserl's talk of a change in attitude, wherein I, for example, shift from attending to the cup I see to my seeing of it, does not sound especially radical or esoteric, Fink nonetheless maintains that 'in the actualizing of the reduction a self-reflection occurs that has a wholly new kind of structure' (ibid.). What is 'wholly new' here is that with the reduction, I am no longer reflecting on my experience as something belonging to a particular empirical being – 'it is not that man reflectively thinks about himself' – but instead 'transcendental subjectivity, concealed in self-objectivation as man, reflectively thinks about itself, beginning *seemingly* as man, annulling itself as man, and taking itself down as man all the way to the ground, namely, down to the innermost ground of its life' (ibid.). All of this leads Fink to pose the question of the motivation to perform the reduction; note especially the stark answer he gives:

In view of this situation, is there still any sense in speaking of *ways* into the transcendental attitude? If we take ways into phenomenology to mean a*continuity in motivation* that begins in the natural attitude and by an inferential force leads into the transcendental attitude, then *there are no such ways.*

(Ibid.: 33)

It might appear from these rather bleak remarks that the answer to the question of who has been waiting for phenomenology is pretty much no one, but it is important to see that Fink does not draw this conclusion. Indeed, what he does offer helps to explain the kind of 'secret longing' Husserl ascribes to modern philosophy and, moreover, why he ascribes it specifically to modern philosophy, as opposed to just anyone and everyone. Despite the radical discontinuity between the natural and phenomenological attitudes, such that nothing in the former provides a ready motivation to take up the latter, Fink maintains (fortunately!) that this 'does not imply, however, that talk of "ways" into phenomenology is altogether senseless' (ibid.). While there is no *continuous* path from the natural attitude to phenomenology, there are in the former glimmers and intimations that are just enough to provide a kind of foothold. The kind of 'self-reflection' that is possible even in the natural attitude can be such as to allow there to 'spring up' a kind of 'transcendental illumination' that points the way towards a radicalization of this initiating reflection: '[O]n the occasion of a decisive and unwavering turn inward into oneself the dispositional possibility is created for catching sight, in a productive, anticipatory way, of the dimension of transcendental radicality' (ibid.). Reflection can create in the natural attitude what Fink refers to as *'extreme situations'*, wherein 'transcendental cognition can flash out' (ibid.: 34).

To get a sense of what Fink has in mind, consider again the reflective turn described above regarding my seeing my coffee cup on the desk before me. The motivation first to engage in such reflection can arise in various ways in the natural attitude: perhaps I have been having trouble with my vision, which prompts me to consider more carefully the contours of my visual experience rather than just the objects of that experience; or perhaps I have been spending a lot of time using the colour picker tool in Photoshop, so that I am struck by just how non-uniform the appearance of what I take to be a uniformly coloured surface is. Such reflections can stay within the natural attitude, leading me to consult an ophthalmologist in the first case and to work harder on colour adjustments to my photographs in the second. But there can be in these moments of reflection an intimation of a more radical kind of thought: if I am struck by the variable and multiform character of the sensuous appearances of my coffee cup, I might be led to wonder where I so much as get the idea that the cup *has* a uniformly coloured surface. What is it about these appearances that leads me to bestow on them the *sense* 'uniformly coloured coffee cup'? What is it about my experience that leads me to think of myself as in touch – or making contact – with a world of stable objects? If I ponder that question for a while, I will come to see that even reference to 'myself' needs accounting for, since I as a *person* am one of those stable and enduring things that populate this world. In coming to see these things, my reflection thereby takes an increasingly radical form, so that what had been a rather quotidian form of reflection thereby becomes 'extreme'.

Descartes, as the founding figure of modern philosophy, provides us with a historical example of what Fink means here by an 'extreme situation'. Consider Descartes' state of mind at the outset of his *Meditations on First Philosophy*. What prompts Descartes' investigation is his 'realizing how numerous were the false opinions that in my youth I had taken to be true' (Descartes 1993: 13). There is nothing markedly unnatural about that realization: while some people never worry all that much about the truth or falsity of their opinions or may never be struck by the idea that things they believed to be true when they were younger turned out not to be true after all, such an idea or worry is certainly available from within the natural attitude. But for Descartes, the realization offers an occasion for a more thoroughgoing investigation of his beliefs and his grounds for them. The initial realization is followed by a second in the very next sentence: 'And thus I realized that once in my life I had to raze everything to the ground and build again from the original foundations, if I wanted to establish anything firm and lasting in the sciences' (ibid.). Already, we can see that the kind of 'flashing out' of transcendental cognition described by Fink, as what Descartes finds himself compelled to do based on his original realization, appears far less natural than what prompted it. In the First Meditation, Descartes does not just declare, but actively demonstrates the extremity of his situation: by enacting the Method of Doubt and proceeding through various 'principles' for the acquisition of beliefs, he first sheds beliefs that even pre-philosophically look a bit suspicious, but then rejects (treats as false) more and more beliefs that seem nearly impossible to doubt: 'I will regard myself as not having hands, or eyes, or flesh, or blood, or any sense, but as nevertheless falsely believing that I possess all these things' (ibid.: 17). We can see here the kind of 'inhuman' turn that Descartes' investigations take, 'beginning *seemingly* as man, annulling itself as man, and taking itself down as man all the way to the ground'.

Although Husserl did not regard Descartes' Method of Doubt as by any means equivalent to the phenomenological reduction, we can nonetheless see in the First Meditation what Fink refers to as 'flashes of transcendental preknowledge that first motivate the performance of the phenomenological reduction' (Fink 1995: 114). Descartes himself did not perform the reduction, but that his thinking contains these 'flashes' helps to secure the idea that the phenomenological reduction constitutes the 'secret longing' of Descartes' philosophy.

While the kind of 'transcendental preknowledge' on display in Descartes' philosophy would appear to allow him to recognize Husserl's phenomenology as what he had indeed been waiting for, further attention to Fink reveals complexities in terms of the kind of recognition at issue here. Fink underscores the way in which 'universal epochē is not only not feasible in the natural attitude, but is senseless' (ibid. 36). As we saw, it is this kind of senselessness that accounts for the discontinuity between the natural and phenomenological attitudes: if the very idea of the phenomenological reduction does not make sense from the perspective of the natural attitude, then there can be no real motivation to perform it. But lack of motivation is only part of the problem, as the problem of senselessness would no doubt extend to any *insights* that the performance of the reduction yields: findings regarding processes that are 'invisible' to the natural attitude will not be understandable to anyone who remains in that attitude. For Fink, this marks a limitation on the utility of phenomenological texts, as they can only really be understood by those who have already had the kinds of insights they attempt to report:

Phenomenological sentences can therefore only be understood if the *situation of the giving of sense* to the transcendental sentences is always *repeated*, that is, if the predicatively explicating terms are always verified again by *phenomenologizing intuition*. There is thus no phenomenological understanding that comes simply by reading reports of phenomenological research; these can only be 'read' at all by re-performing the investigations themselves. Whoever fails to do that just does not read *phenomenological* sentences; he reads queer sentences in natural language, taking a mere appearance for the thing itself to his own self-deception.

(Ibid.: 92)

If anyone who has not already performed the reduction – and so practised phenomenology – only reads 'queer sentences in natural language', in what sense can they recognize *that* as what they had been waiting for? There is, we might say, a fundamental *mismatch* between any terms in which their longing might be couched and the terms in which phenomenology eventually deals.[9] The 'sentences in which the one phenomenologizing makes statements about the phenomenological reduction are not understandable at all if one does not *oneself* perform the phenomenological reduction' (ibid.: 112). Thus, Fink says that such sentences cannot be regarded as 'reports about something which would be pregiven and known in its possibility' (ibid.). For the outsider, phenomenological sentences are no more than '*imperative pointers* to a cognitive action of a hitherto unknown radicality *which can be comprehended only in being itself performed*' (ibid.: 112–13).

WAITING FOR PHENOMENOLOGY: HEIDEGGER

Many readers of Heidegger have no doubt had the feeling that they were reading 'queer sentences in natural language'. Indeed, Heidegger is well aware of the peculiarity of his prose:

With regard to the awkwardness and 'inelegance' of expression in the analyses to come, we may remark that it is one thing to give a report in which we tell about *entities*, but another to grasp entities in their *being*. For the latter task we lack not only most of the words, but, above all, the 'grammar.'

(Heidegger 1962: 63 / 1927: 38–9)[10]

Heidegger considers this 'harshness of expression' (ibid.: 63 / 39) unavoidable because of the poor fit between our familiar vocabulary (and even grammar) and what he wishes to analyse in *Being and Time*, namely, the being of entities. As we saw with Husserl's understanding of sense-bestowing processes as 'invisible' to the natural attitude, what interests Heidegger is something that lies hidden in relation to our ordinary ways of being orientated towards things, while nonetheless giving those ordinary ways their sense:

What is it that phenomenology is to 'let us see'? ... Manifestly, it is something that proximally and for the most part does *not* show itself at all: it is something that lies *hidden*, in contrast to that which proximally and for the most part does show itself; but at the same time it is something that belongs to what thus shows itself, and it belongs to it so essentially as to constitute its meaning and its ground.

(Ibid.: 59 / 35)

For Heidegger, the discoveries of phenomenology thus involve the same direction of movement as for Husserl: what is discovered is something that has been there all along, working 'behind the scenes' in a way that has gone unnoticed. In both cases we are being *led back* to something upon which we have relied, but without really having seen it prior to Heidegger's investigation. Heidegger exploits the etymology behind the word 'reduction' to emphasize this point:

Apprehension of being, ontological investigation, always turns, at first and necessarily, to some being; but then, *in a precise way, it is led away* from that being *and led back to its being.* We call this basic component of phenomenological method – the leading back or reduction of investigative vision from a naively apprehended being to being – *phenomenological reduction.*

(Heidegger 1982: 21)

The hidden character of what interests Heidegger makes for difficulties similar to those raised by Fink concerning the *motivation* to take up the phenomenological perspective: the being of entities may be so hidden that it may never occur to us to seek it out. As Heidegger worries at the very outset of *Being and Time*, not only are we unable to understand the notion of 'being', we are not even bothered by such an inability: 'But are we nowadays even perplexed at our inability to understand the expression "being"? Not at all' (Heidegger 1962: 19 / 1927: 1).

Despite these parallels, there are also significant differences. While it is important not to underestimate the difficulties phenomenology in Heidegger's sense faces, there is a diminishment of the distance, so to speak, between our ordinary ways of being orientated towards the world and the orientation required for phenomenology. Recall that Fink cast the phenomenological reduction as a kind of de-humanizing, 'beginning *seemingly* as man, annulling itself as man, and taking itself down as man all the way to the ground'. For this reason, the motivation for phenomenology from within the natural attitude is severely limited: apart from those rare 'flashes' of 'transcendental preknowledge', there is nothing available from within the natural attitude that points the way towards phenomenology. Heidegger, by contrast, recapitulating the reasoning of Plato's *Meno*, argues that since enquiry 'must be guided beforehand by what is sought', it follows that 'the meaning of being must already be available to us in some way' (ibid.: 25

/ 5). What Heidegger dubs Dasein's *pre-ontological* understanding of being provides the crucial starting point for phenomenology. This kind of understanding is 'always already' operative in our everyday dealings with familiar entities such as hammers, chairs, tables, and pens. As Heidegger puts it, such understanding ' "comes alive" in [Dasein's] dealings with entities' (ibid.: 96 / 67). The job of phenomenology, for Heidegger, is to bring 'to completion, autonomously and explicitly, that understanding of being which belongs already to Dasein' (ibid.).

Since Heidegger's project is to make explicit what 'belongs already to Dasein', both the question of motivation *and* the issue of where we end up would appear to be far less fraught than is the case with Husserlian phenomenology (especially on Fink's construal of it). Rather than something almost entirely unmotivated from within human life, Heidegger even suggests in an early lecture from the years leading up to *Being and Time* that philosophy is in some way *necessary* for it; note especially the link to the idea of the reduction:

> Must there be philosophy? In a sense, yes, if life and existence are supposed to be. 'Supposed'? – They are factually there. Is there a tendency toward fleeing away? The ruinous flight into the world; away from the object; positive sense of Husserl's 're-duction.'
>
> (Heidegger 2001: 31)[11]

Heidegger does not here elaborate further on this notion of a 'positive sense', nor does he say explicitly whether Husserl's original understanding of the reduction would constitute a kind of *negative* sense.[12] Elsewhere, however, Heidegger is much more explicit in distancing his understanding of the phenomenological reduction from Husserl's:

> *For Husserl*, phenomenological reduction, which he worked out for the first time expressly in the *Ideas Toward a Pure Phenomenology and Phenomenological Philosophy* (1913), is the method of leading phenomenological vision from the natural attitude of the human being whose life is involved in the world of things and persons back to the transcendental life of consciousness and its noetic-noematic experiences, in which objects are constituted as correlates of consciousness. *For us*, phenomenological reduction means leading phenomenological vision back from the apprehension of a being, whatever may be the character of that

apprehension, to the understanding of the being of this being (projecting upon the way it is unconcealed).

(Heidegger 1982: 21)

Rather than directing us towards 'the transcendental life of consciousness', Heideggerian phenomenology stays within the perspective of our lives as 'involved in the world of things'. In his earlier lectures, Heidegger insists upon 'the derivation of the phenomenological interpretation out of the facticity of life itself' (Heidegger 2001: 66). What phenomenology aspires to for Heidegger is not something entirely new, lying outside, but mysteriously connected to, our various human ways of making sense of things; its goal is precisely to illuminate the structures of those ways of making sense.[13] These structures may in some sense be hidden, but they are not *elsewhere*. Delineating these structures involves rendering explicit what is otherwise implicit, as 'the "non-explicit" is itself a specifically phenomenological character, one that precisely co-constitutes facticity' (ibid.: 67). Heidegger insists, contrary to the kind of 'annulment' later envisioned by Fink, that phenomenology involves no 'unwarranted forcing', thereby avoiding 'the violence and arbitrariness of a rootless, foreign, and ordering systematization, typologization, or the like' (ibid.: 66). Instead, the structures at issue 'are *alive in life itself* in an original way ... They have their own mode of access, which are not foreign to life itself, as if they pounced down upon life from the outside, but instead are precisely the preeminent way in which *life comes to itself*' (ibid.).

While Husserlian phenomenology risks a gap between the natural and the transcendental attitudes that threatens to undermine any kind of recognition of the latter from the standpoint of the former, Heidegger's recasting of the domain of phenomenology as something *'alive in life itself'* poses its own kind of problem. What I mean here is that whereas the gap in the case of Husserl may be too wide, with Heidegger one might well wonder how there is any gap at all. That is, with Husserl, the motivation to perform the phenomenological reduction proved problematic since where it leads, so to speak, is something entirely screened off from any starting point in the natural attitude; with Heidegger, by contrast, there is likewise a problem of motivation, not because the goal is mysteriously distant, but because there is nowhere to go beyond where we already are.

While this last remark is, in a sense, true, it does not follow that there is *nothing to be learned* about where we already are. That there is still a gap to be overcome is signalled in the lectures I've been citing by Heidegger's appeal there to 'the ruinous flight into the world' that marks our everyday way of being. In *Being and Time*, Heidegger deploys an even more elaborate battery of concepts to characterize our pre-philosophical orientation towards ourselves and the world that accounts for the difficulty of phenomenology: in everydayness, Dasein, as *inauthentic*, is variously *fallen, dispersed,* and *tranquilized*, busily *absorbed* in its tasks, and both *curious* and *fascinated* by the endless *novelty* and *ambiguity* of what surrounds it. These characterizations help to account for the difficulties of phenomenology, as they specify what must be overcome in order to bring the question of being into view. Although I have appealed to Fink prior to discussing Heidegger because of Fink's engagement with Husserl's original conception of phenomenology, his *Sixth Cartesian Meditation* was composed after Heidegger's work in the 1920s. Moreover, Fink attended Heidegger's lectures for several years in that period. Although Fink maintains, *contra* Heidegger, that 'as long as one believes that phenomenology, or phenomenologizing, can be at all *criticized existentially*, one just cannot have understood it' (Fink 1995: 112), he can nonetheless be read as transposing many of Heidegger's 'existential' ideas in order to bridge the gap between the natural and transcendental attitudes. I want to consider two mentioned above that are drawn most directly from Heidegger.

Consider again Fink's appeal to 'extreme situations', wherein 'transcendental cognition can flash out'. Despite his criticisms of existential phenomenology, this appeal echoes Heidegger's account of transition from everydayness to authenticity. What facilitates that transition is a similarly radical disruption of the tranquil complacency of everydayness. Heidegger's appeals to *anxiety, being-toward-death, guilt,* and *conscience* document a kind of crisis whose occurrence facilitates the kind of ontological insights Heidegger describes: 'Anxiety individualizes Dasein and thus discloses it as *"solus ipse"'*, and this 'existential solipsism', rather than engendering a detached worldlessness, brings 'Dasein face to face with its world as world, and thus bring[s] it face to face with itself as being-in-the-world' (Heidegger 1962: 233 / 1927: 188). Through anxiety and its aftermath, Dasein achieves a kind of recognition of itself as a being whose being is an issue. And while there is something transformative about this recognition, it is also retrospective in that Dasein recognizes itself as *having been* that kind of being all along. Were that not the case, it would be entirely unclear how anything like what Heidegger calls the 'call of conscience' could ever *reach* Dasein: in being called, Dasein is brought back to itself, whereby it can fully appreciate for the first time its having been *lost* in everydayness.[14]

But when I am lost in everydayness, I do not feel or take myself to *be* lost. I am simply absorbed in my everyday activity. The *issue* of my own existence is not confronted at all, but instead treated as settled. From that position, which is the position Heidegger must take his audience to inhabit, the appeal of the curious concepts that populate Division II is vanishingly limited. That is, it will be entirely mysterious just what Heidegger is on about and this mystery is something with which his own prose must contend. This brings us to the second notion that Fink borrows from Heidegger. For Fink, sentences that report phenomenological findings are no more than '*imperative pointers* to a cognitive action of a hitherto unknown radicality *which can be comprehended only in being itself performed*'. This appeal to 'imperative pointers' echoes Heidegger's prior notion of *formal indication*, which appears throughout his lectures of the 1920s.[15] Formal indications serve '*the function of drawing attention – from out of* personal existence and *for it*' (Heidegger 2010: 151).[16] While drawing attention, formal indications – as *formal* – only do that: understanding what they draw attention to requires a kind of 'filling in' by phenomenological *experience*. When it comes to the character and significance of the experiences Heidegger indicates, they must be had to be fully appreciated. Heidegger's exposition is limited to such pointings: just what he is pointing to and why will be grasped only by someone who has had the same – or similar – experiences.[17]

In *The History of the Concept of Time* lectures, Heidegger cautions at one point: 'Before words, before expressions, always the phenomena first, and then the concepts!' (Heidegger 1985: 248). Given the priority of phenomena to concepts, any presentation of phenomenology couched in concepts (and how else could it be couched?) will necessarily reverse this imperative. Such concepts can thus *only* be pointers, gesturing towards the phenomena that give them what content they have, and it is those phenomena that must be grasped to appreciate just what those conceptual articulations are all about. Despite Heidegger's efforts to diminish the distance between the perspective afforded by phenomenology and that of everyday experience, the question of whether there can be phenomenological *textbooks* arises just as it does for Husserlian phenomenology. Recall Fink's remark that 'there is thus no phenomenological understanding that comes simply by reading reports of phenomenological research; these can only be "read" at all by re-performing the investigations themselves'. Whatever concepts Heidegger deploys in his texts likewise require that readers 're-perform' the investigations underwriting them. Only then will they be able to recognize in the text something that they had indeed been waiting for.[18]

NOTES

1 One might wonder if Merleau-Ponty has Sartre in mind as one of these 'present-day readers'. Consider the famous anecdote of Sartre turning 'pale with emotion' upon first hearing about phenomenological method from their friend Raymond Aron. According to Simone de Beauvoir, Sartre immediately thereafter purchased a copy of Levinas' early study of Husserl and, upon first reading it, Sartre's 'heart missed a beat'. See (de Beauvoir 1976: 112).

2 For a typical characterization of the natural attitude, see (Husserl 1962: §27).

3 The original German of the entire sentence reads: '*So begreift es sich, daß die Phänomenologie gleichsam die geheime Sehnsucht der ganzen neuzeitlichen Philosophie ist.*'

4 I here pass over many complexities in the phenomenon of nostalgia. While interesting and significant, what matters here is only the temporal direction of the phenomenon, such that being nostalgic for the future is at best oxymoronic and, at worst, nonsensical. For a discussion of the some of the complexities in the phenomenon of nostalgia – and its contrast with more straightforward forms of memory – see (Crowell 1999: 83–104).

5 As both Stephan Käufer and Steven Crowell pointed out to me in discussing Kersten's translation, there is the German word *Nostalgie* that Husserl could have used if that is what he was after (*Sehnsucht* can be translated as 'nostalgia', but it is a secondary meaning). Both Kaufer and Crowell dismissed Kersten's choice here as nothing but a blunder. I am inclined to agree, but I still wish to pursue the idea that the blunder is nonetheless suggestive.

6 This doesn't sound quite right, since surely these causal processes come into view in *some* way; otherwise it would be unintelligible how we ever came to frame such hypotheses at all. Framing such hypotheses must, for Husserl, require abandoning the standpoint of experience in some strong sense, while still leaving room for the idea of such notions becoming legitimate topics in their own right. I take it that what is abandoned is the first-person perspective on one's own experience. So Husserl's claim would involve, for example, denying that the stimulation of my retina is something I can become aware of solely by reflecting on my own visual experience. (It is also worth noting that becoming aware of such causal processes, however that is achieved, would for Husserl remain within the natural attitude.)

7 In appealing to Fink at this juncture, I do not want thereby to suggest that Fink's views are authoritative with respect to Husserlian phenomenology. Although Fink worked closely with Husserl, the latter's marginal comments on the text indicate tensions and disagreements. Nonetheless, I find Fink useful, as he brings these specific issues to the fore in a particularly vivid and compelling manner. For a reading of Fink that questions its Husserlian credentials, see (Crowell 2001b: 244–63).

8 For a succinct formulation of the reduction, see §8 of Husserl's original *Cartesian Meditations*. For extended discussion of the reduction and its possible motivations, see Chapter 2 of (Bernet, Kern, and Marbach 1993).

9 I explore this issue of a 'mismatch' at greater length in (Cerbone forthcoming).

10 I cite both the English and German pagination (English/German).

11 I am indebted to (Crowell 2001a) for drawing my attention to these lectures and underscoring their importance.

12 Later in the lectures, however, Heidegger criticizes the notion of any radical form of detachment as inimical to the practice of philosophy: 'The most convenient thing would surely be to perch oneself, outside of the world and of life, in the land of the blessed and the absolute. Yet it would then be difficult to understand why anyone who had progressed "so far" would still philosophize at all' (Heidegger 2001: 75). While he does not mention Husserl here, it does not strike me as farfetched to connect this remark with what Heidegger might consider a negative sense of reduction.

13 Of course, Husserlian phenomenology aspires to illuminate such sense-making structures as well. The issue, however, is whether the workings of the phenomenological reduction in Husserl's sense make those connections overly obscure.

14 For an insightful discussion that emphasizes the 'temporal slipperiness' of Heidegger's notion of conscience, see (Kukla 2002: 1–34).

15 There has been considerable discussion of this notion in recent years, to which I cannot do justice here. See especially (Kisiel 1993); (Dahlstrom 1994: 775–95); and (McManus 2013: 50–65). See also (Crowell 2001a).

16 I am indebted to Fredrik Westerlund's discussion of formal indication for drawing my attention to this passage. See (Westerlund 2014), especially 87–92.
17 I discuss some of the issues raised by these considerations in greater detail in (Cerbone 2003: 1–26). See also Kate Withy's excellent article, (Withy 2013), which emphasizes the 'therapeutic' dimension of Heidegger's phenomenology.
18 I would like to thank Giuseppina D'Oro, Stephan Käufer, Søren Overgaard, Fredrik Westerlund, and an anonymous reader for helpful comments and suggestions. I would especially like to thank Steven Crowell for his extensive feedback and encouragement at several stages of this project.

16 Existentialist Methodology and Perspective

Writing the First Person

Existentialism is considered by many philosophers to be a part of the history of philosophy, rather than part of its present or future. While phenomenology may lay claim to endure as a living part of the contemporary philosophical landscape, and one that is increasingly in interaction with at least some parts of the putative analytic tradition (cf. Zahavi 2013), existentialism has not been quite so fortunate, despite or perhaps because of its fame around the time of World War Two. Central existential themes have been historicized in a way that has rendered them remnants of a bygone world, notwithstanding that this distinction between phenomenology and existentialism is difficult to render precise.

Without proposing anything quite so grandiose as a return to existentialism, in this chapter we articulate and minimally defend certain core existentialist insights concerning the first-person perspective, the relationship between theory and practice, and the mode of philosophical presentation conducive to best making those points. We do this by considering some of the central methodological objections that have been posed around the role of the first-person perspective and 'lived experience' in the contemporary literature, before providing some neo-existentialist rejoinders. The basic dilemma that contemporary philosophy poses to existentialism, vis-à-vis methodology, is that existentialism is: a) committed to lived experience as some sort of given that might be accessed either introspectively or retrospectively (with empirical science posing *prima facie* obstacles to the veridicality of each); and/or b) it advocates transformative experiences, and the power of philosophy in connection with such experiences, to radically revise our inter-connected web of beliefs. In short, the charge is conservatism on the one hand, radicalism on the other. Each of these concerns will be addressed, utilizing ideas from Kierkegaard (as the source for many existentialist themes, methodological concerns, and formal practices) and from the German and French twentieth-century versions of existentialism. Nonetheless, the commitment to lived experience central to existentialist thought brings in train its own difficulties, which in turn motivate a move to very different forms of philosophical discourse – forms which, in contemporary philosophy, appear to have been largely abandoned. Part of the decline in existentialism may therefore turn out to be not simply because its themes have been superseded or exhausted, but because the forms in which they properly find expression have been excluded from philosophy as a professional praxis.

EXISTENTIALISM AND THE FIRST-PERSON PERSPECTIVE

Existentialism has no readily agreed definition. Many of those philosophers we think of as its key practitioners resisted the label and denied any continuity in their thinking sufficient to constitute a group or movement. Nonetheless, it is arguably overly hasty to dismiss the idea of any philosophical or methodological unity. Family resemblance style definitions can be adduced (cf. Joseph, Reynolds, and Woodward 2011), and methodological matters arguably play a key role in that regard. The method(s) of phenomenology are important for the twentieth-century versions of existentialism in France and Germany, and we also get some methodological clues if we extend our remit further into the beginnings of existentialism, which is often traced to Kierkegaard's philosophy and his opposition to Hegel (or, more precisely, Danish Hegelianism (cf. Stewart 2003)). In both cases, there is concern with existence that focuses predominantly upon our first-personal lived experience of the world. This first-personal dimension is not merely understood as a point about perspective or epistemic limitation, but as an irreducible phenomenal property or aspect of anything that could count as 'experience'. There is, for instance, often claimed to be a basic 'mineness' (*Jeimeinigkeit*) about experience as it is lived, as opposed to described from the outside or a third-person perspective, as with Heidegger's characterization of Dasein's being-in-the-world in *Being in Time*. Likewise, in Sartre's description of 'non-positional consciousness', or non-thetic awareness of awareness, we see a distinctive kind of non-conceptual self-referentiality that is a key aspect of existentialist thought, arguably also going back as far as Kierkegaard (cf. Stokes 2010).

The first-personal givenness of experience, however, is not a uniquely existentialist preoccupation. It also has a place in contemporary phenomenological discussions (e.g., Zahavi 2015), and in some literature in philosophy of mind in the analytic tradition (e.g., Baker 2012), neither of which are usually regarded as 'existential'. What is arguably distinctive is the way in which existentialism indexes that first-personal givenness to a sense of the subject as a concrete, historically, and morally situated being. Whereas phenomenology is often thought to 'bracket' all theoretical and practical commitments in order to get at the immanent structure of experience itself, existentialism constantly refers the philosophizing subject back to their emplacement. Renaudie (2013) has argued that we can see this shift at work in Sartre, in the transition between the phenomenological detachment of *Transcendence of the Ego* to the anxious pessimism of *Being and Nothingness* with its all-encompassing concern with the actuality of freedom. The existentialist subject is a subject whose very existence presents itself as a *problem* and *task* for *the subject herself* – and every reader of existential philosophy is constructed by that philosophy as just such a subject.

Hence the first-personal character of existentialist accounts of subjectivity notoriously finds phenomenally distinctive instantiation in various distinctive experiences. For instance, it is the focus of what Karl Jaspers calls 'limit-situations', and which we might say, using the language of Laurie Paul, is a special sort of epistemic situation (cf. Paul 2014: 2): for Kierkegaard the decision to believe, but, for Paul, the transformational decision to become a vampire (or, only slightly less dramatically, a parent). As both Paul and the existentialists make clear, these are choices and decisions for which none of our prior experiences can adequately prepare us and thus justify a decision about what is in our best interests in a future transformed state. In these kinds of transformative situations, our desires, preferences, *and* epistemic judgements about what is in our interests, and indeed who we are, will shift. No reasons internal to the project of becoming a parent or vampire can be adduced for willing such a transformation, as the transformation itself will change what counts as a reason *for us*; the value of a vampiric or parental life will only be fully accessible to us after making the transition. Moreover, no calculation or weighing of pros and cons can suffice to ameliorate this responsibility, which is revealed via first-personal experiences such as angst, shame, guilt, earnestness, and so on, that are argued to be philosophically significant (by virtue of their world-disclosing power) rather than merely of psychological significance alone. The existentialist position, then, is not (contra Russell 1959) to simply lionize particular idiosyncratic psychological experiences, but to show what they reveal about more general structures of lived-experience, in this case that no wholly impersonal discussion of these phenomena is adequate, precisely because their constitutive first-personal dimension is elided. To give one early example, Kierkegaard claims that we only understand certain key human experiences – sin, death – if we approach them in the right mood (anxiety and earnestness, respectively). By their nature, such experiences resist complete objectification: any analysis that aspires to full objectivity, by removing the analysing subject from its own analysis, will falsify or distort the topic of its enquiry.

One obvious question for the neo-existentialist, then, concerns the claimed irreducibility of this first-personal experience of the world to the third-personal, God's eye view that some scientific naturalists implicitly presuppose. Indeed, it might be protested that first-personal experiences, in general, are not real in any fully fledged metaphysical sense, however significant they appear to us to be from our situated perspective. It is hard to see what *a priori* argument might rule this out. But the burden of proof arguably resides with the putative eliminator (cf. Baker 2012: 116), and there are also genuine worries concerning performative contradiction and the continuing tacit presupposition of such a perspective within the various naturalist projects of elimination and reduction. We cannot settle such debates here, but it is important to recognize that a range of closely related questions are also associated: is self-knowledge equivalent, in form if not in contingent content, to knowledge of others from an external perspective? Without exception, the existentialists will insist on the asymmetry between these two kinds of knowledge, albeit not necessarily by privileging Cartesian introspection as we will see. Another key question concerns just how much we can universalize on the basis of these 'limit situations' and whether the philosophical value of these experiences can be elucidated without recourse to a problematic romanticism/ revisionism in regard to doxastic practice in which the philosopher becomes akin to a prophet unconstrained by common sense.[1]

Of course, the answer one gives to these questions betrays one's view of the aim and purpose of philosophy. One answer might be along the lines of that offered by J. L. Austin, who in response to a talk by Gabriel Marcel, and dying of cancer at the time, reputedly stood up and said: 'we all know we have to die, but why do we have to sing songs about it?' (Scarre 2007: 65). Austin's implied question here might be: why should we think that experiences and moods given to us in the first-person perspective reveal anything about metaphysical structures? Cognitive science provokes slightly different questions: why think that such experiences, and our subsequent descriptions of them, are epistemically or methodologically reliable? Haven't the empirical sciences (e.g., psychology, cognitive science, neurology, etc.) shown us that we should distrust such a perspective, which must either be accessed introspectively, or retrospectively after the experience, approaches which have both been shown to be unreliable? We will attempt to answer these questions, beginning with the role of experience as tribunal for the existentialist.

ERLEBNIS: INTROSPECTION AND RETROSPECTION

Existentialism attempts to proffer a philosophy that is adequate to our existential experience, with that experience usually conceived of as 'given' prior to explicit philosophical reflection. Anathema to existential philosophers are any versions of 'high-altitude' thinking, as Merleau-Ponty calls them in *The Visible and the Invisible*, which survey things from above, as well as any empiricist/reductionist programme that seeks to comprehend and explain experience by breaking it down in terms of its component parts. The focus is hence on description of said experiences, more than the explanation or analysis of those experiences, but there is also a suggestion that the 'view from above' is, at best, partial, or, at worst, mistaken. While it might be possible to curtail one's existentialism in a metaphysically modest manner that is restricted to the semantics of that which presents itself 'for us', usually there is a broader metaphysical and methodological primacy given to experience. A *sub specie aeternitatis* position is understood as wholly unavailable for beings such as ourselves, and a philosophy with pretentions to such a 'view from nowhere', like some versions of scientific realism and speculative realism,[2] are just to that extent abrogations of the existence they claim to comprehend. As Merleau-Ponty nicely presents the consequences of this line of thought: 'no philosophy can be ignorant of the problem of finitude without thereby being ignorant of itself as philosophy' (Merleau-Ponty 2008: 40).

This raises questions about the status of the experience(s) that philosophy is called to attend to. Is this *Erlebnis* just a more holistic version of the 'myth of the given', not an empiricist sense-datum admittedly of the sort influentially criticized by Wilfrid Sellars, but nonetheless still a brute experience that acts as a philosophical justifier? Perhaps, although that label does not decide the fate of existentialism, since perhaps all versions of the given are not equally mythic; some philosophers have come to take seriously the idea of the 'grip of the given', for example, in which we cognitively encounter things directly and pre-discursively in an embodied manner, but they have also argued that such a position need not be vulnerable to Sellars' critique of the myth of the given (see (Hanna 2011) and Hubert Dreyfus' debate with John McDowell on related matters in Schear (2013). Certainly existentialism is committed to an anti-intellectualism about emotions, moods, and other world-disclosing experiences, and at least some have taken this to entail a commitment to non-conceptual content (cf. Ratcliffe 2009: 368). Doing philosophy involves concepts, of course, but the existentialists are committed to that about experience that resists being grasped, comprehended, or known, even if it has in some sense been lived-through. This is a live and ongoing debate, and it is not clear the existentialists are on the wrong side of it. It is apparent, however, that those experiences that are of interest to existentialists must be available (i.e., given) to us in the lived-experience itself, and then also in philosophical reflection upon that experience, even if the reflective relationship to the 'I' or 'Ego' transforms it. Insofar as existentialism takes seriously our experiences of something like 'limit situations', and ontologically significant experiences such as anxiety, shame, and so on, it cannot embrace a constructivism in which we give up the idea that in limit situations we apprehend – however obscurely or pre-reflectively – at least something of the ontological status of our place in the world, and which a philosophy is more or less faithfully able to capture. The existentialist hence invokes experience in a justificatory way, but also in a way that doesn't always ally with common-sense judgements about experience. It is not, for example, akin to the sort of position that we might associate with G. E. Moore, in which some basic dimensions of experience, supported by common sense, are envisaged to trump all kinds of philosophical reflection and, most notably, scepticism about the external world. On the contrary, many of these experiences of 'limit situations' reveal both ourselves and the world to be not quite as we usually take them to be.

We will come back to this revisionary dimension shortly, but for now it is important to ask some questions about this experience, and either the self-knowledge or the worldly knowledge that it makes possible. The dilemma in regard to the primacy that existentialism appears to grant to first-personal experience is that we need an account of our methodological access to the said experience. Indeed, it might be contended that it needs to be accessed via something akin to either introspection or retrospection, with both being said to be problematic empirically. There is, after all, a lot of evidence that suggests that introspective reports are unreliable, often more judgements of plausibility than strict reports (e.g., Nisbett and Wilson 1977; Carruthers 2011: 6). We are prone to frequent confabulation undetectable by the thinker in regard to their own mental states and beliefs, another version of the 'user-illusion' that Benjamin Libet drew our attention to in regard to freedom.

In one sense, this may appear to be no problem for the neo-existentialist who holds that we are often mistaken about ourselves and others, being inevitably liable to bad faith and the stifling and conformist tendencies of what Heidegger calls *Das Man*, and what more broadly we discuss under the headings of conventionalism, reflexive traditionalism, and so on.[3] They would also maintain that our access to experience is not by peering within and observing ourselves as if from outside, as some introspective accounts of self-knowledge hold. Rather than having a pre-existing intention that we might come to be directly aware of (and perceive from the outside in a manner equivalent to perceiving another), or simply as a memory that we access retrospectively after the Owl of Minerva has flown at dusk, we achieve self-knowledge and self-awareness in the intending and (at least attempted) doing of something in the world. Intention and awareness are co-imbricated together in this kind of adverbial account of consciousness that can be associated with existentialism (cf. Romdenh-Romluc 2011: 373). Indeed, this helps to make perspicuous a feature of *Being and Nothingness* that is too often ignored. While he is rightly known as a philosopher of radical freedom, in the material on action Sartre also argues that situation and motivation for pursuing certain projects are indistinguishable (Sartre 1958: 487). Perhaps Sartre's claim is overly dramatic, since we conceptually can and do distinguish between situation and motivation, but for him any act involves a synthetic unity that is partly falsified, when reconstructed in a causal or linear manner that separates a situation, motivation, and end posited. Rather, we pre-reflectively live through such acts in a given emotion or mood, and the authority we have in regard to them – that is, what they reveal about us and the world – is, at best, fleeting, and subsequently compromised by ratiocination and, often, philosophical reflection itself.

While such points are important, they do not rule out the sort of challenge that Carruthers and other philosophers indebted to cognitive science are liable to make. Carruthers (2011), for example, takes the findings about introspection to preclude any kind of transparent, non-behaviourally mediated access to first-person experience; that is not just a claim about introspection narrowly construed but a more general point about any philosophical reliance upon the so-called essential indexical (cf. also Cappelen and Dever 2013). In short, on such views our first-personal experiences are unreliable in themselves, but perhaps especially when we attempt to describe them or articulate them retrospectively, and hence are not the sort of thing that any cognitive science might admit. As Dennett puts a related point, 'we are remarkably gullible theorisers' (Dennett 1991: 68), tending to confuse description of our lived-experiences with theorizing. As has already been noted, the existentialist 'family' is in a complex position here. No existentialist will think judgements about our own beliefs are epistemically reliable, since we tend to be self-deluded, or at least conformist in our reflections upon our own experiences, and in this respect they inherit a lot from the so-called masters of suspicion: Marx, Nietzsche, and Freud. But their suspicion about the role of first-personal experience and description of it in philosophical theorizing doesn't go all the way down. On the contrary, the claim is that our judgements and *ad hoc* theorizing on the fly are conditioned by experiences of another sort, experiences that are not themselves judgements but pre-judicative states or experiences, which are said to depend on certain structures of experience *per se* (such as the structures of temporal experience as elucidated by Husserl in his theory of internal time-consciousness (cf. Zahavi 2005)), but also more characteristically existential pre-judicative experiences like anxiety, dread, shame, and so on. Such experiences are said to reveal something that our after the fact interpretations and hypothesizing about them frequently confabulates about. Data from psychology about this, then, will not strictly contradict existentialism, but it still raises questions about the methods through which the existentialist themselves is able to ascertain the truth of the matter, to see through our procrustean existence to its essential conditions. For the existentialist there is some special or distinctive epistemic significance to at least some of our own experiences, but in attempting to know of them, reflect upon them, or even systematize them, we are liable to betray the said experiences.

Here the methodological naturalist will press back against the existentialist, wanting an account of how the access to brute experience, which serves as a philosophical justifier, might be understood as veridical (or not). If it is not about introspection but rather something that we adverbially live-through, how do we distinguish living-through it veridically (i.e., in an ontologically revelatory way) and living-through it in, say, a deceptive way, or even just in the ontologically superficial way that is characteristic of what Heidegger calls 'average everydayness'? Moreover, if in the activity of philosophizing we are no longer at one, or coinciding with the subject of the said experience, which is playing a justificatory role, the existentialist also seems to need to confront the fragility and permeability of retrospection and memory. And empirical studies regarding the reliability of memory are at least as serious a problem as are those regarding our introspective capacities. The existentialist is likely to respond here that *qua* philosopher it is not a matter of representing a strictly faithful memory of an experience in a 'limit situation', but of promulgating a philosophy that is as adequate as possible to that situation, and taking cognizance of the gap between experience as lived and experience as known. To comprehend or be mindful of the gap, however, presupposes an ability to compare the limit-situation that has been lived through (perhaps in the past), and the philosophical reflection upon it after the said event/experience. Hence this doesn't seem to solve the dilemma of retrospection.

But another way to think about it is to take the existentialist as committed to experience as a justifier, and thus they must endeavour to create this experience for the reader, and thereby enable the reader to remember and imagine related experiences (hence the frequent use of literary techniques, as we will see below). In a way, then, even though we have attempted to present some of the philosophical reasoning behind existentialism, there is a tantalizing and frustrating sense (for the academic philosopher, at least) in which the proof is in the pudding. It works – if it works – by calling upon the reader to imagine, enact, reflect, and remember their own experiences as lived. Avowedly a philosophy of finitude, as we saw Merleau-Ponty note, it also asks the reader to perform a 'situated thought' themselves (cf. Sacks 2005); this is the inter-subjective tribunal that the existentialist appeals to. Can the method be neutrally judged from outside? No. Does that mean it embraces some sort of question-begging dogma in which alternative experiences and reasons cannot count against the philosophy in question? Not necessarily, but it does require one to have a first-personal experience, even if induced by a description or example (hence the ironic manner of dealing with the reader, in, say, Kierkegaard). So, we may dispute the use that Sartre makes of his descriptions of shame, or bad faith, and so on, and think that certain conclusions do not follow. First though, we must attempt to reconstruct the experience, either one related to what we have previously experienced, or using techniques like imaginative variation, or perhaps even engage in a kind of experimental philosophy in the true sense of the word in which we are confronted by limit-situations. Of course, engaging in such matters with a philosophical agenda, to seek to confirm a given description as adequate, is in a way already to corrupt or betray that experience, since there is a sense in which *qua* philosophers one is also always partly withdrawn from the flux of experience on this view. But perhaps that doesn't mean that such experiences can't be engendered adequately in the reader, so much as that the existentialist philosopher is something of a sacrifice on behalf of the reader, alienating herself from her own direct experience in order to bring her reader into a desired encounter with that experiential content.

In the terms of Richard Moran, the general point is to remind us of the philosophical irreducibility of the first-person perspective in regard to the lived-experience. For Moran (who invokes Sartre positively in this context), in choosing, deciding, being responsible, the situated fact that I am choosing, 'cannot be for me a set of data for which I must simply make room in my deliberations, as I may have to accommodate the empirical fact of other people's beliefs and desires' (Moran 2001: 164). As Moran goes on to add:

the attitudes that I bring with me into the situation may well be said to 'frame' the problem for me, but in a given case I may also be obliged to bring them out of the frame and install them within the scope of the problem itself, on the negotiating table, and there my relation to them is unlike anyone else's. Hence they cannot enter into my thinking as the fixed beliefs and desires of someone who just happens to be me.

(Moran 2001: 164)

This, of course, is precisely what many sciences aim for, in bracketing one's situation away and considering oneself as another, but it is also the kind of position presupposed by the philosopher who denies distinctions between self-knowledge and other-knowledge, and between the lived and the known. Whether or not there is a rationalism in Moran's work of a sort that the existentialists deny, they concur with him in rejecting any sort of impersonalism as a moral evasion. For the existentialist, there is an enduring gap or non-coincidence between the lived and the known, and between the first- and third-person perspectives. It is typically dramatized by the existentialists in evocative accounts of dread, shame, and so on, as we have seen, but it also arguably pertains to less radical but still potentially transformative experiences.

Consider John Drummond's interesting characterization of doubt, which aims to show that the act of doubting presupposes some connection with both the action and pre-reflective self-awareness that is not itself bracketed or doubted. This living of doubt (and shame, dread, etc.), he argues, cannot be captured/reconstructed from a third-person perspective alone or bracketed as a mere modal possibility:

One can, of course, explain this experience of doubt from a purely third-person perspective, but such an explanation will fail to capture the experience of doubt as it is lived and, in particular, the manner in which this experience (1) moves away from the simple belief certainty characteristic of perception to a wavering between possibilities exclusive of one another; and (2) at the same time, oscillates between the straightforwardly experienced object, on the one hand, and, on the other, its appearance or sense or meaning, terms that I shall for present purposes consider largely equivalent; and (3) resolves itself in a contrastive apprehension. This movement, oscillation, and resolution characterize the experience as lived, and they have their correlates in the intentional content in the changes in belief modality from actual to possible and back to actual.

(Drummond 2007: 34)

In related fashion, Kierkegaard (1985), in the persona of Johannes Climacus, cites doubt as an experience that discloses the structure of consciousness. He identifies consciousness with 'interest' (interesse) and plays on the Latin roots of this word, inter esse: between being, or being-in-between, caught self-reflexively between the components of ideality and actuality that constitute existence and whose non-coincidence generates the possibility of doubt. He goes on to link subjectivity foundationally with 'infinite', 'passionate interest' in eternal happiness/blessedness [salighed], such that the dispassionate, disinterested objectivity of contemporary philosophy is not an achievement of thought, but its perversion (Kierkegaard 1992). We might also say, with Merleau-Ponty, that for the existentialist we are 'condemned to meaning' (2008: xix). This is to rule out a position outside of meaning (even a naturalistic explanation of meaning), and to insist on this aspect of our lives as ineliminable. If existentialism is right, it thus presents an obstacle to many programmes in scientific naturalism, especially as concerns each of the four Ms sometimes thought to be the key research programmes for scientific naturalism: Mind, Meaning, Morals, and Modality (Price 2004). Might we give a naturalistic account of meaning and morality, for example, that will be adequate to meaning and morality? Again, the existentialist will say no on this score, much as we have seen Drummond and Kierkegaard offer reasons for thinking the experience of doubt to be irreducibly first-personal in a related way. We have not settled this dispute here, of course, but we have suggested that there are at least some reasons to think that existentialism can navigate the charges of introspection and retrospection and the empirical difficulties for each and that it continues to warrant our philosophical interest.

REVISIONISM AND 'RESISTENTIALISM'

Even if that were so, however, there may be another concern about existentialism in terms of its methodology, which is that rather than being overly invested in experience as 'given', it is in fact too disjunct from everyday experience and the manifest image. This is the charge that Philip Pettit (2004) brings in an essay that seeks to navigate between the errors that he takes to be the Scylla and Charybdis of existentialism and scientism. Pettit suggests that existentialism, like scientific naturalism, is overly radical in relation to doxa and practice, allowing for the philosophically inspired to throw off received ideas and practice-bound habits, and live differently. Of course, something like this view is one reason for existentialism's enduring non-academic popularity, but just how committed are the existentialists to this romantic vision in which philosophical considerations are able to trump all other sorts of belief and practice? Is Pettit right to say that the existentialist is committed to the view that 'there is no limit to how far philosophy may lead us to reconstruct ourselves' (2004: 305)? Experience is in fact one limit, as we have seen. Likewise, the contrast between first- and third-person perspectives is another limit. As Sartre points out, we may want to be God but this is not possible. Indeed, we have seen that the ostensible 'authority' of the first-person perspective is of a peculiar sort: hard won, but also not something that endures and grounds certainty thereafter or even a philosophical system or programme (despite the tract that is *Being and Nothingness*). Rather, it is contingent, fallible, difficult to access, prone to ratiocinations and bad faith (cf. Renaudie 2015: 219–20). The authority is largely a negative one, insisting on the inability of a high-altitude perspective to be complete or totalizing. Can we reject the self-deceptive ideas of the folk and simply be authentic? No, since that would be to misunderstand our situated existence. Existentialism may be famously associated with the French resistance in World War Two, but the 'resistentialism' idea is not right. It is far more pessimistic (e.g., there are limits to self-knowledge, there is gap between self- and other-knowledge, our being-for-others is always finally beyond our control) than the endorsing of the capacity of a philosophical idea to suddenly transform all platitudes and doxa.[4] Indeed, as Sartre remarks in Being and Nothingness, 'voluntary deliberation is always a deception' (Sartre 1958: 488). Sartre means this primarily in regard to choosing what we ought to do with our lives, considering the choice to have been made pre-judicatively, but it applies to the relationship between philosophical reflection and our lives too.

There is hence a case that Pettit presents a 'straw man' version of existentialism and its meta-philosophical commitments. In particular, his understanding of the relationship between belief and practice in existentialism is misleading, claiming that 'the direction of determination must run from beliefs to practices' (Pettit 2004: 319). Contrary to such a view, he argues that 'we must reject any easy existentialist optimism about the capacity of philosophy to undo and reform our received practice bound ideas' (Pettit 2004: 320). But optimism is too strong a term here, as anyone familiar with Fear and Trembling, Either/Or, Nausea, Being and Nothingness, and The Ethics of Ambiguity would note. There is no authority for either the first- or third-person perspective for Sartre, but there is an irreducibility of each to the other, a gap that cannot be overcome even if one admits of encroachments in ways that Sartre's dualisms sometimes downplay (cf. Renaudie 2013; Merleau-Ponty 2008). While the existentialist will certainly contend (and call upon the reader to recognize) that there are experiences that we have that might undo and reform our practice-bound ideas, no existentialist thinks they entail that we can remake ourselves ex nihilo in accord with an idea. Even Sartre's discussion of bad faith makes it clear that we cannot change the socially mediated meanings of our choices and actions, whatever choices we might make in relation to them for ourselves. As such, the existentialist claim is less that philosophy undoes our received, practice-bound ideas as Pettit claims, but that life and experience do, and the question is then whether – and indeed how, as we will see – a philosophy can attest to that. It holds that our experience (of norms, of agency, of other people) is not quite as smooth as Pettit might contend. And it appeals to the reader to judge whether or not this is so, whether or not there is anything inflated or grandiose about the descriptions of the said experiences, or whether they capture something fundamental to freedom, agency, normativity; indeed, potentially dimensions of these experiences that are neglected in political philosophy of Pettit's kind. The key question that we have returned to, then, is about the richness of the category of experience, and just how recalcitrant or divergent it is in relation to belief and knowledge. Do, for example, experiences remain separable from beliefs formed on the basis of these experiences? This distinction may be one Pettit is unlikely to draw, but it is one that existentialists will insist on. Whether doxastic or even philosophically well supported, beliefs, understood as propositional and formed at a certain reflective remove, are thought to miss something fundamental about the richness of experience, the actuality of existence; that doesn't mean they don't get at something too, but they are not exhaustive. Existentialism is thus pessimistic about any 'final vocabulary'. Human experience transcends and resists such accounts. Existence always exceeds thought, as both Kierkegaard and Jaspers argued, and the self, as Sartre puts it, is always-already beyond itself whenever it makes itself an object for itself. Versions of this insight about non-self-coincidence crop up in surprising places in contemporary philosophy, in quarters one would not typically think of as neo-existentialist – such as Parfit's (1984) discussions of self-alienation or Galen Strawson's (2009) claim that the self he experiences himself as being right now isn't identical with the person 'GS'.

Pettit's objection, at bottom, is that existentialism asks us to live radically differently, but without being able to give reasons. But recalling L. A. Paul's vampire scenario (Paul 2014: 2), the question remains of how might one choose to be a vampire, or even a parent, rationally, or choose between caring for a sick and vulnerable mother or joining the resistance, in Sartre's scenario. We cannot do so in an exhaustive manner, since the experience of being a vampire, a parent, or in love, is transformative, in both an epistemic and personal sense with respect to one's desires, preferences, and so on. None of this means that we cannot give third-personally couched reasons for becoming or not becoming a vampire or a parent, and probabilistic considerations may be adduced (maybe the social sciences contend that all non-parents rate themselves as happier than parents, or that all vampires attest to being happier in such a post-human state), but this cannot settle the matter 'for us'. Is this an irrationalism in which reason is rendered nothing but the epiphenomenal ratiocination of a blind leap? Sometimes it admittedly appears that way, but there is a more sober side to existentialism that just reminds us of the gap.

EXISTENTIALISM AND THE FORMS OF PHILOSOPHY

The foregoing discussion has given us grounds for thinking that existentialism can overcome at least some of the key difficulties associated with its emphasis on the first-personal, particularly insofar as this might be taken to rely on introspective and retrospective forms of cognition. However, existentialism's appeal to pre-judicative experience creates another problem, already gestured to above: that of non-coincidence. As soon as the subject attempts to catch sight of itself, so to speak, it is already beyond the subject it tries to see; in making itself an object for itself, consciousness always fails to coincide with its object.

Existentialism, as noted, places analysis of certain aspects of experience at the centre of subjectivity's attempt to understand itself. However, the very act of theorizing such experiences already puts us at a distance from the content of experience. This is a problem classical existentialists were not merely aware of, but embraced. In the mid-1930s Jaspers was already insisting that, 'In our research we move about within the encompassing that we are by making our existence into an object for ourselves, acting upon it and manipulating it; but as we do this it must at the same time let us know that we never have it in hand' (Jaspers 1971: 22). The very act of reflection, let alone writing about and then reading about such reflection, opens up a gulf between the subjectivity existentialism aims to capture and its very activity *qua* theorization. Existentialism rejects a 'view from nowhen', but threatens a retreat to just such a position of subjective suspension precisely at the point where it attempts to articulate the experience it tries to encompass. In a sense, the non-coincidence of the subject with itself that Sartre describes is here reduplicated in the very attempt to philosophize existentially *about* topics including that gulf.

While existentialists generally see some form of non-self-coincidence as an inevitable result of the intentional structure of consciousness, this does create a problem for a philosophy that aims to take the existence *of the philosophizing subject herself* as its object. Existentialism refuses both the *sub specie aeternitatis* view of Hegelianism and the 'view from nowhere' of contemporary scientific naturalism and its fellow-travellers in Anglophone metaphysics. But as we've seen, it also rejects the situationally suspended position inherent in at least some construals of the *epochē*; existentialists do not bracket *themselves* as existing, embodied, temporally, socially, and ethically emplaced subjects. The methodological challenge of existentialist philosophy – if that phrase is to avoid being an oxymoron – is to find a way of philosophizing that does not implicitly evacuate its listener, causing them to implicitly view themselves as an abstract, bodiless, ahistorical locus of pure thought. Hence the usual modes of philosophical production, which position the reader as a passive listener, need to be subverted. Equally, though, overtly stating 'the content of this book concerns you as a concrete, free, existing being' is liable to decay immediately into just another proposition for passive, selfless reception, liable to provoke precisely the same sort of world-suspension as the standard modes. Hence the requirement for what Kierkegaard called *indirect communication*, in which the text is calculated to bring the reader into a certain kind of subjective relation to the text – requiring a certain amount of artistic skill on the part of the communicator.

This has implications for the ways in which existentialist philosophy is presented: trying to bring the subject back to a confrontation with the relevant experience (and what it discloses) *itself* rather than simply talking *about* that experience from a place that notionally suspends existence in order to talk about it. Existentialism presupposes, and attempts to engender, a particular subjective orientation on the part of the addressee, without which communication of existential understanding cannot occur. Closely related to this is the problem generated by existentialism's reliance on certain key experiences such as angst, shame, and so on.

What is disclosive in such experiences can't be got across purely through outlining these terms as concepts, but through conceptual elaboration of something implicit in our direct acquaintance with these phenomena. To get any philosophical purchase the existentialist philosopher must assume her reader has had such experiences, in some way or another, or perhaps that a sufficiently vivid description can provide the occasion for direct acquaintance via imagination. Hence the existentialist author needs to be able to *evoke*, not merely to describe, particular subjective states.

Seen in this light, the existentialist emphasis on non-traditional philosophical forms (with the caveat that the formal features of 'traditional' forms are themselves relatively recent, while older forms such as philosophical dialogue have been almost entirely abandoned) is no mere stylistic affectation. Rather, it embodies a vital link between a distinctive philosophical *method* and a corresponding philosophical *form*. While existentialists certainly left behind no shortage of 'traditional' philosophical tomes – dense writings aimed at educated readers and specialists – they also utilized a much wider authorial palate than their philosophical contemporaries. Kierkegaard wrote largely under pseudonyms, and pursued his philosophical and theological project across a range of genres: books, book reviews, newspaper articles, aesthetic essays on the theatre, pamphlets, sermon-like 'edifying' discourses, and texts that subvert the very genres they purport to belong to, for example *Prefaces*, a book composed entirely of prefaces to other, non-existent books. Sartre wrote not only hefty volumes such as *Being and Nothingness* but also plays, novels, memoires, and newspaper pieces – not least those in which he performed his dramatic break with Camus, another existentialist whose philosophical output was predominantly literary rather than expositive in character. This diversity of forms is no accident. Rather, the use of literary forms gives the existentialist the necessary scope to produce a specific relationship between the reader and the text.

Consider the authorial strategy employed in Kierkegaard's *Either/ Or*, his first major publication, and one that is thematically concerned with a number of canonically existentialist concerns: boredom, temporality, choice, decision, and so on. Yet instead of presenting a treatise on these topics, Kierkegaard stages a confrontation between two radically different voices: a jaded young aesthete, 'A', and his older friend, Judge Wilhelm, who provides a long encomium on the ethically integrating effects of choosing commitments such as marriage. This is no simple statement of the primacy of the ethical over the aesthetic: the reader feels the attraction of A's aesthetic life even as we are repulsed by the nihilistic disaffection with which he pursues it. By articulating these life-views from within the well-developed and differently likeable personas of A and Wilhelm, Kierkegaard problematizes the position of the reader herself. She is confronted with two radically different forms of life, and must decide where she stands in relation to what is presented. Moreover, Kierkegaard *himself* will be of no help here, just as Sartre was of no help for principled reasons when he recounts a student coming to him asking whether they ought to join the resistance or care for their dying grandparent. Kierkegaard's work is presented as the papers of A and Wilhelm, though 'The Seducer's Diary' may well be the work of another hand again, while the final chapter is a sermon by a Jutland pastor that Wilhelm presents without, it seems, entirely understanding it. Kierkegaard is not even listed as the editor; that honour falls to one 'Hilarious Bookbinder', whose preface describes in some detail how he came to find A and Wilhelm's correspondence hidden inside a piece of second-hand furniture. Kierkegaard is nowhere to be found in this constellation of pseudonymous voices. These nested deferrals of authorial authority serve to throw the reader back onto her own resources. We cannot simply lose ourselves in a detached understanding of 'what Kierkegaard says', but are instead called to situate ourselves in relation to the disparate voices of the text. The very form of the work calls the reader back to existential engagement, to their own position *qua* existing subject – precisely the position Kierkegaard took the 'objectifying' nineteenth century and its philosophical articulators to be effacing, using the abstracting power of theorizing in a self-defeating attempt to dissolve the existing subject altogether.

It is hard to imagine a book like *Either/Or* finding its way into the review pages of philosophy journals or university syllabi today (or, to be fair, a book like *Tractatus Logico-Philosophicus* either). That may seem like a mere point about philosophical style or contemporary tastes. Philosophers do still communicate in non-traditional forms today – the blog, the podcast, the 'think piece' – but these largely retain the expository character of the journal article and the academic monograph, albeit with a different tone and level of sophistication. But it may also suggest that the conditions which allowed these earlier forms of philosophical production simply don't hold any longer. For one thing, the existentialists were writing for very specific audiences: not (always) professional philosophers, but a philosophically sophisticated educated public. Such a public still exists, but it is not clear that they would be prepared to be confounded by the sorts of genre-defying texts Kierkegaard produced or the sort of philosophically suffused literature of a Sartre or a Camus. Hence the circumstances of the material production of philosophical texts perhaps presents a difficulty for neo-existentialists today. This difficulty needn't be fatal. But it does pose a challenge nonetheless: to connect existentially with subjects where the only available vehicles for philosophical writing pull against that subjectivizing project. Perhaps, in time, new forms will emerge. If existentialism has taught us anything, after all, it is to remain open to radical possibility.

NOTES

1 Paul Jennings published a spoof of Sartre in *The Spectator* in April 1948 under the auspices of the idea of 'resistentialism', making this kind of point. For Jennings, it was partly about the idea that objects resist us, and are recalcitrant to our purposes, as with *Nausea*'s discussion of Antoine Roquentin's encounter with the oak tree, but it is also a spoof about an alleged existentialist resistance to orthodoxy in general.

2 While it is sometimes disputed how much philosophical unity can be ascribed to so-called speculative realism, it is standardly thought to insist on the power of thought to break with any 'correlation' between subject and object. Philosophers like Quentin Meillassoux take phenomenology and existentialism to be problematic philosophies of finitude that, by contrast, tie being to the thinking subject.

3 Variously translated as the herd, the many, the 'they', the crowd, they-self, and sometimes even 'the one', *das Man* refers to those aspects of our lives that are average and anonymous.

4 We cannot just remake ourselves *ex nihilo*. While a footnote in *Being and Nothingness* talks about the possibility of an ethics of radical conversion, Sartre never makes good on this promise. As such, we have to accept a pessimism about existentialism, not a utopianism about us being able to convert our lives and embrace authenticity *tout court*.

17 Hermeneutics and the Question of Method

Right from the beginning of *Truth and Method*, his 1960 *magnum opus*, Hans-Georg Gadamer describes his position as that of *philosophical* hermeneutics, a label that implies the existence of other – non-philosophical? less philosophical? – contributions to this field.[1] In *Truth and Method*, Gadamer seeks to identify these contributions, demonstrate their limitations, and show how they have come to damage our approaches to understanding and interpretation. Gadamer characterizes these strains of hermeneutics as *methodological*.[2] He views methodological hermeneutics as a set of positions indebted to a naive form of Cartesianism that gains influence throughout the Enlightenment and peaks in the works of post-Kantian philosophers such as Friedrich Schleiermacher and Wilhelm Dilthey.[3] Seeking to overcome this paradigm, Gadamer anchors understanding in the ability to establish a continuum of meaning in tradition.[4] Hermeneutics, in his view, is not a method, but a phenomenology of human existence in a historical-cultural world. In fact, as Gadamer sees it, the very call for a hermeneutic method is but a concession to a way of thinking that is fundamentally alien to the *Verstehenswissenschaften*, including philosophy.

Within the European and Anglo-American traditions alike, hermeneutics is often conceived in the spirit of Gadamerian thought (see for instance Rorty 1980; Bernstein 1983; McDowell 1994). Indeed, it would not be an exaggeration to propose that since the publication of *Truth and Method*, Gadamer's hermeneutics has reached a status that nearly ensures identification between his work and the discipline itself. In the following, I would like to challenge this identification and, in particular, the relative consensus about the soundness of Gadamer's rejection of hermeneutic method. I ask if it is possible, after Gadamer, to develop a less categorical way of thinking about the relationship between hermeneutics and method. Returning to Johann Gottfried Herder, an Enlightenment thinker whose significance is generally acknowledged by Gadamer (yet not discussed in much detail),[5] I trace a notion of hermeneutical methodology that is not rooted in the Cartesian ideal that Gadamer so vehemently rejects, but that deliberately seeks to establish an alternative to such a position by grounding hermeneutics in an empirical-anthropological turn.[6] As such, Herder's philosophy offers an alternative notion of what a hermeneutic methodology could look like and how it can help clarify and improve our approaches to understanding and interpretation.

I

For a historically orientated philosopher like Gadamer, hermeneutics must be legitimized by reference to an account of its development in tradition. Along these lines, *Truth and Method* retrieves the historical preamble to philosophical hermeneutics. Drawing on his earlier work, especially *Plato's Dialogical Ethics* (Gadamer 1991 / 1999 V: 3–164), Gadamer outlines a development that begins with Socratic dialogue, Aristotelian *phronesis*, and a neo-Platonic notion of emanation, moves via Augustine, Spinoza, and Vico, and is brought to fruition in the work of Hegel and, ultimately, Heidegger's analysis of the human being in the world.[7] Even though Heidegger hardly counts as a run-of-the-mill humanist,[8] and Plato, Aristotle, and Augustine predate a modern understanding of this tradition, Gadamer suggests that these philosophers offer a particularly helpful way of thinking about the human sciences (*qua* sciences of understanding and interpretation). However, few of these thinkers and positions are subject to in-depth analysis in *Truth and Method* (Plato, Hegel, and Heidegger are discussed in separate studies). This is no oversight. Gadamer's point is not to offer a detailed account of the humanist tradition, but to sketch an informal intellectual horizon that can help him identify a set of questions and concerns with which philosophers have been preoccupied, but that is now, he fears, being marginalized, repressed, or forgotten. Understood in this way, Gadamer's hermeneutics involves an attempt to clarify the promise of the humanist tradition and demonstrate how this tradition has been sidelined by its philosophical competitors.

Gadamer not only takes the humanist tradition to shelter important truths and insights, but also, and more importantly, to exemplify a way of philosophizing.[9] What, then, characterizes this way of philosophizing? While there are many ways to describe what Gadamer is after, I would like to focus on a handful of points that prove particularly significant in that they help to establish the foundation of his own philosophical hermeneutics.

By Gadamer's lights, the humanist tradition emphasizes that the human being is in the world understandingly. While scientists seek to uncover natural laws, the classical humanists view the human being in terms of its self-realization in history and culture. Such a self-realization cannot be explained by reference to causal relations. Thus, the goal of hermeneutics, as a general theory of human being in the world, is to explain this basic capacity for self-realization (*Bildung*) with reference to an even deeper and more comprehensive capacity for self-understanding (Gadamer 1994: 96 / 1990: 101–2). In Gadamer's view, hermeneutics gives us insight into our existence as meaning-producing and understanding agents, whose nature is fundamentally shaped by our participation in and contribution to the historical-cultural world.

Further, the humanist model takes our existence in history and culture to precede a division into different validity spheres, and, relatedly, the division between the natural- and the human sciences. For Gadamer, this translates into a claim about the extension of hermeneutics: it is not a subfield of epistemology or a methodological tool for the human sciences, but covers a fundamental layer of human existence. Hermeneutics becomes, in his words, 'universal in scope' (Gadamer 1994: 264 / 1990: 268).[10]

With reference to a rather loose group of philosophical positions (but especially Plato and Augustine), Gadamer argues that our most basic understanding of the world is mediated by language.[11] This, in turn, has ramifications for the kind of knowledge hermeneutics seeks to generate. In studying the symbolic expressions of the past *and*, by the same token, the human ability to relate to symbolic expression in the first place, hermeneutics discerns a dimension of our being that differs from the perceived target of natural science: human being as it exists in and through historical culture, that is, as an expressive, understanding, and self-interpreting form of life (Gadamer 1994: 276 / 1990: 281).

Finally, in thinking about historical understanding, the humanist philosophers do not see the meaning of art, culture, and historical practice as set once and for all (say, in a past long gone), but as potentially alive and brought to concretion in new and ever richer contexts of interpretation. This has ramifications for our thinking about the object of understanding and interpretation: meaning is shaped in the act of interpretation and, vice versa, the interpreter's self-understanding is coloured by the historical-cultural context of which she is a part. In Gadamer's words, 'understanding is not a method which the inquiring consciousness applies to an object it chooses and so turns it into objective knowledge; rather, being situated within an event of tradition, a process of handing down, is a prior condition of understanding. Understanding proves to be an event [*ein Geschehen*]' (Gadamer 1994: 309 / 1990: 314). That which is understood is discovered in light of a concrete situation and thus in ever new and evolving ways. In short, understanding is always application (ibid.). As the meaning of the work is realized within ever-new contexts, it also reflects the particular characteristics of that context itself. This, in turn, takes us back to the point about the hermeneutic goal of self-understanding.[12]

For Gadamer, these insights – insights that, albeit derived from the history of philosophy, serve to define hermeneutics – have been overshadowed by an alternative, in Gadamer's mind far less attractive, way of explaining historical meaning and our nature as symbol-producing and understanding beings. Gadamer traces this strand of thought back to the beginning of the modern era as it reaches its philosophical articulation in Descartes and later Enlightenment philosophy.[13]

For anyone familiar with the tradition of phenomenology, the proper name 'Descartes' will invoke far more than a reference to a historical figure or a particular body of work. Husserl and Heidegger had viewed Descartes as a representative of a new and genuinely modern way of doing philosophy. Husserl points out the limits of this paradigm, yet endeavours to rescue its methodological potential (Husserl 1988: 43, 48).[14] Heidegger is more ambivalent and soon abandons his early (Husserlian) attempts at productively *abbauen* the Cartesian system in favour of a more black and white approach,[15] in which Descartes comes to represent more than he ever bargained for, namely the entire worldview of modern natural science (Heidegger 1996 / 2006 §§18–22).

Gadamer is visibly influenced by this view of modern philosophy. In his work, we find strange generalizations such as the claim that '[s]cientific certainty always has something Cartesian about it' (Gadamer 1994: 238 / 1990: 243). He posits, further, an absolute opposition between Cartesianism and historical awareness. Much can be said about this way of dealing with Cartesian thought – about Gadamer's reconstruction of Descartes' relationship to tradition (or, rather, lack of such),[16] and about the contradiction inherent to his claim that we are always already situated in tradition and his (Gadamer's) desire, nonetheless, to abandon the entire Cartesian chapter of philosophy. Further, questions can be raised about Gadamer's approach to the natural sciences and his claim that they reflect a problematic methodological monism. However, what matters more in our context is how Gadamer constructs his argument about the Cartesian-methodological usurpation of the human sciences. For it is this argument that will indeed lead to his rejection of methodology in hermeneutics.

Gadamer's narrative of the methodological usurpation of the human sciences is sweeping, and, again, he targets a set of general tendencies rather than seeking to account in much detail for any one particular theory formation. The trend he describes can be summarized in the following way. In the wake of Descartes' emphasis on a methodological approach to philosophy and knowledge, the human sciences, in order to justify themselves *as* sciences, were encouraged to shape themselves with reference to an objectivity-establishing methodology (rather than a context-sensitive understanding of the humanist kind). As Gadamer describes the case of Wilhelm Dilthey (in a quote that demonstrates, yet again, his tendency to identify the Enlightenment with Cartesianism), '[f]or Dilthey, a child of the Enlightenment, the Cartesian way of proceeding via doubt to the certain is immediately self-evident' (Gadamer 1994: 239 / 1990: 243). A focus on enriching and meaningful experience, the kind of experience that all the same reflects and facilitates a profound understanding of the cultural-historical world of which the interpreter is herself a part, is replaced by the search for a procedure through which interpretative objectivity can be ensured (by regulating our subjective attitudes or approaches to tradition). This, Gadamer points out, is the beginning of modern hermeneutics – hermeneutics as a methodological discipline.

In his discussion of modern hermeneutics, Gadamer is particularly interested in what he sees as an influential, Romantic tradition that he traces back to Friedrich Schleiermacher. Gadamer argues that Schleiermacher's hermeneutics fundamentally alters the goal, extension, knowledge, and object of understanding, reducing a broader humanist concept of historical-cultural existence to a narrow, methodologically orientated theory of interpretation. Each of these points begs further explanation.

In Gadamer's view, methodological hermeneutics springs out of a paradigm that overlooks the continuity of tradition and thus erroneously assumes that '[t]he need for a hermeneutics is given precisely with the decline of self-evident understanding' (Gadamer 1994: 183 / 1990: 187). On this view, the goal of hermeneutics – and, consequently, of the human sciences, understood as sciences of interpretation – is to overcome this alienation.[17] Gadamer describes this as a hermeneutics of *reconstruction*, which he contrasts with his own hermeneutics of *integration* (Gadamer 1994: 166 / 1990: 171–2).

Further, methodological hermeneutics understands itself as a subfield of philosophy. It is complemented by, and closely affiliated with, epistemology, criticism, dialectics, and so on. On this model, the extension of the term 'hermeneutics' is no longer co-determined with that of philosophy (hermeneutics is no longer 'universal' in its scope), but is seen as an interpretational tool or device. In Gadamer's words, Schleiermacher seeks to 'isolate the procedure of understanding' and make it an 'independent method of its own' (Gadamer 1994: 185 / 1990: 189).

As Gadamer sees it, methodological hermeneutics assumes a need for a standard against which any given interpretation will be put to test. It wants, in Gadamer's words, to replace 'the unity of the content of the tradition' with 'the unity of a procedure [*Verfahren*]' (Gadamer 1994: 179, 194–5 / 1990: 182, 198–9). With reference to a method mastered by the interpreter, this position aspires to secure knowledge of the point of view an other. At stake is no longer a process of on-going, historical self-understanding, insight into a shared tradition that unifies interpreter and work, but an objectivized notion of subjective intent – 'the individuality of the Thou', as Gadamer puts it (Gadamer 1994: 179 / 1990: 187).

In seeking to reconstruct subjective intent, the interpreter, true to the assumption that knowledge is reached by way of a methodological procedure that stands under the control of the interpreting subject, endeavours to bracket his or her own beliefs, values, and culturally mediated points of view. That is, the interpreter seeks neutrality vis-à-vis the text or expression at stake (Gadamer 1994: 188 / 1990: 192). As such, we encounter what Gadamer deems a methodological abstraction from the thick, pre-reflective context of the lifeworld (Gadamer 1994: 197 / 1990: 201).

Unfortunately, Gadamer mischaracterizes the positions of Schleiermacher, Dilthey, and later hermeneuticians in their vein. In particular, he is wrong in claiming that this kind of hermeneutics is committed to a naive and rigid Cartesianism of the kind described above (see Gjesdal 2006). He is right, however, in pointing out that late eighteenth-century and early nineteenth-century hermeneutics is concerned with the need for a reflective, methodological consciousness, though that does not imply that it is *Cartesian* in nature (at least not in Gadamer's meaning of the term).

Facing Gadamer's criticism of methodological hermeneutics, later philosophers, especially those of a non-Gadamerian disposition, have asked, first, if his description of methodological hermeneutics is correct (Frank 1977) and, second, if Gadamer's own alternative is tenable (Habermas 1990 / 1982; Apel 1997).[18] In this context, I will pursue a different approach. I will sketch, albeit briefly, a counter-narrative, an alternative genealogy of hermeneutics that, I hope, can serve as a basis for a discussion of the strengths and limitations of the criticism Gadamer and his followers launch against the notion of a hermeneutic method. The point of departure for my counter-narrative is, again, a contrast between a narrow (for Gadamer: quasi-Cartesian) methodology, on the one hand, and hermeneutics, on the other. Yet, this hermeneutic alternative is not, as in Gadamer's work, to be understood as opposed to methodology. At stake, rather, is an attempt to formulate a broader notion of methodology, one that develops out of the empirical-anthropological turn that was part of the transition from a more mechanistic (some would say Newtonian) worldview to a broader naturalist paradigm in German philosophy in the second half of the eighteenth century.[19] A central figure in this narrative is Johann Gottfried Herder,[20] whose work would play an important role for the development of nineteenth-century hermeneutics, the positions of Schleiermacher and Dilthey included.[21]

II

We have seen that Gadamer presents philosophical hermeneutics as an alternative to what he sees as a problematic Cartesian tradition in philosophy. In so doing, he rejects the idea of philosophical method. Herder, too, is worried about a certain Cartesian influence in modern philosophy (see for instance Herder 2002a: 181 / 1887– VIII: 266).[22] Yet he does not abandon a commitment to hermeneutic method,[23] but seeks, rather, to reshape the very idea of what a hermeneutic methodology is and can be. In order to see how Herder's position is of relevance to the question of hermeneutic method, we thus need to survey his critique of what he takes to be the dominant approaches to philosophy, look at his construction of hermeneutic methodology, and discuss how it enables a view of hermeneutics as contributing to human *Bildung*.

Herder's interest in hermeneutics is part of a larger concern about the development of philosophy as an academic discipline. He observes how philosophy has been forced to defend its validity and relevance; philosophy, as he puts it in 1765, is 'in the process of getting condemned' (Herder 2002a: 7 / 1985–: 109). The status of deductive science, especially mathematics, is not subject to the same kinds of pressures, nor, for that matter, is the kind of philosophy that bases its method solely or primarily on the model of mathematics (Herder 2002a: 3 / 1985–: 104). Hence there is a temptation, Herder fears (and here he follows the pre-critical Kant), for philosophers naively to lean on the methodological ideals of mathematics. Critical of his own contemporary culture, but especially the rationalist school philosophy of his day, Herder traces this tendency back to a 'German disease of leading everything, whether it really follows or not, from purely formal propositions' (Herder 1985– IX/2: 110).

According to Herder, this tendency is reproduced in philosophical teaching. There is, he worries, less and less room for independent thought – *Selbstdenken* – which he, in the spirit of the

Enlightenment, views as a necessary aspect of philosophy.[24] Thus, Herder claims, we should replace '[l]ogic and moral theory [in the narrow meaning of the terms]' with 'a philosophical spirit [that] forms the human being in independent thought [dem Menschen im Selbstdenken (bildet)]' (Herder 2002a: 19 / 1985– I: 122). In Herder's view, the lack of independent thought is not simply a problem for the discipline of philosophy, but is a tendency that deprives society of an important source of critique and reflection. If philosophy, in naively mimicking other disciplines, abandons its commitment to independent thought, then a core aspect of enlightened discourse is at risk. However, if philosophers turn their backs on the resources of science, they would be in equally bad shape and end up as the *Schöngeister* that Herder also criticizes (see Herder 2006: 6 / 1985– I: 108 and Herder 2006: 335–47 / 1985– IV: 215–33).[25]

Herder does not believe that modern thought is fundamentally saturated by a Cartesian spirit, but his reflections concern, more modestly, what he takes to be a problematic development in the discipline of philosophy: its tendency to establish a dichotomy of objectivism and aestheticism.[26] Since this is, for Herder, an internal philosophical problem, his solution also works at an internal, philosophical plane. At stake, though, is not an attempt to abandon methodology, but an effort to reshape it. That is, Herder's critique of one kind of methodology (associated with rationalist school philosophy) does not imply that he is against the idea of methodology as such, neither in philosophy, nor in hermeneutics more specifically. Rather, Herder highlights the risks of letting the methods of one discipline or disciplinary subfield monopolize other disciplines or subfields. Herder is also not against interdisciplinary scholarship (Herder 2002a: 255 / 1985– I: 148–9). Yet, he would argue that genuinely interdisciplinarity is only possible to the extent that each discipline reflects on its status and epistemic foundation.

How, then, does this larger, philosophical framework affect Herder's discussion of understanding and interpretation? In order to respond to this question, we need to see how, for him, the philosophical challenges of understanding and interpretation are related to historical development, cultural diversity, and linguistic variation.

Against prevailing theories of the divine origin of language (Johann Peter Süßmilch and others (see Forster 2010: 63–4)), Herder argues that humans have a natural capacity for language, and that they actualize themselves in and through culture (Herder 2002a: 57 / 1985– I: 607). He asks, '[w]hat is more worthy and important for human beings than to investigate productions of human forces, the history of human efforts, and the births of our understanding?' (Herder 2002a: 58 / 1985– I: 608). Culture, however, is not one. Just as nature varies geographically and changes over time, so culture is defined by its diversity of manifestations. In facing cultural diversity (but also a wave of European colonialism and exploitation), Herder seeks to develop strategies for non-monopolizing, non-reductive approaches to others. Hermeneutics is part of this effort. Herder emphasizes that an interpreter should strive to acknowledge the uniqueness of the interlocutor's outlook, culture, and context of life.[27] As he warns his readers, whoever tries to rob an author of the 'birthmarks of his time' risks depriving her of her individuality (*Eigenheit* is Herder's term; Herder 2002a: 172 / 1985– II: 579).[28] Just as a grasp of the manifold of natural forms is crucial to natural science, so a grasp of cultural diversity is crucial to our understanding of humanity. And, as an implication of this, even self-understanding (as it includes understanding of humanity) depends, in a certain sense, on the understanding of others (Herder 2002a: 168–9 / 1985– II: 572–3).

In the period in which Herder develops his hermeneutic philosophy, often through interpretation of particular texts and discussion of their reception (see Mayo 1969 and Kelletat 1984), he also writes separate works in philosophy of language, philosophy of history, political philosophy, and other subfields. However, his larger, methodological concern of this period is reflected in his aesthetics. In critiquing his fellow art-historians and aestheticians, Herder does not completely break with them – in the case of Winckelmann and Lessing, their discussions, centred on the sculpture Laocoön, deal precisely with methodological issues (such as the relationship between empirical and inductive research). Herder here draws a parallel between diversity in nature and diversity in culture and calls for a 'natural method' of interpretation (Herder 1985– VII: 576).[29] In his writings, hermeneutics is a theory of interpretation and interpretation, in turn, is based in a capacity for sympathy as well as scholarship, critique, and reflection. While an interpreter sympathetically discloses the point of view presented as an expression of a possible, human standpoint,[30] the initial hypothesis about its meaning is followed up (confirmed, modified, or rejected) by reflection and scholarly work. For Herder, such a fallibilist, bottom-up approach serves as a corrective to what he calls a natural desire towards establishing systematic order, even at the cost of such order misrepresenting or unduly simplifying a complex and manifold reality. In his own philosophy, he explains, he 'did not set out to present a doctrinal system [*Lehrgebäude*]' (Herder 1992: 97 / 1985– I: 174). As he remarks, the desire for systems is a human weakness, and so also is the inability to complete them (Herder 1985– I: 657). Herder thus criticizes philosophers who speak of reason as a self-operating machine. He points out that reason does not fall from heaven, but is gradually formed (Herder 1985– IX/ 1: 391). This formation (*Bildung*) takes place in history and across cultures. Hence, Herder's approach to hermeneutics does not oppose science and methodology, but, rather, requires a methodology that is sensitive to the particular challenges and gains of the human sciences as sciences through which a human being understands itself as realized in language, culture, and history.

Herder emphasizes the need to situate texts and symbolic utterances in their original historical and cultural context. Such an undertaking, he argues, requires that an interpreter, in his or her engagement with a given historical material or culturally distant expressions, is willing to critique tradition and the possible prejudices to which it has given rise. As Herder puts it in *Ideas for the Philosophy of History of Humanity*, tradition is a great 'institution of nature', but if it comes to dominate politics and educational institutions, it can preclude progress and serve as an opium of the mind (*Opium des Geistes*, Herder 1985– VI: 512).

Herder develops his critical hermeneutic theory in a number of texts throughout the late 1760s, 1770s, and beyond. Yet, it is his activity as an interpreter that offers the most solid evidence of his methodology and his call, in the name of a reflected relation to traditional meaning-content, for an approach that involves sympathy as well as criticism. One example of this is his contribution to the eighteenth-century Shakespeare debate. In a climate of classicism and Francophile aesthetic preferences, critics were fundamentally unsure about how best to respond to Shakespearean drama, which was gaining increasing attention across Europe. While the strictest classicists, Aristotle in hand, had condemned his work without further ado, more moderate voices had tried, on the one hand, to accommodate Shakespeare's work to the classicist taste (by rendering his drama in alexandrines, streamlining his characters, and editing out supposedly un-dramatic sections of his plays), and, on the other, to offer a broader and more inclusive reading of Aristotle's poetics so as to accommodate works that did not comply with the rules and criteria of classicist aesthetics.

In a series of drafts and essays, drawing on his early philosophy of literature, Herder criticises the stifling dominance of the classicist tradition. Turning the classicist cannon against its vindicators, he shows that Aristotle, albeit helpfully elucidating the nature of ancient Greek drama, neither can nor should be taken as providing a set of trans-historical standards. Just like the ancient tragedians, Aristotle, too, is situated in a particular time and in a particular culture. And, what is more, so is the modern critic who defends a classicist repertory against alternative aesthetic canons. Thus, the challenge of interpretation – of, say, Shakespeare's drama – must move beyond and question existing prejudices (e.g., the fairly unanimous prejudices against Shakespeare) and seek to situate the relevant works within their original contexts, thus also trying to ferret out their internal measures of success and coherence. Herder never claims that this is an easy undertaking. Nor does he claim, by reference to criticism and hermeneutic sympathy, to have developed a watertight hermeneutic methodology. While he is, most of the time, remarkably fair and even-handed in his interpretations (even of work with which he disagrees, such as Lessing's *Laocoön*), he sometimes stumbles and falls back into plain prejudices. What he does claim, though – and, I suggest, justly so – is that philosophical hermeneutics needs to proceed by reference to critical standards (method) and awareness of how the tradition, through which the works of the past and other cultures are typically handed down to us, both enables and prevents interpretation.

Herder hopes that this kind of hermeneutic reflection and practice can help facilitate a society that is open to human self-realization for all. (He especially mentions that women should get access to philosophy and praises non-canonical art forms such as indigenous poetry.) In order to do so, hermeneutics must place the human being, in its diversity of orientations and ways of life, at its centre; it ought, in short, to conduct what Herder, in his early work, speaks of as an *anthropological* turn (Herder 2002a: 29 / 1985– I: 134). In his later work, especially in *Ideas for the Philosophy of History of Humanity*, this is related to a basic epistemic modesty, a willingness to let go of the aspiration to take up a god-like position of certainty (Herder 1985– VI: 632).

As Herder anticipates a later Humboldtian approach to education, he emphasizes, in this context, the role of the university as a place of dynamical research – a place where there can emerge 'out of every criticized error a new reason, a new view of the truth' (Herder 2002a: 370 / 1985– VII: 322). In contributing to such an environment, an anthropologically grounded hermeneutics must address a wide range of cultural practices and preferences. It must take into account a diversity of human ways of realizing oneself. Hand in hand with this, it must acknowledge that any attempt to pin down one set of practices as representing *the* good, *the* right, or *the* human risks not only quelling the diversity of life forms but also presenting an illegitimate attempt to universalize one particular culture, tradition, or set of beliefs.

Through an engagement with the symbolic expressions of others, hermeneutic activity represents for Herder an attempt to break through prejudices and false beliefs and see the world from a different point of view.[31] He would therefore be suspicious of models in which the object of understanding (the meaning of a given practice, text, or work of art) is realized or co-constituted by the interpreter.[32] As Herder puts it, '[i]t is impossible for us to translate and emulate [*nachahmen*] [others] before we understand them' (Herder 1992: 186 / 1985– I: 292). True to this position, Herder not only theorizes the process and gains of understanding, but also, in the spirit of practical-hermeneutic work, collects, translates, and distributes art and poetry that fall outside of mainstream taste (see for instance Herder 1985– III: 9–429).

Such is the critical ethos of Herder's Enlightenment hermeneutics, as it seeks, descriptively, to characterize the processes of everyday understanding and, prescriptively, to facilitate better understanding through a methodology of genealogical critique of one's own prejudices and beliefs, and an openness and on-going effort to take seriously the view-points of others. A hermeneutic openness of this kind does not, however, force us to accept the other's point of view. This is clear from Herder's critique of cannibalism (see Herder

1985– VI: 377 and 548), but also, in a more local historical context, in his engagement with Lessing's *Laocoön*, which he, in the same spirit, seeks to understand and criticize (Herder 1985– II: 205–6).

In Herder's books, human beings are characterized by a capacity for understanding, yet an increasingly diversified world makes it ever more imperative to cultivate, *Bilden*, understanding not only within, but also across traditions. In Herder's view, a hermeneutic methodology – not understood as an objectifying procedure, but as an endorsement of a set of critical standards and regulative ideas for interpretation – helps serve this larger goal. Herder does not articulate his method at the level of a detailed, book-length discussion. Yet, as he, in his work as a philosopher as well as interpreter of art and literature, develops his critique of the infusion of history with ideological premises, his call for sympathy in interpretation, and his advocacy of the need to understand an author or language-user in the context of his or her own original culture, Herder gives us a horizon from within which the notion of a broader (to stick to Gadamer's terminology: non-Cartesian) methodology can be conceived.

III

While Herder and Gadamer develop their models two centuries apart, they share an interest in exploring the dialectics between self-understanding and understanding of others, an ideal of education in culture (*Bildung*), *and* they share a worry about objectivizing methodologies in the human sciences. However, precisely because of this overlap it is productive to ask why their contributions, representing, respectively, an Enlightenment ethos and the sensibilities of late phenomenology, present such different approaches to the possibility of a hermeneutic method: Gadamer's rejection of methodological hermeneutic as being, by definition, Cartesian in nature and Herder seeking to develop, precisely, a non-Cartesian methodology.

In *Truth and Method*, Gadamer sets out to describe the dynamic movement of tradition. How is it, he asks, that we are drawn to certain works of art and try to realize their meaning in ever new contexts of interpretation? How is it that works such as Sophocles' *Oedipus*, Shakespeare's *Hamlet*, and Goethe's *Faust* keep being experienced as profoundly true and meaningful? His is a model that seeks to describe our sustained indebtedness to the great works of the tradition, not to formulate a set of critical standards, which would, in his view, be tantamount to a concession to Cartesianism.[33] Herder, on his side, is interested in how we, as finite human beings, understand expressions from other cultures and time-periods and he emphasizes that understanding can only be reached through an effort to articulate and sustain an empirically motivated and anthropologically sensitive methodology. Hermeneutics, in my view, should have room for both of these approaches, though recognize that they are based on different kinds of philosophical questions to which different kinds of responses are called for.

Gadamer's model seeks to offer a phenomenological account of how the works that we count as fundamental to a given tradition do indeed gain such a paradigmatic status and how this status is maintained. This is a legitimate and valuable undertaking. However, in articulating his philosophical hermeneutics above and beyond the concerns of methodology, Gadamer fails to ask, critically and reflectively, whether the works of the tradition do indeed deserve their status. In his orientation towards the great, Western canon, he also downplays the question of what works were pushed aside, ignored or forgotten as this tradition was established. Finally, in emphasizing the continuity of tradition, he does not ask what critical-methodological resources are at hand when assessing if the ruling understanding of the works of tradition, as it has developed in and through this tradition itself, is just, right, and adequate.

In Gadamer's version, philosophical hermeneutics should help us keep tradition alive. As articulated in *Truth and Method*, his hermeneutics provides an account of what it is to be a being whose life is lived in and through historical time. However, in phenomenologically describing the self-understanding that traditional (or, as he puts it, great) works afford, Gadamer has a tendency to universalize this kind of understanding, thereby, in effect, preventing the discipline from discussing alternative approaches (which need not, as we have seen, be 'Cartesian' in spirit). Unlike Herder, he does not ask whose traditions these are, what alternative patterns of identification are suppressed by their rise to prominence, and to what extent the meaning of the works of the past has been sufficiently grasped. These are the kind of questions

Herder's hermeneutics can help us articulate. And they are, in my view, questions that are crucial to hermeneutics' continued relevance as a philosophical discipline.

From the point of view of such a perspective, an attempt to expand the field of hermeneutics and bring back the methodological discussions that were part of the discipline in its initial, modern formulation is indeed important. While this project might well go against the letter of Gadamer's work, it does not necessarily go against its spirit. For if it is true, as Gadamer contends, that tradition only lives in constant renewal, then hermeneutics – being part not simply of our thinking about tradition, but also of this very tradition itself – is in need of ongoing revision.

Both historically and systematically speaking, hermeneutics holds within it more possibilities than what is entailed by Gadamer's now fairly standardized narrative of methodological (Cartesian) versus philosophical hermeneutics. I have sought to point out that, in the wake of the Enlightenment and the developments in eighteenth-century science, there emerges a method- and diversity-oriented strand of hermeneutics that is deserving of renewed attention. Whether or not this anthropologically grounded model is more attractive than ontological hermeneutics may be an open question. What is not, however, an open question is that the example provided by Herder's philosophy of interpretation demonstrates a need for a return to earlier models of hermeneutics and a willingness to ask how the notion of methodology, once we depart from its more narrow (again, with Gadamer, Cartesian) formulations, can be of help to our understanding of history, tradition, ourselves, *and* of philosophy as one of the ways in which we can make sense of history and our place in tradition.

NOTES

1 In the 'Foreword to the Second Edition', Gadamer clarifies his aspirations: 'My real concern was and is philosophic: not what we do or what we ought to do, but what happens to us over and above our wanting and doing' (Gadamer 1994: xxviii, see also 512 / 1990: 438, see also 394).

2 For his description of methodological hermeneutics, see (Gadamer 1994: 182–242 / 1990: 185–246).

3 For Gadamer's account of the Cartesian roots of the turn to method in the human sciences, see (Gadamer 1994: 277–85 / 1990: 281–9). His goal, as he

puts it, is 'to detach [himself] from the Cartesian basis of modern science' (Gadamer 1994: 461 / 1990: 465). For a discussion of this dimension of Gadamer's work, see (Rorty 1980) and (Bernstein 1983). For a recent review of Cartesian strands in modern philosophy, see (Toulmin 1992).

4 Gadamer argues that 'the human sciences are connected to modes of experience that lie outside science: with the experiences of philosophy, of art, and of history itself. These are all modes of experience in which a truth is communicated that cannot be verified by the methodological means proper to science' (Gadamer 1994: xxii / 1990: 1–2).

5 In fact, the only text Gadamer dedicates to Herder's work is a problematic speech given to French prisoners during World War Two (Gadamer 1942). This speech was later modified and published as the introduction to Herder's *This Too a Philosophy of History* (Gadamer 1999 IV: 318–36).

6 The importance of this turn has often been overlooked. This, however, is not to claim that Herder has been completely neglected. Dilthey recognizes Herder's hermeneutic significance (see fn. 21), Emerson kept Herder's important hermeneutic work *The Spirit of Hebrew Poetry* among his favourite books (Clark 1955: 295), and the Neo-Kantian Hermann Cohen offers the following praise: 'Aber der Begriff der Literatur, menschlich und wissenschaftlich, wie er ist, hat auch hier Hilfe gebracht. Und unser Herder darf hier als sittlicher Befreier genannt werden' (Cohen 1904: 316–17). In a more recent context, Wellek (1981) views him as an important forerunner of modern criticism, and Franz Boas (1989) takes him to be a predecessor to cultural anthropology. Frederick Beiser emphasizes the importance of Herder's work for our understanding of political philosophy in the eighteenth century (Beiser 1992: 189–222) and through the work of Charles Taylor, Michael Forster, and others, Herder's philosophy of language has gained traction (Taylor 1995: 79–100; Forster 2010: 55–91).

7 I discuss Gadamer's affiliation with Heidegger in (Gjesdal 2009). In *Truth and Method*, Gadamer, while presenting his work as fundamentally indebted to Heidegger, distinguishes himself from his mentor in the following way: 'Heidegger entered into the problems of historical hermeneutics and critique only to explicate the fore-structure of understanding for the purpose of ontology. Our question, by contrast, is how hermeneutics, once freed from the ontological obstructions of the scientific concept of objectivity, can do justice to the historicity of understanding' (Gadamer 1994: 265 / 1990: 270).

8 For his critique of humanism, see (Heidegger 1998: 262–3 / 1976: 315–17).

9 In a similar vein, *Truth and Method* seeks 'to present the hermeneutic phenomenon in its full extent. It is a question of recognizing in it an experience of truth that not only needs to be justified philosophically, but which is itself a way of doing philosophy' (Gadamer 1994: xxiii / 1990: 3). The emphasis on the need to change the way philosophy is done, which also reverberates in Gadamer's Plato studies (Gadamer 1991: xxxii–xxxiii / 1999 V: 161–2), is taken over from Heidegger (Heidegger 2001: 1985).

10 In *Truth and Method*, Gadamer leads this point back to Heidegger. This, though, differs from his analysis of the universality of experience, which draws on Aristotle (Gadamer 1994: 350–1 / 1990: 356–7).

11 On his books, '[v]erbal form and traditionary content [überlieferter Inhalt] cannot be separated in the hermeneutic experience' (Gadamer 1994: 441 / 1990: 445).

12 Following Heidegger, Gadamer thus speaks of a hermeneutic circle, though this circle is not vicious, but designates the way in which historical self-understanding is gained through engagement with a tradition of which the interpreter herself is part. See (Gadamer 1994: 266–7 / 1990: 270–1).

13 Gadamer does not clarify what Enlightenment movement(s) he has in mind (the Scottish, French, German Enlightenment, or all of them?). Nor does he discuss particular Enlightenment works in much detail. For a discussion of Gadamer's critique of the Enlightenment, see (Gjesdal 2008).

14 See also (Husserl 1964), (Husserl 1956: 6–8), and (Husserl 1973). It is worth noting that Husserl and later Heidegger connect the allegedly untenable aspects of Descartes' position to his indebtedness to a Scholastic paradigm in philosophy. I discuss the phenomenological reception of Descartes in (Gjesdal 2011).

15 For Heidegger's early discussions of Descartes, see (Heidegger 2005 / 1994; 2004 / 1995; 2001 / 1985).

16 For a discussion of Descartes that emphasizes his relationship to tradition (especially Augustine), see (Menn 1998), (Matthews 1992), (Gilson 1967), and (Gaukroger 1997). For an account that also ascribes to Descartes a broader interest in education (or even *Bildung*), see (Garber 1998).

17 According to Gadamer, Schleiermacher claims that misunderstanding follows automatically (Gadamer 1994: 185 / 1990: 189–9). Gadamer reads this in a polemical and ahistorical fashion, failing to view it as a reflection of a broader Enlightenment sensitivity to cultural difference.

18 It goes without saying that this hermeneutic query is and has been accompanied by non-hermeneutic efforts to complete the far too narrow picture of Descartes that Gadamer provides and also to offer a more nuanced picture of the humanist tradition.

19 For an account of this transition, see (Gaukroger 1995) and (Reill 2005).

20 In a broader, European context, we should also mention Denis Diderot and his fellow encyclopaedists, some of whom Herder met during his visit in Paris (see Haym 1954 I: 373–4).

21 See (Dilthey 1996: 89 / 1914– XIV: 649) and (Dilthey 1985: 175–223 / 1914– VI: 242–87).

22 Herder's philosophical context should here be kept in mind. He was a student of Kant and also worked with Johann Georg Hamann (Zammito 2002). Further, French and Scottish enlightenment philosophy was significant for his development. For a general discussion of Scottish philosophy in Germany, see (Kuehn 1987) and (Bultmann 1999). Herder also draws on the rationalist tradition, including the Leibnizian notions

of individuality and pluralism (Cassirer 1961: 115–17) and embodiment (DeSouza 2012).

23 This possibility is discussed in (Berlin 2000: 169).

24 In viewing Herder as an Enlightenment thinker, I follow (Norton 1991); (Beiser 1992); (Zammito 2002); (Forster 2010). Gadamer, however, contrasts Herder and the Enlightenment, which he characterizes in negative terms: the 'extremism of the Enlightenment' and its 'abstract and revolutionary' nature (Gadamer 1994: 280–1 / 1990: 285).

25 For a study of Herder's interest in and indebtedness to natural science, see (Nisbet 1970); (Bollacher 1987); (Heinz and Clairmont 2009).

26 Later, Gadamer develops his own version of this argument. See (Gjesdal 2009: 48–81).

27 This is not simply a theoretical principle, but also extends to *de facto Realpolitik*. Herder notes how an ever expanding European colonization leads to a situation in which '*[t]hree parts of the world [are] laid waste* and *civilly administered* by us' (Herder 2002a: 328 / 1985– IV: 74). Moreover, the ideology of Western rationality is distributed with less than rational means: '[T]he more [non-Europeans] become fond of our brandy and luxury', Herder notes, the more they 'become *ripe* for our *conversion* too!' (Herder 2002a: 325 / 1985– IV: 71). Trade, Herder reflects, allows for no genuine recognition of difference, but is '*all-embracing*' (Herder 2002a: 328 / 1985– IV: 74).

28 A similar point is later found in Schleiermacher (see Gjesdal 2014).

29 Herder, however, does not sublate philosophy into empirical science. Here I diverge from the reading defended in (Zammito 2002: 3), though the argument is modified at (Zammito 2002: 172); see also (Gjesdal 2013).

30 For a discussion of this aspect of the Enlightenment, see (Frazer 2010).

31 Here I deviate from (Wright 2015), who envisions the possibility of an improved notion of intercultural understanding from *within* Gadamer's point of view. (Janz 2015) marks the limits of such a position (see especially 479–80). Janz, however, discusses Gadamer's own neglect of non-European cultures. My approach is different in that it, at a principled level, discusses the versatility (or lack of such) of philosophical hermeneutics upon encountering such contexts of interpretation.

32 Herder, though, insists that we do not seek to understand an author's mind as inner and hidden, but as it appears in human practice: 'we do not even know ourselves from within […] it follows that the historian must all the more study his author *from without* in order to scout out his soul in *words and deeds*' (Herder 2002a: 169 / 1985– II: 573).

33 It is the very goal of his work to address the deepest, pre-predicative understanding of tradition. However, there is, in my view, something potentially unsatisfactory about a theory-formation that ends at this point rather than asking how we, against the background of such initial understanding, can distinguish between good and not so good ways of engaging, as scholars and reflective readers, the expressions of culturally or temporally distant others.

18 Critical Theory's Philosophy

Critical Theory has an uneasy relationship to philosophy, and it is a complex question whether it constitutes a philosophical position at all: it both aims to leave philosophy behind and insists on the need for it.

On the one hand, Critical Theory stands in the tradition of Marx (and Engels), who famously wrote in *The German Ideology* that '[w]e know only a single science, the science of history' (MECW 5:28 / MEW 3: 18);[1] in the tradition of Kierkegaard and others who are suspicious of the success of and need for certain discursive grounding; and in the tradition of Hegel, who insisted on philosophy as always coming second to practical innovations and historical developments; in the tradition of Nietzsche, with his attack on many forms of philosophy; as well as in the tradition of Freud, with his calling into question some of the most fundamental notions of modern philosophy (such as the self and its autonomy). At the very least, this results in a commitment to a truly interdisciplinary approach, and in some authors (such as Adorno) it even leads to a certain anti-philosophical stance, where partisanship is not philosophically grounded and the very idea of a philosophical system is seen as anathema.

On the other hand, the very same authors (including notably Adorno) insist on the continued need for philosophy and require critique of philosophical positions to be, in important senses, internal to philosophy, explicitly rejecting criticisms of these positions simply in terms of the interests and social positions of their adherents. The relentless self-reflexivity mandated by Critical Theory also pushes its proponents in the direction of what has traditionally been described as philosophy – conceptual investigation into conditions of possibility. Similarly, while traditional metaphysics and logical positivism are rejected unanimously among proponents of Critical Theory, when it comes to Kantian transcendental philosophy and fundamental ontology these proponents take different, sometimes opposing views (as they do in relation to religion and metaphysics). One further complication is that some of the proponents change their view of philosophy across time – for example, Habermas thinks of philosophy in 1971 mainly in terms of a critique of scientism, but by 1983 it has become a programme of justification.[2]

In this chapter, I will investigate Critical Theory's uneasy relationship with philosophy. I will do so mostly by way of a case study (of Adorno's Critical Theory). I adopt the case study approach for a number of reasons, notably two related ones: a more in-depth focus is better suited to illuminate the complexity of this uneasy relationship, and there already exist a number of overview accounts (whether thematic or chronological),[3] such that there is no pressing need for another one.

Still, as a starting point, it is necessary to take more of a bird's eye view. When asking about the (meta)philosophical stance of Critical Theory, an initial difficulty that one encounters is *typological*: what characterizes Critical Theory and who should be counted among its proponents?

A sort of litmus test here is whether Foucault's work is counted in or out. On the one hand, one could be easily excused for thinking that Foucault stands clearly outside this tradition – the fierce criticisms of his work by Habermas and those influenced by Habermas (such as Fraser and McCarthy) would suggest as much.[4] And often Critical Theory is defined narrowly in terms of 'the German tradition of interdisciplinary social theory, inaugurated in Frankfurt in the 1930s' (Allen 2016: xi). This 'Frankfurt School' tradition is then understood in family terms along generations:[5] with Horkheimer, Adorno, and Marcuse as key figures of the first generation; Habermas as the leading figure of the second generation; and Honneth as the most prominent member of the third, which, however, now has expanded beyond Germany, with McCarthy, Fraser, and Benhabib as overseas 'children' of Habermas. In line with family analogy, the generations would continue: just as Habermas was assistant to Adorno and Honneth to Habermas, some of the assistants and doctoral students of third-generation thinkers (such as Allen and Jaeggi) would then make up the fourth generation, and so on.

On the other hand, if one takes a broad view, such that Critical Theory is 'any politically inflected form of cultural, social or political theory that has critical, progressive, or emancipatory aims' (Allen 2016: xi), then Foucault certainly counts as one of its proponents. Indeed, in a late interview he said that he wished he had read the work of Frankfurt School theorists (presumably he has here particularly the works of the first generation in mind) as this would have saved him a lot of work (Foucault 1994: 117). Also, Foucault contests that he is an anti-Enlightenment thinker, and, contrary to Habermas' criticism and much more like the Frankfurt School, places himself in its tradition of critically interrogating the present.[6] And at least from Honneth onwards, there has been a much less confrontational relation to Foucault's work among Frankfurt School theorists. Moreover, a narrow, institutional understanding of Critical Theory can come apart from its broader notion, such that at least some of the successor theorists might no longer be doing Critical Theory – despite what the institutional stalwarts say, one could argue that Foucault is more of a core case of Critical Theory than Habermas or Honneth.[7]

Perhaps this typological question does not allow for a conclusive answer – at least not in terms of necessary and sufficient conditions. Some views and theorists will be core examples; many will subscribe to some shared elements (such as a commitment to emancipation or a Hegelian notion of reason), but even so the differences in how they interpret these elements will often be more important; some theorists and approaches will seem more peripheral; others still will clearly fall outside; and there will be hard cases (perhaps Foucault is one). Just as in a morphing sequence, a number of (often small) changes can cumulatively lead to configurations that are fundamentally different – such that Adorno, who rejected discursive grounding, stands at one end and Forst, who combines Habermas and Rawls in such a way as to make discursive grounding the centrepiece of any Critical Theory, at the other.[8]

A clear core case – indeed, in many ways, setting the agenda – is Horkheimer's 1937 text 'Traditional and Critical Theory' (and its 'Postscript' published a few months later).[9] According to Horkheimer, the traditional conception of theory – not just in philosophy but in all of the academic disciplines – abstracts from the social functions and preconditions of theorizing as well as its actual processes. In the pursuit of objectivity and impartiality, these matters seem of secondary importance – at best, they can be ignored altogether and, at worst, they are obstacles to be negotiated or conditions to be optimized, but even then, ultimately, they leave the core of theorizing untouched. Similarly, the ideal is a transhistorical notion of truth – historical contexts might prevent people from seeing it, but this does not change the fact that truth itself is non-historical in nature and theory aims to track it. Moreover, on the traditional conception of theory, there is a social division of labour between academic, scientific work and politics, whereby the former either is value-free or takes the existing value orientations as external givens. Critical Theory, as Horkheimer introduces it, differs along all three of these dimensions: its proponents deny that the social function of theorizing can be neatly distinguished from its content and nature, requiring us to take a self-reflective stance on the process of theorizing and its social preconditions (Horkheimer 1972: 197, 205–6, 209, 216–17 and 244);[10] they conceive of Critical Theory and of truth as deeply historical (Horkheimer 1972: 240);[11] and they reject the notions of value-free science and are 'suspicious of the very categories of better, useful, appropriate, productive, and valuable, as these are understood in the present order', refusing 'to take them as non-scientific presuppositions about which [Critical Theory] can do nothing' (ibid.: 207).

Horkheimer in this takes his orientation from two earlier notions of critique: Kant's 'critical philosophy' and Marx's 'critique of political economy'. Like the former, he thinks that the object and the subject of cognition are pre-constituted in a certain way; but, unlike Kant, he thinks that this pre-constitution is socio-historical:

> It is not only in clothing and appearance, in outward form and emotional make-up that human beings are the product of history. Even the way they see and hear is inseparable from the social life-process as it has evolved over the millennia. The facts which our senses present to us are socially preformed in two ways: through the historical character of the object perceived and through the historical character of the perceiving organ.
>
> (Ibid.: 200)[12]

If anything the debts to Marx are bigger still – indeed, Horkheimer remarks that calling the theorizing he has in mind 'critical' is meant 'less in the sense it has in the idealist critique of pure reason than in the sense it has in the dialectical critique of political economy' (ibid.: 206, n14). We can begin to see this, if we consider how the distinguishing features of Critical Theory mentioned above are united in a slogan from Marx (contained in a published letter to Ruge): the 'task for the world and us' is 'the self-clarification (critical philosophy) of the struggles and wishes of the age' (MECW 5: 15 / MEW 3: 7). Here theorizing is not conceived independently from political struggle, but as integral to it; theorizing also has a clear function, which is explicitly articulated and presumably something that itself is subject to theoretical reflection; and there is a clear historical index.

At this point, the question arises in which way, if any, Critical Theory, so conceived, is still philosophy or employs philosophical methods. Marx famously noted, in the eleventh Feuerbach Thesis, that '[t]he philosophers have only *interpreted* the world in various ways; the point is to *change* it' and if Critical Theory is understood as self-clarification of the struggle to effect this change, then this seems to put it into contrast with philosophy. There has been much debate about Marx's attempt to leave philosophy behind,[13] but, whatever is the case with Marx, Horkheimer in 1937 clearly does not want to suggest that Critical Theory is completely discontinuous with philosophy.

This becomes clearer as a consequence of Marcuse's 'Philosophy and Critical Theory', written in response to Horkheimer's initial piece. Marcuse picks up and expands on one point contained in it: Horkheimer suggests that philosophy labours under a mistaken self-image of theorizing as self-sufficient and independent, but that, nonetheless, it also contains a 'camouflaged utopia' in its 'hypostatization of Logos' insofar as 'reason should actually determine the course of events in a future society' (Horkheimer 1972: 198).[14] In the same vein, Marcuse argues that idealist philosophy is both ideological and utopian: it is ideological in individualizing the quest of realizing reason and freedom and in suggesting that they have been (fully) realized in the social world; but it also has an utopian and critical element in insulating itself from this world, and thereby pointing beyond it – 'abstractness saves its truth' (Marcuse 2009: 112). Critical Theory here is not conceived as philosophy, but as social theory, and yet it draws on the 'truth content' of idealist philosophy: Critical Theory makes use of its notion of reason, which as general points beyond any specific contexts and the interests predominant in them; Critical Theory can even rely on the individualized notion of freedom to criticize notions and practices of 'false collectives' (Marcuse is presumably thinking of the Soviet Union here); and it inherits philosophy's 'obstinacy [*Eigensinn*]' and fantasy, both of which are crucial for a critical stance (ibid.: 103, 104, 106, 109, 113).[15] Crucially, in all this, Critical Theory, according to Marcuse, does not commit itself to eternal truths: it accepts that philosophy can help us to think beyond the socially given, but this transcending does not equate to or require universal truths (ibid.: 112).

Horkheimer and Marcuse do not just present Critical Theory as heir to philosophy in the medium of social theory. Rather, as critique of political economy, Critical Theory also continues as 'a philosophical discipline':

For its content is the transformation of the concepts which dominate the economy in its opposites: fair exchange into a deepening of social injustice, a free economy into monopolistic control, productive work into rigid relationships which hinder production.

(Horkheimer 1972: 247)

The idea here is that social processes (like the commodity exchanges at the heart of the capitalist economy) cannot be neatly separated from their conceptualization – the latter are not merely brought externally to the subject matter, but are, in a sense, in them: the social processes in questions are 'real abstractions' – concepts, like 'commodity', play a role in how they function insofar as these processes, while happening in one sense behind the back of the participants (insofar as the participants do not adequately understand or control them), are also in another sense mediated by the conceptual grasp of these participants. When we, say, buy bread at our local bakery, we are – and cannot but be – operating (implicitly) with the categories of political economy. Otherwise what we would do would not be a business transaction. As a consequence, if the concepts governing social processes turn into their opposites (and it is such dialectical inversions that Horkheimer above suggests Critical Theory should investigate), then this does not leave the practices untouched, but signifies that they misfire too. This need not imply idealism – that is, the thesis is not that the misfiring of the concepts *causes* the misfiring of the practices. The point is rather that the analysis of the concepts in question can reveal something that is indicative of social tendencies. Accordingly, conceptual analysis here is understood as always implying social analysis – it is both deeply philosophical (in that conceptual work is traditionally seen as the *métier* of philosophy) and gives up on philosophy as an autonomous domain. Indeed, in Horkheimer's 1931 address as the new Director of the Frankfurt Institute of Social Research, it is this latter aspect that he highlights: following Hegel, social processes should be studied as historical manifestations of reason, but, contrary to Hegel, philosophy does not settle the decisive problems and is not immune to revision on the basis of the insights of the empirical disciplines – philosophical analysis and empirical insight have to work in tandem.

The entwinement of philosophical and empirical analysis with a view towards the 'self-clarification of the struggles and wishes of the age' has then taken different twists and turns in the hands of different proponents and 'generations' of Critical Theory. From Habermas onwards, the dominant strand in Frankfurt has understood this task mainly in terms of a *reconstructive* methodology: the rational potential of social practices is meant to be reconstructed, such that its participants can become aware of the grammar of these practices, be it – as in Habermas – along a split into lifeworld and system (and communicative and instrumental action) or – as in Honneth – in terms of spheres of recognition. In this, historical and social analysis dominates, although conceptual work still has its place (notably by way of conceptual innovation, such as Habermas' adapting the distinction between lifeworld and system). Still, reconstruction is not meant to stand on its own – the moral validity of the reconstructive normative contents has to be secured too, according to Habermas and Honneth. Here elements more traditionally associated with philosophy come to the fore: while traditional metaphysics is rejected, accounts of truth and validity take on importance (notably in Habermas' project of securing what Kant's *Groundwork*, at least on some interpretations, tried but failed to provide: a non-moral ground for morality); philosophical anthropology is revived (by Habermas and Honneth); philosophy of history is resurrected, supposedly along non-metaphysical lines (as in Honneth's more recent work); or (metaethical) constructivism is added to the picture (in Forst's attempt to radicalize Rawls, O'Neill, and Scanlon, such that a right to justification becomes the recursive ground of the normative contents of Critical Theory). In a number of ways, these various projects depart from Horkheimer's (and Marcuse's) original proposal – be it in their separation between scientist and citizen (which, as mentioned, Horkheimer sees as one of the hallmarks of Traditional Theory), in integrating system theory (Habermas 1981b),[16] in broadening the causes of the present distress beyond capitalism (Habermas 1981b; Honneth 2011), or in narrowing of the normative vocabulary to moral terms, most importantly justice.[17]

Instead of tracing these twists and turns, I will now move to a case study of Adorno's work. After being central to the revival of Critical Theory in post-WWII Germany, it came increasingly under fire from the late 1960s onwards and then was largely side-lined, but recently experienced something of a renaissance. Even irrespective of this ebb and flow, Adorno's case is particularly illuminating for the complex relationship between Critical Theory and philosophy, including because – as already suggested at the beginning – he seems to go furthest in an anti-philosophical direction. (My emphasis will be particularly on the influence of Hegel and Marx, but this is not to deny that the works of Kierkegaard, Nietzsche, and Freud also play into this.)

Adorno (1903–69) fully enters the (German) academic scene with his inaugural lecture of 1931. Its theme is whether philosophy is still a suitable, topical endeavour (whether it has 'actuality [*Aktualität*]'). It begins with a sobering statement:

Whoever chooses philosophy as a profession today must first reject the illusion that earlier philosophical enterprises began with: that the power of thought is sufficient to grasp the totality of the real.

(Adorno 1977: 120)

Adorno claims that the history of philosophy itself bears witness to this being an illusion: this history is littered with failed attempts of showing that thought can grasp 'the totality of the real', and this reveals the doomed nature of the very enterprise. In this lecture, he concentrates not so much on the historical attempts – we find such discussion in later works on Husserl, Hegel, Kant, and (mainly in his lectures) Plato and Aristotle. Rather, he criticizes the dominant philosophical schools of his day: Neo-Kantianism, Positivism, and Phenomenology (especially Heidegger's version thereof). This reflects his view that 'one of the first and most actual tasks' is 'the radical criticism of the ruling philosophic thinking' (ibid.: 130).

The nature of this radical criticism is such that one might think Adorno wants to liquidate philosophy. He admits that this is how it will seem:

> For the strict exclusion of all ontological questions in the traditional sense, the avoidance of invariant general concepts (including, for instance, the concept of human being), the exclusion of every conception of a self-sufficient totality of mind [*Geist*], or of a self-contained 'history of mind'; the concentration of philosophical questions on concrete inner-historical complexes from which they are not to be detached – these postulates indeed become extremely similar to a dissolution of that which has long been called philosophy.
>
> (Ibid.: 130)[18]

Adorno operates here with a certain picture of traditional philosophy – as concerned with essences, which are conceived as invariant and eternal and expressible in conceptual frameworks with universal, timeless validity, and as the activity of philosophy as an autonomous expression of a *res cogitans* that unfolds over time. The thought is not that all traditional philosophers explicitly sign up to all elements of such picture, but rather that each subscribes to some of such elements, whether explicitly and knowingly or not. And in contrast to this picture of what philosophy is, what he proposes would seem to abandon philosophy. His alternative seems to make good on Marx and Engels' claim that the only science is history with its emphasis on 'concrete inner-historical complexes' (such as the events for which the name 'Auschwitz' stands, from which, Adorno thinks, ethical questions cannot and should not be detached). In that sense, he could have added that it would also seem he liquidates philosophy by thinking of it not as an autonomous discipline, but as deeply intertwined with other subjects, especially history and sociology (but also aesthetics).

However, in an important sense, the impression that Adorno wants to leave philosophy behind is mistaken. For all his debts to Marx and sociology, Adorno rejects – already in the inaugural lecture but also throughout the career that followed – attempts to reduce the criticism of philosophy to sociology of knowledge, that is, to (often debunking) accounts of works in terms of their historical, social, and biographical context. It might well be true that, for example, the fact that Kant was a bourgeois, male individual with a Pietistic background might have explanatory value in accounting for the particular contents and approach of his works. Yet, for Adorno such explanations play, at most, a supplementary ('metacritical') role: they can contribute to explaining why certain (philosophical) errors, despite the intelligence and good intentions of those who commit them, occur.[19] They supplement philosophical critique, 'for the truth content of a problem is in principle different from the historical and psychological conditions out of which it grows' (ibid.: 128).

We will return to the distinctively philosophical nature of the critique of (philosophical) systems below. For now, I want to note two aspects of how Adorno delineates philosophy, while denying its complete autonomy vis-à-vis the natural and social sciences. First, Adorno thinks that philosophy differs from the sciences not in the objects and problems of study, but in virtue of how it approaches them. While, 'the separate sciences accept their findings, at least their final and deepest findings, as indestructible and static', this is not so in philosophy, which instead 'must proceed interpretively without ever possessing a sure key to interpretation' (ibid.: 126).[20] The answers to philosophical problems are not already given, merely needing to be discovered; and the correctness criteria for its answers are also not independent of the enquiry itself, but depend on the 'interpretation [Deutung]' adopted, without thereby (Adorno would claim) being merely arbitrary and subjective either. Second, and relatedly, this also means that philosophy cannot simply take the categories of the sciences – such as, notably, sociology – as givens. Prefiguring what Horkheimer and Marcuse would write six years later, Adorno suggests that the specific philosophical contribution to unravelling the problems presented by our social world (taken up in the social sciences and philosophy) is by way of 'exact fantasy' in the construction and combination of concepts. (Exact in that it 'abides strictly within the material which the sciences present to it' and fantasy in that it 'reaches beyond them only in the smallest aspects of their arrangement: aspects, granted, which fantasy itself must originally generate' (ibid.: 131).)[21] He speaks of such combination of concepts (following Benjamin) in terms of 'constellations' (ibid.: 127).[22] He emphasizes the trial character of such attempts and that there is not (as the sciences presuppose) an already existing answer to be found, but a construction of an answer by way of a transformation of social reality – somewhat like the night sky, where the stars, while existing independently of us, form constellations only as a result of a successful interpretation.

This task of transforming (social) reality is not something that philosophy can accomplish on its own (ibid.: 129). Here we see another of the elements highlighted by Horkheimer: the way philosophy is not completely separate from political praxis, but could only be realized by way of it. Adorno remains committed to this thought, but there is less optimism associated with it than there is in 1931. The 'Introduction' of what is widely regarded as Adorno's magnum opus, *Negative Dialektik* [1966], begins as follows:

Philosophy, which once seemed obsolete, keeps itself alive because the moment of its realisation was missed. The summary judgement that it had merely interpreted the world, that resignation in the face of reality had crippled it in itself, becomes a defeatism of reason after the transformation of the world miscarried.

(Adorno 1966: 15 / 1973: 3)[23]

Adorno still accepts that philosophy is something that could be realized and perhaps thereby come to an end in some sense. But he now thinks the opportunity for such a realization has passed – in part because '[p]erhaps the interpretation which promised the transition did not suffice' (ibid.).[24] And, as a result – contrary to Marx's dictum – there still is a role for philosophy, for interpreting the world.

As in 1931, Adorno reserves a central role for philosophy 'ruthlessly to criticize itself' (ibid.).[25] This is not meant as a navel-gazing exercise, but is in the service of trying to break the hold certain conceptual structures have on us (and thereby the hold on us of social practices in part constituted by these conceptual structures). The relationship to the praxis of changing the world is, thus, complex: Adorno insists both on not subordinating philosophy to political struggle (such subordination tends to be to the detriment of that struggle itself because it tends to involve silencing critical voices which could provide checks on misdevelopments);[26] and on philosophy's remaining orientated by that struggle and ultimately depending on the political struggle's success for its own success. In a nutshell, Adorno's proposal is that philosophy should contribute in its own domain and with its own weapons to this struggle.

Adorno tends to speak of 'dialectic' to denote the tracing and unfolding of problems internal to philosophical theories:

Dialectic is not a third standpoint [in addition to positivism and fundamental ontology] but rather the attempt, by means of an immanent critique, to develop philosophical standpoints beyond themselves and beyond the despotism of a thinking based on standpoints.

(Adorno 1998: 12)

The first aspect here is the notion of dialectic as 'immanent critique': demonstrating that theories fail by their own ambitions and standards. For instance, he argues not just that Kant's examples reflect a bourgeois stance, but also that there is a central tension in Kant between downplaying the role of examples for justifying his theory (which is meant to have *a priori* validity) and the weight they then end up having (but failing) to bear.[27] (Consider, for instance, how the famous gallows example in the *Critique of Practical Reason* is pivotal in Kant's argument, but how telling it is that it centrally involves compulsion to demonstrate freedom and how unconvincing it is to claim that no desire can be so strong that one would want it to be satisfied, even at the price of being executed immediately afterwards.)

The second aspect – the claim that dialectic is beyond standpoints – is more puzzling, but one thing he means is that dialectic is not a method that can be separated from its object. Generally, Adorno is highly critical of those philosophical theories which separate method and substance, or form and content. He does not deny that we can make local distinctions between these two purported poles. Rather, his point is that we should be highly suspicious when such distinctions are absolutized – that form is separable from specific content in a particular context does neither imply that it is separable from that specific content in all contexts, nor that it is separable from all content.

One index of the fact that Adorno does not think of dialectic as a self-standing method is that he presents it as historically indexed: dialectic is not apt in all historical contexts. Rather, it is apt specifically in our context because that context is one in which not only philosophical theories present themselves as systems which are, in fact, riddled with contradictions, but because our social world also is such a system.[28] In that sense, 'dialectics is the ontology of the wrong state of things'; and '[T]he right one would be emancipated from it, as little system as contradiction' (Adorno 1966: 22 / 1973: 11).[29]

Here we also begin to see the difference to Hegel, whose work exerted a decisive influence on Adorno's. The historical index of dialectic to our modern world already breaks with Hegel's notion of dialectic (as something that involves historical unfolding but is not restricted to one historical epoch). A related, but perhaps even more important, break is that Adorno eschews both the *telos* of absolute identity of mind and world and the trust in progress that he sees as essential to Hegel's dialectic. That is why Adorno speaks of '*negative* dialectic' (Adorno 1966: 145, 398 / 1973: 141, 406; my emphasis) – nothing in the dialectic process guarantees a positive resolution of contradictions, especially not a culmination in 'absolute knowledge'; and the existing totality of which dialectic is the ontology stands forth not as reconciled state, but as 'triumphant calamity' (Horkheimer and Adorno 2002: 1), and this ought to cure us of any attempts to squeeze positive meaning out of history (Adorno 1966: 354 / 1973: 361).[30] For all the benefits modern civilization brings, it is – according to Adorno – a 'triumphant calamity' because it is characterized by a decoupling (or even inversion) of means and ends that is most clearly exemplified in the death camps of Auschwitz and the creation of the atom bomb, but also inherent in its general structures and tendencies. (I return below to the decoupling of means and ends.)

Hegel, according to Adorno, breaks with his own idea of dialectic by smuggling in (however, inadvertently) external criteria by which to orientate the dialectical process. However, here one might object that even if this were right about Hegel, how can Adorno avoid doing the same? Wouldn't ruthless self-criticism of philosophy otherwise become too fragmented and disjointed, resulting in a whole raft of immanent critiques, which all point in different directions? Moreover, isn't immanent critique too limited an approach? Even if one succeeds in demonstrating how a theory falls short of its standards, this does not yet tell us whether the theory should be modified so that it meets its standards or modified by abandoning them. Nor does it tell us how, all things considered, we should proceed (perhaps a theory that falls some distance short of its own standards is still the least bad option available).

Intriguingly, Adorno himself notes the limitations of immanent critique:

> What is immanently argumentative is legitimate where it registers the integrated reality become system, in order to oppose it with its own strength. What is on the other hand free in thought represents the authority which is already aware of what is emphatically untrue of that context. Without this knowledge it would not come to the breakout, without the appropriation of the power of the system the breakout would fail.
>
> (Adorno 1966: 40 / 1973: 30)[31]

We encounter here again the idea that immanent critique (and hence dialectic) is appropriate ('legitimate') because of the particular historical situation we are in (characterized as 'integrated reality'). This situation is one of untruth – untruth not in the sense that we face a world of delusion created by a Cartesian evil demon. Just the opposite: the problem is that the social world is factually existent – it genuinely shapes and dominates us. Untrue, rather, in the sense that the social world is a system of domination when it need not be and in the sense that it gives rise to false consciousness about its nature and constitution (following broadly Marx's idea of ideology). Yet the latter also means that immanent critique cannot stand on its own – it presupposes and needs to be orientated by knowledge of this untruth.

This raises at least two questions: whereby do we gain such knowledge? And how does Adorno fare better than Hegel whom he accuses of importing something external into the dialectical unfolding of immanent critique? In answer to the first of these questions, Adorno answers that negative experiences, particularly suffering, acquaint us with untruth. Such experiences range from physical pain inflicted directly as part of social domination or socially caused ills (such as anti-Semitic or racist violence) to experiences of negativity resulting from highly intellectual engagement with art and metaphysical ideas.[32] While such experiences will often be mediated by a complex theoretical apparatus, their validity is not a matter of ultimate justification at the level of theorizing. Indeed, Adorno is highly critical of such 'discursive grounding' – viewing it as unnecessary (we do not need theorizing to know that domination is an evil, even if we might need theorizing in order to recognize, analyse, explain, and overcome instances of it). He even claims that attempting to provide such grounding can be an 'outrage [Frevel]' – for it wrongly implies, for example, that events associated with the name 'Auschwitz' are not paradigms of evil and could only be legitimately judged to be evils if something else held true which grounds this judgement (say Kant's original categorical imperative or that the very act of engaging in communication ineluctably but appropriately commits one to certain norms). Moreover, it also wrongly implies that these events might not be negative – depending on whether *or not* that something else that is said to be required as a ground could legitimate them as evils. The mere fact that most grounds are intended to legitimate them as such and would do so on reasonable interpretations is not sufficient here – for one can get the appropriate outcome for the wrong reasons (just as the mere fact that Utilitarianism might not actually licence the killing of innocent people in a particular situation does not suffice to defend it). Leaving open certain possibilities – even if only theoretically – is a sign of bad character or theory.

At this point, it may seem as if Adorno is just importing a negative orientation into his dialectic where Hegel (according to Adorno) imported a positive one, and neither is more justified in doing so than the other – Hegel's discursive grounding fails according to Adorno (in a nutshell because it begs the question by assuming from the beginning what is meant to be proven), but by rejecting such grounding, it seems as if Adorno cannot really offer anything more. The question is whether anything else might be said in favour of Adorno's negative dialectic over Hegel's positive one. One point Adorno makes is that there is a closer link between negative experiences and philosophy, indeed thinking at all, than with positive experiences. He claims that pain and negativity are 'the motor of dialectical thought' (Adorno 1966: 202 / 1973: 202).[33] To cut a long story short, Adorno subscribes to a 'natural-historical' account of how conceptual thought and reason emerged: with the human animal exposed to an often hostile natural environment, they emerged out of physical impulses and drives – most generally put, the drive for self-preservation – in the face of negative experiences.[34] Moreover, while genesis and validity cannot simply be equated, Adorno thinks that something from any genesis remains inscribed in and structures to a certain extent what has emerged – indeed, (practical) reason becomes irrational when it leaves behind its mooring in 'naked physical fear, and the sense of solidarity with what Brecht called "tormentable bodies"' (Adorno 1966: 281 / 1973: 286). (This is the key to Adorno's rejection of discursive grounding.)[35]

Such (on the face of it implausible) claims would deserve careful and detailed discussion. Here I can only offer a high-altitude sketch. Adorno particularly highlights three elements: (a) instrumental rationality; (b) capitalism; and (c) 'identity thinking [*Identitätsdenken*]'. The first is familiar enough, and it is fairly clear how it fits into the kind of naturalist story hinted at above: reasoning over what means are required to achieve an end is a powerful tool for human beings to navigate the challenges they face in surviving; its emergence plausibly is linked with various impulses and drives, which it both channels and keeps in check (typically taking means for ends involves postponing satisfying our immediate impulses in the service of more long-term satisfaction of these impulses or drives that go beyond them).

Capitalism – as a way of organizing production and society – is (for Adorno) one particular manifestation of our drive for self-preservation and instrumental rationality. It is a very sophisticated 'tool' humans developed (not by some conscious, plan-directed collective effort on our part, but as the consequence of human history understood on the secular model of natural growth – purposeful, but without conscious design or control). Adorno harbours no illusion of a pre-capitalist golden past and recognizes that there are material and other advances this 'tool' has enabled us to secure. However, Adorno also thinks that – as in Goethe's well-known ballad '*Der Zauberlehrling* [The Sorcerer's Apprentice]' (and the even better known Disney adaption of this featuring Mickey Mouse) – this tool no longer serves us, but has come to overwhelm, even dominate us. A means–end reversal has happened of the sort often envisaged in dystopian science-fiction stories, whereby the machines meant to serve us have taken over and we serve them (perhaps without realizing it).

Finally, 'identity thinking' is another such tool. Adorno suggests that all conceptual thinking is identifying – trying to grasp a particular as falling under a concept (or set of concepts). And such identifying is powerful – it allows us to shape the world in such a way that it becomes more manageable to us (allowing us to impose patterns on it, to try out different solutions to what can be identified as recurring problems, and the like).[36] Yet, once again, Adorno thinks that this tool has come to dominate us, and the point where this happened is when mere thinking in terms of identity became 'identity thinking', where this shaping of the world became forgetful of the fact that there is something lost in merely saying what a particular falls under (even if what it falls under is not simply one concept, but a whole conceptual scheme) and that imposing patterns, schemas, and systems on particulars distorts them, which – in the case of sentient beings – also causes suffering. Thus, even if all conceptual thought involves identifying, not all such thought need be identity thinking. Negative dialectic does not (and cannot) escape operating by way of conceptual identification, but is different from identity thinking in not ossifying this operation. It is mindful of what is not identical to the conceptual schemes we impose, and tries to recover it and make amends inasmuch as our conceptual tools allow us to do so.

Again much more would need to be said to unpack and defend this set of claims, but the important point for our context is that Adorno presents all of the three elements as already connected to negative experiences, such that bringing the latter into the critique of the former is, in one sense, not to import something external into the dialectical process, though in another sense it is. Adorno is not simply applying the standards inherent in identity thinking, but bringing to this endeavour negative experiences of the 'untrue whole' – in this sense, his critique is not simply immanent. Still, implicit in the very logic of what he criticizes are negative experiences – identity thinking and instrumental rationality are not simply manna from heaven, but historically developed and developing responses to the pain, loss, and terror humans felt (and continue to feel) in navigating their world. Indeed, if Adorno is correct, implicit in the very logic of both capitalism and identity thinking (and, by extension, theories manifesting their logic) is their own demand for something else: capitalism constitutively aims for – in the words of Adam Smith – 'a well-governed society', in which 'universal opulence [...] extends itself to the lowest ranks of the people',[37] so that if it cannot deliver this (whether it be, say, because of its inherent tendencies towards immiseration or because it leads to the destruction of the environmental conditions for human flourishing), then it calls for a different organization of production and social life. Similarly, identity thinking constitutively aims at grasping fully what is being identified, and insofar as it cannot achieve this, it also calls for being transcended.

Tracing and revealing such contradictions requires a particular mode of presentation. Adorno suggests that we should write in such a way that each sentence is equidistant to the centre of the subject matter under discussion (Adorno 1951: §44), and he often seems to come close to this ideal. As a consequence, one finds little argument that is developed along one continuous, linear path – if anything such a procedure is rejected as inadequate,[38] not least because the object of enquiry (the modern social world and its thought forms) is itself antagonistic and as such resists 'continuous presentation' (Adorno 1984: 163–4).

Often, it seems as if arguments are lacking altogether and we are just faced with striking and suggestive conclusions, leaving it to the reader to construct arguments in support of them – the text is meant as a trigger for reflection, not as reporting about reflection that has taken place. Adorno's approach is one of *'disclosing critique'*, meant to make us see the particular phenomena and the social world of which they are part in a new way. The use of exaggeration is not accidental to it – as Adorno puts it memorably in *Minima Moralia*: 'The splinter in your eye is the best magnifying glass' (Adorno 1951: §29).

Engaging in immanent critique also complicates the task of presentation (and interpretation). What Adorno says in the course of an immanent critique need not represent his own views at all, but merely serves the purpose of this critique. Moreover, he often uses the complex terminology and ideas of the authors he discusses (such as Kant, Hegel, or Heidegger), which then require their own decoding, a task made more difficult by the fact that Adorno transfigures the terms and ideas in the course of the discussion. In general, Adorno denies that philosophical ideas can be captured in neat definitions that provide necessary and sufficient conclusions.[39]

Adorno also eschews examples whenever they remain completely external or inconsequential to what they are meant to illustrate – whenever they are *mere illustrations*. Instead he advocates what he calls 'models': working through an issue in the particular way it appears in a paradigm case (say freedom in Kant's philosophy in the 'first model' of *Negative Dialektik*). Similarly, his anti-systematic stance is also reflected in his use of aphorisms (especially *Minima Moralia*) and, most importantly of all, the use of the essay form. He adopts the latter both for its openness as literary form and for signalling (by way of its French root of '*un essai*') the fallibility of philosophical endeavours (in contrast to the certainty which (some) traditional philosophy claims for itself).

It is, however, a mistake to understand Adorno's anti-system as anti-logical – as so caught up in presenting contradictions and *aporias* that it ends up flouting the rules of logic, infinitely deconstructing and erasing every step as soon as it is taken. As he puts it in relation to the essay form:

For the essay is not situated in simple opposition to discursive procedure. It is not unlogical; rather it obeys logical criteria in so far as the totality of its sentences must fit together coherently. Mere contradictions may not remain, unless they are grounded in the object itself. It is just that the essay develops thoughts differently from discursive logic. The essay neither makes deductions from a principle nor does it draw conclusions from coherent individual observations. It co-ordinates elements, rather than subordinating them; and only the essence of its content, not the manner of its presentation, is commensurable with logical criteria.

(Adorno 1984: 169)

Just because one rejects discursive grounding and the idea that the world can be captured in top-down deductively organized conceptual frameworks, does not mean one foregoes stringency, exactness, clarity, structure, or even bindingness. Adorno denies that these qualities can be had only within (and thereby at the cost of) a system. Just as (musical) composition has its own stringency and logic without thereby having to be a deductive system or algorithm, so does thinking, even where it turns against its own tendencies to petrify the world and our experiences into rigid systems.

So far this case study of Adorno's theory has been an exploration that neither entered into scholarly debates around interpretation nor provided much by way of critical scrutiny. I will conclude by highlighting one crucial critical junction. There is a fundamental interpretative question as to whether Adorno's negative dialectic contains, however implicitly, a positive core; and a fundamental philosophical question as to whether it should contain it, such that if it were missing, this would undermine, even invalidate his theory. The literature is divided along both questions, but the majority of interpretations involve ascribing a positive core of some sort to Adorno's theory.[40] Perhaps in good part this is because it is widely accepted that a positive core is required. However, this widespread commitment is, in fact, problematic – or so I have argued elsewhere.[41] In particular, it overlooks the plausibility and cogency of 'metaethical negativism' – the view that the bad or wrong has normative force of its own, which can be recognized without reference to the good and the right, and which at least on occasion is sufficient for us to come to all-things-considered judgements about what to do and refrain from doing (recall how Auschwitz functions as a negative paradigm for Adorno). Also, it mistakenly assumes that every form of criticism has to be constructive in the sense of providing a positive alternative or substitute – while it might well be desirable that critique can point to such an alternative, it is not a requirement, neither in philosophy (flicking through any philosophy journal would provide illustration for that), nor outside it (would we really require of Jean Améry that he provides his torturers with a positive alternative in order for him to be permitted to criticize what they subject him to?). If this is correct, then Adorno's negative dialectic could do without a positive core, and Adorno is right not to be afraid of 'the reproach of unfruitful negativity' (Adorno 1977: 130).

However, if this is mistaken, and if – as many of his successors within the Critical Theory tradition also think – Adorno's theory lacks the resources to provide a positive core of the right kind, then subsequent developments within this tradition would be vindicated in taking a different approach. Crucially, these developments thereby also change the conception of and relation to philosophy – making Critical Theory dependent on universal pragmatics or normative reconstructions of our social spheres and a reconfigured philosophy of history or constructivist accounts of justification. As noted from the outset, this chapter does not aim to trace the morphing sequences that Critical Theory's (relationship to) philosophy has undergone, but provides a case study of one of its exemplifications – a 'model' in Adorno's sense.

Where does this leave Critical Theory's uneasy relationship with Philosophy? In the model case I focused on – Adorno's work – the relationship is one where critique of philosophy is combined with insistence on the need for it. Adorno's critique is directed against philosophy in the sense of theory that is committed to some combination of the following elements: the possibility of capturing the world fully in our conceptual schemes; timeless essence(s); philosophy's having to be a system; the requirement for and possibility of ultimate grounding (including of our ethical judgements); a stark division between method and substance; and the separation of philosophy from other disciplines. Adorno insists on the need for self-critical reflection about these elements (or the works of authors which exemplify their combination). Such critique of philosophy should, thus, be in a sense internal (rather than, for example, a sociology of knowledge or a neuroscientific account that presents these thought constructions as epiphenomena). It also operates by way of conceptual innovation and rearrangement – and thereby is an heir to traditional philosophy. The need for self-critical reflection arises because Adorno thinks our existing conceptual schemes reflect and even mediate our (social) reality and thereby contribute to its wrongness, such that criticizing them has to be part of social critique. In a word, he advocates philosophizing with and because of a bad conscience – including, crucially, a bad conscience about the nature and function of philosophy itself.[42]

NOTES

1 There is some controversy around attributing this claim to Marx and Engels insofar as this passage is crossed out in the manuscript – it is an open and contestable issue whether this indicates that they dropped the claim on reflection or merely decided against bringing it in at this particular point in the text.

2 'Does Philosophy Still Have a Purpose' [1971] in (Habermas 1981a: 15–37); and 'Discourse Ethics – Notes on a Program of Philosophical Justification [*Begründungsprogramm*]' in (Habermas 1983: 53–125).

3 See, notably, (Honneth 2008) and (Wiggershaus 1994).

4 See (Habermas 1985: Lectures IX–X); (Fraser 1989: Part 1); and (McCarthy 1990).

5 See, for example, (Anderson 2011).

6 Notably (Foucault 1994); see also (Kelly 1994).

7 This seems to be the (implicit) upshot of (Allen 2016).

8 See, notably, (Adorno 1966: 358 / 1973: 365); and (Forst 2015). (There are no reliable translations of *Negative Dialektik*. I refer first to the German original and then to the most commonly used translation.)

9 Both reprinted and translated in (Horkheimer 1972: 188–252).

10 See also (Marcuse 2009: 115).

11 Not all proponents of Critical Theory reject a transhistorical notion of truth. Indeed, some commentators would probably even deny that Horkheimer rejects such a notion in his seminal text, for example (Forst 2015).

12 Translation amended. This kind of historicizing of Kant's transcendental philosophy is also what Foucault, at least on some interpretations – see, notably, (Han-Pile 2002) – aims to do.

13 See, notably, (Brudney 1998).

14 Translation amended.

15 Horkheimer also mentions obstinacy and fantasy (indeed fantasy's obstinacy) as something critical theorists must have (Horkheimer 1972: 220).

16 See also (McCarthy 1985); (Fraser 1989: Ch. 6).

17 Honneth was, for a certain period, an outlier, but recently he has reconfigured his critique of accounts of justice in such a way that he is no longer emphasizing 'the other of justice', but rather a wider, non-procedural conception of justice. See, notably, (Honneth 2011).

18 Translation amended.

19 On Adorno's notion of metacritique, see (Jarvis 1998). Within texts, the metacritical elements can precede the philosophical critique. I return below briefly to Adorno's thoughts on the construction of texts.

20 Translation amended.

21 'Fantasy' refers here to a use of the imagination that need not be tainted, contrary to what the word, in English, nowadays suggest, that

is delusions, mere wishful thinking, and so on (in German, the latter
would be '*Phantasterei*' not '*Phantasie*').

22 On Adorno's relationship to Benjamin, see the seminal study by (Buck-
Morss 1977).

23 Translation amended. See also Adorno 1998: 13–14.

24 Redmond's online translation used.

25 Adorno 1966: 15 / 1973: 3.

26 That is why, for Adorno, not to undertake philosophy is 'practically
criminal [*praktischer Frevel*]' (Adorno 1966: 243 / 1973: 245). See also
(Freyenhagen 2014).

27 See, notably, (Adorno 1966: 222–5 / 1973: 223–6).

28 Despite important changes since his death (including the fall of the Soviet
bloc), Adorno, if he were alive, would view today's existing context as
fundamentally continuous with the one he described in his works.

29 Translation amended.

30 For a detailed discussion of progress and Critical Theory, see (Allen 2016).

31 Redmond's online translation used and amended. See also (Adorno
1966: 183 / 1973: 181–2).

32 On metaphysical experience, see (Skirke 2012) and (Hulatt forthcoming).
To say that negative experiences play a pivotal role in Adorno's theory
is not to say that Adorno understands them as encountering theory-
independent facts that could be appealed to in order to arbitrate between
different theories. This would be to slip into the kind of foundationalist
framework that Adorno urges us to avoid – along with what he sees
as the crude empiricism of Logical Positivism or the appeal to pure
immediacy in Heidegger.

33 Redmond's online translation used.

34 See notably (Horkheimer and Adorno 2002). Adorno's notion of 'natural
history' is meant to denote the intertwining of nature and history –
see, for example, (Cook 2011). Such natural history cannot be decoded
simply by way of the natural sciences, though it is broadly compatible
with them. Nietzsche's idea of genealogy and Freudian psychoanalysis
as well as (particularly the early) Marx play a background role here.

35 See (Freyenhagen 2013: Ch. 5 and especially Ch.7).

36 This is a *shaping* of the world, not simply taking it in as it is. Otherwise,
it would be mysterious why 'identity thinking' is (for Adorno) both a
useful tool *and* – as we will see shortly – getting the world terribly wrong.

37 (Smith 1993 [5th edn 1789]: Vol. I, Bk. I. Ch. 1, para. 10).

38 See, for example, (Adorno 1966: 44 / 1973: 33).

39 See, for example, (Adorno 1984: 159–60).

40 See, for example, (Finlayson 2002) and (Seel 2004).

41 See (Freyenhagen 2013: Ch. 8).

42 My thanks for critical comments on earlier drafts to the editors, a reader
for the Press, Christian Skirke, Dan Watts, and the members of the
Critical Theory Colloquium at Essex.

19 An Extension of Deconstructionist Methodology

Influenced by Nietzsche and Heidegger, French thought at the end of the 1960s defined itself by the task of reversing Platonism, that is, by reversing the positing of and belief in a transcendent world behind or above the actual world (Deleuze 1995: 59–66). Deleuze and Derrida, in particular, spoke respectively of destroying and deconstructing metaphysics (Derrida 2011: 64; Deleuze 1990: 266).[1] The attempt to deconstruct metaphysics, however, is not simple. Because we can never escape metaphysical language – our words are sedimented with meaning inherited from Plato – we can never establish a presuppositionless starting point for a method. Therefore, when Derrida, at the end of the 60s, spoke of deconstruction, he defined it as a strategy (Derrida 1997b: 157–64). As we shall see, not only must we strategize to escape the metaphysical system, but also we must undergo a transformative experience.

For Derrida, the strategy of deconstruction consists of two phases (Derrida 1982: 135–6; Derrida 1981: 41–2).

First, metaphysical hierarchies, which are conceptual and really axiological, must be reversed. For instance, at this moment, Derrida saw a hierarchy that subordinated writing to speech. Likewise, Deleuze saw a hierarchy that subordinated accidents to essences. Both argued that there are grounds to reverse these established and acquired hierarchies, making writing and accidents prior to speech and essences, making writing and accidents even *a priori*. However, deconstruction is not satisfied with merely reversing the hierarchy. In a second phase, both Derrida and Deleuze tried to reach the absolute foundation from which the hierarchies themselves derived. The search for the absolute foundation implies that both Derrida

379

and Deleuze belong to the Kantian tradition of transcendental philosophy. However, unlike Kant, both defined the absolute or transcendental foundation in terms of difference, but difference really means time (*différance* in Derrida and *Aion* in Deleuze).[2] In our experience of time, the flow differentiates itself into the past and future. Making the experience of time fundamental transforms the concept of foundation. Instead of permanence, we have a differentiating flow. Both Derrida and Deleuze tried to show that the difference within the flow of time makes the experience of time unstable. The difference makes anything like a reconciliation of opposites impossible. The irreconcilable difference in the foundation presents deconstruction with its most difficult task. One must find a mode of expression that is adequate to the temporal and yet absolute foundation. Derrida spoke of creating paleonyms, while Deleuze spoke of creating new concepts. The task of expressing the unstable foundation is so difficult, verging on the impossible, that we are never certain we have really escaped from the hierarchies. As we already pointed out, Derrida always defines deconstruction as a strategy (Derrida 1982: 135). We must speak of strategy (and not a method).

In his early writings, Derrida called deconstruction a strategy because deconstruction aims to avoid, in particular, two pitfalls that make one relapse into the hierarchies being deconstructed. The two pitfalls correspond to the two phases of deconstruction. First, if the Western metaphysical tradition has always (at least on the surface) consisted in hierarchies, and thus in inequalities, deconstruction, in order not to fall back into such hierarchies, aims at a kind of equality and balance, or even something like justice (Derrida 1992: 15).[3] At the least, it aims not at oppression. Second, if below the metaphysical hierarchies the foundation is unstable and unbalanced, then deconstruction strategizes to avoid modes of expression that betray the foundation. Since the foundation is difference in the experience of time, expressions that betray the foundation are expressions of identity and permanence. How one should *not think* is found in these kinds of expressions.[4] One has to avoid these expressions, which include common-sense expressions, in order to find a way of thinking and a way of speaking that differs from all of these accepted expressions. Therefore, deconstructionist thinking strives to be *creative*. It aims to be, and produce, free thinking.

As the subtitle of this essay indicates, what follows attempts to creatively extend deconstructionist thought. The extension takes place by moving through four components, which are like four steps in a method. Here are the four steps in a nutshell; they structure this essay. The *first* step is an encounter. The encounter is a kind of intuition that disrupts all the usual and accepted modes of thinking. The encounter is the starting point for thinking otherwise. It opens the way through which one is able to discover an absolute foundation. The *second* step turns to the foundation. Following phenomenological methodology (in particular, the *epochē* and the reduction which I shall explain below), the foundation discovered is non-mundane or prior to the world, or even the origin of the world. *Third*, the foundation is subjective (inner experience), but the subjectivity to which we are led is temporal. As we shall see, the experience of time is self-contradictory. At once and inseparable in the experience of time, there is the singularity of an event and the universality of a repetition. Something that is singular in the strict sense is an event that is not repeatable and therefore not universalizable. Similarly, to have something that is universal in the strict sense is something that is only repeatable and therefore not singular.[5] *Fourth*, deconstructionist thinking expresses the experience of time in concepts or statements that are themselves self-contradictory. The self-contradictory nature of the deconstructionist discourse gives off the appearance of irrationality. However, it is not irrational. While self-contradictory, the discourse the thinking produces – which we believe is genuine philosophical discourse – makes sense. In fact, it attempts to make a new sense, an event in thinking that differs from all prior thinking. Even more, it aims to produce undecidability, on the basis of which one is able to make a non-programmed and therefore free decision. As we shall see, genuine philosophical discourse aims to bring the one to whom it is addressed to such a free decision. It aims at free thinking – and free behaviour.

I. FIRST STEP: THE ENCOUNTER

Both Plato and Aristotle claimed that all philosophy begins in the experience of wonder. This astonishment explains why we spoke above of an intuition. If we go to Bergson, perhaps the greatest philosopher of intuition in the twentieth century, we see that the word 'intuition' has two senses. On the one hand, for Bergson, intuition refers to a method (Deleuze 1991: 13–35). Negatively, in intuition one does *not* remain outside of the thing one is considering. The positive formula for the method of intuition is to enter into the thing (Bergson 1992: 159). Bergson provides the image of either standing outside of a city in order to look at it or walking around within the city to experience it. Of course, one learns more about the city from within the city, than from outside the city. Therefore, in Bergson, unlike the psychologist who observes a patient's inner life from the outside, one must enter into the continuous, inner flow of time. As is well known, Bergson called the inner flow of time 'the duration'. When one has entered into the duration, one is able to learn how the continuous flow is differentiated (and looks to be an opposition as, for instance, between the soul and the body), and one is able to learn how to integrate the differences back into the continuity. We should note that the method of intuition – entering in, and differentiation-integration – includes the expression of the duration. Bergson claims frequently that traditional philosophical concepts are not adequate to the duration; what is required is a fluid language which corresponds to the flow of the duration. We'll return to the problem of expression below in the fourth step.

Bergson's second sense of intuition is more controversial. For Bergson, intuition means a mystical vision (Bergson 1977: 230). However, the intuition in Bergson is not only vision. Bergson stresses that what precedes the vision is 'a call' or 'a voice' (ibid.: 34, 230). Indeed, the call and the vision come upon us with such force that, as Bergson says, it produces a disequilibrium in the mind (ibid.: 245). The disequilibrium upsets common sense and customs. Because of the disequilibrium, the mystical vision and the mystic resemble madness and the madman. In *The Two Sources of Morality and Religion*, Bergson explains at length how mysticism differs from madness. Mystics who are actually mad, Bergson says, are charlatans; they speak and speak, but make no sense; they remain in the disequilibrium. In contrast, the true mystic overcomes the disequilibrium resulting in a new and different equilibrium. Responding to the voice, the true mystic speaks, makes sense, and makes changes in the world. Bergson's example of a great mystic is Joan of Arc. It is precisely the expression of the experience in words and actions that distinguishes the madman from the mystic. The expressions of the great mystic do something.

Perhaps, like Deleuze, Bergson should have called the mystical experience an encounter (Deleuze 1995: 139). Without appealing to religion, we can imagine an experience of extreme intensity. This would be an experience so intense that it outstrips our sensibility and our ability to cognize. It produces a disequilibrium, as Bergson says, among the faculties of the mind, forcing us to think otherwise than how we have been thinking. Experiences that produce mental disequilibrium are experiences of suffering. Indeed, there are many experiences of suffering that are intense enough to disrupt our faculties, for instance, the experience of hate crimes. These experiences are not only visions; they cry out to us and require a response. It is only when we hear *the call* that we are able to start to think (and behave differently). If therefore we can assume that we have experienced something like wonder or better an intuition, if we can assume an encounter and shock to our faculties, then we can turn to the next step. The second step is the phenomenological method of the *epochē*.

II. SECOND STEP: THE PHENOMENOLOGICAL *EPOCHĒ*

Because the encounter comes upon us without warning – no one can will an intuition to happen[6] – we can claim that the shock to our faculties disturbs our presuppositions. As is well known, Husserl required that philosophy be presuppositionless. The phenomenological method attempts to dismantle all presuppositions, which Husserl puts under the general category of 'the natural attitude'. The 'natural attitude' is the general thesis, belief, or presupposition that the world exists in itself (mind-independent), expressed by the simple sentence 'The world is.' The purpose of the dismantling (or the deconstructing) lies in discovering, as we said in the Introduction, the foundation on which the thesis 'the world is' rests. The foundational purpose explains why Husserl speaks of transcendental philosophy. The methodology leads one to *transcend* the world to its origin (Fink 1970: 92).

In order to deconstruct the thesis that the world exists, and find a way towards the origin of the world, Husserl takes up Cartesian doubt (Husserl 2014: 53–4). Phenomenological methodology owes a lot to the idea of Cartesian doubt, which, as is well known, results for Descartes in the certainty of the 'I think'. However, Husserl's appropriation of Cartesian doubt is complicated. Husserl states that the *epochē* does not strictly doubt the general thesis of the world's existence. Instead of speaking of doubt, Husserl speaks of 'suspending' or 'bracketing' the general thesis of the world's existence. The words 'suspension' and 'bracketing' are used to indicate that the natural thesis is still functioning, and as still functioning, the phenomenologist aims to discover how it comes into existence. What we learn through the *epochē* is that the general thesis of the world's existence is generated from subjective acts. The world is then seen as relative to consciousness. We can see what is vital in the *epochē* only if we associate these terms with the idea that the *epochē*, for Husserl, is 'a total change of the natural attitude of life' (Husserl 1970: 148). Indeed, what is most difficult to understand is the 'totality', or better, 'the universality' of the *epochē*. The universality of the suspension means that all modes of thinking, and especially common sense, all existential beliefs that we think are valid, all of the natural, psychological, and human sciences, all genera and species of being – all of these are put in suspense. And the universality of the *epochē*, Husserl stresses – in contrast to Descartes – does not occur piecemeal. It sweeps away 'with one blow' all of our mundane presuppositions (ibid.: 150). This 'with one blow' explains why Husserl calls the *epochē* 'a total transformation', 'a thoroughly new way of life', making 'an immense difference' (ibid.: 137, 176). As we stated above, the outcome of the immense difference is that the world is relativized to subjectivity. Relativized, the world becomes the correlate of subjectivity. The world's objectivity therefore is reduced to being a phenomenon, that is, an appearing to a subject.

The 'one blow' occurs through what Husserl calls 'the phenomenological reduction'. Husserl uses the word 'reduction' because the independent being of the world, its objectivity, is reduced to being a phenomenon, an appearance to consciousness. The reduction functions through certain kinds of argumentation (or thought experiments). The reduction's argumentation takes the *epochē*'s relativization of the world to subjective experience much further, through which it resembles more closely Cartesian doubt. We see the argumentation in Husserl's 1923–4 lecture course, *Erste*

Philosophie (*First Philosophy*) (Husserl 1959).[7] The demonstration proceeds by Husserl describing our natural attitude life in the world. In general in our life directed by the natural attitude the world is a harmonious system of things and their perceptions. Nevertheless, the occurrence of optical illusions shows that we never have certain evidence for our belief in a thing's existence. However, as Husserl points out, empirical illusions are always disclosed as illusions and after the disclosure our perceptions continue harmoniously. The harmony is able to be reestablished because the world is harmonious. In contrast, after the *epochē* and our radical transformation, the world's existence becomes a 'transcendental illusion' (Husserl 1959: 53). Husserl calls the transcendental illusion an 'illusion', because the world is reduced from being a world true in itself to being only an appearance, 'a mere appearance' (ibid.). Since the harmonious world is 'a pure appearance', the belief in the world being grounded in something like God or eternal laws must vanish. As a pure appearance, with the word 'appearance' meaning a semblance, it is thinkable or imaginable that the world might be different from what it seems to be. In fact, nothing in the appearance-semblance of the world being harmonious contradicts the possibility that the world might turn into 'a senseless and pure chaos' (ibid.: 64, 65). Husserl then calls the transcendental illusion 'transcendental', because this illusion of a chaotic world differs from every empirical illusion. An empirical illusion always includes an anticipation that the harmony of perceptions will be restored. However, this 'end of the world' illusion does not involve the probability of an anticipation (ibid.: 54). While the world assures us in advance that empirical illusions will be disclosed and corrected, the transcendental illusion cannot be corrected. As 'the end of the world' image suggests, the phenomenological reduction is, as he says in *Ideas 1*, 'world-annihilation' (Husserl 2014: 88–9).

To summarize, the *epochē* suspends our belief in a world true in itself. The reduction reduces the world to a pure appearance which, as such, could always be otherwise; the world's existence is contingent. The harmony of the world could disappear at any moment and take on the appearance of chaos. The mundane harmony that we encounter in the natural attitude therefore can only be explained by subjective activities. The question becomes: what is the status of the constituting subject? More precisely, if the one who is meditating by means of the phenomenological method is a human being, how is it possible for an object in the world, a human being, to be also the subject of the world? It seems that a part of the world has 'swallowed up' the whole world (Husserl 1970: 180).

In order to eliminate this appearance of a part being larger than the whole, the subject who constitutes the world's meaning as harmony must be differentiated from an empirical subject. If the subject is non- or extra-mundane, beyond the world, if it is a transcendental subject, then the subject is not a part of the world. The differentiation between empirical subject and transcendental subject had already been anticipated in the *epochē*'s universality: the existence of all things in the world, including humans, and our knowledge of them has been suspended. Even more, in the world annihilation, other humans are in chaos. The world annihiliation also includes me as a human; I do not exist, or, as Husserl claims, in transcendental subjectivity, 'nothing human is to be found' (ibid.: 183). If the humans, including me as a human, like the world, are gone, then the result of the phenomenological method is solitude (ibid.: 184). Again, producing a difference, Husserl stresses that this solitude is not that of someone who has cut himself off from society, as in a shipwreck. It is not Robinson Crusoe's solitude, the solitude of someone who still knows that he is a member of a society. This radical solitude seems to isolate the subject completely. In transcendental solitude, Husserl says, 'I am not an ego, who still has his you, his we, his total community of co-subjects' (ibid.). The 'I' or 'ego', Husserl even says, is not even a personal pronoun. The residue left behind after the annihilation of the world is 'a sphere of ownness' unlike any empirical sphere of solitude (Husserl 1977: 92). Husserl calls this sphere 'solipsism' (Husserl 1959: 64; 1977: 89).

III. THIRD STEP: THE EXPERIENCE OF TIME

Thus, through the reduction, Husserl has tried to show us that the transcendental level is really different from the empirical level. In the reconstruction we just completed we saw two differences: the transcendental illusion differs from all empirical illusions because the transcendental illusion cannot be corrected; and transcendental solitude differs from empirical solitude since the transcendental solitude has no community to which the phenomenologist had previously belonged. Perhaps, these differences can be questioned. Nevertheless, they point us in the direction of the absolute foundation. The differences at least give us a hint of what the absolute foundation would look like. Husserl's attempt to differentiate the absolute foundation from the empirically founded is based on his recognition of a problem that menaces all transcendental philosophy. In the laying out and expression of the foundation, we transcendental philosophers make use, usually unbeknownst to ourselves, of precisely those elements that are in question (Husserl 1959: 92). In Heidegger's terminology, the problem lies in us defining being (*Sein*) by means of things that exist (*Seiende*) (Heidegger 2010: 1–3). Thus, there is a principle that responds to this problem of circular thinking. The principle is given its most precise formulation by Deleuze: the foundation must never resemble what it founds (Deleuze 1990: 99). After the event of the intuition, philosophy must obey this principle if it wants to avoid circular reasoning. So, in the recognition that for Husserl, all transcendental phenomenology, and indeed all transcendental philosophy, strives to obey the non-resemblance principle, we see ourselves placed at the most fundamental and absolute level of experience.

Here we take up Derrida's argumentation from *Voice and Phenomenon*, Chapter Five (Derrida 2011: 51–9). It is Derrida who has taught us the most about how to appropriate the phenomenological method (Derrida 2005: 140, 158–60). Kant (and perhaps Aristotle prior to him and Bergson after him) had already shown that all experience is conditioned by time. The claim that all experience is temporally conditioned seems incontestable. We must therefore describe the form of time or how time flows at the bottom of experience. And, if we want to maintain ourselves at the transcendental level, the description of time must be distinguished from empirical time. So, at the outset, we must show how fundamental time is not calculable succession. In order to reach the form of fundamental time, we must abstract from time all empirical content. Or, we must vary the experience of time across a wide variety of contents. If we have done the variation, we discover that every 'now-point', as Husserl says, that is, every 'right now, here before my eyes', is conjoined with an immediate recollection or 'retention'. Like Husserl, Bergson had also discovered that a kind of double of the present appears immediately with the now (Bergson 2007: 106–48).

In addition, what is right now here before my eyes is conjoined with an immediate anticipation or 'protention'. In order to help us see this conjunction, Husserl refers us to the experience of a melody, where retention and protention are more apparent than in ordinary experience. If we vary the experience of a melody, we see that it is impossible to hear the melody unless we have retained the prior musical phrase and have anticipated the phrase's return later in the melody. The impossibility of hearing the melody without retentions and protentions means that the present moment is, as Husserl says, 'thick'. In other words, the now-point is inseparably connected to retentions and protentions. We cannot imagine any experience that does not involve retentions and protentions. Therefore, while it may seem that the ordinary succession of time is simple, it is not: fundamental time is complicated.

We can draw *five implications* from the complication within the experience of time. *First*, as we can see now thanks to the varied experience of a melody, the retentional phase of the present moment is defined by repeatability (Derrida 2011: 58). As the word indicates, re-tention retains; it retains a form that is repeatable; the form's repeatability sets up protentions and anticipations. Like any form, the retained one can be repeated indefinitely, and, at the limit, a repetition can be universalized. Undoubtedly, the experience of boredom is based on the indefinite repeatability of retentions. However, if the retentional phase possesses the possibility of a quasi-permanence over temporal change (what Husserl calls 'omnitemporality'), then the now right here before my eyes is at least different from the retentional phase (Derrida 2011: 56). While, as Husserl shows, the retentional phase is an essential component of the present as we live it, it is a reproduction of what is no longer present. And as a reproduction, the retention is repeatable into the future, which is later and elsewhere. In contrast, the experience of what is here right now before my eyes is here and now; it is really present; it is not elsewhere and later. Therefore, what is fundamental, at the deepest level of the experience of time, is the difference between presence and non-presence, or, more precisely, between retention as the source of universalization and the singularity of the now. Since the difference in the experience of time already implies a lack of sameness, the difference also implies alterity. Thanks to temporal experience, we are never alone. In a moment, we shall see more clearly how alterity enters into the apparently isolated self.

Second, although we can see how the experience of time is continuous due to the retentional and protentional phases, especially when their relationship is harmonious, the difference between the now and the retentional phase is profound. Between universalization and singularlization, there is a difference so deep that we must think of it as an abyss. The foundation is essentially a non-foundation because it is fractured. The conjunction of retentions and the now point is essentially out of joint. Being out of joint, the difference between universalization and singularization is so extreme that the two poles of experienced time do something like violence to one another. (The use of the word 'violence' here extends its normal meaning. The violence at the fundamental level of experience is of course not real violence. However, this fundamental or transcendental violence is the condition for the possibility of real or empirical violence (see Lawlor 2016). We shall return to transcendental violence in the fourth step.) In logical terms, we would have to say that the form of experienced time is self-contradictory. It is as if at the fundamental level there are two voices forever calling out to one another with opposite and unreconcilable commandments: 'Do not singularize! Universalize!'; 'No, do not universalize! Singularize!'

The *third* implication extends the fundamental self-contradiction. As we have seen, the self-contradiction is based in the form of experienced time. But as the form of experienced time, the relations between the retentional and protentional phases and the now are irreducible, essential, necessary, and not contingent. In short, it is impossible to imagine any experience that does not include retentions and protentions surrounding the now. But if there is not and never has been and never will be an experience of an isolated now, then we cannot imagine that the retentional phase is a repetition of a primal now. We cannot find a truly first now; the now has always already been repeated. Or we have to say that the repetition is a repetition of nothing that is absolutely pre-given. Essentially, the now, which looks to be an *arche*, always finds itself in the context of a past. Time, as we experience it, therefore is 'an-archic' in the literal sense of having no first *arche* or origin, or first principle. The origin of the world is itself 'an-archic', in the sense of lacking an *arche*.

Fourth, the 'anarchy' of the origin gives the repetition great power. As repeating no primal now or presence, the repeatable form can be repeated in an indefinite and almost unlimited number of ways. As repeating nothing like a first principle, the repetition essentially contains innumerable possibilities, possibilities that cannot be predicted and calculated. Again, we are far from the calculable succession of ordinary time. The formal container of repetition – an image, for example, but also a musical refrain – with its indefinite and unforeseeable scope, must therefore be open to all content, even the content that is the repeated image's opposite. It must be essentially open to an event that disharmonizes and disrupts the harmony and the universality. Essentially it must be open to all empirical content, including the accidents that we would like to avoid. In other words, if the container already contains and includes the possibilities of accidents and events, of being otherwise, it includes the possibility of the disruption of harmony, something like death. Heidegger of course has stressed my death is an essential possibility of existence. As one of my essential possibilities, death is part of my life. I am, as Derrida would say, a spectre, neither strictly alive nor strictly dead (Derrida 1994). The fact that life includes death, which is something very different from life, allows us to see better how alterity cannot be excluded from the sphere of ownness. As soon as I imagine myself alone, all alone, the image I form of myself is not the self I am at this very moment. It is different or other than the 'me' I am now. In addition, the repeatability of that image is open to being used by others, even if I never externalize the image. In my head, I imagine (or remember) my 'self', and this image means that others are there in my head with me. As was anticipated, we must say that we are never strictly alone.[8]

Fifth, solipsism has been deconstructed. Although we had to pass through transcendental solitude, the openness of time to alteration has placed us in something like a transcendental un-solitude. We cannot call the transcendental un-solitude a community since the others in me are present to me only through the mediation of the image. Not only is every now-point irreducibly connected to retentions, and not only is every retention open to indefinite repetition, but also: if the image is an image of another person or sentient being, it is necessarily the case that the living being's inner life is absent from me. Given to us in the Fifth Cartesian Meditation

(Husserl 1977: 108), the phenomenological insight that the experience of others is always mediated, indicating a non-accessible interior life, implies that we have an irreducible and even absolute non-knowledge of others. Since the others are in us (through the images we make of ourselves which are different or other from what I am now), we must also recognize that we have an absolute non-knowledge of our own interior life.[9] The images we form of ourselves mediate our own self-knowledge. As in interior monologue, the absolute non-self-knowledge takes the form of a question: 'Why did you do that? You've gone wrong.' As Plato claimed in the *Theaetetus*, all interior life of persons is a kind of monologue. However, given the difference in the fundamental experience of time, the monologue is in fact and necessarily dialogical. And this dialogue is not tranquil. The voices in us are of such an intensity to demand that we respond to them. The demand, which is a call, is the root of responsibility.

IV. FOURTH STEP: EFFECTIVE PHILOSOPHICAL DISCOURSE

The demand at the root of responsibility points in the direction of the experience of the call. It seems probable that the call is the fundamental unit of language. We can claim that the call is the fundamental unit of language because, even if the discourse seems to be a simple report of facts, even if it seems to be composed for no one, at the least it is addressed to a future 'me'. When I write, I have to read what I wrote. But as *addressed* at least to 'me', the report is, fundamentally, a call. And since the call is always repeatable, the call necessarily calls to indeterminate readers. It may appear that the fundamental unit of language is the proposition. It may appear that the primary purpose of language is information and communication. Nevertheless, below the level of every constative statement, there is always and necessarily a performative. No matter how reportive and no matter how objective, the statement does something by calling out to indefinite addressees.

What is a call? By answering this question we are in fact elaborating on the idea of the encounter presented in the first step. Thus, to answer the question of the call, we must say that the call's structure resembles the form of time. A call calls someone to presence in the here and now; and yet, the call calls someone to presence because the one called is not present (the one called has not yet been reached or has already disappeared). The one called is at once present and absent; the addressee comes near without coming near. The structure of the call, therefore, consists of an unstable conjunction of presence and absence. Therefore, the primary purpose of the call is to have an effect on the potential hearer, to call the hearer close by and in proximity. But the purpose of the call can never be completely fulfilled since the mediate nature of another's interior life keeps the other at a distance. Although through my speaking I may call out to others and bring them near, the structure of the experience of others keeps them at a distance from me. Likewise, as someone hearing (and not making) a call, I can never know precisely that for which someone else is calling to me; I can never get close enough to know for certain. Even if the call is only implicit in a report, I cannot know precisely that for which I am being called because I have no direct access to the speaker's interior life. Therefore, the unstable conjunction of presence and absence – the one called remains distant while being near and the one calling remains distant while being near – opens up possibilities of speaking that exaggerate the distance. These exaggerated possibilities of speaking define the mode of expression required by the method we have laid out so far. These possibilities are at the heart of the deconstructive strategy. We can understand these possibilities in two ways.

First, we can think about concept formation. Following the idea of synthetic judgements, the concepts we form must unify heterogeneous components. It is important to keep in mind that the thinking we are describing is creative. In order to be creative, in order to be new, a concept must unify ideas that are very different from one another, as, for instance Descartes did, when he combined thinking with being. Although unifying heterogeneous elements, the concept must also make those elements be consistent. And yet, the components themselves must remain heterogeneous. In other words, the discourse we compose must make sense; it must say something, even if what is said is paradoxical. While this is a strange image, the concepts formed must resemble reinforced concrete, combining very different elements like cement and steel (Deleuze and Guattari 1987: 329). Although this image hardly suggests the fluid concepts that   Bergson demanded and it hardly suggests an unstable and non-solid foundation, at least the image of reinforced concrete shows us a consistent combination of heterogeneous elements. From this image, we can move to an example.

The transcendental violence we mentioned above in step two could be conceived in the following way. First, the idea of a willed and therefore immoral violence must be negated. Transcendental violence is *not* ethical violence. Then, unlike ethical or willed violence, we see that transcendental violence happens unwillingly and necessarily. It happens necessarily because we cannot imagine any experience of another person (understood as a true individual) that ever excludes the recognition of that other person as other. In other words, the experience always includes the subsumption of the other person under the general category of alterity. And since the other person is a singularity, the subsumption under a generality violates the other person (or other living being). Here through the necessity of subsumption, we have transcendental violence. Nevertheless, and likewise, the recognition of another as other, albeit a violation, makes possible all the forms of understanding of others that we can imagine. We cannot imagine the experience of helping another, making peace with him or her, without the recognition of that other person as other and therefore as different from me. Therefore, the concept of transcendental violence is at once heterogeneous and consistent. We discovered necessities by means of imaginatively varying experiences: recognition and subsumption are inseparable from the experience of others. Conditions of possibility were then put in place; recognition and subsumption are the necessary conditions for understanding others. And from those conditions, we drew consequences. However, the consequences that necessarily follow from these conditions are heterogeneous. What is synthesized in the concept of transcendental violence is both violence and non-violence. Even more, from this particular concept formation, we can see a possibility of speaking. We can imagine a speaking that would exaggerate the violence of the subsumption to the point where the other would feel forced to flee the subsumption relationship. As Derrida has convincingly shown, the form found in Aristotle's reputed statement 'Oh my friends, there is no friend' calls others friends but then negates the very possibility of friendship so that the statement seems to say at once 'I love you' and 'I hate you' (Derrida 1997a: 206–18). The expression alienates the other, but that alienation also liberates the other, and carries the other away into the distance.

The other way through which we can understand the exaggerated possibilities of speaking appears through the form of experienced time outlined above in step two. As we saw, the iteration (retention) in time includes indefinite possibilities; it is open even to those possibilities that seem to contradict it. In order to be adequate to the form of experienced time, that is, to be adequate to its openness, the composition of the philosophical discourse must be equally open. To include all these possibilities, even those that negate the discourse's sense, the statements that compose the discourse must say 'yes'. In addition, in order to be adequate to the openness of experienced time, the discourse must negate everything that plays the role of a universal or constant in a natural language, displaying the constants and universals not as necessary laws but as statistical averages. The negation of universals and constants explains why one finds so many 'neither–nor' expressions in deconstructive texts. These negative formulas are essential for the liberation of the forms of expression, in other words, *for speech that is creative and free*. When these supposed principles and origins have been annihilated – recall that time is an-archic – linguistic forms are able to multiply but they do not multiply as a repetition of the same; the multiplication of the liberated forms differentiate themselves from one another.

For instance, we can complicate the simple word 'and'. Because the 'and' is a 'syncategoreme' (and not a 'categoreme'), it has no basic meaning or signified (Derrida 2000: 292; Husserl 1977: 508–50). In other words, the 'and' does not have a constant or universal to which it corresponds. Its sole function is to join statements or words together, regardless of the statements' content. Thus, in the composition of a philosophical discourse, the 'and' can be either inclusive, establishing relations of tautology, or exclusive, establishing relations of heterology. In its undecideable status, the 'and' produces a thread, perhaps a quite thin thread, of continuous sense, while at the same time it produces discontinuities that disrupt the sense. The 'and' can disrupt the continuity to the point of self-contradiction. In other words, the conjunction can continue to the point of stating one idea essentially includes its opposite: good and (is) evil.[10]

Therefore, we can imagine a discourse that first destroys all the supposed invariants and rigid oppositions found within the idea of goodness: 'Goodness is *neither* happiness *nor* obedience to the law.' The 'neither–nor' 'abstracts' goodness from what appear to be its constants. 'Goodness' becomes nothing more than a minimal form, perhaps nothing more than the form of the word. Then, goodness, minimized, is able to be proliferated. Passing through each conjunction, which asserts that goodness *is* this, goodness passes through differences: 'goodness is happiness, but *not* quite happiness; *and* goodness is obedience to the law, but *not* quite obedience; *and* goodness is care but *not* quite care, etc.' As the differences appear, they rebound onto the first assertion implying a kind of overarching sense. But at the limit, like the relation of a circle and a tangent, goodness approximates something entirely different from itself: 'goodness is pleasure, but not quite pleasure. Does that non-pleasure imply that goodness is suffering? Does suffering imply that goodness is actually evil?' Consequently, evil comes to be connected, and consistently connected, to goodness so that no separation can be established between goodness and evil. Through the proliferations of conjunctions, goodness ends up contradicting itself. But then, importantly, we see that anyone, a philosopher, who has composed this discourse would have to decide, on the basis of the undecidability of the conjunction between good and evil, whether to argue that a penalty like the death sentence cannot be applied in the name of goodness since the idea of goodness is necessarily contaminated by evil or to argue that the death sentence must be applied in the name of goodness since the evil of death is contaminated with goodness. By making the conjunction between good and evil undecidable, only through that undecidability does one make a decision that is worthy of the name – a decision that is free and not programmed by constants and universals. When a philosophical discourse aims to effectuate this decision, it is a genuine philosophical discourse.

V. CONCLUSION: HOW NOT TO THINK

A method by which to philosophize aims to avoid certain pitfalls to thinking. The deconstructionist method outlined here aims to avoid first of all mundaneity. In other words, it aims not to think in terms of established and acquired concepts and kinds of knowledge. In particular, it aims to avoid common sense and consensus. Thinking in terms of consensus only ever results in confirming what has already been accepted. To be clear, thinking otherwise advocates change, not conformism. The avoidance of common sense and consensus is a strategy for transcending the actual world in order to discover its foundation. If, through the phenomenological *epochē*, one is able to arrive at the foundation of mundane experience, then one will have avoided the confusion between the founding and the founded. If we have avoided this confusion, then we see that the accepted universals, constants, and invariants are only statistical averages and imposed norms of the founded or empirical world. Instead of these supposed founded or empirical invariants, we have seen two foundational or transcendental invariants. On the one hand, there is the invariant of the content-less form of experienced time: an irreducible struggle between universalization and singularization. On the other hand, there is the invariant of the experience of others: no immediate access to the interior life of others. As we saw, both invariants produce paradoxical consequences. The invariant of experienced time contains an abyss (an *Abgrund*) that turns the foundation or ground into a non-foundation. The invariant of others is the irreducible mediation of the experience of others. It is this abyss and this mediated accessibility that philosophical discourse must respect. In order to compose such a philosophical discourse (at least one based on the thinking presented here), one must avoid all oppositional logics; these logics fall with the avoidance of mundaneity. Instead, if one has avoided these mundane logics, one must rework negation in order to make affirmations proliferate. One must rework the very idea of consistency. Most importantly, in order that a philosophical discourse is *effective*, the author of the discourse must strategize to change the ones to whom it is addressed. It must bring the addressee to the point of undecidability so that he or she is able to make a free decision. The goal of the thinking called deconstructionist lies in changing the addressees' mode of thinking – and behaviour – so that it is free and creative.

NOTES

1 Through fundamental similarities in Derrida's and Deleuze's ways of conceiving the experience of time, I have merged their respective ways of thinking under the title 'deconstruction'. However, between Derrida's

and Deleuze's ways of thinking, there are also fundamental differences. See (Lawlor 2003), in particular, 123–41.

2 Here Derrida and Deleuze rely on the achievement of Heidegger's interpretation of Kant's *Critique of Pure Reason* (Heidegger 1997).

3 Derrida's use of the words 'justice' and 'injustice' to refer to the fundamental structure of the experience of time is based on an ancient way of speaking. Simplicius claims that Anaximander said: 'Whence things have their origin, there they must also pass away according to necessity; for they pay penalty and be judged for their injustice, according to the ordinance of time.' This fragment is quoted in (Heidegger 1975: 13). Derrida mentions Heidegger's interpretation of the Anaximander fragment in (Derrida 1982: 64 and 51 n31).

4 In addition, deconstruction avoids formal logic and especially oppositional logic, and even Hegel's logic of contradiction.

5 The opposition between universality and singularity does not correspond to the type–token distinction. A singularity is a strict event, unrepeatable and unlike anything else. It is not a particular instantiation of a universal type or essence. Similarly, what I am calling universality here does not correspond to an unchangeable type or essence. Since the universalization is based in repetition, the repeatable form is open to variation. It is this dis-unified but inseparable relation between two agencies – universalizability and singularity – that both Derrida and Deleuze have discovered in the experience of time, which they call respectively 'aporetical' and 'paradoxical' (Derrida 1993: 68; Deleuze 1990: 1–3).

6 The starting point in an intuition subverts the very idea of a philosophical methodology. There is no way to will oneself into the intuition. It only ever comes upon us, without warning, perhaps like Bergson's mystic vision. The unpredictability of the encounter means that we really cannot describe it with more than the few words we wrote above. The unpredictability also means that one must prepare for the encounter. One prepares for it by attempting to think beyond all accepted hierarchies.

7 No English translation of this book exists.

8 This claim does not mean that isolation in the normal sense is impossible. We are examining a fundamental structure below the normal course of experience.

9 Freudian psychoanalysis had already demonstrated this claim of absolute non-knowledge.

10 This point is clearer in French: 'le bien est (et) le mal.' The French words 'est' ('is') and 'et' ('and') are phonologically the same.

20 Pathological Experience:

A Challenge for Transcendental Constitution Theory?

INTRODUCTION

Husserl's theory of transcendental constitution relies on the idea that the intentional subject – particularly the subject of motor acts orientated towards a goal – has within itself the resources needed to make sense of objects and, in general, of all salient aspects, all configurations and formations invested with meaning in his lifeworld (*Lebenswelt*). Already anticipating the naturalization of phenomenology as embodied cognition (Petitot 1999; Petit 2015), transcendental constitution places special emphasis on the role of kinaesthesia, the body's intimate feeling of doing, and in so doing, it makes of the kinaesthetic system the source of the meaning structures of the *Lebenswelt*, and the guide to its systematic description. From a narrowly naturalistic point of view one might object to this programme on the grounds that it remains dependent upon the transcendental idealism of the Cartesian tradition, to the extent that it seems to suppose that the subject of motor acts necessarily enjoys an optimal control of the use of its motor system, as if it were exempt from disabilities. Hence the objection: surely the programme of transcendental constitution simply makes of successful voluntary movement the rule for all of human experience without regard to the pathological experience? This despite the fact that the empirical approach of biomedical sciences shows how very precarious and limited our capabilities to make sense are using only the normal resources of the body.

In this contribution I am going to try and defuse just this kind of objection and, more precisely work out a defence against a possible critique of the Husserlian kinaesthetic theory of transcendental constitution, focusing on the example of Parkinson's disease as a selective impairment of the kinaesthetic system. My key idea is that the empirical approach cannot afford to completely eviscerate any normative dimension of the description of the physiological foundations of motivation and action without creating difficulties for itself in the attempt to move back up from the fundamental level of physiological systems and functions (and dysfunctions) towards the phenomenological description of normal and abnormal behaviour. This claim will be supported by scientific literature on Parkinson's, which will be taken up at two levels. 1) At the level of clinical diagnosis, I note that if the symptom differs from normal motor behaviour, it is not on account of some deviation from an average but rather of the deficient realization of an ideal norm: from which I infer that the statistical analysis upon which the diagnosis depends cannot replace, at least in clinical practice, the phenomenological description of lived experience to the extent that the latter is centred on intentionality. 2) At the level of etiological research, the mechanistic explanation seems to be engaged in an infinite regression, where the postulation of the existence of certain physiologically dysfunctional mechanisms cascades down towards multiply embedded, and always more elementary mechanisms, while postponing the integration of all mechanisms in a mutually compatible way in the unity of behaviour, whether normal or abnormal. Here again, the mechanisms assumed to explain anomalies implicitly refer to an ideal of normality that eludes any explanation by mechanisms.

Interpreting pathological experience is a challenge for phenomenology, to the extent that the latter seeks to retain this experience within the field of meaning, the normal world of perception and action, while medical statistics tend to classify it under the laws of chance, and biological research envisages it in the perspective of the chaos of elementary particles. My thesis is the following: that however reticent the empirical approach might be with regard to the admission of any kind of normativity, the concepts of Parkinson's syndrome and motor neurodegeneration cannot be understood without referring to the transcendental norm of a kinaesthetic activity underlying the sense conferred by the subject to its lived experience.

My claim is that a satisfactory compatibility has to be found between phenomenology and the *practice* of biomedical science – if not its standard ideology, a physicalism averse to phenomenology. Thus, at the same time as the researcher officially has to do with level after level of blind, automatic subpersonal mechanisms, he or she cannot but entertain some tentative interpretation of the possible function of such mechanisms. In field parlance one might well say: 'Such and such mechanism is normally (or fails to be in case of anomaly) *for* such and such function – a function which is in turn *for* such and such component of behaviour, which in turn is *for* the living being to sustain its normal relationships in the *Lebenswelt*.' So the way the scientist thinks of the mechanisms as being *for* something ultimately refers us to normal human life and the functional norms that are part and parcel of it – including the norms of voluntary, free movement. Thus, the entire chain of references is ultimately anchored in the intentionality of the lifeworld – the phenomenologist's home ground.

A KINAESTHETIC SUBJECT?

If the return to the thinking subject as foundation of the sense of experience is a familiar theme in traditional transcendental philosophy, it might, on the other hand, seem hopeless to want to derive from so disembodied a principle as the thinking subject the sense of being of anything whatsoever. Could we credit Husserl with having found a way out of this dilemma by opting for an incarnate conception of the foundation of subjectivity? His theory of transcendental constitution would then be freed from the idealist premises of a constituting subject surveying the entire domain of sense from an unconditionally elevated position inconsistent with our existence as natural beings. Sense constitution would then become a process for which the responsible subjective instance would no longer be an 'I think' (*cogito*) but an 'I act', an 'I' activating the movements of its body. By transferring responsibility for sense constitution from a thinking subject to an acting subject, the requirement that there should be a subjective foundation for transcendental constitution would be met, without detriment to naturalism. As an acting subject, the pole of a kinaesthetic system capable of feeling itself doing, this subjective activity would no longer be disassociated from the deployment by a living being of a sensorimotor apparatus. 'Constantly kinaesthetic', whether engaged in activating its body and so learning from its success or failure in moving its limbs, or remaining in a posture of rest, the principle governing motor activity would be granted an irreproachable anchorage in the body.

In this article I hope to show that transcendental idealism has effectively been surmounted through a kinaesthetic theory of constitution; or at least that whatever element of idealism cannot be eliminated from this theory remains compatible with a naturalistic approach. But if we think of the acting subject as the pole of a kinaesthetic system rooted in an organism, we still need to ask: will it normally be exposed to the vicissitudes of the sensorimotor system, in just the same way as the anatomical and psychophysiological functions are so exposed? Or will its status as a transcendental source confer upon the acting subject a mysterious exemption from the stigmatism of its living incarnation? Surely, the dysfunctioning of the sensorimotor apparatus, underlying the working of the kinaesthetic system, would disturb the constitution of the sense of anything encompassed by the horizon of the *Lebenswelt* if the sense in question resulted from the investment of a subjective activity into the kinaesthetic animation of a living body?

In reflections found in his manuscript materials on the phenomenological status of a sensory anomaly (Daltonism), Husserl only manages to save the unity of the *Lebenswelt* at the cost of tracing back the abnormal experience to a variation of normal visual experience. For him, abnormal experience necessarily derives its sense from normal experience, whether we are talking about the child, the animal, or even of madness. If one wants to explore the origin of sense, one always has to go back to what sense *is* for the normal subject. The constitutive privilege of normal experience, in turn, relies upon the fact that the ordinary resources of the kinaesthetic system of an incarnate subject (its intimate sense of 'moving itself' in voluntary action) suffice for the constitution of one's own body as a permanent formation in the experiential flux. One's own body is that which can be activated at will by the subject through constituting operations making use of its kinaesthetic system: one hand touching another and so on. This kind of self-constitution of the own body appeals to a relation of absolute immediacy as between the subject of the voluntary intention and the corporeal movement. The sense of having or of being a body is born of *doing* something with one's body, actualizing a 'can do', whether innate or acquired.

But constitution theory faces a challenge here, since it needs to overcome its persistent idealism in order to be able to account for pathological experience. That this is a real challenge is indicated by a certain ambiguity in the transcendental status of kinaesthesia, acknowledged in the perplexities (quoted below) expressed by Husserl himself. It is the constituting role of kinaesthesia that anchors the subjective activity in the own body, even though this anchorage is not devoid of ambiguity: incarnation or naturalization? The ambiguity is due to the fact that kinaesthesia can be traced back to a phase of motivation which precedes voluntary action and consciousness, a phase in which desire is mingled with intention and volition:

So there is no distinction to be understood between desire and will, no more than there is between will and acting in general. But let's not lose sight of the kinaesthesiae. As an active Ego – and as conscious I am always active, therefore continually affected – I am in a constant 'I move', I am 'kinetic'. It is the latter (or any originary sphere in the same perspective), which is the kinaesthesia (the problem being to determine whether kinaesthesia is foundational for all moving oneself – all subjective process).

(Husserl 2006: 320)

Along the same lines, one is tempted to confer a dimension of intentionality upon the instinctual impulse of desire as preceding voluntary action, thereby finishing up with a questionable transfer of constitutive functions to the instinctive processes of the organism:

What we should say is that the instinct effective in kinaesthesia leads right up to the constitution of the mastered system as the unity of one possible mode of access, the possibility of freely reproducing each posture ... each kinaesthetic system being an instinctive connection which can be actualized for itself.

(Ibid.: 328)

The result is an unresolved tension between kinaesthetic automatism, that aspect of the motor system which is actually operative, and the subjective, *a priori* dimension of the intentional activity and voluntary action of the Ego:

What then are these kinaesthesia in themselves and what relation is there between them and the leading acts of an I that persists right through them throughout their unfolding? Could it be that this way of understanding acts as leading kinaesthesia is not already misleading?

(Husserl: D10, 60a)[2]

Between a complete immersion of the subject and the overseeing of the kinaesthetic flux by the latter, Husserl's hesitation is patent, as shown in the following quote:

So what is the special affinity of these kinaesthetic processes to the I in its activity? ... But is the 'I' something alongside its concrete acts in the actualization of life, and can the concrete acts be thought in any other way than as a process through which something is actively produced, something that could even have passively happened of itself, and, in the end, as a core that immediately and actively moves out from itself and can be activated with equal immediacy[?]

(Husserl: D10, 62a)

In the very fact that certain kinaesthesiae are privileged as 'kinaesthesiae of the I' – which suggests that the subject surveys those kinaesthesiae from above, as it were – one notes the temptation to treat the constituting subject as self-constituting. The implied idea is that all sense giving has to originate unconditionally – and so un-motivationally – in the I itself. But if we think about the deterioration of the neurophysiological conditions of voluntary movement, we are forced to reconsider the hidden presuppositions of the theory of the kinaesthesiae of the Ego as a refuge for the self-constitution of the constituting subject. The slow movement (so-called bradykinesia) and loss of movement (akinesia) characteristic of Parkinson's disease attest to the relativity of voluntary movement with regard to an unstable equilibrium between activation and inhibition of the neuronal circuits responsible for the initiation of motor activity. This state of activation itself relates less to the auto-activity of the subject than to the final result of a series of inhibitions exerted by subcortical inhibitory interneurones upon the innervation of pyramidal neurones of the corticospinal pathways responsible for the motor command sent out to the muscles. In this condition movements are difficult to initiate because motor commands are interfered with by inhibitory internal signals. Since one cannot attribute the activation of the neuronal circuits to 'the subject', the question arises how the subject might uphold its claim to be originally constituting. In order to understand how the intentionality underlying the motor intention can actually come to grips with the motor organs, and through them with the environment, one has to recur to an endless circularity of motivational feedback loops, thereby reducing the constituting subject to redundancy. After all, surely an incarnate subject is an empirical subject, and as such remains quite incapable of upholding the claim to being the constituting instance with regard to the sense of whatever happens?

We should however be careful not to allow our understanding of the kinaesthetic theory of transcendental constitution to be dictated by an empirical model drawn from biological sciences, as if it were a matter of projecting the functioning of the motor system upon the effective behaviour of the individual. Even though it does make an important move in the direction of physiology, the kinaesthetic theory of transcendental constitution remains an explicitly phenomenological approach and, as such, one that is regulated by the norm of intentional directedness within the horizon of a relation of the subject to the world. The pathways opened up by kinaesthetic initiatives do not simply result from a clearing of the pathways of nerve conduction thanks to the alternation of muscular tension and relaxation as the organism departs from and regains its rest posture. From within the immanence of subjective experience, the only paths opened up are those that are continually cleared by a goal-orientated intentionality. Both form of percept and aim of action feature a *telos* whose ideal character is isolated from the vicissitudes of the organism's functioning. The ocular movements are orientated in such a way as to make it possible for the subject to focus on the object of interest in the most convenient way. A triviality in any other context, that a normally sighted person sees *better* than a visually impaired person is an observation worth making here.

Kinaesthetic activity cannot be reduced to the actual state of the body, whether moving or at rest. In the same way, a perceived thing cannot be reduced to its lateral presentation in the visual field. That side of a thing which is actually visible is inscribed in the intentional horizon of a continuous variety of its other aspects, anticipated in advance as possible modes of presentation, and as a function of a constant subjective-objective correlation between the field of vision and the postures and possible movements (felt from within) of the sensorial and motor organs of a subject who is both perceiving and acting. As a result, what is taken to be real acquires its sense for the subject from something that is not observable, if only because it is virtual and not actual, and comprehends all the other possible modes of presentation that might result from a change in the position of the body or of its members. The complete kinaesthetic system, including all its kinaesthetic initiatives and transitional rest postures, subjects to a transcendental schematization the sensorial material which, without the kinaesthesia in question, would be indistinguishable from a fugitive impression. It would have to figure as a sensory illusion, to the extent that the relevant impression would be withdrawn from the framework of an experience allowing for something that remains the same across the variety of its modes of presentation. So the idea is that it is the kinaesthetic system that accounts for the sense I have of seeing a thing with a rear side, and so on, since my sense of the rear side is the sense of something that I *would* experience if I moved in such-and-such ways.

That the physiological concept of kinaesthesia is integrated in the phenomenological description of subjective experience means that the world, as kinaesthetically constituted, is a fully intentional world, endowed with all the layers of sense that it can acquire for an inhabitant. As a result, the incarnation of the theory of constitution made possible by enlisting the kinaesthetic system safeguards some elements of transcendental idealism. For the sense of things is enfolded within the horizon of a world common to many subjects whose sensorial and motor equipment is taken to be variable from one to the other, proceeding as it does from an individual development and personal history, all this within limits which are also those of mutual understanding, and which include, amongst other things, those who are handicapped, not just from the standpoint of sensory experience but also from that of motricity. From here it is also possible to reach up towards the dimension of the 'Spirit' of the constituted world, inasmuch as the sense of the configurations it displays is not limited to correlations between the effective functioning of the organs of perception and the actual bodily movements of the biological individual. For this world is common to all and so cannot be conceived except as intersubjective, and so cannot be understood from the incommensurable standpoints of subjects locked up in the solipsistic prisons of their own material body, whether these organisms are physiologically functional or not.

In other words, the transcendental idealism that persists in Husserl's thinking is less Cartesian than it is Augustinian. It is not the subject dominating empirical reality from a superior stance who is the constituting subject but rather the subject 'who rises all of one piece to the call of truth' (Augustine 2009: VIII, §9).

PHENOMENON AND SYMPTOM

When I am no longer able to reach out with my hand towards something, grasp it, take hold of and manipulate it as I please; when I can no longer go up to it and walk around it; when I have lost the tempo of fluidly linked movements and tire of trying to command each elementary segment separately; when tracing out the letter I am writing blocks any anticipation of the movement needed to pass on to the next letter; when I become unable to lift my foot off the ground without freezing, then, both locomotion and the displacement of members of my body lose the familiarity, fluidity, and elegance of a gesture. My inability to take part in the movements going on all around me, to intervene appropriately in a general conversation, alienate me from the world – a condition known as *akinetic mutism*. Depressed, apathetic, nothing motivates me any more. Immobile in my chair, the world, having ceased to be the locus of my intervention, ceases even to interest me as a spectacle. The effort needed to adjust my extraocular muscles with a view to looking at people and things directly demands an expenditure of energy I am unwilling to commit. My four limbs paralyzed in a hypertonic contraction, my life remains fixed in a 'now' lacking any protentional horizon. Disarmed by the arrival of anything unknown, I anxiously hold on to an indefinitely repeated 'now'.

The contrast with phenomenology, the kingdom of sense, whose horizon takes in the *Lebenswelt*, could not be greater. Phenomena make sense at their own level: shapes, a face, a melody, a sentence, the aim of an action are all given to the perceiving and acting subject with a meaningfulness that is directly evident. On the other hand, the symptom is ambiguous even for the subject whose symptom is in question. 'What's happening to me?': loss of control over my hand, reluctance to extend my hand towards an object, difficulty in bringing my hand to my face, inability to change the constantly flexed position of my arm, an unsteady gait ... The symptoms only make sense within the etiological perspective of the doctor, who explains what the patient says in terms of underlying causal mechanisms. A given set of symptoms may only make sense in the framework of a syndrome without any other unity to hold them together except that of characterizing the majority of observed cases. As an emphasis on the fuzziness of that condition, let's only remember that diagnosing Parkinson's disease, for example, can never be more selective than the detection of a 'Parkinsonian syndrome', covering similar behavioural traits whose pathologies may be quite different.

A paradoxical relation obtains between the subjective aspect of the description of experience given by the patient and the medical typology of the expression in terms of symptoms of underlying causes of dysfunction. Afar from the solitary drama of a self betrayed by itself in its frustrating, because ineffectual, efforts to make movements; the identification of symptoms adopts the detour of medical statistics on numerous patients selected on the basis of the usual diagnostic questionnaires. Husserl tells that our subjective certainty of the coexistence of the *Lebenswelt* and of our own body is *apodictic*. For it functions as the continuous background against which the coherence of appearances constantly gets re-established in the further course of experience, in spite of any locally encountered disruption. Cut off from this ground of certainty, the interpretation of symptoms across the detour of a medical hermeneutics moves in the sphere of the probable, relying on the fact that the body of subjects considered remains sufficiently representative with regard to the usual statistical criteria. But even the experts recognize that these routine thresholds of significance afford no guarantee for the possibility of reproducing the published results (Johnson 2013; Ioannidis 2005). A symptom only makes sense if it is rooted in a multidimensional representational substrate-space whose dimensions have to be differentiated empirically – by comparing competing scales of measurement, reflecting the different aspects of the illness, and the possible approaches – but which also reflect the sociological spectrum of the institutions who promote these scales of measurement.[3]

After 200 years of diagnosis and fifty years of treating Parkinson's disease, the relevant nosological category has still not acquired the strict definition of a Fregean concept, without, for all that, collapsing into a Wittgensteinian family resemblance. Taken as an 'umbrella concept', its extension is stretched between regrouping and/or dividing tendencies and so raises the question: 'What is Parkinson's?' (Jenner 2013). The symptoms only have the approximate unity of a flexible whole distributed across time. Ranging over varying degrees of gravity and successive steps in the development of the disease, the traits in common between Parkinson's, Lewy body dementia and Alzheimer's disease argue in favour of the existence of a continuum of degenerative neuropathologies running from Parkinson's to Alzheimer's, without excluding the possibility of an accumulation of the pathologies with age. Not all cases present all the symptoms, even those most representative of the disease, if not of its gravity (the trembling at rest at the root of its description as *shaking palsy* or *paralysis agitans* by James Parkinson (1817)). While traditional clinical classifications talk of a disorder that is basically motor, further progress in research now tends to classify it with neuropsychiatry. The animal taken as a model (transgenetic mouse) does not exhibit the behavioural symptoms of the Parkinson's shown by humans. The usual remedy – doses of dopamine, a provisional palliative without protective implications for the neurones – does improve bradykinesia for a while, but ends up causing abnormal movements (*dyskinesia*) and hallucinations, and is unable to stop, or even slow down, the deterioration of neurones. Kinesitherapy, finally, relies on brain plasticity. But by the time the disease takes hold, brain plasticity has perhaps already reached its limits. The late appearance of motor symptoms in the evolution of the disease might just be recording the exhaustion of the resources upon which neurones of parallel motor circuits of a brain deprived of dopamine afferents relied to draw the energy needed to compensate the deficit over the asymptomatic period of time.

In sum, the occurrence of a symptom diminishes subjects' capabilities to make sense of their own experiences. Nevertheless and even while recognizing the opacity it introduces into experience, the symptom, in its turn, retains an intermediary status between phenomenology and mechanism, one which indicates that in spite of everything it still belongs on the phenomenal plane. The contrast between the divergence of the paths of research on mechanisms responsible for cellular death and the integration of symptoms within the unity of behaviour attests to a gap in explanation, and makes it difficult to discern any smooth transition from given dysfunctions of systems to such and such pathological symptoms, implying a failure in the self-confidence of an objectivity cut off from subjective experience. Between phenomenology and symptomatology, the to-and-fro might well turn out in favour of the former, by making it possible to fill the gaps in our usual thinking about the phenomena due to a disregard for pathological experience, and so to open the way to an exhaustive and systematic phenomenology extended across the borders of normality. If one does not want to have to deal with an overly idealized constituting subject, the pathologies in question, together with their motor disorders, have to be reintegrated into the kinaesthetic theory as constitutional operators. But, how is this possible, given that the symptom does not disclose – as does the phenomenon – the sources of its own significance?

CROSSING THE PHENO-ONTIC FRONTIER

'My brain', Paul Ricoeur affirmed, 'cannot be fitted into my bodily experience. It's an object of science' (Ricoeur in Changeux and Ricoeur 1998: 64). In other words, a pheno-ontical frontier separates any description developed in the light of reflective evidence and the ontic domain, in this case, that of statistics bearing on populations of individuals and hypotheses on the underlying mechanisms. Nevertheless, the explanatory narrow dependency of pathological experience on dysfunctional brain systems looks like a denial of that descriptive closure of normal experience, requiring that we try to cross one way or another this pheno-ontical frontier.

Kinaesthetic experience is the place where the physiological constraints of motivation and action are brought to conscious awareness – or rather to that horizon of feeling enveloping the attentional focus of consciousness. Ideally, an immanent description of the kinaesthetic experience would be called upon to accompany the process of motivation and realization of action in all its stages. But no one thinks of attributing to the intuition and reflection of the phenomenologist an imaginary power of insight into the underlying mechanisms. The pheno-ontic frontier is not a transparent window behind which the subject might be able to observe its own organism. And in any case, the reality of the mechanisms remains that of models under discussion in the present state of research, a condition far removed from anything like a visionary contemplation. Nevertheless, there should be an alternative to the confrontation between a Cartesianism of the subject shut up in the citadel of consciousness and an imperialism of neurosciences in search of subjective territory to take over.

But in following this route, the *a priori* character of the transcendental theory of kinaesthetic constitution will have to come to terms with certain *events* in the history of medicine: so many empirico-transcendental precipitates in the process of objectifying pathological experience. The description of shaking palsy by James Parkinson (1817), the discovery of proteinaceous inclusions in the nerve cells of patients by Franz Lewy (1912), the description of Parkinson's syndrome in accidentally intoxicated drug addicts (Langston *et al.* 1983), the discovery of a mutation of the gene α-synuclein associated with Parkinson phenotype in the genotype of an Italian family (Polymeropoulos *et al.* 1997), discoveries of this kind prolong the long shadow of Galileo, 'this revealing-concealing genius' whose intervention shattered the *Lebenswelt*, 'where the earth does not move', precipitating it onto a physico-geometrical space (Husserl 1976: §9). These are the phases of objectification of my ill-being in a world that has become too constrained, in the form of a clinical syndrome currently being explained by the dysfunctioning of mechanisms of the motor system, the causal outcome of the neurodegeneration of a brain, itself no more than a society of cells in neuronic man.

The pathology of voluntary activity represented by Parkinson's motor disorders highlights the exceptional character of the normal functioning of living beings and the uniqueness of the emergence of a sense-giving activity at the very heart of a Nature, otherwise indifferent to sense. And this because it is the multiplicity of ways in which organisms can fail to function, the greater probability of disorder and nonsense over order, which is precisely what confers value upon sense. When drawn from the resources of the kinaesthetic system of the agent, transcendental constitution prolongs 'the effort after meaning' (Barlow 1985), from cellular metabolism to behaviour. Moving in the reverse direction, complementary to that of constitution, let us embark upon the limitless descent towards those levels of organization (and risk factors of disorganization) which make it possible to envisage a constitutive role for kinaesthesia. Given the impossibility of retracing all levels distinguished by neurosciences, I will make do with two complementary approaches, the integrative neurophysiology of the motor system and molecular and cellular biology – with regard to which it should be added that the causal connection is far from having been established between the molecular alterations in nerve cells, the dysfunctioning of the motor system and the behavioural disturbances (Caviness 2014).

The causes of Parkinson's disease are multiple and their impact can be either divergent or convergent. Exogenous causes: the intoxication of addicts by an adulterated drug; the exposure of agricultural workers to herbicides and pesticides; the exposure of the population at large to environmental pollutants; cerebral traumatism and so on. Endogenous causes: the mutation of certain genes predisposes the organism to produce proteins of an abnormal kind whose toxic accumulation in nerve cells induces an irreversible process of degeneration and death. The best identified causes only take account of the most infrequent cases (Polymeropoulos 1997; Gasser 2011). For the common cases of Parkinson's known as sporadic or idiopathic, the recognition of risk factors (to the extent they are plurigenetic) will depend on further progress in sequencing the coding sequences of genes, or even on sequencing the complete genome. Regarding these heterogeneous causes, a synergy of influences is probable, but has yet to be established. Similar processes can be found in distinct pathologies (Lewy bodies in brain tissues of Parkinson's patients have their homologues in the senile amyloidal plaques found in Alzheimer's disease). What we know about the mechanisms of cell death does not explain the selective failure of the dopaminergic neurones of *substantia nigra*[4] in Parkinson's.

Classically, the brain pathways of voluntary motricity branch off on leaving the motor cortex in two ways: a pyramidal tract heading towards the spinal cord conveys motor commands to the muscles, and an extrapyramidal closed circuit goes through a series of subcortical nuclei before returning to the cortex. It is assumed that the extrapyramidal circuit controls the pyramidal activity by fostering the crossing of spinal cord inhibition by the motor command once made the selection of movement parameters. The disappearance of the regulatory function of *substantia nigra* (pars compacta) on the activity of the basal ganglia[5] brings with it an excessive inhibition of the thalamus,[6] reducing its normally reinforcing influence on motor cortex for the initiation of voluntary movements. This inhibition is brought about by an intermediary loop connecting the entry to (putamen)[7] and the exit from the basal ganglia (internal globus pallidus[8] and substantia nigra pars reticulata). There are two paths of projection to accomplish this task, one direct and excitatory and the other inhibitory and indirect (it runs across the external globus pallidus and the subthalamic nucleus).[9] From which it follows that the initiation of movements is less an originally auto-motor, positive phenomenon and more the result of equilibrium between excitatory and inhibitory pathways within a cerebral circuit too complex to remain functional for long (Delong 1990). A knowledge of the physiological constraints of motivation and action preparation is all the more welcome to the phenomenologist in that it calls his attention to the horizon of consciousness of acting, where voluntary activity meets passivity and inertia, where contrary tensions counterbalance each other until clearing the way of motor intention to the movement's target.

Focusing now on the cell level, its metabolism is regulated by a large number of interwoven circular causal loops. A disturbance in any one of these loops can be the micro-event triggering a catastrophic process of neurodegeneration leading to cellular death. As a result, the researcher is confronted with a Hitchcockian situation: a crime scenario that could be re-written almost indefinitely starting out with a number of different suspects. The cell's sources of energy are energetic molecules used for the brain functions. Their production in mitochondria,[10] intracellular organelles specialized in the process of respiration through oxido-reduction, generates toxic derivatives (calcium, free radical oxygen) that accumulating in the cells expose them to oxidative stress. The mitochondria have to be carried by motor proteins along the cell's skeleton and from the axon right up to presynaptic terminals, locus of the greatest demand for energy. But free radicals damage these cytoskeletal proteins and disturb the transfer of mitochondria, resulting in an energetic crisis threatening the cell's survival (Mattson and Liu 2002)

The gene PARK-1 expresses α-synuclein:[11] a phosphorous protein of helicoidal structure abundant in presynaptic terminals, where it performs a regulatory function on the secretion of neurotransmitters by dumping (*exocytosis*) synaptic vesicles into the synapse. The overproduction, or the mutation, of PARK-1 results in an alteration of spatial structure (aggregation or fibrillation) of the said protein in the form of Lewy bodies (Polymeropoulos 1997) and their inclusion as insoluble formations into the fluid contents (*cytoplasm*) of neurones. Moreover, the presence of α-synuclein in presynaptic terminals favours the permeability of vesicles with a leakage of dopamine in the cytoplasm, which is stressful for the neurone (Dauer and Przedborski 2003).

The infiltration of fibrillar α-synuclein of cytoplasm into the mitochondrial matrix (Hashimoto *et al.* 2003) blocks the chain of transport of electrons into mitochondria's internal membrane by inhibiting the transmembranal proteins, which normally get hydrogen ions to permeate the membrane in such a way as to re-establish the concentration in ions following upon the depolarization due to neuronal discharge. The resulting fall in electrical potential of the membrane reduces the excitability of the neurone (Mattson and Liu 2002; Dauer and Przedborski 2003).

The high excitability of the spontaneously active neurones of *substantia nigra* is maintained, thanks to the conductance (probability of being open) of ion calcium channels, transducers of membrane potential. The mitochondria control the level of intracellular calcium by interacting with organelles responsible for its secretion, the *endoplasmic reticulum*,[12] sequestrating this calcium. This regulation is under the control of other genes, whose mutations also pose a risk of Parkinson's, as they contribute to the accumulation of calcium. This dyshomeostasy of calcium results in the mitochondria losing energy (Reeves *et al.* 2014; Hirsch *et al.* 2013).

Free radicals, oxidative stress, dysfunctioning mitochondria all contribute to the aggregation of α-synuclein. The degradation of abnormal proteins through enzymes is ensured in barrel shaped organelles specialized in the elimination of waste material: the *proteasome*,[13] or in spherical organelles containing dissolving enzymes: the *lysosome*.[14] The dysfunctioning of this waste disposal system results in an accumulation of abnormal proteins in the cytoplasm, a vicious circle bringing with it neurodegeneration and cellular death (Dawson *et al.* 2010). Mimicking human society at large, doomed by its incapacity to eliminate or recycle the disposals it cannot but generate, the biology of cell metabolism emphasizes the deeply contradictory character rather than the sustainability of the living being. With such a pit of nonsense overflowing inside, it is difficult to see how it could be – what in fact it is – capable of 'making sense of' any natural or cultural environment.

PHENOMENOLOGY VINDICATED

The scientistic policy of ignoring the subject's immanental point of view over his or her own kinaesthetic experience in acting and perceiving in favour of mechanical explanations that make no reference to subjectivity left the researcher with a loss of criteria of *normality*. That this threat is serious becomes clear just as soon as we review the indices of incompatibility between rival claims advanced for the disassociation of the experience of the voluntary agent, whether normal or pathological, each of which proposes underlying mechanisms for motor behaviour. To take simply the current controversy in physiopathology on the function of basal ganglia, their role is differently interpreted depending on the laboratories: sometimes as regulator of the balance of inhibition and reinforcement in the extrapyramidal circuit (Delong 1990); sometimes as selector of a motor programme (Kreitzer and Malenka 2008); sometimes as provider of an internal reward whose lack which would lead to anhedonism (Wise 1985); sometimes as energizer of action correlate of the 'strength of will' (Salamone *et al.* 2007); sometimes as synchronizer of neuronal oscillations in the motor system preventing a non selective synchronization responsible for trembling (Wichmann *et al.* 2011); sometimes as storekeeper clearing the way for new actions once learned actions have been stored in the repertories of long term memory (Yin and Knowlton 2006); sometimes as a bottleneck of channels of cortical information, a cause of increase in local potential due to their desegregation and linkage under the effect of compression (Brown 2007: 659); sometimes as cost/benefit estimator of the energy required by the movement, eventually resulting in a 'decision' of slowing down in bradykinesia (Mazzoni *et al.* 2007). And so on, and so forth.

This does not mean that it would be enough to simply pay attention to lived experience to be in a position to determine the functions of the basal ganglia. Rather, it means that the discovery of a functional interpretation able to integrate the different models currently competing is likely to take more years of research. Alternatively our ideas of action and perception are simply condemned to remain without any determinate correlates at the cerebral level, inasmuch as the investigation of substructures of the isolated brain fails to provide any access to the holistic characteristics of the kinaesthetic interaction between an acting subject and the *Lebenswelt*.

From the foregoing, it appears that the functional normality of the totality of subsystems of a living creature definitely is a transcendental idea. There is no *a priori* necessity that the interaction between elements of the organism, reduced to its physico-chemical composition, suffices to keep movement going in the interval between hypokinesia and hyperkinesia, and so across the life-time of the individual. It might well be possible to postulate a law of evolution (still to be discovered (Berthoz and Petit 2014; Berthoz 2009)) according to which a living creature does not get drowned in the complexity of its all too numerous, and all too entangled, anatomical circuits and functions, in spite of the length, the slowness, and the intricate pathways of communication of information in the restricted space of the skull. But a rational reformulation of the teleology implicit in the normal functioning of living beings can best be worked out with reference to the idea of *kinaesthesia* enabling us to understand life in the light of the sense it brings to the world through its own activity.

To recapitulate: normal functionality is that mode of action of the kinaesthetic system of an organism allowing permanent things to appear in its environment, the organism in question being, for itself, an animate body among other such bodies, all these things – along with the un-thinglike things that other subjects are – belonging together within a common world. Such normality is not determined (or not exclusively) at the level of the functional mechanism's underlying behaviour. For, from a strictly mechanistic point of view, such 'normal' functioning has no reason to be preferred to malfunctioning. It is only from the point of view of the living creature itself, as perceiving and acting subject standing in relation to a lifeworld sufficiently stable to support a lastingly congruent experience, that one can talk about and define functional norms for biological mechanisms. Behaviour – as not reducible to its observable and measurable external aspects – has to be apprehended originally in its lived dimension. Behaviour, which culminates in the field of the conscious experience of the subject in the domain of its practical intervention, remains the sole criterion as soon as one refuses to be satisfied with an apologetic teleology disguised as a law of natural evolution. With regard to the functionality of the mechanisms postulated in the explanation, lived experience, through its phenomenological description, remains the norm. For the latter raises to the level of explicit expression the *a priori* hidden in normal physiology.

So it would be naive, or at least premature, to claim that the knowledge acquired by research into the causes of motor neurodegeneration could not only supplement but even supplant, the phenomenology of behaviour. Whatever the functional limitations due to the anomalies might be, as long as it is still possible to execute actions, a set of conditions are still available, whose reflective examination will bring to light the transcendental structures of the experience of the free and voluntary agent. No matter how revealing of the nature of human action it might be, the *dexterity* of movements in athletes or craftsmen (Bernstein 1996) simply exemplifies the optimal realization of a more fundamental structure of all living beings, therefore equally applicable to those suffering from deficient modalities. Acting, doing, being able, wanting, deciding, trying, realizing, and so on, all these concepts of action bring to verbal expression a *cogito* of the acting subject, which is not simply the pole of virtual reference of the semantic apparatus of discourse, no matter how under-determined it might appear to be from the physiological standpoint. To the extent that it covers the practical field of intentions, goals, and means of the agent, my voluntary act initiates a causal chain which is, in a certain sense, quite new, without this novelty standing in the way of an explanation in terms of underlying causal circuits. Trusting or not my ability to do, I aim at goals across kinaesthetic pathways made occasionally difficult by obstacles, or handicaps, or as prescribed by the internal articulation of the objects to be constituted. 'Not only is the whole world held within that horizon led by my kinaesthetic activities,' Husserl emphasizes, 'but even though I am actually hindered by paralysis or any physical restraint, that does not prevent a world of surrounding things appearing, things which are in principle accessible to me' (Husserl: D3, 9b).[15]

NOTES

1 Translation by Christopher Macann.
2 Quoted with permission from the Husserl Archives Leuven.
3 *NMSS*: Non-Motor Symptoms Scale in Parkinson's disease; *CISI-PD*: Clinical Impression of Severity Index for Parkinson's Disease; *SCOPA-M*: Scales for Outcomes in Parkinson's Disease – Motor; *UPDRS*: Unified Parkinson's Disease Rating Scale; *PDQ-39*: Parkinson's Disease Quality of Life Questionnaire, and so on.
4 *Substantia nigra*: midbrain structure, its *pars compacta* contains dopaminergic neurons whose death shortens the supply of dopamine neurotransmitter, a cause of motor dysfunction that characterizes Parkinson's disease.
5 *Basal ganglia*: subcortical nuclei at the basis of forebrain, the release of their continuous inhibitory influence on motor systems of the cortex makes possible the selection and switching of the motor programmes of behaviour.
6 *Thalamus*: pair of central brain nuclei, a relay of sensory and motor signals between cortex and the body.
7 *Putamen*: nucleus of basal ganglia with projections to *substantia nigra*, a regulator of movements and learning.
8 *Globus pallidus*: nucleus of basal ganglia, regulator of voluntary movements through inhibition of thalamus.
9 *Subthalamic nucleus*: nucleus of basal ganglia, a central pacemaker implied in tremor and control of impulse.
10 *Mitochondria*: intracellular organelles, powerplants of the metabolism of neurones.
11 *α-synuclein*: neuronal protein regulator of dopamine supply and release. Parkinson's is a synucleinopathy.
12 *Endoplasmic reticulum*: network-like intracellular organelle important for the proteins properly folding and transport and the level of calcium regulation in the cell.
13 *Proteasome*: intracellular complex protein dedicated to the enzymatic degradation of damaged cell proteins.
14 *Lysosome*: enzyme containing vesicular intracellular organelle, another powerful waste disposal of the cell.
15 Quoted with permission from the Husserl Archives Leuven. The ability to form motor intentions would be retained in cases of paralysis through spinal lesion: when imagining manual movements (touching its nose or its mouth) a tetraplegic patient can induce in its posterior parietal cortex patterns of neuronal activity coding the goal and the trajectory, thereby enabling it to realize the willed movement through robotic prostheses (see Aflalo *et al.* 2015).

BIBLIOGRAPHY

Ackerman, F. 1992. 'Does Philosophy Only State What Everyone Admits? Discussion of the Method of Wittgenstein's *Philosophical Investigations*', *Midwest Studies in Philosophy* 27, 246–54.

Adorno, T. W. 1951. *Minima Moralia*. Frankfurt a.M.: Suhrkamp [trans. E. F. N. Jephcott. London: NLB, 1974].

Adorno, T. W. 1966. *Negative Dialektik*, Frankfurt a.M.: Suhrkamp [trans. as *Negative Dialectics*, by E. B. Ashton, London: Routledge and Kegan Paul, 1973]. Alternative translation, by D. Redmond, available online: www.efn.org/~dredmond/ndtrans.html; last accessed 22 August 2011.

Adorno, T. W. 1977. 'The Actuality of Philosophy'[1931], *Telos* 10 (1) 120–33.

Adorno, T. W. 1984. 'Essay as Form', trans. B. Hullot-Kentor and F. Will, *New German Critique* 32, 151–71.

Adorno, T. W. 1998. 'Why Still Philosophy'['Wozu noch Philosophie', 1963], trans. H. W. Pickford in *Critical Models*. New York: Columbia University Press, 5–17.

Aflalo, T. *et al.* 2015. 'Decoding Motor Imagery from the Posterior Parietal Cortex of a Tetraplegic Human', *Science* 348 (6237), 906–10.

Alcock, J. 2013. *Animal Behavior: An Evolutionary Approach*, 10th edn. Sunderland, MA: Sinauer Associates.

Alexander, J. 2012. *Experimental Philosophy: An Introduction*. Cambridge: Polity Press.

Alexander, J. 2016. 'Philosophical Expertise', in *A Companion to Experimental Philosophy*, eds J. Systma and W. Buckwalter. Oxford: Wiley-Blackwell, 555–67.

Alexander, J., and J. Weinberg 2007. 'Analytic Epistemology and Experimental Philosophy', *Philosophy Compass* 2, 56–80.

Alexander, J., and J. Weinberg 2014. 'The "Unreliability" of Epistemic Intuitions', in *Current Controversies in Experimental Philosophy*, eds E. Machery and E. O'Neill. Abingdon and New York: Routledge, 128–44.

Allen, A. 2016. *The End of Progress: Decolonizing the Normative Foundations of Critical Theory*. New York: Columbia University Press.

Anderson, J. 2011. 'Situating Axel Honneth in the Frankfurt School Tradition', in *Axel Honneth: Critical Essays*, ed. D. Petherbridge. Leiden: Brill Academic Publishers, 31–58.

Andrews, K. 2015. *The Animal Mind*. Abingdon: Routledge.

Apel, K.-O. 1997. 'Regulative Ideas or Truth-Happening? An Attempt to Answer the Question of the Conditions of Possibility of Valid Understanding', trans. R. Sommermeier, in *The Philosophy of Hans-Georg Gadamer*, ed. L. E. Hahn. Chicago: Open Court, 67–95.

Aristotle 1955. *Aristotelis Fragmenta Selecta*, ed. W. D. Ross. Oxford: Clarendon Press.

Augustine 2009. *Confessions*, ed. and trans. P. de Labriolle, Paris : Les Belles Lettres.

Austin, J. L. 1962. *Sense and Sensibilia*. London: Oxford University Press.

Austin, J. L. 1970. *Philosophical Papers*, 2nd edn. Oxford University Press.

Ayer, A. J. 1952. *Language, Truth and Logic*. New York: Dover.

Ayer, A. J. 1956. *The Problem of Knowledge*, London: Macmillan.

Baddeley, A., M. W. Eysenck, and M. C. Anderson 2009. *Memory*. Hove and New York: Psychology Press.

Baggott, J. M. D., and M. Duff 2013. 'A Theory of Everything ... Has Physics Gone Too Far?' *The Guardian*, 16 June 2013. Online: www.theguardian.com/science/2013/jun/16/has-physics-gone-too-far

Baker, L. R. 2000. *Persons and Bodies: A Constitution View*. Cambridge University Press.

Baker, L. R. 2012. *Naturalism and the First-person Perspective*. Oxford University Press.

Barlow, H. B. 1985. 'The Role of Single Neurons in the Psychology of Perception', *The Quarterly Journal of Experimental Psychology* 37A, 121–45.

Barnes, B. 1977. *Interests and the Growth of Knowledge*. London: Routledge.

Bealer, G. 1998. 'Intuition and the Autonomy of Philosophy', in *Rethinking Intuition: The Psychology of Intuition and its Role in Philosophical Theorizing*, eds M. DePaul and W. Ramsey. Lanham, MD: Rowman and Littlefield, 201–39.

Bealer, G. 1998. 'Intuition and the Autonomy of Philosophy', in *Rethinking Intuition*, eds M. DePaul and W. Ramsey. Rowman and Littlefield, 201–40.

Beebe, J., and J. Shea 2013. 'Gettierized Knobe Effects', *Episteme* 10, 219–40.

Beiser, F. C. 1992. *Enlightenment, Revolution, and Romanticism: The Genesis of Modern German Political Thought, 1790–1800*. Cambridge, MA: Harvard University Press.

Bell, J., A. Cutrofello, and P. Livingston (eds) 2015a. *Beyond the Analytic–Continental Divide: Pluralist Philosophy in the Twenty-First Century*. London: Routledge.

Bell, J., A. Cutrofello, and P. Livingston 2015b. 'Introduction: Contemporary Philosophy as Synthetic Philosophy', in *Beyond the*

Analytic–Continental Divide, eds J. Bell, C. Cutrofello, and P. Livingston. London: Routledge, 1–13.

Bengson, John. 2013. 'Experimental Attacks on Intuitions and Answers', *Philosophy and Phenomenological Research* 86 (3), 495–532.

Bennett. K. 2009. 'Composition, Colocation and Metaontology', in *Metametaphysics*, eds D. J. Chalmers, D. Manley, and R. Wasserman. Oxford University Press, 38–76.

Bennett, K. 2015. 'There is No Special Problem with Metaphysics', *Philosophical Studies*. DOI 10.1007/s11098-014-0439-0.

Bennett, M. R., and P. M. S. Hacker 2003. *Philosophical Foundations of Neuroscience*. Oxford: Blackwell.

Bergson, H. 1977. *The Two Sources of Morality and Religion*, trans. R. A. Audra and C. Brereton, with the assistance of W. H. Carter. Notre Dame, IN: University of Notre Dame Press.

Bergson, H. 1992. *The Creative Mind*, trans. M. L. Andison. New York: The Citadel Press.

Bergson, H. 2007. *Mind-Energy*, trans. H. Wildon Carr. New York: Palgrave Macmillan.

Berlin, I. 2000. *Three Critics of the Enlightenment: Vico, Hamann, Herder*, ed. H. Hardy. Princeton University Press.

Bernet, R., I. Kern, and E. Marbach 1993. *An Introduction to Husserlian Phenomenology*. Evanston: Northwestern University Press.

Bernstein, N. 1996. 'On Dexterity and Its Development', in *Dexterity and Its Development*, eds M. L. Latash and M. T. Turvey. Mahwah, NJ: Lawrence Erlbaum Associates.

Bernstein, R. J. 1983. *Beyond Objectivism and Relativism: Science, Hermeneutics, and Practice*. Philadelphia: University of Pennsylvania Press.

Berthoz, A. 2009. *La Simplexité*. Paris: Odile Jacob.

Berthoz, A., and J.-L. Petit (eds) 2014. *Complexité-Simplexité*. Paris: Collège de France.

Bertram, C. 2012. 'Jean Jacques Rousseau', *The Stanford Encyclopedia of Philosophy* (Winter 2012 Edition), ed. E. N. Zalta, available online at URL = <http://plato.stanford.edu/archives/win2012/entries/rousseau/>.

Bird, A. 2010. 'Social Knowing: The Social Sense of "Scientific Knowledge"', *Philosophical Perspectives* 24 (1), 23–56.

Blackburn, S. 1993. 'Review of Paul Johnston's Wittgenstein and Moral Philosophy', *Ethics* 103, 588–90.

Blattner, W. D. 2000. 'Life Is Not Literature', in *The Many Faces of Time*, eds J. B. Brough and L. E. Embree. Dordrecht: Kluwer, 187–201.

Boas, F. 1989. 'The History of Anthropology', in *A Franz Boas Reader*. The University of Chicago Press, 23–36.

Bogen, J., and J. Woodward 1988. 'Saving the Phenomena', *Philosophical Review*, 97, 303–52.

Boghossian, P. 1996. 'Analyticity Reconsidered', *Nous* 30 (3), 360–91.

Bollacher, M. 1987. '"Natur" und "Vernunft" in Herders Entwurf einer Philosophie der Geschichte der Menschheit', in *Johann Gottfried Herder 1744–1803*, ed. Gerhard Sauder. Hamburg: Felix Meiner, 114–24.

BonJour, L. 1998. *In Defense of Pure Reason*. Cambridge University Press.

Bookchin, M. 1995. *Social Anarchism or Lifestyle Anarchism*, available online at URL = <http://dwardmac.pitzer.edu/Anarchist_Archives/bookchin/soclife.htm>.

Bourget, D., and D. J. Chalmers 2014. 'What do Philosophers Believe?', *Philosophical Studies* 170 (3), 465–500.

Boyd, K., and J. Nagel 2014. 'The Reliability of Epistemic Intuitions', in *Current Controversies in Experimental Philosophy*, eds E. Machery and E. O'Neill. Abingdon and New York: Routledge, 109–27.

Bradley, F. H. 1897. *Appearance and Reality*, 2nd edn. Oxford: Clarendon Press.

Brandom, R. 1994. *Making It Explicit: Reasoning, Representing, and Discursive Commitment*. Cambridge, MA: Harvard University Press.

Brandom, R. B. 2011. *Perspectives on Pragmatism*. Cambridge, MA: Harvard University Press.

Braver, L. 2007. *A Thing of This World: A History of Continental Anti-Realism*. Evanston: Northwestern University Press.

Bricker, P. forthcoming. 'Realism without Parochialism', in *Modal Matters: Essays in Metaphysics*. Oxford University Press.

Brown, P. 2007. 'Abnormal Oscillatory Synchronization in the Motor System Leads to Impaired Movement', *Current Opinion in Neurobiology* 17, 656–64.

Brudney, D. 1998. *Marx's Attempt to Leave Philosophy*. Cambridge, MA: Harvard University Press.

Buck-Morss, S. 1977. *The Origin of Negative Dialectics: Theodor W. Adorno, Walter Benjamin, and the Frankfurt School*. Hassocks, Sussex: Harvester Press.

Buckwalter, W. forthcoming. 'Epistemic Contextualism and Linguistic Behavior', in *The Routledge Handbook of Epistemic Contextualism*, ed. J. Ichikawa. Abingdon: Routledge.

Bultmann, C. 1999. *Die biblische Urgeschichte in der Aufklärung. Johann Gottfried Herders Interpretation der Genesis als Antwort auf die Religionskritik David Humes*. Tübingen: Mohr Siebeck.

Burgess, A., and D. Plunkett 2013a. 'Conceptual Ethics I', *Philosophy Compass* 8 (12), 1091–101.

Burgess, A., and D. Plunkett 2013b. 'Conceptual Ethics II', *Philosophy Compass* 8 (12), 1102–10.

Burke, T. F. 2013. *What Pragmatism Was*. Bloomington: University of Indiana Press.

Cappelen, H. 2011. 'Against Assertion', in *Assertion: New Philosophical Essays*, eds J. Brown and H. Cappelen. Oxford University Press, 21–48.

Cappelen, H., and J. Dever 2013. *The Inessential Indexical: On the Philosophical Insignificance of Perspective and the First Person*. Oxford University Press.

Cardwell, M. 1996. *Dictionary of Psychology*. Chicago: Fitzroy Dearborn.

Carnap, R. 1950. 'Empiricism, Semantics and Ontology', *Revue Internationale de Philosophie* 4 (2), 20–40.

Carnap, R. 1956a. *Meaning and Necessity*, 2nd edn. University of Chicago Press.

Carnap, R. 1956b. 'Empiricism, Semantics, and Ontology' [1950]. Reprinted in *Meaning and Necessity*, 2nd edn. University of Chicago Press, 205–21.

Carruthers, P. 2011. *The Opacity of Mind*. Oxford University Press.

Carus, A. W. 2007. 'Carnap's Intellectual Development', in *The Cambridge Companion to Carnap*, eds M. Friedman and R. Creath. Cambridge University Press, 19–42.

Cassirer, E. 1961. *Freiheit und Form. Studien zur deutschen Geistesgeschichte*. Darmstadt: Wissenschaftliche Buchgesellschaft.

Cavell, S. 1969. *Must We Mean What We Say*. Cambridge University Press.

Cavell, S. 1979. *The Claim of Reason: Wittgenstein, Skepticism, Morality, and Tragedy*. Oxford University Press.

Cavell, S. 2002. *Must We Mean What We Say? A Book of Essays*, updated edn. Cambridge University Press.

Caviness, J. N. 2014. 'Pathophysiology of Parkinson's Disease Behaviour – a View from the Network', *Parkinsonism and Related Disorders* 20 (Suppl. 1), S39–S43.

Cerbone, D. R. 2003. 'Distance and Proximity in Phenomenology: Husserl and Heidegger', *The New Yearbook for Phenomenology and Phenomenological Philosophy* III, 1–26.

Cerbone, D. R. forthcoming. 'Making Sense of Phenomenological Sense-Making: On Moore on Husserl', in *Philosophical Topics*.

Chalmers, D. J. 2011. 'Verbal Disputes', *Philosophical Review* 120 (4), 515–66.

Chalmers, D. J. 2012. *Constructing the World*. Oxford University Press.

Chalmers, D. J. 2015. 'Why Isn't there More Progress in Philosophy?', *Philosophy* 90 (1), 3–31.

Chalmers, D. J., and F. Jackson 2001. 'Conceptual Analysis and Reductive Explanation', *Philosophical Review* 110 (3), 315–60.

Chalmers, D., D. Manley, and R. Wasserman (eds) 2009. *Metametaphysics*. Oxford and New York: Oxford University Press.

Chang, J. 1993. *Wild Swans: Three Daughters of China*. London: Flamingo.

Changeux, J.-P., and P. Ricoeur 1998. *Ce qui nous fait penser. La nature et la règle*. Paris: Odile Jacob.

Chase, J., and J. Reynolds 2011. *Analytic versus Continental: Arguments on the Methods and Value of Philosophy*. Durham: Acumen.

Cheney, D. L., and R. M. Seyfarth 2007. *Baboon Metaphysics*. University of Chicago Press.

Chisholm, R. 1989. *Theory of Knowledge*, 3rd edn. Englewood Cliffs, NJ: Prentice-Hall.

Chomsky, N. 1957. *Syntactic Structures*. Amsterdam: Mouton.

Chroust, A.-H. 1969. *Aristotle, Protrepicus: A Reconstruction*. Notre Dame, IN: University of Notre Dame Press.

Clark, R. T. 1955. *Herder: His Life and Thought*. Berkeley: University of California Press.

Clarke, D. 2012. 'Blaise Pascal', *The Stanford Encyclopedia of Philosophy* (Fall 2012 Edition), ed. E. N. Zalta, available online at URL = <http://plato.stanford.edu/archives/fall2012/entries/pascal/>.

Cohen, H. 1904. *Ethik des reinen Willens*. Berlin: Bruno Cassirer.

Collingwood, R. G. 1993. *The Idea of History* [1946]. Revised edition, with an introduction by J. Van der Dussen. Oxford University Press.

Collingwood, R. G. 1998a. *An Essay on Metaphysics with an Introduction and Additional Material*, ed. R. Martin. Oxford University Press.

Collingwood, R. G. 1998b. *An Essay on Metaphysics* [1940]. Revised edition with an introduction by R. Martin. Oxford University Press.

Collingwood, R. G. 1999. *The Principles of History*, eds W. H. Dray and Jan Van der Dussen. Oxford University Press.

Collingwood, R. G. 2005a. *An Essay on Philosophical Method with an Introduction and Additional Material*, eds J. Connolly and G. D'Oro. Oxford University Press.

Collingwood, R. G. 2005b. *An Essay on Philosophical Method* [1933]. Revised edition with an introduction by J. Connelly and G. D'Oro. Oxford University Press.

Conant, J. B. (ed.) 1950. *The Overthrow of the Phlogiston Theory: The Chemical Revolution of 1775–1789*. Cambridge, MA: Harvard University Press.

Cook, D. 2011. *Adorno on Nature*. Durham, UK: Acumen.

Crowell, S. G. 1999. 'Spectral History: Narrative, Nostalgia, and the Time of the I', *Research in Phenomenology* 29, 83–104.

Crowell, S. G. 2001a. 'Question, Reflection, and Philosophical Method in Heidegger's Early Freiburg Lectures', in his *Husserl, Heidegger, and the Space of Meaning*. Evanston: Northwestern University Press, 129–51.

Crowell, S. G. 2001b. 'Gnostic Phenomenology: Eugen Fink and the Critique of Transcendental Reason', in his *Husserl, Heidegger, and the Space of Meaning*. Evanston: Northwestern University Press, 244–63.

Crowell, S. (ed.) 2012. *The Cambridge Companion to Existentialism*. Cambridge University Press.

Curley, E. 1996. 'Kissinger, Spinoza and Genghis Khan', in *The Cambridge Companion to Spinoza*, ed. D. Garrett. Cambridge University Press, 315–82.

Dahlstrom, D. 1994. 'Heidegger's Method: Philosophical Concepts as Formal Indications', *The Review of Metaphysics* 47, 775–95.

Dauer, W., and S. Przedborski 2003. 'Parkinson's Disease: Mechanisms and Models', *Neuron* 39, 889–909.

Davies, D. 2004. *Art as Performance*. Oxford: Blackwell.

Dawson, T. M. *et al.* 2010. 'Genetic Animal Models of Parkinson's Disease', *Neuron* 66, 646–61.

de Beauvoir, S. 1976. *The Prime of Life*, trans. P. Green. New York: Harper & Row.

Deleuze, G. 1990. *Logic of Sense*, trans. M. Lester with C. Stivale, ed. C. Boundas. New York: Columbia University Press.

Deleuze, G. 1991a. *Empiricism and Subjectivity: An Essay on Hume's Theory of Human Nature*, trans. C. V. Boundas. New York: Columbia University Press.

Deleuze, G. 1991b. *Bergsonism*, trans. H. Tomlinson and B. Habberjam. New York: Zone Books.

Deleuze, G. 1994. *Difference and Repetition*, trans. P. Patton. New York: Columbia University Press.

Deleuze, G. 1995. *Difference and Repetition*. New York: Columbia University Press.

Deleuze, G., and F. Guattari 1987. *Capitalism and Schizophrenia, Vol. 2: A Thousand Plateaus*, trans. B. Massumi. London: Continuum.

Deleuze G., and F. Guattari 1987. *A Thousand Plateaus*, trans. B. Massumi. Minneapolis: University of Minnesota Press.

Deleuze, G., and F. Guattari 1994. *What is Philosophy?*, trans. Hugh Tomlinson and Graham Burchill. London: Verso.

Delong, M. R. 1990. 'Primate Models of Movement Disorders of Basal Ganglia Origin', *Trends in Neurosciences* 13 (7), 281–5.

Dennett, D. C. 1971. 'Intentional Systems', *Journal of Philosophy* 68 (4), 87–106.

Dennett, D. 1991. *Consciousness Explained*. New York: Little, Brown and Co.

Derrida, J. 1981. *Positions*, trans. A. Bass. University of Chicago Press.

Derrida, J. 1982. *Margins of Philosophy*, trans. A. Bass. University of Chicago Press.

Derrida, J. 1992. 'Force of Law: The Mystical Foundation of Authority', trans. M. Quaintance, in *Deconstruction and the Possibility of Justice*, eds D. Cornell, M. Rosenfeld, and D. G. Carlson. New York: Routledge, 3–67.

Derrida, J. 1993. *Aporias*, trans. T. Dutoit. Stanford University Press.

Derrida, J. 1994. *Specters of Marx*, trans. P. Kamuf. New York: Routledge.

Derrida, J. 1997a. *Politics of Friendship*, trans. G. Collins. London: Verso.

Derrida, J. 1997b. *Of Grammatology*, corrected edn, trans. G. Spivak. Baltimore: The Johns Hopkins University Press.

Derrida, J. 2000. 'Et Cetera', in *Deconstructions: a User's Guide*, ed. Nicholas Royle. New York: Palgrave, 282–303.

Derrida, J. 2001. *A Taste for the Secret*, trans. G. Donis. London: Polity Press.

Derrida, J. 2005. *Sovereignties in Question: The Poetics of Paul Celan*. New York: Fordham University Press.

Derrida, J. 2011. *Voice and Phenomenon*, trans. L. Lawlor. Evanston: Northwestern University Press.

Descartes, R. 1993. *Meditations on First Philosophy*, trans. D. Cress. Indianapolis: Hackett Publishing Company.

DeSouza, N. 2012. 'Leibniz in the Eighteenth Century: Herder's Critical Reflections on the Principles of Nature and Grace', *The British Journal for the History of Philosophy* 20 (4), 773–95.

Devitt, M. 2010. *Putting Metaphysics First*. Oxford University Press.

Dewey, J. 1969–91. *The Collected Works of John Dewey: The Early Works, The Middle Works, The Later Works*, 37 vols, ed. J. A. Boydston. Carbondale: Southern Illinois University Press.

Dietrich, E. 2010. 'There Is No Progress in Philosophy', *Essays in Philosophy* 12, (2), 9.

Dillon, R. S. 2007. 'Arrogance, Self-Respect and Personhood', *Journal of Consciousness Studies* 14 (5-1), 101–26.

Dilthey, W. 1914–. *Gesammelte Schriften*, 26 vols. Göttingen: Vandenhoeck and Ruprecht.

Dilthey, W. 1985. 'Three Epochs of Modern Aesthetics', trans. Michael Neville, in *Selected Works*, eds R. Makkreel and F. Rodi, vol. V, *Poetry and Experience*. Princeton University Press, 175–222.

Dilthey, W. 1996. *Selected Works*, eds R. A. Makkreel and F. Rodi, vol. IV, *Hermeneutics and the Study of History*, trans. T. Nordenhaug *et al.* Princeton University Press.

Doris, J., and the Moral Psychology Research Group (eds) 2010. *The Moral Psychology Handbook*. Oxford University Press.

D'Oro, G. 2002. *Collingwood and the Metaphysics of Experience*. London and New York: Routledge.

D'Oro G. 2011. 'Davidson and the Autonomy of the Human Sciences', in *Dialogues with Davidson: New Perspectives on his Philosophy*, ed. J. Malpas. MIT Press, 283–96.

D'Oro, G. 2012. 'Reasons and Causes: the Philosophical Battle and the Meta-philosophical War', *Australasian Journal of Philosophy* 90 (2), 207–21.

D'Oro, G. 2015. 'Unlikely Bedfellows? 'Collingwood, Carnap and the Internal/External Distinction', *British Journal for the History of Philosophy* 23 (4), 802–17.

D'Oro, G., and C. Sandis 2013. 'From Anti-Causalism to Causalism and Back' in *Reasons and Causes: Causalism and Anti-Causalism in The Philosophy of Action*, eds G. D'Oro and C. Sandis. Basingstoke: Palgrave Macmillan, 7–48.

Douven, I. 2011. 'Abduction', in *The Stanford Encyclopedia of Philosophy* (Spring 2011 Edition), ed. E. N. Zalta, available online at URL = <http://plato.stanford.edu/archives/spr2011/entries/abduction/>.

Dray, W. H. 1957. *Laws and Explanation in History*. London: Oxford University Press.

Dray, W. H. 1963. 'The Historical Explanation of Actions Reconsidered', in *Philosophy and History*, ed. S. Hook. New York University Press, 105–35.

Drummond, J. 2007. 'Personal Perspectives', *The Southern Journal of Philosophy* 45 (1), 28–44.

Dummett, M. 1978. 'Can Analytical Philosophy Be Systematic, and Ought It to Be?'[1975] reprinted in his *Truth and Other Enigmas*. Cambridge, MA: Harvard University Press, 437[3n]58.

Dupré, J. 2002. *Humans and Other Animals*. Oxford University Press.

Eichenbaum, H. 2008. *Learning and Memory*. New York: Norton.

Einstein, A. 1950. 'On the Generalized Theory of Relativity', *Scientific American* 182 (4), 13–17.

Eklund, M. 2013. 'Carnap's Metaontology', *Nous* 47 (2), 229–49.

Eklund, M. 2015. 'Intuitions, Conceptual Engineering, and Conceptual Fixed Points', in *Palgrave Handbook of Philosophical Methods*, ed. C. Daly. Basingstoke: Palgrave Macmillan, 363–85.

Feltz, A., and E. Cokely 2009. 'Do Judgments about Freedom and Responsibility Depend on Who You Are? Personality Differences in Intuitions about Compatibilism and Incompatibilism', *Consciousness and Cognition* 18 (1), 342–50.

Feyerabend, P. 1975. *Against Method: Outline of an Anarchistic Theory of Knowledge*. London: Verso.

Fink, E. 1970. 'The Phenomenological Philosophy of Edmund Husserl and Contemporary Criticism', in *The Phenomenology of Husserl*, ed. R. O. Elveton. Chicago: Quadrangle Books, 73–147.

Fink, E. 1995. *Sixth Cartesian Meditation: The Idea of a Transcendental Theory of Method*, trans. R. Bruzina. Bloomington: Indiana University Press.

Finlayson, J. G. 2002. 'Adorno on the Ethical and the Ineffable', *European Journal of Philosophy* 10 (1), 1–25.

Fischer, E., P. E. Engelhardt, and A. Herbelot 2015. 'Intuitions and Illusions: From Explanation and Experiment to Assessment', in *Experimental Philosophy, Rationalism, and Naturalism*, eds E. Fischer and J. Collins. London: Routledge, 259–92.

Fleischacker, S. 2013. *What is Enlightenment?* London: Routledge.

Fodor, J. A. 2003. *Hume Variations*. Oxford University Press.

Forst, R. 2015. *Normativität und Macht. Zur Analyse sozialer Rechtfertigungsordnungen*. Berlin: Suhrkamp.

Forster, M. N. 2010. *After Herder: Philosophy of Language in the German Tradition*. Oxford University Press.

Forster, P. 2011. *Peirce and the Threat of Nominalism*. New York: Oxford University Press.

Foucault, M. 1965. *Madness and Civilization*, trans. R. Howard. New York: Vintage Books.

Foucault, M. 1994. 'What Is Enlightenment?'[1984] in *The Foucault Reader*, ed. P. Rabinow. New York: Pantheon, 32–50.

Foucault, M. 2001. *The Order of Things: An Archaeology of the Human Sciences*, trans. A. Sheridan. London: Routledge.

Frances, B. forthcoming. 'The Epistemically Troubling Philosophical Survey'.

Frank, M. 1977. *Das individuelle Allgemeine*. Frankfurt am Main: Suhrkamp Verlag.

Fraser, N. 1989. *Unruly Practices: Power, Discourse and Gender in Contemporary Social Theory*. Minneapolis: University of Minnesota Press.

Frazer, M. L. 2010. *The Enlightenment of Sympathy: Justice and the Moral Sentiments in the Eighteenth Century and Today*. Oxford University Press.

Freyenhagen, F. 2013. *Adorno's Practical Philosophy: Living Less Wrongly*. Cambridge University Press.

Freyenhagen, F. 2014. 'Adorno's Politics: Theory and Praxis in Germany's 1960s', *Philosophy & Social Criticism* 40 (9), 867–93.

Gadamer, H.-G. 1942. *Volk und Geschichte im Denken Herders*. Frankfurt am Main: Klostermann.

Gadamer, H.-G. 1990. *Wahrheit und Methode*. Tübingen: J. C. B. Mohr.

Gadamer, H.-G. 1991. *Plato's Dialectical Ethics. Phenomenological Interpretations Relating to the Philebus*, trans. R. M. Wallace. New Haven: Yale University Press.

Gadamer, H.-G. 1994. *Truth and Method*, trans. J. Weinsheimer and D. G. Marshall. New York: Continuum.

Gadamer, H.-G. 1999. *Gesammelte Werke*. Tübingen: J. C. B. Mohr.

Garber, D. 1998. 'Descartes, or the Cultivation of the Intellect', in *Philosophers on Education: Historical Perspectives*, ed. A. O. Rorty. London: Routledge, 124–39.

Gasser, T., *et al.* 2011. 'Milestones in PD Genetics', *Movement Disorders* 26 (6), 1042–8.

Gaukroger, S. 1995. *Descartes: An Intellectual Biography*. Oxford University Press.

Gaukroger, S. 2010. *The Collapse of Mechanism and the Rise of Sensibility: Science and the Shaping of Modernity, 1680–1760*. Oxford University Press.

Gerken, M. ms. *On Folk Epistemology*.

Gettier, E. 1963. 'Is Justified True Belief Knowledge?' *Analysis* 23, 121–3.

Gilson, E. 1967. *Etudes sur le rôle de la pensée médiévale dans la formation du système cartésien*. Paris: Vrin.

Gjesdal, K. 2006. 'Hermeneutics and Philology: A Reconsideration of Gadamer's Critique of Schleiermacher', *British Journal for the History of Philosophy* 14 (1), 133–56.

Gjesdal, K. 2008. 'Between Enlightenment and Romanticism: Some Problems and Challenges in Gadamer's Hermeneutics', *Journal of the History of Philosophy* 46 (2), 285–306.

Gjesdal, K. 2009. *Gadamer and the Legacy of German Idealism*. Cambridge University Press.

Gjesdal, K. 2011. 'Heidegger, Husserl, and the Cartesian Legacy in Phenomenology', in *Acta Philosophica Fennica*. Special issue: *Rearticulations of Reason*. ed. L. Haaparanta, 117–43.

Gjesdal, K. 2013. 'A Not Yet Invented Logic: Herder on *Bildung*, Anthropology, and the Future of Philosophy', in *Die Bildung der*

Moderne, eds M. Dreyer, M. Forster, K.-U. Hoffmann, and K. Vieweg. Tübingen: Francke-Verlag, 53–69.

Gjesdal, K. 2014. 'Hermeneutics, Individuality, and Tradition: Schleiermacher's Idea of *Bildung* in the Landscape of Hegelian Thought', in *The Relevance of Romanticism*, ed. Dalia Nassar. Oxford University Press, 92–109.

Glock, H.-J. 1996. *A Wittgenstein Dictionary*. Oxford: Blackwell.

Glock, H.-J. 2003. *Quine and Davidson on Language, Thought and Reality*. Cambridge University Press.

Glock, H.-J. 2008. *What is Analytic Philosophy?* Cambridge University Press.

Goldman, A. 1992a. 'What is Justified Belief?' [1979], reprinted in his *Liaisons: Philosophy Meets the Cognitive and Social Sciences*. Cambridge, MA: MIT Press, 105–26.

Goldman, A. 1992b. 'Psychology and Philosophical Analysis' [1989], reprinted in his *Liaisons: Philosophy Meets the Cognitive and Social Sciences*, Cambridge, MA: MIT Press, 143–53.

Goldman, A. 2007. 'Philosophical Intuitions: Their Target, Their Source, and Their Epistemic Status', *Grazer Philosophische Studien* 74, 1–26.

Gopnik, A. 1993. 'How We Know Our Minds: The Illusion of First-Person Knowledge of Intentionality', *Behavioral and Brain Sciences* 16, 1–15.

Gregory, R. 1987. 'In Defense of Artificial Intelligence – a Reply to John Searle', in *Mindwaves*, eds C. Blakemore and S. A. Greenfield. Oxford: Blackwell, 235–44.

Griffin, D. 1981. *The Question of Animal Awareness*, 2nd edn. New York: Rockefeller University Press.

Haack, S. 1993. *Evidence and Inquiry*. Oxford: Blackwell.

Habermas, J. 1981a. *Philosophisch-politische Profile*. Frankfurt a.M.: Suhrkamp. Extended edn [trans. as *Philosophical-Political Profiles* by F. G. Lawrence, Cambridge, MA: MIT Press, 1983].

Habermas, J. 1981b. *Theorie des kommunikativen Handelns*. Vol. 1: *Handlungsrationalität und gesellschaftliche Rationalisierung*. Vol. 2: *Zur Kritik der funktionalistischen Vernunft*. Frankfurt a.M.: Suhrkamp [trans. as *The Theory of Communicative Action*. Vol. I: *Reason and the Rationalization of Society*; Vol. II: *Lifeworld and System* by T. McCarthy. Boston: Beacon, 1984; 1987].

Habermas, J. 1982. *Zur Logik der Sozialwissenschaften*. Frankfurt am Main: Suhrkamp.

Habermas, J. 1983. *Moralbewußtsein und kommunikatives Handeln*. Frankfurt a.M.: Suhrkamp [trans. as *Moral Consciousness and Communicative Action* by C. Lenhardt and S. Weber Nicholsen, Cambridge, MA: MIT Press, 1990].

Habermas, J. 1985. *Der philosophische Diskurs der Moderne: Zwölf Vorlesungen*. Frankfurt a.M.: Suhrkamp [trans. as *Philosophical Discourse of Modernity: Twelve Lectures* by F. Lawrence, Cambridge, MA: MIT Press, 1987].

Habermas, J. 1990. 'The Hermeneutic Claim to Universality', trans. J. Bleicher, in *The Hermeneutic Tradition: From Ast to Ricoeur*, eds G. Ormiston and A. D. Schrift. Albany, NY: SUNY Press, 245–72.

Hacker, P. M. S. 1996. *Wittgenstein's Place in Twentieth Century Analytic Philosophy*. Oxford: Blackwell.

Hacker, P. M. S. 2007. *Human Nature: The Categorial Framework*. Oxford: Wiley-Blackwell.

Hamilton, A. 2014. *Interpreting On Certainty*. London: Routledge.

Hanfling, O. 2000. *Philosophy and Ordinary Language*. New York: Routledge.

Hanna, R. 2001. *Kant and the Foundations of Analytic Philosophy*. Oxford University Press.

Hanna, R. 2011. 'The Myth of the Given and the Grip of the Given', *Diametros* 27, 25–46.

Hanna, R. 2015a. *Cognition, Content, and the A Priori: A Study in the Philosophy of Mind and Knowledge*. Oxford University Press.

Hanna, R. 2015b. *Kantian Ethics and Human Existence: A Study in Moral Philosophy* (unpublished ms, Winter 2015 version), available online at URL = <www.academia.edu/11991023/Kantian_Ethics_and_Human_Existence_A_Study_in_Moral_Philosophy_Winter_2015_version_comments_welcomed>.

Hanna, R. 2015c. *Deep Freedom and Real Persons: A Study in Metaphysics* (unpublished ms, Fall 2015 version), working draft available online at URL = <www.academia.edu/14493090/Deep_Freedom_and_Real_Persons_A_Study_in_Metaphysics_Fall_2015_version_comments_welcomed>.

Hanna, R. 2016a. 'Kant, the Copernican Devolution, and Real Metaphysics', in *Kant Handbook*, ed. M. Altman. London: Palgrave Macmillan.

Hanna, R. 2016b. 'Directions in Space, Non-Conceptual Form, and the Foundations of Transcendental Idealism', in *Kantian Non-conceptualism*, ed. D. Schulting. London: Palgrave Macmillan.

Hanna, R. 2016c. 'You Must Reject and Exit the State, For God's Sake, *Or*, The Gap Between Right and Virtue in Kant's Practical Philosophy' (unpublished ms, Spring 2016 version), available online at URL = <www. academia.edu/24118385/You_Must_Reject_and_Exit_the_State_For_Gods_Sake_Or_The_Gap_Between_Right_and_Virtue_in_Kants_Practical_Philosophy_Spring_2016_version_comments_welcomed>.

Hanna, R., and A. Chapman 2016. *Kant, Agnosticism, and Anarchism: A Theological-Political Treatise* (unpublished ms, Spring 2016 version), available online at URL = <www.academia.edu/15300656/Kant_Agnosticism_and_Anarchism_A_Theological-Political_Treatise_Spring_2016_version_comments_welcomed>.

Hanna, R., and M. Maiese 2009. *Embodied Minds in Action*. Oxford University Press.

Han-Pile, B. 2002. *Foucault's Critical Project: Between the Transcendental and the Historical*. Stanford University Press.

Hashimoto, M., *et al.* 2003. 'Role of Protein Aggregation in Mitochondrial Dysfunction and Neurodegeneration in Alzheimer's and Parkinson's Diseases', *NeuroMolecular Medicine* 4, 21–35.

Haslanger, S. 2012. *Resisting Reality*. Oxford University Press.

Haug, M. (ed.) 2014. *Philosophical Methods: The Armchair or the Laboratory?* London: Routledge.

Haug, M. C. (ed.) 2014. *The Armchair or the Laboratory?* New York: Routledge.

Haugeland, J. 1998. *Having Thought: Essays in the Metaphysics of Mind*. Cambridge, MA: Harvard University Press.

Hawking, S., and L. Mlodinow 2012. *The Grand Design*. London: Bantam.

Haym, R. 1954. *Herder*, 2 vols. Berlin: Aufbau-Verlag.

Heidegger, M. 1927a. *Being and Time*. New York: Harper & Row.

Heidegger, M. 1927b. *Sein und Zeit*. Tübingen: Max Niemeyer Verlag.

Heidegger, M. 1962a. *Being and Time*, trans. J. Macquarrie and E. Robinson. Oxford: Blackwell.

Heidegger, M. 1962b. *Being and Time*, trans. J. Macquarrie and E. Robinson. New York: Harper and Row.

Heidegger, M. 1975. *Early Greek Thinking*, trans. D. F. Krell and F. A. Capuzzi. New York: Harper and Row.

Heidegger, M. 1976. *Wegmarken. Gesamtausgabe*, vol. 9. Frankfurt am Main: Vittorio Klostermann.

Heidegger, M. 1982. *Basic Problems of Phenomenology*, revised. edn, trans. A. Hofstadter. Bloomington: Indiana University Press.

Heidegger, M. 1985a. *The History of the Concept of Time: Prologomena*, trans. T. Kisiel. Bloomington: Indiana University Press.

Heidegger, M. 1985b. *Phänomenologische Interpretationen zu Aristoteles. Einführung in die phänomenologische Forschung*, eds W. Bröcker and K. Bröcker-Oltmanns, *Gesamtausgabe*, vol. 61. Frankfurt am Main: Vittorio Klostermann.

Heidegger, M. 1994. *Einfuhrüng in die Phenomenologische Forschung. Der Beginn der neuzeitlichen Philosophie, Gesamtausgabe*, vol. 17. Frankfurt am Main: Vittorio Klostermann.

Heidegger, M. 1995. *Phänomenologie des religiösen Lebens*, eds M. Jung, T. Regehly, and C. Strube, *Gesamtausgabe*, vol. 60. Frankfurt am Main: Vittorio Klostermann.

Heidegger, M. 1996. *Being and Time*, trans. J. Stambaugh. Albany, NY: SUNY Press.

Heidegger, M. 1997. *Kant and the Problem of Metaphysics*, 5th edn, enlarged, trans. R. Taft. Bloomington: Indiana University Press.

Heidegger, M. 1998. 'Letter on Humanism', trans. F. A. Capuzzi, in *Pathmarks*, ed. W. McNeill. Cambridge University Press, 239–77.

Heidegger, M. 2001a. *Phenomenological Interpretations of Aristotle: Initiation into Phenomenological Research*, trans. R. Rojcewicz. Bloomington: Indiana University Press.

Heidegger, M. 2001b. *Phenomenological Interpretations of Aristotle: Initiation into Phenomenological Research*, trans. R. Rojcewicz. Bloomington: Indiana University Press.

Heidegger, M. 2004. *The Phenomenology of Religious Life*, trans. M. Fritsch and J. A. Gosetti-Ferencei. Bloomington: Indiana University Press.

Heidegger, M. 2005. *Introduction to Phenomenological Research*, trans. D. O. Dahlstrom. Bloomington: Indiana University Press.

Heidegger, M. 2006. *Sein und Zeit*. Tübingen: Max Niemeyer Verlag.

Heidegger, M. 2010a. *Phenomenology of Intuition and Expression*, trans. T. Colony. London: Continuum.

Heidegger, M. 2010b. *Being and Time*, trans. D. J. Schmidt. Albany, NY: The SUNY Press.

Heil, J. 2003. *From an Ontological Point of View*. Oxford University Press.

Heinz, M., and H. Clairmont. 2009. 'Herder's Epistemology', in *A Companion to the Works of Johann Gottfried Herder*, eds H. Adler and W. Koepke. Rochester, NY: Camden House, 43–64.

Hempel, C. 1942. 'The Function of General Laws in History', *Journal of Philosophy* 39, 35–48.

Hempel, C. 1966. *Philosophy of Natural Science*. Englewood Cliffs, NJ: Prentice-Hall.

Herder, J. G. 1887–. *Sämtliche Werke*, eds B. L. Suphan *et al.* Berlin: Weidmann.

Herder, J. G. 1985–. *Werke in zehn Bänden*, eds G. Arnold *et al.* Frankfurt am Main: Deutscher Klassiker Verlag.

Herder, J. G. 1992. *Selected Early Works, 1764–1767*, eds E. A. Menze and K. Menges, trans. E. A. Menze and M. Palma. University Park, PA: The Pennsylvania State University Press.

Herder, J. G. 2002a. *Philosophical Writings*, ed. and trans. M. N. Forster. Cambridge University Press.

Herder, J. G. 2002b. *Sculpture: Some Observations on Shape and Form from Pygmalion's Creative Dream*, ed. and trans. J. Gaiger. The University of Chicago Press.

Herder, J. G. 2006. *Selected Writings on Aesthetics*, ed. and trans. G. Moore. Princeton University Press.

Herder, J. G. 2008. *Shakespeare*, ed. and trans. G. Moore. Princeton University Press.

Herman, L., and P. Morrel-Samuels 1990. 'Knowledge Acquisition and Asymmetry Between Language Comprehension and Production: Dolphins and Apes as General Models for Animals', in *Interpretation and Explanation in the Study of Animal Behavior*, vol. 1, eds M. Beckoff and D. Jamieson. Boulder, CO: Westview, 283–312.

Hetherington, S. 2012. 'The Gettier-illusion: Gettier-partialism and Infallibilism', *Synthese* 188, 217–30.

Hirsch, E. 2009. 'Ontology and Alternative Languages' in *Metametaphysics*, eds D. Chalmers, D. Manley, and R. Wasserman. Oxford and New York: Oxford University Press, 231–59. [Reprinted in Hirsch 2011a.]

Hirsch, E. 2011a. *Quantifier Variance and Realism*. Oxford University Press.

Hirsch, E. 2011b. 'Quantifier Variance and Realism', in his *Quantifier Variance and Realism*. Oxford University Press, 68–95.

Hirsch, E. 2011c. 'Physical Object Ontology, Verbal Disputes and Common Sense', in his *Quantifier Variance and Realism*. Oxford University Press, 144–77.

Hirsch, E. C., *et al.* 2013. 'Pathogenesis of PD', *Movement Disorders* 28 (1), 24–30.

Hofweber, T. 2009. 'Ambitious Yet Modest Metaphysics', in *Metametaphysics*, eds D. Chalmers, D. Manley, and R. Wasserman. Oxford and New York: Oxford University Press, 260–89.

Honneth, A. 2008. 'Critical Theory', in *The Routledge Companion to Twentieth Century Philosophy*, ed. D. Moran. London and New York: Routledge, 784–813.

Honneth, A. 2011. *Das Recht der Freiheit: Grundriß einer demokratischen Sittlichkeit*. Berlin: Suhrkamp [trans. as *Freedom's Right: The Social Foundations of Democratic Life* by J. Ganahl. Cambridge: Polity Press, 2014].

Hookway, C. 2000. *Truth, Rationality, and Pragmatism*. New York: Oxford University Press.

Hookway, C. 2012. *The Pragmatic Maxim*. New York: Oxford University Press.

Horkheimer, M. 1972. *Critical Theory: Selected Essays*, trans. M. J. O'Connell. New York: Herder and Herder.

Horkheimer, M., and Adorno, T. W. 2002. *Dialectic of Enlightenment*[1944, 1947] trans. E. Jephcott. New York: Herder & Herder.

Horne, Z., and J. Livengood 2015. 'Ordering Effects, Updating Effects, and the Specter of Global Skepticism', *Synthese* 1–30.

Hulatt, O. forthcoming. *Adorno's Theory of Aesthetic and Philosophical Truth: Texture and Performance*. New York: Columbia University Press.

Husserl, E. 1956. *Erste Philosophie. 1 Theil, Husserliana VII*. The Hague: Martinus Nijhoff.

Husserl, E. 1959. *Erste Philosophie (1923/24), Zweiter Teil. Theorie der Phänomenologischen Reduktion*. The Hague: Martinus Nijhoff.

Husserl, E. 1962. *Ideas: General Introduction to Pure Phenomenology*, trans. W. R. Boyce Gibson. New York: Collier.

Husserl, E. 1964. *The Paris Lectures*, trans. P. Koestenbaum. Dordrecht: Martinus Nijhoff.

Husserl. E. 1970a. *The Crisis of European Sciences and Transcendental Phenomenology: An Introduction to Phenomenological Philosophy*, trans. D. Carr. Evanston: Northwestern University Press.

Husserl, E. 1970b. *The Crisis of European Sciences and Transcendental Phenomenology*, trans. D. Carr. Evanston: Northwestern University Press.

Husserl, E. 1973a. *Cartesian Meditations*, trans. D. Cairns. The Hague: Martinus Nijhoff.

Husserl, E. 1973b. *Cartesianische Meditationen und Pariser Vorträge. Husserliana I*, ed. S. Strasser. The Hague: Martinus Nijhoff.

Husserl, E. 1976. *Die Krisis der Europäischen Wissenschaften und die Transzendentale Phänomenologie*, Husserliana VI. The Hague: Martinus Nijhoff.

Husserl, E. 1977. *Cartesian Meditations*, trans. D. Cairns. The Hague: Martinus Nijhoff.

Husserl, E. 1981. *Shorter Works*, eds P. McCormick and F. Elliston. Notre Dame, IN: University of Notre Dame Press.

Husserl, E. 1982. *Ideas Pertaining to a Pure Phenomenology and to a Phenomenological Philosophy*, trans. F. Kersten. Dordrecht: Kluwer Academic Publishers.

Husserl, E. 1988. *Cartesian Meditations: An Introduction to Phenomenology*, trans. D. Cairns. Dordrecht: Martinus Nijhoff.

Husserl, E. 2006. *Späte Texte über Zeitkonstitution (1929–1934). Die C-Manuskripte*, ed. D. Lohmar, Husserliana Materialien VIII. Dordrecht: Springer.

Husserl, E. 2014. *Ideas 1*, trans. D. O. Dahlstrom. Indianapolis: Hackett Publishing.

Hutto, D. 2003. *Wittgenstein and the End of Philosophy: Neither Theory nor Therapy*. Basingstoke: Palgrave Macmillan.

Hutto, D. 2009. 'Philosophical Clarification, its Possibility and Point', *Philosophia* 37 (4), 629–52.

Ichikawa, J. 2010. 'Explaining away Intuitions', *Studia Philosophica Estonica* 2, 94–116.

Ioannidis, J. P. A. 2005. 'Why Most Published Research Findings are False', *PLoS Medicine* 2 (8 (e124)), 696–701.

Irwin, T. 1977. *Plato's Moral Theory: The Early and Middle Dialogues*. Oxford University Press.

Jackson, F. 1994. 'Armchair Metaphysics', in *Philosophy in Mind, Philosophical Studies Series*, 60, eds M. Michaelis and J. O'Leary Hawthorne. Dordrecht: Kluwer, 23–42.

Jackson, F. 1998. *From Metaphysics to Ethics: A Defence of Conceptual Analysis*. Oxford University Press.

Jackson, F. 1998. *From Metaphysics to Ethics*. Oxford University Press.

Jackson, F. 2002. 'Critical Notice of *Knowledge and Its Limits* by T. Williamson', *Australasian Journal of Philosophy* 80, 516–21.

Jackson, F. 2010. *Language, Names, and Information*. Malden, MA: Wiley-Blackwell.

Jackson, F. 2011. 'On Gettier Holdouts', *Mind and Language* 26, 468–81.

Jackson, F. forthcoming. 'In Defence of Reductionism in Ethics', in *Does Anything Really Matter? Parfit on Objectivity*, ed. P. Singer. Oxford University Press.

James, W. 1977. *The Writings of William James*, ed. J. J. McDermott. University of Chicago Press.

Janz, B. 2015. 'Hermeneutics and Intercultural Understanding', in *The Routledge Companion to Hermeneutics*, eds J. Malpas and H.-H. Gander. London: Routledge, 474–85.

Jarvis, S. 1998, *Adorno – A Critical Introduction*. Cambridge: Polity.

Jaspers, K. 1971. *Philosophy of Existence*, trans. R. F. Grabau. University of Philadelphia Press.

Jenkins, A., D. Dodell-Feder, R. Saxe, and J. Knobe 2014. 'The Neural Bases of Directed and Spontaneous Mental State Attributions to Group Agents', *PLoS ONE* 9 (8), e105341.

Jenner, P., *et al.* 2013. 'Parkinson's Disease – the Debate on the Clinical Phenomenology, Aetiology, Pathology and Pathogenesis', *Journal of Parkinson's Disease* 3, 1–11.

Johnson, V. E. 2013. 'Revised Standards for Statistical Evidence', *Proceedings of the National Academy of Sciences* 110 (48), 19313–17.

Jones, K. 2012 'The Politics of Intellectual Self-Trust', *Social Epistemology* 26 (2), 237–52.

Joseph, F., J. Reynolds, and A. Woodward (eds) 2011. *Bloomsbury Companion to Existentialism*. London: Bloomsbury.

Joughin, M. 1990. 'Translator's Preface' to G. Deleuze, *Expressionism in Philosophy: Spinoza*, trans. M. Joughin. New York: Zone Books.

Joyce, R. 2006. *The Evolution of Morality*. Cambridge, MA: MIT Press.

Kahneman, D., P. Slovic, and A. Tversky 1982. *Judgment under Uncertainty: Heuristics and Biases*. New York: Cambridge University Press.

Kant, I. 1933. *Critique of Pure Reason*, trans. N. K. Smith, 2nd edn. London: Macmillan.

Kant, I. 1950. *Prolegomena to any Future Metaphysics*. Indianapolis: Bobbs-Merrill.

Kant, I. 1964. *Groundwork of the Metaphysics of Morals* [1785], trans. H. J. Paton. New York: Harper Torchbooks.

Kant, I. 1985. *Critique of Pure Reason* [1781], trans. N. K. Smith. London: Macmillan.

Kant, I. 1992a. 'On the Form and Principles of the Sensible and Intelligible World (Inaugural Dissertation)', in *Immanuel Kant: Theoretical Philosophy: 1755–1770*. Cambridge University Press, 373–416.

Kant, I. 1992b. 'The Jäsche Logic', trans. J. M. Young, in *Immanuel Kant: Lectures on Logic*. Cambridge University Press, 519–640.

Kant, I. 1996a. 'An Answer to the Question: 'What is Enlightenment?'' trans. M. Gregor, in *Immanuel Kant: Practical Philosophy*. Cambridge University Press, 17–22.

Kant, I. 1996b. 'Groundwork of the Metaphysics of Morals', trans. M. Gregor, in *Immanuel Kant: Practical Philosophy*. Cambridge University Press, 37–108.

Kant, I. 1996c. 'Critique of Practical Reason', trans. M. Gregor, in *Immanuel Kant: Practical Philosophy*. Cambridge University Press, 139–272.

Kant, I. 1997. Critique of Pure Reason, trans. P. Guyer and A. Wood. Cambridge University Press.

Kant, I. 1998. *Critique of Pure Reason*, trans. and eds P. Guyer and A. Wood. Cambridge University Press.

Kant, I. 1999. *Immanuel Kant: Correspondence*, trans. A. Zweig. Cambridge University Press.

Kant, I. 2000. *Critique of the Power of Judgment*, trans. P. Guyer and E. Matthews. Cambridge University Press.

Kant, I. 2004. *Prolegomena to Any Future Metaphysics*, trans. G. Hatfield. Cambridge University Press.

Kant, I. 2007a. 'Idea for a Universal History with a Cosmopolitan Aim', trans. A. Wood, in *Immanuel Kant: Anthropology, History, and Education*. Cambridge University Press, 107–20.

Kant, I. 2007b. 'The Idea for a Universal History with a Cosmopolitan Aim', in *Anthropology, History and Education*, eds G. Zoller and R. Loundon. Cambridge University Press, 107–20.

Kekes, J. 1980. *The Nature of Philosophy*. Totowa, NJ: Rowman & Littlefield.

Kelletat, A. F. 1984. *Herder und die Weltliteratur. Zur Geschichte des Übersetzens im 18. Jahrhundert*. Frankfurt am Main: Peter Lang.

Kelly, M. (ed.) 1994. *Critique and Power: Recasting the Foucault/Habermas Debate*. Cambridge, MA: MIT Press.

Kelly, T. (2016) 'Disagreement in Philosophy: Its Epistemic Significance', in *The Oxford Handbook of Philosophical Methodology*, eds H. Cappelen, T. S. Szabó, and J. Hawthorne. Oxford University Press, 374–94.

Kelly, T., and S. McGrath forthcoming. 'Are there any Successful Philosophical Arguments?' in *Being, Freedom, and Method: Themes from van Inwagen*, ed. J. Keller. Oxford University Press.

Kierkegaard, S. 1985. *Philosophical Fragments and Johannes Climacus*, trans. H. V. Hong and E. H. Hong. Princeton University Press.

Kierkegaard, S. 1992. *Concluding Unscientific Postscript to Philosophical Fragments*, trans. H. V. Hong and E. H. Hong. Princeton University Press.

Kim, M., and Y. Yuan 2015. 'No Cross-cultural Differences in the Gettier Car Case Intuition: A Replication Study of Weinberg *et al.* 2001', *Episteme* 12 (3), 355–61.

Kisiel, T. 1993. *The Genesis of Heidegger's Being and Time*. Berkeley and Los Angeles: University of California Press.

Kitcher, P. 1978. 'Theories, Theorists and Theoretical Change', *Philosophical Review* 87, 519–47.

Kitcher, P. 1983. *The Nature of Mathematical Knowledge*. Oxford University Press.

Kleingeld, P., and E. Brown 2013. 'Cosmopolitanism', *The Stanford Encyclopedia of Philosophy* (Fall 2013 Edition), ed. E. N. Zalta, available online at URL = <http://plato.stanford.edu/archives/fall2013/entries/cosmopolitanism>.

Knobe, J. 2010. 'Person as Scientist, Person as Moralist', *Behavioral and Brain Sciences* 33, 315–29.

Knobe, J. 2016. 'Experimental Philosophy is Cognitive Science', in *A Companion to Experimental Philosophy*, eds J. Systma and W. Buckwalter. Oxford: Wiley-Blackwell, 37–52.

Knobe, J., and S. Nichols (eds) 2008. *Experimental Philosophy*. New York: Oxford University Press.

Koopman, C. 2009. *Pragmatism as Transition: Historicity and Hope in James, Dewey, and Rorty*. New York: Columbia University Press.

Kornblith, H. 1998. 'The Role of Intuition in Philosophical Theorizing', in *Rethinking Intuition*, eds M. DePaul and W. Ramsey. Lanham, MD: Rowman and Littlefield, 129–41.

Kornblith, H. 2002. *Knowledge and its Place in Nature*. Oxford University Press.

Kornblith, H. 2006. 'Appeals to Intuition and the Ambitions of Epistemology', in *Epistemology Futures*, ed. S. Hetherington. Oxford University Press, 10–25.

Kornblith, H. 2007. 'How to Refer to Artifacts', in *Creations of the Mind: Essays on Artifacts and their Representations*, eds E. Margolis and S. Laurence. Oxford University Press, 138–49.

Kornblith, H. 2009. 'Review of *The Philosophy of Philosophy* by T. Williamson', *Analysis* 69, 109–16.

Kornblith, H. 2012. *On Reflection*. Oxford University Press.

Kornblith, H. 2014. 'Is There Room for Armchair Theorizing in Epistemology', in *Philosophical Methods: The Armchair or the Laboratory?*, ed. M. C. Haug. London: Routledge, 195–216.

Kornblith, H. forthcoming. 'Philosophy, Science, and Common Sense', in *Scientism*, eds R. Peels and R. van Woudenberg. Oxford University Press.

Korsgaard, C. M. C. 1983. 'Two Distinctions in Goodness', *The Philosophical Review* 92 (2), 169–95.

Kreitzer, A. C., and R. C. Malenka. 2008. 'Striatal Plasticity and Basal Ganglia Circuit Function', *Neuron* 60, 543–54.

Kriegel, U. 2013. 'The Epistemological Challenge of Revisionary Metaphysics', *Philosopher's Imprint* 13 (12), 1–30.

Kripke, S. 1980a. *Naming and Necessity*. Oxford: Basil Blackwell.

Kripke, S. A. 1980b. *Naming and Necessity*. Cambridge, MA: Harvard University Press.

Kroon, F. 1987. 'Causal Descriptivism', *Australasian Journal of Philosophy* 65, 1–17.

Kropotkin, P. 1910. 'Anarchism', *Encyclopedia Britannica* [1910], available online at URL = <www.marxists.org/reference/archive/kropotkin-peter/1910/britannica.htm>.

Kuehn, M. 1987. *Scottish Common Sense in Germany, 1768–1800: A Contribution to the History of Critical Philosophy*. Montreal: McGill-Queen's University Press.

Kuhn, T. 1970. *The Structure of Scientific Revolutions*, 2nd enlarged edn. University of Chicago Press.

Kukla, R. 2002. 'The Ontology and Temporality of Conscience', *Continental Philosophy Review* 35, 1–34.

Kunda, Z. 1999. *Social Psychology: Making Sense of People*. Cambridge, MA: MIT Press.

Kusch, M. 2002. *Knowledge by Agreement: The Programme of Communitarian Epistemology*. Oxford University Press.

Lackey, J. 2014. 'Socially Extended Knowledge', *Philosophical Issues* 24 (1), 282–98.

Langston, J. W., *et al.* 1983. 'Chronic Parkinsonism in Humans Due to a Product of Meperidine-analog Synthesis', *Science* 219, 979–80.

Larmore, C. 2002. 'Attending to Reasons', in *Reading McDowell on Mind and World*, ed. N. Smith. New York: Routledge, 47–66.

Lawlor, L. 2003. *Thinking through French Philosophy*. Bloomington: Indiana University Press.

Lawlor, L. 2016. *From Violence to Speaking out*. Edinburgh University Press.

Lazerowitz, M. 1970. 'A Note on "Metaphilosophy"', *Metaphilosophy* 1, 91.

Levi, I. 1991. *The Fixation of Belief and its Undoing*. Cambridge University Press.

Lewis. C. I. 1923. 'A Pragmatic Conception of the A Priori', *The Journal of Philosophy* 20, 169–77.

Lewis, D. 1986. *On the Plurality of Worlds*. Oxford: Blackwell.

Lewis, D. 1990. 'Noneism or Allism', *Mind* 99, 23–31.

Lewy, F. J. 1912. 'Paralysis agitans. I. Pathologische Anatomie', in *Handbuch der Neurologie*, ed. M. Lewandowski. Berlin: Springer, 920–33.

Liao, S. M., A. Wiegmann, J. Alexander, and G. Vong 2012. 'Putting the Trolley in Order: Experimental Philosophy and the Loop Case', *Philosophical Psychology* 25 (5), 661–71.

Lieberman, D. 2011. *Human Learning and Memory*. Cambridge University Press.

Lipton, P. 1991. *Inference to the Best Explanation*. London: Routledge.

Locke, J. 1964. *An Essay Concerning Human Understanding*[1690]. Glasgow: Collins and Sons.

Lowe, J. 1998. *The Possibility of Metaphysics*. New York: Oxford University Press.

Macarthur, D. 2014. 'Cavell on Skepticism and the Importance of Not-Knowing', *Conversations: The Journal of Cavellian Studies* 2, 2–23.

Macarthur, D. forthcoming. 'The Ethical Significance of Metaphysical Quietism: Remarks on the Wittgenstein–Malcolm Incident Involving an Alleged British Plot to Kill Hitler', in *Later Wittgenstein Now*, ed. A. Malachowski. London: Blackwell.

Machery, E. 2011. 'Thought Experiments and Philosophical Knowledge', *Metaphilosophy* 42 (3), 191–214.

Machery, E. 2012. 'Expertise and Intuitions about Reference', *THEORIA. Revista de Teoría, Historia y Fundamentos de la Ciencia* 27 (1), 37–54.

Machery, E., R. Mallon, S. Nicols, and S. P. Stich 2004. 'Semantics, Cross-Cultural Style', *Cognition* 92, B1–B12.

Machery, E., J. Sytsma, and M. Deutsch 2015. 'Speaker's Reference and Cross-Cultural Semantics' in *On Reference*, ed. A. Bianchi. Oxford: Oxford University Press, 62–76.

Machery, E., S. Stich, D. Rose, A. Chatterjee, K. Karasawa, N. Struchiner, S. Sirker, N. Usui, and T. Hashimoto forthcoming-a. 'Gettier was Framed!' in *Epistemology for the Rest of the World: Linguistic and Cultural Diversity and Epistemology*, eds E. McCready, M. Mizumoto, J. Stanley and S. Stich. Oxford University Press.

Machery, E., S. Stich, D. Rose, A. Chatterjee, K. Karasawa, N. Struchiner, S. Sirker, N. Usui, and T. Hashimoto forthcoming-b. 'Gettier across Cultures', *Noûs*.

Mackie, J. L. 1977. *Ethics: Inventing Right and Wrong*. Harmondsworth: Penguin.

Maddy, P. 2007. *Second Philosophy: A Naturalistic Method*. Oxford University Press.

Magee, B. 1982. *Talking Philosophy: Dialogues with Fifteen Leading Philosophers*. Oxford University Press.

Malcolm, N. 2001. *Ludwig Wittgenstein: A Memoir*. Oxford University Press.

Malpas, J., and H.-H. Gander (eds) 2015. *The Routledge Companion to Hermeneutics*. London: Routledge.

Manley, D. 2009. 'Introduction: A Guided Tour of Metametaphysics', in *Metametaphysics*, eds D. Chalmers, D. Manley, and R. Wasserman. Oxford and New York: Oxford University Press, 1–37.

Marcuse, H. 2009. 'Philosophie und Kritische Theorie' [1937], in his *Negations: Essays in Critical Theory*, trans. J. J. Shapiro. London: MayFlyBooks, 99–118.

Marx, K., and F. Engels 1956–90. *Marx Engels Werke*[MEW]. Berlin: Dietz Verlag.

Marx, K., and F. Engels 1975–2005. *Marx Engels Collected Works*[MECW]. Moscow: Progress Publishers.

Matthews, G. B. 1992. *Thought's Ego in Augustine and Descartes*. Ithaca, NY: Cornell University Press.

Mattson, M. P., and D. Liu 2002. 'Energetics and Oxidative Stress in Synaptic Plasticity and Neurodegenerative Disorders', *NeuroMolecular Medicine* 2, 215–31.

Mayo, R. S. 1969. *Herder and the Beginnings of Comparative Literature*. Chapel Hill: The University of North Carolina Press.

Mazzoni, P., *et al.* 2007. 'Why Don't We Move Faster? Parkinson's Disease, Movement Vigor, and Implicit Motivation', *The Journal of Neuroscience* 27 (27), 7105–16.

McCarthy, T. 1985. 'Complexity and Democracy, or the Seducements of Systems Theory', *New German Critique* 35, 27–53.

McCarthy, T. 1990. 'The Critique of Impure Reason: Foucault and the Frankfurt School', *Political Theory* 18 (3), 437–69.

McDowell, J. 1996. *Mind and World*. 2nd edn. Cambridge, MA: Harvard University Press.

McDowell, J. 1994. *Mind and World*. Cambridge, MA: Harvard University Press.

McDowell, J. 2002. 'Reply to Larmore', in *Reading McDowell on Mind and World*, ed. N. Smith. New York: Routledge, 294–6.

McDowell, J. 2009. 'Wittgensteinian Quietism', *Common Knowledge* 15 (3), 365–72.

McGinn, C. 1993. *Problems in Philosophy: The Limits of Inquiry*. Oxford: Blackwell.

McGinn, C. 2002. *The Making of a Philosopher: My Journey Through Twentieth Century Philosophy*. New York: Perennial.

McManus, D. 2013. 'The Provocation to Look and See: Appropriation, Recollection, and Formal Indication', in *Wittgenstein and Heidegger*, eds D. Egan, S. Reynolds, and A. Wendland. London: Routledge, 50–65.

Menn, S. 1998. *Descartes and Augustine*. Cambridge University Press.

Merleau-Ponty, M. 1962. *Phenomenology of Perception*, trans. C. Smith. London: Routledge and Kegan Paul.

Merleau-Ponty, M. 2008. *Phenomenology of Perception*, trans. D. Landes. London: Routledge.

Merricks, T. 2000. 'No Statues', *Australasian Journal of Philosophy* 78 (1), 47–52.

Misak, C. 1991. *Truth and the End of Inquiry*. New York: Oxford University Press.

Misak, C. 1995. *Verificationism: Its History and Prospects*. New York: Routledge.

Misak, C. 2013. *The American Pragmatists*. New York: Oxford University Press

Moore, A. W. 1997. *Points of View*. Oxford University Press.

Moore, A. W. 2012. *The Evolution of Modern Metaphysics: Making Sense of Things*. Cambridge University Press.

Moore, G. E. 1903. *Principia Ethica*. Cambridge University Press.

Moore, G. E. 1955. 'Notes on Wittgenstein's Lectures, 1930–33', *Mind* 64 (253), 1–27.

Moran, R. 2001. *Authority and Estrangement: An Essay on Self-Knowledge*. Princeton University Press.

Morgan, C. L. 1894. *An Introduction to Comparative Psychology*. London: Walter Scott.

Nado, J. 2014. 'Philosophical Expertise', *Philosophy Compass* 9, 631–41.

Nado, J. 2015. 'Intuition, Philosophical Theorizing, and the Threat of Skepticism', in *Experimental Philosophy, Rationalism, and Naturalism*, eds E. Fischer and J. Collins. London: Routledge, 204–21.

Nagel, J. 2012. 'Intuitions and Experiments: A Defense of the Case Method in Epistemology', *Philosophy and Phenomenological Research* 85, 495–527.

Nichols, S., N. Pinillos, and R. Mallon 2016. 'Ambiguous Reference', *Mind* 125 (497), 145–75.

Nietzsche, F. 1974. *The Gay Science: With a Prelude in Rhymes and an Appendix of Songs*, ed. W. A. Kaufmann. New York: Vintage Books.

Nisbet, H. B. 1970. *Herder and the Philosophy and History of Science*. Cambridge University Press.

Nisbett, R.E., and T.D. Wilson 1977. 'Telling More than We Can Know: Verbal Reports on Mental Processes', *Psychological Review* 84 (3), 231–59.

Noë, A. (ed.) 2007. 'Special Issue on Dennett and Heterophenomenology', *Phenomenology and the Cognitive Sciences* 6 (1–2), 1–270.

Nolan, D. 2015. 'The A Posteriori Armchair', *Australasian Journal of Philosophy* 93, 211–31.

Norton, R. E. 1991. *Herder's Aesthetics and the European Enlightenment*. Ithaca, NY: Cornell University Press.

Nozick, R. 1981a. *Philosophical Explanations*. Cambridge, MA: Belknap Press.

Nozick, R. 1981b. *Philosophical Explanations*. Cambridge, MA: Harvard University Press.

Overgaard, S., P. Gilbert, and S. Burwood 2013. *An Introduction to Metaphilosophy*. Cambridge University Press.

Pagin, P. forthcoming. 'Problems with Norms of Assertion', *Philosophy and Phenomenological Research*, DOI: 10.1111/phpr.12209.

Papineau, D. 2009. 'The Poverty of Analysis', *Aristotelian Society Supplementary Volume* 83, 1–30.

Parfit, D. 1984. *Reasons and Persons*. Oxford University Press.

Parkinson, J. 1817. *An Essay on the Shaking Palsy*. London: Sherwood, Neely, and Jones.

Paul. L. A. 2014. *Transformative Experiences*. Oxford University Press.

Peirce, C. S. 1931. *Collected Papers*, Vol. II, ed. C. Hartshorne and P. Weiss. Cambridge, MA: Harvard University Press.

Peirce, C. S. 1931–58. *The Collected Works of Charles Sanders Peirce*, 8 vols. Cambridge, MA: Harvard University Press.

Peirce, C. S. 1934. *Collected Papers*, Vol. V, Cambridge MA: Harvard University Press.

Peirce, C. S. 1955. 'The Fixation of Belief', in *Philosophical Writings of Peirce*, ed. J. Buchler. New York: Dover, 5–22.

Petit, J.-L. (dir.) 2015. 'La naturalisation de la phénoménologie 20 ans après', *Les Cahiers Philosophiques de Strasbourg*, 38.

Petitot, J., F. Varela, B. Pachoud, and J.-M. Roy (eds) 1999. *Naturalizing Phenomenology: Issues in Contemporary Phenomenology and Cognitive Science*. Stanford University Press.

Petitot, J., *et al.* (eds) 1999. *Naturalizing Phenomenology*. Stanford University Press.

Pettit, P. 2004. 'Existentialism, Quietism, and the Role of Philosophy', in *The Future of Philosophy*, ed. B. Leiter. London: Routledge, 304–27.

Philp, M. 2013. 'William Godwin', in *The Stanford Encyclopedia of Philosophy* (Summer 2013 Edition), ed. E. N. Zalta, available online at URL = <http://plato.stanford.edu/archives/sum2013/entries/godwin/>.

Piercey, R. 2003. 'Doing Philosophy Historically', *Review of Metaphysics* 56 (June), 815–36.

Piercey, R. 2009a. *The Crisis in Continental Philosophy: History, Truth and the Hegelian Legacy*. London: Continuum.

Piercey, R. 2009b. *The Uses of the Past From Heidegger to Rorty: Doing Philosophy Historically*. Cambridge University Press.

Piercey, R. 2010. 'Metaphilosophy as First Philosophy', *International Philosophical Quarterly* 50 (3) (September), 335–50.

Plant, B. 2012. 'Philosophical Diversity and Disagreement', *Metaphilosophy* 43 (5), 567–91.

Plato, 1927. *Charmides, Alcibiades 1 and 2 Hipparchus, the Lovers, Theages, Minos, Epinomis; with an English Translation*, trans. W. R. M. Lamb, ed. T. E. Page. Vol. 201, Loeb Classical Library. London: Heinemann.

Plato, 1971. *Gorgias*, trans. W. Hamilton. Harmondsworth: Penguin.

Plato, 1981. *Meno*, trans. G. M. A. Grube, in *Five Dialogues*. Indianapolis: Hackett Publishing Company.

Pleasants, N. 1999. *Wittgenstein and the Idea of a Critical Social Theory: A Critique of Giddens, Habermas and Bhaskar*. London: Routledge.

Plunkett, D. 2015. 'Which Concepts Should We Use?: Metalinguistic Negotiations and the Methodology of Philosophy', *Inquiry* 58 (7–8), 828–74.

Plunkett, D., and T. Sundell (2013). 'Disagreement and the Semantics of Normative and Evaluative Terms', *Philosopher's Imprint* 13 (23), 1–37.

Polymeropoulos, M. H., *et al.* 1997. 'Mutation in the α-Synuclein Gene Identified in Families with Parkinson's Disease', *Science* 276, 2045–47.

Popper, K. R. 1968. *Conjectures and Refutations: The Growth of Scientific Knowledge*. New York: Harper & Row.

Popper, K. R. 1975. 'How I See Philosophy', in *The Owl of Minerva: Philosophers on Philosophy*, eds C. J. Bontempo and S. J. Odell. New York: McGraw-Hill, 41–55.

Prado, C. (ed.) 2003. *A House Divided: Comparing Analytic and Continental Philosophy*. Amherst, NY: Humanity Books.

Price, H. 2003. 'Truth as Convenient Friction', *Journal of Philosophy* 100, 167–90.

Price, H. 2004. 'Naturalism Without Representationalism', in *Naturalism in Question*, ed. D. Macarthur and M. de Caro. Cambridge, MA: Harvard University Press, 71–88.

Price, H. 2009. 'Metaphysics after Carnap: The Ghost Who Walks?' in *Metametaphysics*, eds D. Chalmers, D. Manley, and R. Wasserman. Oxford and New York: Oxford University Press, 320–47.

Price, H. 2011. *Naturalism Without Mirrors*. New York: Oxford University Press.

Pust, J. 2000. *Intuitions as Evidence*. New York: Routledge.

Putnam, H. 1975a. 'The Meaning of 'Meaning', in his *Mind, Language and Reality: Philosophical Papers*, vol. 2. Cambridge University Press, 215–71.

Putnam, H. 1975b. *Mathematics, Matter and Method: Philosophical Papers*, vol. 1. Cambridge University Press.

Putnam, H. 1975c. *Mind, Language and Reality*. Cambridge University Press.

Putnam, H. 1975d. *Philosophical Papers (Vol. 1): Mathematics, Matter and Method*. Cambridge University Press.

Putnam, H. 1987. *The Many Faces of Realism*. LaSalle, IL: Open Court.

Putnam, H. 1995. 'Pragmatism', *Proceedings of the Aristotelian Society* 95, 291–306.

Putnam, H. 1997. 'A Half Century of Philosophy', *Daedalus* 12, 175–208.

Putnam, H. 2012. *Philosophy in an Age of Science: Physics, Mathematics and Skepticism*, eds M. De Caro and D. Macarthur. Cambridge, MA: Harvard University Press.

Quine, W. V. 1951. 'Two Dogmas of Empiricism', in his *From a Logical Point of View*. Cambridge, MA: Harvard University Press, 20–46.

Quine, W. V. O. 1960. *Word and Object*. Cambridge, MA: MIT Press.

Quine, W. V. 1966. 'Mr. Strawson on Logical Theory' [1953], reprinted in his *The Ways of Paradox and Other Essays*. New York: Random House.

Quine, W. V. O. 1969. 'Epistemology Naturalized', in his *Ontological Relativity and Other Essays*. New York: Columbia University Press.

Quine, W. V. 1970. 'Philosophical Progress in Language Theory', *Metaphilosophy* 1, 2–19.

Quine, W. V., and J. S. Ullian 1978. *The Web of Belief*, 2nd edn. New York: Random House.

Ratcliffe, M. 2009. 'The Phenomenology of Mood and the Meaning of Life', in *Oxford Handbook of Philosophy of Emotion*, ed. P. Goldie. Oxford University Press, 349–72.

Reeves, A., *et al.* 2014. 'Ageing and Parkinson's Disease: Why is Advancing Age the Biggest Risk Factor?' *Ageing Research Reviews* 14, 19–30.

Reill, P. H. 2005. *Vitalizing Nature in the Enlightenment*. Berkeley: The University of California Press.

Renaudie, P.-J. 2013. 'Me, Myself and I: Sartre and Husserl on Elusiveness of the Self', *Continental Philosophy Review* 46 (1), 99–113.

Renaudie, P.-J. 2015. 'A Pebble at the Bottom of the Water. Sartre and Cavell on Self-knowledge', in *Pre-reflective Consciousness: Sartre and Contemporary Philosophy of Mind*, eds S. Miguens, G. Preyer, and C. B. Morando. London: Routledge, 208–24.

Rescher, N. 1973. *Conceptual Idealism*. Oxford: Blackwell.

Rescher, N. 1978. 'Philosophical Disagreement: An Essay Towards Orientational Pluralism in Metaphilosophy', *Review of Metaphysics* 32 (2), 217–51.

Rescher, N. 1985. *The Strife of Systems*. University of Pittsburgh Press.

Rescher, N. 1992. *A System of Pragmatic Idealism*, 3 vols. Princeton University Press.

Rescher, N. 1994. *Metaphilosophical Inquiries*. Princeton University Press.

Rescher, N. 2000. *Standardism: An Empirical Approach to Philosophical Methodology*, University of Pittsburgh Press.

Rescher, N. 2001. *Philosophical Reasoning*. Oxford: Blackwell.

Rescher, N. 2006a. *Studies in Metaphilosophy*. Frankfurt: Ontos.

Rescher, N. 2006b. *Philosophical Dialectics: An Essay on Metaphilosophy*. Frankfurt: Ontos.

Rescher, N. 2014. *Philosophical Progress: And Other Philosophical Studies*. Boston: De Gruyter.

Ricoeur, P. 1974. 'Freedom in the Light of Hope', trans. Robert Sweeney, in *The Conflict of Interpretations*, ed. D. Ihde. Evanston: Northwestern University Press, 402–24.

Rilke, R. M. 1989. *The Selected Poetry of Rainer Maria Rilke*, ed. and trans. S. Mitchell. New York: Vintage.

Romdenh-Romluc, K. 2011. 'Time for Consciousness: Intention and Introspection', *Phenomenology and Cognitive Sciences* 10, 369–76.

Rorty, R. 1979. *Philosophy and the Mirror of Nature*. Princeton University Press.

Rorty, R. 1980. *Philosophy and the Mirror of Nature*. Oxford: Blackwell.

Rorty, R. 1982. *Consequences of Pragmatism*. Minneapolis: University of Minnesota Press.

Rorty, R. 1984. 'The Historiography of Philosophy: Four Genres', in *Philosophy in History*, eds R. Rorty, J. B. Schneewind, and Q. Skinner. Cambridge University Press, 49–75.

Rorty, R. 1989. *Contingency, Irony, Solidarity*. Cambridge University Press.

Rorty, R. 1999. 'Trotsky and the Wild Orchids', in his *Philosophy and Social Hope*. London: Penguin.

Rorty, R. 2007. *Philosophy as Cultural Politics: Philosophical Papers Volume 4*. Cambridge University Press.

Russell, B. 1959. *Wisdom of the West*, ed. P. Foulkes. London: Rathbone.

Russell, B. 1967. *The Problems of Philosophy*. [1912] Oxford University Press.

Ryle, G. 1949. *The Concept of Mind*. University of Chicago Press.

Ryle, G. 1970. 'Autobiographical', in *Ryle*, eds O. P. Wood and G. Pitcher. New York: Doubleday and Co, 1–15.

Ryle, G. 1971. *Collected Essays*. Vol II. London: Hutchinson.

Ryle, G. 2009. *Collected Papers, Volume 2: Collected Essays 1929–1968*. London: Routledge.

Sacks, M. 2005. 'The Nature of Transcendental Arguments', *International Journal of Philosophical Studies* 13 (4), 439–60.

Salamone, J. D., *et al.* 2007. 'Effort-related Functions of Nucleus Accumbens Dopamine and Associated Forebrain Circuits', *Psychopharmacology* 191, 461–82.

Sartre, J.-P. 1958. *Being and Nothingness*, trans. H. Barnes. London: Routledge and Kegan Paul.

Sartwell, C. 1991. 'Knowledge is Merely True Belief', *American Philosophical Quarterly*, 157–65.

Scarre, G. 2007. *Death*. Montreal: McGill-Queen's University Press.

Schear, J. K. (ed.) 2013. *Mind, Reason, and Being-in-the-World: The McDowell-Dreyfus Debate*. London: Routledge.

Schiller, F. C. S., C. A. Mace, and J. L. Stocks 1933. 'Symposium: Must Philosophers Disagree?' *Aristotelian Society Supplementary Volume* 12, 118–49.

Schulz, E., E. Cokely, and A. Feltz 2011. 'Persistent Bias in Expert Judgments about Free Will and Moral Responsibility: A Test of the Expertise Defense', *Consciousness and Cognition* 20, 1722–31.

Schwitzgebel, E., and F. Cushman 2015. 'Philosophers' Biased Judgments Persist Despite Training, Expertise and Reflection', *Cognition* 141, 127–37.

Schwitzgebel, E., and J. Rust 2014. 'The Moral Behavior of Ethics Professors: Relationships among Self-reported Behavior, Expressed Normative Attitude, and Directly Observed Behavior', *Philosophical Psychology* 27 (3), 293–327.

Seel, M. 2004. *Adornos Philosophie der Kontemplation*. Frankfurt a.M.: Suhrkamp.

Sellars, J. 2011. *The Art of Living: The Stoics on the Nature and Function of Philosophy*, 2nd edn. London: Duckworth.

Sellars, W. 1956. 'Empiricism and the Philosophy of Mind' in *Minnesota Studies in the Philosophy of Science*, vol. I, eds H. Feigl and M. Scriven. Minneapolis: University of Minnesota Press, 253–329.

Sellars, W. 1963. *Science, Perception, and Reality*. London: Routledge & Kegan Paul.

Sellars, W. 1991. *Science, Perception, and Reality*. Atascadero, CA: Ridgeview.

Sextus Empiricus 1994. *Outlines of Scepticism*, trans. and eds J. Barnes, and J. Annas. Cambridge University Press.

Shettleworth, S. 2010. *Cognition, Evolution, and Behavior*, 2nd edn. Oxford University Press.

Shieber, J. 2012. 'A Partial Defense of Intuition on Naturalist Grounds', *Synthese* 187, 321–41.

Shope, R. 1983. *The Analysis of Knowledge: A Decade of Research*. Princeton University Press.

Sider, T. 2011. *Writing the Book of the World*. Oxford University Press.

Skirke, C. 2012. 'Metaphysical Experience and Constitutive Error in Adorno's "Meditations on Metaphysics"', *Inquiry* 55 (3), 307–28.

Smart, J. J. C. 1993. 'Why Philosophers Disagree', *Canadian Journal of Philosophy* 23 (supp 1), 67–82.

Smith, A. 1993. *The Wealth of Nations* [first published 1776; 5th edn 1789]. Oxford University Press.

Smith, N. (ed.) 2002. *Reading McDowell on Mind and World*. New York: Routledge.

Sosa, E. 2007. 'Experimental Philosophy and Philosophical Intuition', *Philosophical Studies* 132 (1), 99–107.

Sosa, E. 2008. 'Experimental Philosophy and Philosophical Intuition', in *Experimental Philosophy*, eds J. Knobe and S. Nichols. Oxford University Press, 231–40.

Spinoza, B. de 2002a. *Ethics*, in his *Spinoza: Complete Works*, ed. M. L. Morgan and trans. S. Shirley. Indianapolis: Hackett Publishing.

Spinoza, B. de 2002b. *Theological-Political Treatise*, in his *Spinoza: Complete Works*, ed. M. L. Morgan and trans. S. Shirley. Indianapolis: Hackett Publishing.

Stanovich, K., and R. West 2007. 'Natural Myside Bias is Independent of Cognitive Bbility', *Thinking & Reasoning* 13 (3), 225–47.

Starzak, T. 2016. 'Interpretations without Justification', *Synthese*, 1–21.

Stern, D. G. 2004. *Wittgenstein's Philosophical Investigations: An Introduction*. Cambridge University Press.

Stewart, J. 2003. *Kierkegaard's Relation to Hegel Reconsidered*. Cambridge University Press.

Stich, S. 1990. *The Fragmentation of Reason: Preface to a Pragmatic Theory of Cognitive Evaluation*. Cambridge, MA: MIT Press.

Stich, S. 2013. 'Do Different Groups Have Different Epistemic Intuitions? A Reply to Jennifer Nagel', *Philosophy and Phenomenological Research* 87, 151–78.

Stirner, M. 1982. *The Ego and His Own*, ed. J. J. Martin and trans. S. T. Byington. Sun City: West World Press.

Stokes, P. 2010. *Kierkegaard's Mirrors: Narrative, Self, and Moral Vision*. Houndmills: Palgrave.

Strawson, P. F. 1959. *Individuals: An Essay in Descriptive Metaphysics*. London: Methuen.

Strawson, P. F. 1963. 'Carnap's Views on Constructed Systems vs. Natural Languages in Analytic Philosophy', in *The Philosophy of Rudolf Carnap*, ed. P. A. Schilpp. Illinois: Open Court, 503–18.

Strawson, P. 1992. *Analysis and Metaphysics: An Introduction to Philosophy*. Oxford University Press.

Strawson, G. 2009. *Selves: An Essay in Revisionary Metaphysics*. Oxford University Press.

Strawson, P. F. 2011. *Philosophical Writings*, eds G. Strawson and M. Montague. Oxford University Press.

Strohminger, N., and S. Nichols 2014. 'The Essential Moral Self', *Cognition* 131, 159–71.

Sunstein, C. R. 2005. 'Moral Heuristics', *Behavioral and Brain Sciences* 28 (4), 531–41.

Swain, S., J. Alexander, and J. Weinberg 2008. 'The Instability of Philosophical Intuitions: Running Hot and Cold on Truetemp', *Philosophy and Phenomenological Research* 76 (1), 138–55.

Szubka, T. 2010. 'Richard Rorty and the Analytic Tradition: Radical Break or Partial Continuity?', *Diametros* 25 (September), 146–58.

Talbot, B. 2013. 'Reforming Intuition Pumps: When are the Old Ways the Best?' *Philosophical Studies* 165 (2), 315–34.

Talisse, R. B. 2001. 'A Pragmatist Critique of Rorty's Hopeless Politics', *Southern Journal of Philosophy* 39 (4), 611–26.

Talisse, R. B. 2007. *A Pragmatist Philosophy of Democracy.* New York: Routledge.

Talisse, R. B. 2012. *Pluralism and Liberal Politics.* New York: Routledge.

Talisse, R. B., and S. F. Aikin 2008. *Pragmatism: A Guide for the Perplexed.* London: Continuum.

Tanesini, A. 2004. *Wittgenstein: A Feminist Interpretation.* Cambridge: Polity Press.

Tanesini, A. 2015. 'Nietzsche on the Diachronic Will and the Problem of Morality', *European Journal of Philosophy* 23 (3), 652–75.

Tanesini, A. 2016. '"Calm Down Dear": Intellectual Arrogance, Silencing and Ignorance', *Proceedings of the Aristotelian Society*, Supplementary Volume 90, 71–91.

Taylor, C. 1984. 'Philosophy and its History', in *Philosophy in History*, eds R. Rorty, J. B. Schneewind, and Q. Skinner. Cambridge University Press, 17–30.

Taylor, C. 1995. 'The Importance of Herder', in his *Philosophical Arguments.* Cambridge, MA: Harvard University Press, 79–100.

Taylor, C. 2007. *A Secular Age.* Cambridge, MA and London: Belknap Press of Harvard University Press.

Thomasson, A. 2001. 'Geographic Objects and the Science of Geography'. *Topoi* 20, 149–59.

Thomasson, A. L. 2007a. *Ordinary Objects.* New York: Oxford University Press.

Thomasson, A. L. 2007b. 'Modal Normativism and the Methods of Metaphysics', *Philosophical Topics* 35 (1&2), 135–60.

Thomasson, A. 2009. 'Answerable and Unanswerable Questions', in *Metametaphysics*, eds D. Chalmers, D. Manley, and R. Wasserman. Oxford and New York: Oxford University Press, 444–71.

Thomasson, A. L. 2012. 'Experimental Philosophy and the Methods of Ontology', *The Monist* 95 (2), 175–200.

Thomasson, A. L. 2013. 'The Nancy D. Simco Lecture: Norms and Necessity', *Southern Journal of Philosophy* 51 (2), 143–60.

Thomasson, A. L. 2015. *Ontology Made Easy.* Oxford and New York: Oxford University Press.

Thomasson, A. L. 2016. 'Metaphysical Disputes and Metalinguistic Negotiation', in *Analytic Philosophy*. doi:10.1111/phib.12087.

Tobia, K., W. Buckwalter, and S. Stich 2013. 'Moral Intuitions: Are Philosophers Experts?' *Philosophical Psychology* 26 (5), 629–38.

Tomasello, M., and J. Call 1997. *Primate Cognition.* Oxford University Press.

Toulmin, S. 1992. *Cosmopolis: The Hidden Agenda of Modernity.* The University of Chicago Press.

Travis, C. 2013. *Perception: Essays After Frege*. Oxford University Press.

Turri, J. 2014. 'Problem of ESEE Knowledge', *Ergo* 1, http://dx.doi.org/
10.3998/ergo.12405314.0001.004

Turri, J. 2016. 'Knowledge Judgments in Gettier Cases', in *A Companion
to Experimental Philosophy*, eds J. Systma and W. Buckwalter.
Oxford: Wiley-Blackwell, 337–48.

Unger, P. 1979a. 'There Are No Ordinary Things', *Synthese* 41 (2), 117–54.

Unger, P. 1979b. 'Why There Are No People', *Midwest Studies in Philosophy*
4 (1), 177–222.

Unger, P. 2014. *Empty Ideas: A Critique of Analytic Philosophy*. Oxford and
New York: Oxford University Press.

Van Inwagen, P. 1990. *Material Beings*. Ithaca, NY: Cornell University Press.

Van Inwagen, P. 2004. 'Freedom to Break the Laws', *Midwest Studies in
Philosophy* 28 (1), 334–50.

Van Inwagen, P. 2008. 'How to Think about the Problem of Free Will',
Journal of Ethics 12 (3/4), 327–41.

Velleman, J. D. 2006. *Self to Self: Selected Essays*. Cambridge University Press.

Ward, P. 1995. 'Madam Guyon in America: An Annotated Bibliography',
Bulletin of Bibliography 52 (2), 107.

Weigel, C. 2011. 'Distance, Anger, Freedom: An Account of the Role
of Abstraction in Compatibilist and Incompatibilist Intuitions',
Philosophical Psychology 24 (6), 803–23.

Weinberg, J. 2007. 'How to Challenge Intuitions Empirically without
Risking Skepticism', *Midwest Studies in Philosophy* 31, 318–43.

Weinberg, J. 2015. 'The Methodological Necessity of Experimental
Philosophy', *Discipline Filosofiche* 25, 23–42.

Weinberg, J. forthcoming. 'Knowledge, Noise, and Curve-fitting.
A Methodological Argument for JTB?' in *Explaining Knowledge: New
Essays on the Gettier Problem*, eds R. Borges, C. de Almeida, and
P. Klein. Oxford University Press.

Weinberg, J., S. Nichols, and S. Stich 2001. 'Normativity and Epistemic
Intuitions', *Philosophical Topics* 29, 429–60.

Weinberg, J., J. Alexander, C. Gonnerman, and S. Reuter 2012.
'Restrictionism and Reflection: Challenge Deflected, or Simply
Redirected?' *The Monist* 95, 200–22.

Wellek, R. 1981. *A History of Modern Criticism 1750–1950*, vol.
1. Cambridge University Press.

Westerlund, F. 2014. *Heidegger and the Problem of Phenomenality*,
Philosophical Studies from the University of Helsinki, vol. 45.

Wheeler, S. 2000. *Deconstruction as Analytic Philosophy*. Stanford
University Press.

Wichmann, T., *et al.* 2011. 'Milestones in Research on the Pathophysiology
of Parkinson's Disease', *Movement Disorders* 26 (6), 1032–41.

Wiggershaus, R. 1994. *The Frankfurt School: Its History, Theories and
Political Significance* [1986], trans. M. Robertson. Cambridge: Polity.

Williams, B. 1993. *Ethics and the Limits of Philosophy*. London: Fontana.

Williams, B. 2003. 'Contemporary Philosophy: A Second Look', in *The Blackwell Companion to Philosophy*, eds N. Bunnin and E. P. Tsui-James. Oxford: Blackwell, 23–34.

Williams, B. 2006. *Philosophy as a Humanistic Discipline*, ed. A. W. Moore. Princeton and Oxford: Princeton University Press.

Williams, B. 2006a. 'The Human Prejudice', in his *Philosophy as a Humanistic Discipline*, ed. A. W. Moore. Princeton University Press.

Williams, B. 2006b. 'Philosophy as a Humanistic Discipline', reprinted in his *Philosophy as a Humanistic Discipline*, ed. A. W. Moore. Princeton University Press.

Williams, B. 2006c. 'What Might Philosophy Become', in his *Philosophy as a Humanistic Discipline*, ed. A. W. Moore. Princeton University Press.

Williams, B. 2006d. 'Wittgenstein and Idealism', reprinted in his *The Sense of the Past: Essays in the History of Philosophy*, ed. M. Burnyeat. Princeton University Press.

Williams, B. 2006e. *Ethics and the Limits of Philosophy*. London: Routledge.

Williams, B. 2014. 'What Hope for the Humanities?' reprinted in his *Essays and Reviews 1959–2002*. Princeton University Press.

Williams, M. 2004. 'Is Knowledge a Natural Phenomenon?' in *The Externalist Challenge*, ed. R. Schantz. Berlin and New York: de Gruyter, 193–209.

Williamson, T. 2000. *Knowledge and its Limits*. Oxford University Press.

Williamson, T. 2007. *The Philosophy of Philosophy*. Oxford: Blackwell.

Williamson, T. 2013. *Modal Logic as Metaphysics*. Oxford University Press.

Wilson, T. 2002. *Strangers to Ourselves: Discovering the Adaptive Unconscious*. Cambridge, MA: Harvard University Press.

Wise, R. A. 1985. 'The Anhedonia Hypothesis: Mark III', *Behavioral Brain Science* 8, 178–86.

Withy, K. 2013. 'The Strategic Unity of Heidegger's *The Fundamental Concepts of Metaphysics*', *The Southern Journal of Philosophy* 51, 161–78.

Wittgenstein, L. 1958. *Philosophical Investigations* [1953], trans. G. E. M. Anscombe. Oxford: Blackwell.

Wittgenstein, L. 1961a. *Tractatus Logico-Philosophicus*, trans. D. F. Pears and B. F. McGuiness. London: Routledge & Kegan Paul.

Wittgenstein, L. 1961b. *Tractatus Logico-Philosophicus* [1921], trans. and eds B. McGuiness and D. Pears. London: Routledge.

Wittgenstein, L. 1963. *Tractatus Logico-Philosophicus*, trans. D. F. Pears and B. F. McGuinness. New York: Routledge and Kegan Paul.

Wittgenstein, L. 1967a. *Philosophical Investigations*, trans. G. E. M. Anscombe, 3rd edn. Oxford: Blackwell.

Wittgenstein, L. 1967b. *Zettel*, trans. G. E. M. Anscombe. Oxford: Blackwell.

Wittgenstein, L. 1969a. *The Blue and the Brown Books*, 2nd edn. Oxford: Blackwell.

Wittgenstein, L. 1969b. *On Certainty*, trans. G. E. M. Anscombe and Denis Paul. Oxford: Blackwell.

Wittgenstein, L. 1993. *Philosophical Occasions: 1912–1951*, eds J. Klagge and A. Nordmann. London: Hackett.

Woolgar, S. 1988. *Knowledge and Reflexivity*. London and Beverly Hills, CA: Sage.

Wright, C. 2001. *Rails to Infinity: Essays on Themes from Wittgenstein's Philosophical Investigations*. Oxford University Press.

Wright, J. C. 2010. 'On Intuitional Stability: The Clear, the Strong, and the Paradigmatic', *Cognition* 115 (3), 491–503.

Yablo, S. 2002. 'Coulda, Woulda, Shoulda', in *Conceivability and Possibility*, eds T. S. Gendler and J. Hawthorne. Oxford University Press, 441–92.

Yin, H. H., and B. J. Knowlton 2006. 'The Role of the Basal Ganglia in Habit Formation', *Nature Reviews Neuroscience* 7, 464–76.

Zahavi, D. 2005. *Subjectivity and Selfhood: Investigating the First-Person Perspective*. Cambridge, MA: MIT Press.

Zahavi, D. (ed.) 2013. *Oxford Handbook of Contemporary Phenomenology*. Oxford University Press.

Zahavi, D. 2015. *Self and Other: Exploring Subjectivity, Empathy, and Shame*. Oxford University Press.

Zahavi, D. 2016. 'The End of What? Phenomenology and Speculative Realism', forthcoming in *International Journal of Philosophical Studies*.

Zammito, J. H. 2002. *Kant, Herder, and the Birth of Anthropology*. The University of Chicago Press.

INDEX

CPSIA information can be obtained
at www.ICGtesting.com
Printed in the USA
LVHW04s2115020818
585757LV00026B/438/P

9 781107 547360